Cachar under British Rule in North East India

Cachar
under
British Rule
in
North East India

Jayanta Bhusan Bhattacharjee

RADIANT PUBLISHERS

First Published 1977 by
Radiant Publishers
E-155 Kalkaji, New Delhi-110019

The publication of the book was financially supported by the
Indian Council of Historical Research. The responsibility
for the facts stated, opinions expressed, or conclusions
reached, is entirely that of the author and the
Indian Council of Historical Research
accepts no responsibility for them.

Printed in India by Granth Bharti, Delhi-110032

Contents

List of Appendices

Preface

Cachar, or the kingdom of Heramba, which was annexed to
the British territory in India in 1832, has failed to attract
adequate attention of the historians. Dr. A.C. Banerjee in his
Eastern Frontier of British India has discussed the policy of the
East India Company towards Cachar and her neighbouring
states in North East India till the end of the First Anglo-
Burmese War. The circumstances which led to the British
annexation of Cachar have been discussed by Dr. R.M. Lahiri
in his *The Annexation of Assam.* Dr. H.K. Barpujari has ex-
haustively described the administrative reforms introduced by
the British Government in South Cachar immediately after the
annexation of the area, besides elaborating the political developments since 1826 to the occupation of the erstwhile kingdom in
three instalments, in his *Assam: In the Days of the Company.*
The contributions of these learned scholars are, however,
limited to the first half of the 19th century. The history of
Cachar before and after this period naturally remains to be
studied.

The present book intends to provide a comprehensive history
of Cachar from 1765 to 1947, in the context of British rule in
India and British policy in the north-eastern sentinel of the
country. The ultimate object, however, is to reveal the original
materials available for critical studies, particularly the local
records, and to explore areas of further research. Chapter One
opens with the geographical, ethnological and historical background. The policy of the East India Company towards
Cachar and her neighbouring states and territories in North

East India, the successive Manipuri and Burmese occupation of Cachar, expulsion of the Burmese by the British, reinstatement of Govindachandra as the ruler of a protected state have been discussed in Chapter Two. The next Chapter deals with internal problems of Cachar, strained relations of the Raja with his over-ambitious neighbours, ill-conceived policy of the British and their indulgence to the Raja of Manipur leading to the assassination of Govindachandra, and the rise of British para-mountcy in Cachar. The administrative measures of the Colonial Government in supercession of the native institutions and customs, particularly the unique agricultural communes, problem of the frontier tribes and repeated appropriations of Cachar's territory to the adjacent units, with their effects on the people find elaboration in Chapters Four and Five. Chapter Six deals with the consolidation of the British rule and Chapter Seven with material progress of Cachar during the above period while the political, social and economic impact of the colonial rule is examined in Chapter Eight. Chapter Nine provides an outline of Cachar's share in the national struggle for freedom from British yoke.

The study is mainly based on the official documents preserved in the National Archives of India, New Delhi, West Bengal State Archives, Calcutta, Assam Secretariat Records Office, Shillong and Cachar District Records Room, Silchar. Besides official reports, minutes, gazetteers, contemporary and semi-contemporary works as well as chronicles in Bengali and Assamese have been consulted and utilised, the details of which are appended in the bibliography towards the end of the volume.

My acknowledgements are due to the authors whose works I have consulted, and to the Director of the National Archives of India, Director of Archives, Government of West Bengal, Director of Historical and Antiquarian Studies, Government of Assam, Keeper of Records, Assam Secretariat; Keeper of Records, Cachar District Records Room; Librarian and Staff, Assam State Central Library for allowing access to the materials in their custody. I am thankful to the Indian Council of Historical Research for the generous grant towards the publication of the volume, and to Radiant Publishers, New Delhi, for undertaking the publication. My thanks are also due to those friends and colleagues who encouraged me to complete the work, but would go unnamed. It goes without saying that a pioneering work is bound to contain many shortcomings, and I would ungrudgingly crave the indulgence of the readers for the irregularities. My labour would be considered rewarded if some enthusiastic scholars can be drawn to the study of North East India.

NEHU, Shillong   J.B. Bhattacharjee

Introduction

Cachar, now a district of Assam, is situated between Longitude 92.15" and 93.15" East and Latitude 24.8" and 25.8" North, covering an area of 6,941.2 square kilometres, and is bounded on the north by the North Cachar Hills District of Assam and Jaintia Hills District of Meghalaya, on the east by Manipur, on the south by Mizoram and on the west by Tripura and the Sylhet District of Bangladesh.[1] But on the eve of British annexation, the present North Cachar Hills District and Hojai Davaka areas of the Nowgong District of Assam and Jiri Frontier Tract of Manipur formed parts of Cachar, then known as *Heramba Rajya* ; while the modern Karimganj Sub-division was included in the Sylhet District of Bengal. To quote Hamilton[2]:

> West from Manipur and its dependencies, on the frontier of Assam, is the territory of the Kachhar Raja, which borders with Assam from nearly opposite to Koliyabar to the river Kopili, which enters the Kolong about the middle of its course. The length of this frontier is therefore about thirty miles. At the Kopili, Kachhar reaches with a corner to the Kolong; but in general it does not descend into the plains on the bank of that river. It extends a little south of the Surma, which passes Silhet or Srihatta in Bengal, and therefore to about 24.30' of north Latitude, while its northern extremity is in about 26.20' north giving 110 geographical miles for its length.

Cachar thus consisted of two distinct divisions, *viz.* North Cachar Hills, which were a continuation of the Assam range

or Meghalaya plateau, and Cachar Plains,* that formed the
eastern extremity of the alluvial valley of Surma and was
"geographically; historically and ethnically an extension of
Gangetic Bengal."[3] But the latter division was also dotted with
hills. In addition to the southern belt of the Barail range, with
an average width of six or seven miles, containing peaks
between three and six thousand feet in height, on the eastern
frontier lay the Bhuban range, a continuation of the Lushai
Hills that ran almost due north to the junction of the Jiri and
Barak rivers and at places over 3,000 feet above the sea level;
while on the west of the Hailakandi valley the Chatachura or
Saraspur hills stretched in a continuous line to the Barak. The
hills division, consisting mainly of the Barail range, from
Jaintia Hills to a point little to the west of A̓salu formed a
continuous wall of mountains, gradually increasing in height
towards the east. Kalangtam, where the range entered Cachar,
was 4,336 feet above the level of the sea, the next important
peak being Jentahajum (5,127 feet), while Sherfaisif, a little to
the north, was 5,617 feet. To the north east of Haflong there
were three peaks over 5,617 feet in height, where the chain
took a sharp turn towards the north and reached its greatest
elevation at Hampeopet (6,143 feet), but from this point it
gradually declined in height, and at Laikek, a little before it
entered Naga Hills, the altitude was only 2,628 feet.[4]

Most of these hills were rugged and precipitious into which
innumerable rivers cut deep gorges as they descended upon the
plains. The mountainous character of the country rendered the
intercommunication extremely difficult, while most of the
rivers would remain unnavigable even in the rainy seasons.
Barak, the principal river, took its rise a little to the west of
Maothana on the southern slopes of the lofty range which
was the northern boundary of Manipur. Having a south-
westerly move from its source near Tipaimukh, it turned
sharply to the north and for a considerable distance formed
the boundary line between Cachar and Manipur. After its junction with Jiri, the principal affluent to join it, which too for a

* Cachar Plains consisted of the Silchar and Hailakandi Sub-divisions
of the modern district. This region was generally known as South
Cachar.

considerable area acted as the Cachar-Manipur border, at Jiribam, it turned again to the west and flowing through the heart of Cachar reached Badarpur. From Badarpur to Haritikar it provided the boundary between Cachar and Sylhet. At Haritikar the river became divided into two branches, *viz.* Surma and Kushiara. The latter branch entered Sylhet at the junction, while the former continued to form the frontier of Cachar as far as Jalalpur and then across Sylhet confluenced with the old stream of Brahmaputra near Bhairab Bazar in Mymensing. In addition to Jiri, the Barak received numerous tributaries from the hills through which it made the way. A little to the west of Lakhipur, it was joined by Chiri that took its rise on the southern slopes of the Barial near Haffong, while Madhura, rising from the same range, joined near Silchar. Jatinga, which rises south of Haflong, debouched in the plains at Panighat and then through Barkhola, receiving Dalu on the left bank, fell into Barak beyond Jaynagar. The principal rivers in South Cachar were Sonai, Dhaleswai and Katakhal, while in the north it was Dayan. The Hajoi-Jamunamukh-Davaka area was known as Central Cachar, and Kapili was the most important river there. Most of these rivers were dried up during winters, but in summer Barak and her tributaries would rise up in high spate and, as in these days, caused inundations almost every year.[5]

The hills were clothed with dense forest, and the Valley of Barak was dotted with hollows, *beels* and swamps.[6] The hills were rich in timber, mineral and tusked elephants, and the valley reared fertility and the *beels* abounded with palatable fish; but the climate was extremely enervating. The region was a dumping ground for malarial fever, and *kalazar*, cholera and small pox usually levied huge toll on human life. The physiography had thus imposed a formidable barrier, but the plains tract being only a continuation of Bengal was never unaccessibile to the people of Sylhet. However, the frequent raids and superstitious customs of the dwellers of the neighbouring hills, the ravages caused by the wild animals, the devastating floods and unhealthy climate had hitherto acted as a serious check on the growth of population. No wonder, therefore, the Valley of Barak was known to the Bengalees as Kachhar, meaning, according to the local dialect of Sylhet, a stretch of land on the foot of mountains.[7]

The picturesque valley of Barak is a natural continuation of the vast Bengal plains, and was included in the various kingdoms that had emerged during the pre-historic and early historic periods like Gauda, Vanga and Samatata.[8] In ancient time Cachar Valley, Sylhet and Chittagong were colonised by the Aryans and the area was known as *Pratyanta Desha*.[9] The *Varaha Purana* and *Vayu Purana* referred to Barak (*Barabakra*) as a Holy River,[10] while *Yogini Tantra* and *Kalika Purana* mentioned about the Bhubanesar Temple.[11] A tradition suggests that, Kapila, the celebrated author of *Shankhya*, had his *ashram* on the bank of Barak at Siddheswer near Badarpur.[12] *Kamakshya Tantra*, a Sanskrit work, shows that Cachar was included in the *Sapta-Khanda Kamarupa*.[13] According to an inscription of Lokenath, a *Samanta* ruler of East Bengal, issued in the seventh century A.D., he constructed the temple and image of *Ananta Narayana* at Subang, near Bikrampur. The reference in this inscription to *Jayatunga-Versa* and *Su-Vanga visaya* suggests that Jatinga Valley was a *Varsa* or feudatory state under Samatata and Subang was a *Visaya* or district.[14] During seventh to the tenth centuries the region might have been included in the Harikela Kingdom which comprised Sylhet and the adjacent territories.[15] In the thirteenth century, the Barak Valley was ruled by the Tipperahs, a section of the Bodos,[16] whose territory, in addition to present Tripura, included a considerable portion of modern Sylhet and Comilla districts of Bangladesh, and once the capital of the kingdom was at 'Khalangsha' in Cachar.[17] Khalangsha was perhaps the ancient name of Rajghat, on the bank of Rukni, where old roads, tanks and brick-built plinths are still in existence.[18] But the Tipperahs gradually moved eastward and in the Cachar Valley an independent kingdom was established of which Tulashidvaj was the reigning prince in the 15th century A.D. Raja Tulashidhvaj fought several wars with Pratapgarh in the west.[19] However, in the beginning of the 16th century Cachar was annexed to Tripura.[20]

The North Cachar Hills were then included in the territory of the Dimachas, another section of the Bodos, now popularly

known as the Kacharis. They are the earliest known inhabitants of the Assam Valley[21] and claim their descent from
Ghatotkach, the son of Bhima, the hero of *Mahabharata*,
through Hidimba. Although their history from Ghatotkach has
not yet been reconstructed, the Dimachas "exercised their
sovereignty in Assam in different names and in different
places."[22] In the beginning of the Christian Era, they were the
ruling power of Kamarupa and were expelled from there by
Pushyavarman, the founder of the Varman Dynasty, in the
fourth century A.D.[23] The Dimachas then established a kingdom at Sadiya where they ruled for several centuries and
gradually extended their jurisdiction over a vast territory that
extended beyond the river Dishang upto Namsang in the Naga
Hills and included modern North Cachar Hills, with headquarters at Dimapur on the bank of the river Dhansiri.[24]

Meanwhile, the Ahoms, an off-shoot of the Tai or Shan
race of Upper Burma, wandered into the eastern extremity of
the Brahmaputra Valley. Obviously, they came into conflict
with the Dimachas, and Sukapha, the leader of the Ahom
invaders (1228 A.D.), encountered the latter at the foot of the
Naga Hills.[25] Realising the difficulty of overcoming the defenders, Sukapha concentrated himself in subduing the Morans
and the Barahis in the north and north-east of the Dimacha
territory. But Suteupha, the son and successor of Sukapha,
occupied the Dimacha territory upto Namdang towards the end
of the thirteenth century, which came to be recognised as the
boundary between the two neighbours for about two hundred
years.[26] In 1490, the Ahom army crossed Dikhu and erected a
fort which was suddenly sacked by the Dimachas who forced
the invaders, chased upto Tangsu, to sue for peace offering an
Ahom princess as bride to the Dimacha Raja with two elephants
and two slaves as dowry.[27] However, in 1526, Suhungmung,
the Ahom monarch, sent an expedition that immediately
reclaimed the territory upto Dikhu which also for sometime
came as the boundary between the two kingdoms. The Dimachas were next pushed back to Namdang, and their refusal to
surrender the city of Dergaon led to several encounters ultimately resulting in the Ahom occupation, in December 1526, of
the Dimacha city.[28] In 1531, Khunkara, the Dimacha Raja,

opposed the construction of a fort by the Ahoms at Marangi. As a result, a serious conflict broke out in which the Dimachas were completely routed. The Ahoms pursued them upto their capital at Dimapur and the river Dhansiri became the boundary.[29] Before long, Dersongpha, the Dimacha Raja, resented the loss of territory and the Ahoms, in 1536, sacked Dimapur and Dersongpha was put to death. Retreating further, the Dimachas put their new capital at Maibong. Madan Kumar, son of Dersongpha, was proclaimed as the Raja with the name of Nirbhoynarayan. He married an Ahom princess and promised to pay an annual tribute, while river Kalong was recognised as the Ahom-Dimacha boundary.[30] The new capital was adorned with built-up and rock-cut temples in which the images of *Ranachandi, Durga* aad *Basudeva* were installed.[31] Notwithstanding, the pressure from the other side of the Kalong continued to threaten the existence of the Dimachas, while the Jaintias in the west also began hostility with them.[32]

These frontier disputes between the neighbours, however, subsided for sometime due to the imperial adventures of the Koch rulers. Naranarayan, the Raja of Koch Behar, despatched an expedition in 1562 under Sukladhvaj, popularly known as Chilarai, his brother and general, which subdued the Ahom and the Dimacha kingdoms as well as Jayantia, Khyriem, Dimarua, Manipur, Sylhet and Tripura. The defeated rulers acknowledged the Koch suzerainty and agreed to pay annual tributes, besides war indemnities and presents. Durlabhnarayan, the Dimacha Raja, made over eighty elephants and other valuable presents to Chilarai and agreed to pay an annual tribute of seventy thousand rupees, one thousand gold *mohars* and sixty elephants. A strong battle was fought between Chilarai and the Raja of Tripura at Longai in the southern border of Cachar. The Raja of Tripura was defeated and killed. The son of the vanquished king ascended the throne of Tripura and undertook to pay the Raja of Koch Behar an annual tribute of ten thousand rupees, one thousand gold *mohars* and thirty horses.[33] The authority of Tripura in Cachar came to an end, and Chilarai left a contingent of Koch soldiers at Brahmapur, later known as Khaspur, in Cachar Valley, while Longai came to be recognised as the boundary between the Koch and

Tipperah territories. Cachar was surrounded by the con-
quered states of Jayantia, Khyriem, Sylhet, Tripura, Manipur
and the Dimacha territory. The Koch authorities, therefore,
might have considered it advantageous to convert Cachar into
a 'crown colony' under a Governor who would be responsible
for maintaining diplomatic relations with the adjoining subsi-
diary states and the collection of tributes. Accordingly, Kamalnarayan, popularly known as Gosain Kamal, another brother
of Naranarayan, whose name is associated with the construction of a 350-mile road, several tanks and other works of art
in Lower Assam, was appointed as the Governor of Cachar.[34]
Similarly, the Ahom interference in the affairs of the Dimachas
was stopped, both the Ahoms and Dimachas being now tributary to Koch Behar. However, taking the advantage of the
reverses that the Koches faced during their expedition in
Bengal, the rulers of the north eastern states reasserted themselves. Meghanarayan, the Dimacha Raja, proclaimed himself
as a sovereign ruler. But the Ahoms immediately began to
demand tribute from the Dimachas, which was discontinued
since the defeat of both the Ahoms and the Dimachas at the
hands of the Koches. Jasanarayan, the Dimacha Raja, however,
successfully resisted the Ahom pressure and evaded the payment.[35]

In South Cachar, however, the Koches continued to rule for
more than a century. Kamalnarayan, the Koch Governor, was
a pious and peaceful administrator. He had established a
number of religious shrines in Cachar, of which *Kali* temple at
Thaligram and *Kancha-Kanti* at Udharband have survived the
stress and strain of time and circumstances. He also settled
some Brahmins as priests and few Koches as *Devagrihi* or
Sabayat. After the collapse of the Koch supremacy in North
East India, the Governor of Brahmapur was deprived of his
diplomatic functions. As a result, the Koch territory in Cachar
emerged as a petty kingdom. Two rulers ruled in Cachar after
Kamalnarayan. The third ruler was an oppressive monarch.
Ultimately, the nobles in the kingdom conspired against him
and the Raja was assassinated. Udita, the general, was then
proclaimed as the Raja by the people and his successors ruled in
Cachar for seven generations. The seventh ruler, Bhim Singha,

had no son, but only one daughter named Kanchani. She was married to Laksmichandra, who belonged to the ruling Dimacha family of North Cachar. Laksmichandra was appointed by Bhim Singha as the Governor of a division of the kingdom and the headquarters of this division later came to be known as Lakhipur. However, after the death of Bhim Singha, Laksmichandra became the Raja of South Cachar and in course of time South Cachar merged with the Dimacha territory in North Cachar Hills.[36] Some historians wrongly believed that a Dimacha Raja from North Cachar had contracted an alliance with the Raja of Tripura by marrying the latter's daughter and the Cachar Valley was transferred to the Dimachas as part of the dowry.[37] As a matter of fact, the Tripura rule in Cachar had come to an end with latter's defeat, at the hands of Chilarai and a Koch state in the valley had developed under Kamalnarayan, the Koch Governor. There was a Koch colony in Cachar during both Heramba and British rule, and the Koches were known as *Dehans* after *Dewan* or the Governor. They were "reputed to be descendants of some Koches who accompained Chilarai's army amd remained in the country. They enjoyed special privileges in the days of the Kachari rule, and their chief, or Senapati, was allowed to enter the king's courtyard in his palanquin."[38]

On the other hand, Jasanarayan, the Dimacha ruler of North Cachar Hills, had to reckon with tremendous pressure from the Ahoms and the Jaintias ever since the Koch supremacy over the region had collapsed. There was persistent demands from the Ahom monarch to renew the allegiance, while the Jaintias indulged in frontier troubles. Danamanik, the Raja of Jayantia (1580-96), refused to allow the Dimachas to trade with Sylhet through his territory. Under the instigations of the Raja, some Jaintias plundered the commodities of the Dimacha traders at Mulagul. In retaliation, the Dimachas killed some Jaintias on the bank of Kapili.[39] To make matters worse, Danamanik seized Prabhakar, the Chief of Dimarua, a vassal to the rulers of Maibong. Prabhakar appealed to his overlord for rescue, and Jasanarayan demanded his release from Dhanamanik who ignored the demand. Ultimately, Jasanarayan led an army into Jayantia. Dhanamanik was compelled to release Prabhakar, to acknowledge the Dimacha suzerainty and undertake to pay annual tributes. He also offered two Jaintia princesses to Jasanarayan and made over Jasamanik, his nephew and heir-apparent, as hostage. To commemorate the victory, Jasanarayan assumed the title of Arimardhan.[40] This was immediately followed by the death of Dhanamanik, whereupon Jasamanik was released and installed as the vassal ruler of Jayantia.[41]

Meanwhile, the political dialogues continued between the Dimacha and the Ahom courts. Jasanarayan was determind to maintain his hold in the Kapili-Jamuna and Doyang-Dhansiri valleys on equal terms with the Ahom monarch, but the latter always persisted on the servitude of the Dimacha Raja.[42] On the other hand, Jasamanik, the Jayantia Raja, resented the suzerainty of Maibong and taking advantage of the Ahom-Dimacha embroils wanted to drag the two to a war considering that the Ahom supremacy will definitely prevail. He offered a princess to the Ahom monarch, Pratap Singha, on the condition that she would be escorted to the Ahom capital through Dimacha territory. This proposal was strongly opposed by Jasanarayan who did not find any justification for the deviation from the traditional route between Assam and Jaintia through Gobha, a feudatory state under Jayantia. Failing to persuade the authorities at Maibong, Pratap Singha, in 1606, deputed one Sundar Gohain, an Ahom General, at the head of a powerful army, who succeeded in occupying several Dimacha garrisons on the way. But when the Ahoms approached Maibong, the Dimachas, under Bhimbal Kumar, the General, fell upon the invaders and assassinated the Gohain himself.[43] The death of Sundar Gohain was a heavy shock to the Ahom monarch, while Jasanarayan added insult to injury by sending a message that he had carefully preserved Gohain's scalp which could be taken back if needed for any ceremony in the Ahom capital. But the Ahoms were then engaged in war with the Mughals and, consequently, could not send another punitive expedition against Maibong.[44]

The success against the Ahoms was undoubtedly a great achievement which the Dimachas had every reason to rejoice. Jasanarayan now assumed the title of Pratapnarayan, and

changed the name of Maibong into Kirtipur. With this termi-
nated the vivasory of the Dimachas, and Jasanarayan declared
himself as an independent sovereign, styled as *Herambesvara* or
'Lord of Heramba'. He claimed his descent from Hidimba of
Mahabharata, and the Dimacha territory has since then been
known as Heramba Kingdom. Jasanarayan was, therefore, the
founder of a historically known independent and sovereign
kingdom of the Dimachas. A silver coin issued by Jasanarayan
claiming himself as *Herambesvara* and "a worshiper of Hara,
Gauri, Siva and Durga" is the earliest available coin of the
dynasty.[45] The term 'Heramba' had for the first time appeared
in this historic coin, but since then it had frequently occured
in inscriptions, coins and other records. There is no evidence
to show that the Dimachas had used it on any occasion prior
to the reign of Jasanarayan. Sir Edward Gait, therefore,
believed that the name was given to the Dimacha territory by
the Brahmins. To quote him :[46] "...it seems more likely that
Hidimba was an old name of Cachar, which the Brahmans
afterwards connected with the Kachari dynasty, just as in the
Brahmaputra Valley they connected successive dynasties of
aboriginal potentates with the mythical Narak."

The emergence of Heramba as an independent and powerful
kingdom, on the other hand, had drawn the attention of the
Imperial Mughals who had made themselves the rulers of
Bengal and were making repeated endeavours to conquer
Assam and Tripura. Jasanarayan, however, defended the
sovereignty of his kingdom by successfully repulsing the
invaders.[47] Jamal Khan, the Commander of the Mughal Army,
was given to believe that the Raja of Heramba was anxious for
his friendship and persuaded to wait for valuable presents. The
Dimachas then in a mid-night coup suddenly pounced upon
the waiting Mughal soldiers and taking them quite unwares
thoroughly massacred the entire contingent. Jamal Khan himself was slain.[48] However, the second Mughal invasion, in
1612, under Quasim Khan, the Governor of Bengal, gave a
completely opposite verdict. The Heramba forts at Asuratikri
and Pratapgarh were captured. To check further advance of
the Mughals, Jasanarayan made peace by offering forty
elephants and one lakh rupees for the emperor, five elephants

and rupees twenty thousand for the *Subahdar*, and two elephants and rupees twenty thousand for the *Thanadar* of Bandasal who was in immediate command of the invading contingent. The river Surma had since become the boundary between Heramba Kingdom and Bengal, and a Mughal *Thanadar* was posted at Badarpur.[49]

Naranarayan, who succeeded Jasanarayan, maintained the integrity and prestige of the kingdom intact, while Bhimbalnarayan, the next Raja, resolved to recover the territory upto Dimapur and encouraged the Dimachas to indulge in raids and plunders in the Ahom country. The Ahoms, who were then more concerned with defending their territory from the Mughals realised the expediency of conciliating the Heramba rulers and started negotiations for peaceful coexistence. An Ahom princess was offered to Biradarpanarayan, the Raja of Heramba (1644-1682), but the latter did not give up his hostile attitude and sacked Baghergaon in the Ahom territory. To prevent further incursions, the Ahom authorities settled a number of villages along the Heramba frontier. However, the death of Biradarpa, in 1682, offered an opportunity to the Ahoms to resume the negotiations with the Heramba Government which continued throughout the reign of Makaradhvajanarayan (1682-1695). Meanwhile, the Ahoms were relieved of the Mughal-fobia, and had no difficulty to open rupture with Heramba.[50]

On the other hand, Tamradhvajnarayan, Raja of Heramba (1695 to 1707), who had strengthened his position by marrying Chandraprava, daughter of the Raja of Koch Behar, sent a letter to the Ahom monarch demanding the restoration of the territory upto Mohong. He also boldly asserted the independence of his kingdom and refused to acknowledge the Ahom hegemony. In retaliation, Rudra Singha, the Ahom monarch, determined to reduce the Herambas to submission. In 1706, he despatched two strong divisions of Ahom soldiers to Maibong. The first numbered over 37,000 men and was commanded by the *Bar Baruah* through the Dhansiri route, while the 34,000 strong second army under *Pani Phukan* proceeded by the Kapili route. The Dimachas offered gallant resistance to the advancing Ahom forces under *Bar Baruah* in the Dhansiri frontier. Although they were required to take shelter in the hills due to the superiority of the Ahom soldiers, the Dimachas ambuscaded several small parties of the Ahoms which were engaged in clearing the jungle. However, the Dimachas were defeated in heavy encounters at Lathia, Amlakhi and Tarang. The Ahom army made further advance and ultimately occupied Maibong. Tamradhvaj fled to Khaspur* which since then had become the capital of the Heramba Kingdom. A huge amount of booty, including a cannon and 700 guns had fallen into the hands of the invaders.[51] Meanwhile, the army under *Pani Phukan* had reached Demera, by cutting a forty-one miles road from Raha, through dense jungle, and having sacked on the way the prosperous villages of Salgaon, Lambur and Dharmapur. The Dimachas endeavoured to repel the invasion without success, and the invaders reached Maibong without much difficulty.[52]

The initial success took the morale of the Ahoms very high and Rudra Singha, the Ahom monarch, encamped himself at Raha to keep direct contact with the commanders in the frontier. But sickness broke out in the Ahom camp at Maibong due to the pestilential climate, while the provisions began to run short. As a result, the vigour with which the campaign was undertaken began to decline. On the other hand, the Dimachas took advantage of the situation and harrassed the invaders in several ways. Nevertheless, Rudra Singha repeatedly ordered the commanders to proceed to Khaspur. The *Pani Phukan*, according marched upto Sempani, while the *Bar Baruah*, who was seriously ill, undertook his return journey and died on the way. The death of the commander broke the morale of the Ahoms and, in March 1707, their monarch was persuaded to abandon the expedition against Khaspur. The *Pani Phukan* withdrew the troops from Sempani and Maibong, but demolished the brick fort and burned down the houses at Maibong. A strong garrison was left at Demera and fortifica-

---

* Some scholars, however, believe that Tamradhvaj had taken a temporary shelter elsewhere during the sack of Maibong and he and two of his successors had ruled from Maibong, and that the capital was shifted to Khaspur about 30 years after this invasion. (See Guha, n. 9, p. 82). On the other hand, Gait contended that Tamradhvaj had fled to Bikrampur in Cachar and there he was captivized by the Raja of Jayantia and taken to Jayantiapur. Ultimately, however, both the Rajas were take to the Ahom capital, and eventually Tamradhvaj proceeded to his new capital at Khaspur. (See Gait, n. 21, p. 179).

tions were constructed there. For sometime, Demera became the outpost between the two states. But with the outbreak of the rainy season, the sickness and mortality amongst the soldiers became so alarming that the Ahoms were compelled to withdraw finally from the Dimacha territory.[53]

Tamradhvaj from his camp in South Cachar, where he fled during the occupation of Maibong, had appealed to Ram Singh, the Raja of Jayantia, for help. As a matter of fact, Jayantia was a tributary to the Raja of Cachar, as has already been mentioned, since the reign of Jasanarayan, and the rising power of the overlord had suppressed for long the spirit of the Jaintias to reassert themselves. Realising that the Raja of Heramba was in trouble, Ram Singh resolved to capitalise the situation. The Heramba army was dispersed by the Ahoms immediately after the occupation of Maibong. Ram Singh, therefore, considered that if he could seize the person of Tamradhvaj the Heramba kingdom would be annexed to Jayantia. He collected a large army, but before the commencement of the journey Tamradhvaj informed him that the Ahoms have withdrawn from North Cachar Hills and that his help was no longer necessary. Despite, Ram Singh marched to Mulagul, and pretended to make common cause with Tamradhvaj against the Ahoms. He invited Tamradhvaj to a friendly meeting at Balesvar under the pretext of concerting measures to attack Assam, but treacherously captivized the Raja of Heramba and took him to the Jaintia Capital at Jaintiapur as a prisoner. Chandraprava, the queen of Heramba, communicated the conduct of Ram Singh to the Ahom monarch and requested the latter to rescue her husband.[54] Rudra Singa, the Ahom monarch, took advantage of the situation to compel the Heramba monarch to acknowledge the suzerainty of the Ahoms, and demanded immediate release of Tamradhvaj from the Raja of Jayantia. But Ram Singh refused to comply, while the Ahoms closed the market at Gobha on which the people in Jaintia Hills depend for the supply of essential commodities. In December 1707, two Ahom forces marched against Jaintiapur, one under the *Bar Baruah* through the Kapili and Cachar valleys, while the other under *Bar Phukan* across Gobha and Jaintia Hills. The 43,000 strong column under *Bar Baruah* was cordially received

by the people in North Cachar Hills as well as in South
Cachar, and could easily reach Bikrampur and begin operations
against Jayantia. The Jaintia outposts at Balesvar, Dalagaon
and Mulagul, in Surma valley, were all sacked. The Ahom
army eventually reached Jaintiapur; and Ram Singh had no
alternative but to surrender. On the other hand, the advance of
the contingent under *Bar Phukan* was repeatedly, hampered by
the Jaintias who offered gallant resistance to the invaders and
harrassed them all the way. However, the Ahom soldiers
succeeded in overcoming the opposition and joined the other
column at Jaintiapur.[55] Ram Singh and his *Juvaraj* as well
as Tamradhvaj were taken to Bishnath and produced before
the Ahom monarch. Tamradhvaj confirmed his allegiance to
the Ahoms and ceded territory upto Jamuna river. Ram Singh
died of illness, and the *Juvaraj*, Jaynarayan, was nominated as
the Raja of Jayantia. Thus both Cachar and Jayantia became
tributary to the Ahoms.[56]

Ever since Khaspur had become the capital of Heramba,
the kingdom was called by the people of Sylhet as 'Cachar'
and the ruling Dimacha tribe as 'Kacharis.' The Bodos living
in different parts of Brahmaputra Valley also came to be
known by the same name and owed their moral allegiance to
the Raja of Cachar. Although Sir Edward Gait contended that
Cachar got its name from the Kacharis, he himself had noted
that the "word Kachar is derived from a Sanskrit word meaning a broadening region."[57] As a matter of fact, not only the
ruling Dimacha tribe but even the Bengalees in Cachar were
known to the people of Sylhet as Kacharis. The historians
with local knowledge have, therefore, strongly established that
the Valley of Barak was always known to the Bengalees as
Cachar and the ruling race appeared in the British records as
Kacharis only after the country where the ruling family belonged
to their tribe. To quote P.N. Bhattacharjee[58] :

> Mr. Gait is of opinion that 'the Kacharis have given their
> name to the district' of Cachar. We might as well be told
> that the Romans gave the name Rome. The fact is that the
> name has been given to the district by the Bengalis of
> Sylhet, because it is an outlying place skirting the moun-
> tains. The word 'Kachhar' is still used in Sylhet in desig-
> nating a plot of land at the foot of a mountain. It is

derived from Sanskrit 'Kachchha' which means 'a plain near mountain' or 'a place near water' whence is the name of the state of Katch in Bombay. The 'Kachharis' are naturally the natives of Kachar as Bengalees are of Bengal.†

Nevertheless, the occupation of Cachar had opened a new chapter in the history of the Heramba Kingdom. As Dr. Bhuyan observed, "it is only in Cachar that the Kacharis experimented the arduous task of state-building."[59] The kingdom now extended from the river Dhaleswai in South Cachar to Jamuna in Nowgong. Tamradhvajnarayan, Raja of Cachar, having ceded the territory upto the river Jamuna to the Ahoms, the said river came to be recognised as the boundary between the Ahom territory and the kingdom of Heramba. The Ahom outpost was at Mohong on the west bank of the river, while on the east bank was the outpost of Cachar at Dijua. This meeting place of the two states was popularly known as Mohong-Dijua* and had developed as an important market where the people from Cachar, Assam, Manipur and Naga Hills traded with each other. The prosperous village of Mohong+ was subsequently, recovered by the rulers of Khaspur and on the eve of the British annexation formed part of Cachar.[60] The North Cachar Hills, peopled by the Dimachas, was placed under a Deputy or *Senapati* by the Raja, while the Jamuna Valley including the slopes of the Mikir Hills, popularly known as Central Cachar, was supervised by a Governor.[61]

Tamradhvajnarayan died in September, 1708, and was succeeded by his son Suradarpanarayan who was only 9 years old. As a result, the actual administration was run by his mother, Chandraprava. She was a great patron of learning, and a large number of Sanskrit works were translated into Bengali under her patronage. According to *Deshavali*, a

---

† To quote Robinson : "The country of Kachar is bounded on the west by Sylhet and Jaintia; on the north by Assam; on the east by Manipur; on the south by Tripurah. It was originally divided into three portions; two of which lie on the northern side of the great mountain chain, which, sweeping round from the north-eastern extremity of the Manipur territory, forms the western termination of the Garo Hills; the third division is on the southern side of this lofty barrier. These divisions were severally distinguishe,d by the names of Northern, Central, and Southern Kachar". See Robinson W., *A Descriptive Account of Assam*, 399.

* About sixteen miles to the West of Diphu Railway Station.

+ Latitude 25.59 North and Longitude 90.30 East.

Sanskrit work composed in 1728 A.D., Suradarpa's territory extended from Kamrup in the north to Manthara in South and Manipur in the east to Sialkot in the west, while the important political divisions in the kingdom were Khaspur, Dharmapur, Sialkot, Tiladrinal, Phulchand, Jaynagar, Chapghat, Bandashil, Lohato, Chatsati and Baoyaganj.[62] Suradarpa had set himself to reorganise the kingdom. A brick-built palace and several temples were constructed in Khaspur, the new capital, and the image of *Ranachandi*, the tutelar deity of the Dimachas, was installed in one these temples. On the other hand, the rock-cave temple of *Hara-Parvati* in the Bhuban Hills, originally constructed by the Tipperahs, was regularly maintained by the Raja and kept up in good condition. Rungrang, in the eastern frontier of the kingdom, during this time had developed as a flourishing business centre where the people of Cachar, Manipur Lushai Hills and Tripura traded in cloth, brass and bell-metal utensils, paddy, cotton and vegetables.[63]

Attempts were also made to attract more settlers from neighbouring Bengal in the fertile but thinly populated valley of the Barak. As a matter of fact, the Bengalee population in Cachar had begun to increase since the Koch rule in the valley. Some Brahmins from Sylhet were appointed as the priests in the temples of *Kancha-kanti* and *Shyama* in Udharband. Besides, a large number of Brahmins were also settled in different parts of the Kingdom. During the reign of Laksmichandra, the son-in-law and successer of the Koch ruler Bhim Singha, one Jaganath Tarkabachaspti, a great Sanskritist, was granted 50 *hals* of rent-free *Brahmattara* land in Kalain. The ancestors of this scholar belonged to the village of Kanchadia on the bank of Padma in East Bengal, but in course of time the village was washed away by the river and Ramjeeban Sharma, the grandfather of Jagannath migrated towards the east.[64] Cachar was an extention of the Gangetic Bengal and even before the Koch rule several Bengalee settlements had developed in Cachar as a result of the natural movement of the people towards the east. No wonder, therefore, the official language of the kingdom was Bengali, while the coins and inscriptions of the Heramba rulers were inscribed in Sanskrit in Bengali script. The earliest Bengalee inhabitants of the valley belonged to agrarian classes; the *Patnis*, for example.

However, during the reign of Laksmichandra the population had increased unexpectedly and the villages of Berenga, Dudpatil, Banskandi and Udharband were established during this period. *Nath*, a very populous community in Cachar, had also immigrated during the reign of Laksmichandra. With the shifting of the capital from Maibong to Khaspur, the Brahmin priests and scholars in the royal court also migrated to South Cachar and their descendants are still to be found in Jatrapur, Tarapur, Barkhola and Phulbari.[65] In the beginning of the 18th century one Bikram Roy was granted a rent-free estate which after him came to be known as Bikrampur *Pargana*. Bikram Roy came from Dacca and was granted the estate to encourage more Bengalee immigration from the west. He was followed by Ashu Thakur from Pratapgarh in Sylhet and Gulal Khan Choudhury from Tripura.[66] There was, however, a general influx during the reign of Harishchandranarayan,* son and successor of Suradarpa, who granted land to the cultivators on nominal gross revenue. The Brahmins and high caste people from Bengal also rushed to Cachar seeking employment. The development of the country enabled the Government to throw off the allegiance to the Ahoms, while the appointment of the Bengalees as *Vakeels*, ministers and to other high posts added to the efficiency of the state. By the time Kirtichandranarayan, the next Raja, ascended the throne the size of the new settlers had become considerable. As a result, in 1736, he appointed one Maniram Laskar of Barkhola as the *Uzir* to deal with the settlement of the new-comers from Bengal.[67] The immigrants also encroached upon the Tripura territory in the Dhaleswari Valley in the south, and the area† was ultimately annexed to Cachar in 1736 A.D.[68] This might have provoked the invasion from Tripura during the reign of Ramachandranarayan, the successor of Kirtichandra, who made peace by paying compensation to the Raja of Tripura.[69] Ramachandra also reiterated the sovereign status of Heramba Government in the face of the persistent demand of the Ahom

* An inscription on a rock-cut temple at Maibong suggests that it was excavated in the *Saka* year 1643 (1721 A.D.) during the reign of Harishchandranarayan who has been described in the said inscription as the 'Lord of Heramba'.

† Parts of modern Hailakandi Subdivision

monarch to renew the allegiance. He was succeeded by Harishchandranarayan Bhupati who was, in turn, succeeded by Krishnachandra Narayan and the latter by Govindachandra Narayan* during whose reign Cachar was annexed by the British. The circumstances leading to this annexation have been discussed in the next two chapters.

---

* An undated coin of Govindachandra claims himself as the 'Lord of Heramba'. J.A.S.B., Vol. VI.

CHAPTER II

Early Contacts

The grant of the *Dewani* of Bengal by Shah Alam II, the Mughal Emperor, to Robert Clive, in 1765, secured for the East India Company, 'the Superintendency of all lands and the collection of all revenues' of the presidency of Bengal. The western portion of the Surma Valley forming the Sylhet *Sarkar* of Bengal *Subah* passed under the authorities at Fort William in Calcutta. But the British accesion being limited to the Mughal territory, Cachar, like Jayantia, remained independent. On the other hand, early in the same year, Ramchandra, Raja of Cachar, who had for long thrown off the allegiance to the Ahom Government, detained the messengers calling upon him to appear before Rajeswar Singh, the Ahom monarch. This led to the Ahom expedition against Cachar; Ramchandra had to re-affirm his allegiance to the Ahoms.[1]

Nevertheless, the common border between Cachar and Sylhet, existence of the sizable Bengalee population in Cachar plains having regular intercourse with their counterparts in Lower Province and rise of British interest in the affairs of the native states on the North eastern frontier—partly induced by the question of defence and partly for their potentialities—brought the kingdom of Heramba into contact with the British. As a matter of fact, Cachar had attracted the attention of the Company soon after the Battle of Plassey. This was occasioned by the Burmese occupation of a portion of Manipur.[2] Jai Singh, Raja of Manipur, appealed, simultaneously, to the Ahom monarch and the British authorities to save his country from

Burmese inroads. To the former, he offered his daughter, Kuranganayani, and to the latter promised a rent free grant of 12,000 square feet of land in the capital city for the British Residency and also undertook the liability of all expenditure in connection with the military help.[3] Unfortunately, however, the Ahom contingent sent under Haranath Phukan missed the route in the Naga Hills and had at last to return mid-way being oppressed by pestillence.[4] Similarly, the authorities at Fort Wiiliam had ordered Captain Verelst, the Chief of the Company's administration in Chittagong, to proceed to Manipur with six companies of sepoys to assist the Raja against Burmese. The latter, on his way, reached Khaspur in April 1763 and encamped there for nealy a year; but was prevented by the difficulties of communication rendered by the hills beyond Barak, heavy rainfall and much sickness in his troops, and was finally recalled.[5]

Poor Jai Singh went in exile, while the Burmese placed one Goursham on the throne. However, Jai Singh organised a strong army with the help of the Ahom monarch, and recovered his throne in 1768. But the installation of the Burmese rule in Manipur had some far-reaching effects upon the history of Cachar. In 1765, they made an attack on Cachar, when Sandhikari made a show of submission by handing over to the victorious Burmese general a tree bound in their native clay which signified that 'the land and person of the Raja were at the disposal of the King of Ava.[6] The Ahoms and the British alike were indifferent to the Burmese intrigue in the affairs of Cachar. As a matter of fact, this enabled Sandhikari to finally shake off the Ahom yoke with the disappearance of the Burmese. Harishchandra Narayana, the next Raja, constructed the Royal Palace at Khaspur, in 1771, and issued an inscription claiming himself as the 'Lord of Heramba' and reigned peacefully like a sovereign without any interference from any quarter.[7] Same spirit marked the early career of Krishnachandra, who succeded his father, Harishchandra. in 1780 ; but the latter being a weak and unscrupulous ruler, Cachar became the arena of conflict for her neighbours.[8] He married Indraprabha, daughter of Jai Singh, Raja of Manipur, and under latter's influence was intitiated to *Vaisnavism*.[9] The Brahmins who were invited from

Sylhet to attend the initiation ceremony were granted rent-free lands and settled in different parts of Cachar, particularly in Khaspur, Udharband and Bihara. Krishnachandra also constructed two *Vishnu* temples at Khaspur, and the pious Raja was always guided by the Brahmins in state affairs.[10]

But the piety of the Raja dragged the kingdom into complications with Manipur which followed in the succeeding years. His desire to visit the Holy shrines like Varanasi and Gaya, on the other hand, compelled him to oblige the British Government.[11] The latter were not likely to misuse the opportunity of obliging the Raja since the resources of Cachar had already evoked the interest of the British officers in Sylhet. In return of minor compliances, the Company's officers and British merchants carried on flourishing trade in the Cachar borders. But when their exactions surpassed reasonable limit, the Raja could not but appeal to the Company's Government for justice. In 1790, he addressed a letter to Lord Cornwallis, the Governor-General stating that since the beginning of the Company's administration in Bengal under the succesive Collectors of Sylhet, *viz.* Messers Sumer, Thackery, Holland, Lindsay and Willies, the relations between his Government and the East India Company were cordial; but the sixth Collector, Henry Lodge, wanted a monopoly in the trade in tusks, wax, cane, and bamboos, and with this intention he posted sepoys on the borders to prevent all transactions between the Company's territory and Cachar. This country consisted mainly of hills and jungles and the *ryots* subsisted on the sale of grass and bamboos.[12] Even the Raja's officers and the *Zamindars* used to make *Khedas* and sell their elephants to the British merchants in Sylhet on attractive prices. Also, merchants themselves would visit Cachar and purchase elephants.[13] Obviously, the restrictions threatened to crush the country economically. The Board of Revenue thereupon instructed the Collector of Sylhet to abolish the trade restrictions between Cachar and Sylhet.[14] The restoration of the free trade, made the Raja more favourably disposed towards the British Government, and he now looked upon the latter for help and protection whenever he was involved in any problem. In 1799, a Mughal adventurer, named Aga Mahammad Reza, entered Cachar from Sylhet and for a time succeeded in

making himself the master of the country. Baffled in his attempt
to resist the intruder, Krishnachandra took refuge in the hills.
Puffed up at the initial success, Aga declared that he was the
twelfth *Imam* destined to liberate India from the yoke of the
British merchants. He could easily win over a large section of
the local Muslims and many crossed over the British frontier
from Sylhet, Comilla and Mymensingh to join the *Imam*. Meanwhile, Krishnachandra sent an appeal to the authorities at
Fort William for help. In response, the latter sent some sepoys.
Aga was captured in 1801, and remanded to Calcutta.[15] Again,
in 1804, one Kalyan Singh, a dismissed *Subehdar* of the Company's Army, collected a large body of *Barkandazes* and
commenced plunder and atrocities in Cachar. The Raja appealed to the Collector of Sylhet and the latter despatched a Company of soldiers who succeeded in expelling the adventurers.[16]
Krishnachandra also suspected that he had some enemies in
the neighbouring territories of Manipur, Tripura and Jayantia.
Although he possessed an extensive territory, the revenue of
the state was not sufficient to keep a standing army. The Raja,
therefore, on several occasions requested the Government to
station some companies of the British sepoys in his country
and at times even wanted to place his *Raj* under the British
control.[17] But the policy of the Government towards the native
states at the time being strictly one of non-intervention all
appeals of the Raja of Cachar for military assistance went in
vain.

To make matters worse, circumstances compelled Krishnachandra to be entangled in a conflict with the Ahoms. During
the Moamaria Rebellion* in Assam many rebels clubed in Cachar
and in collaboration with the people of North Cachar carried
on depredations in the Ahom territory. Kamalesvar Singha,
tae Ahom monarch, demanded the surrender of the recalcitrants from the Raja of Cachar, but the latter denied any hand

---

* The Moamarias were a socio-religious sect and, according to Gait,
it consisted "mainly of persons of low social rank, such as *Domes*, Morans,
Kacharis, Horis and Chutias and, as they denied the supremacy of the
Brahmins, they were naturally the special aversion of the orthodox Hindu
hierarchy". Gait, n. 10, 60 ; for further details see S.K. Bhuyan, *Anglo-
Assamese Relations*, 217-37 and 585-7 ; A.C. Banerjee, *The Eastern Frontier
of British India*, 13 and 25.

in the matter. This resulted in a series of skirmishes from 1803 to 1805. However, a decisive defeat was inflicted by the Ahoms on the rebel 'Kacharis' and their Moamaria allies on the bank of the river Kalong and the Moamaria Rebellion was finally suppressed.[18]

About the same time, in 1807, Krishnachandra had a dispute with the Collector of Sylhet regarding the boundary between Sylhet and Cachar. The *Amins* of Sylhet laid down a line which the *ryots* in Cachar did not recognise, and when the crops had ripened the Raja's people crossed the line and forcibly carried away the grains.[19] Stringent orders were then issued by the Collector to the native officer of Badarpur *thana* to prevent such tresspass into British territory.[20] But subsequently it was revealed that the line laid down by the *Amins* included certain portion of Cachar, which was then restored.[21]

Inspite of the occasional bitterness created by the questions of trade and boundaries, it is clear that Krishnachandra was dependent on the British authorities for his security. The Raja was granted, in 1809, passport to visit the Holy shrine at Varanasi, Gaya and Calcutta and was escorted by the British sepoys. Due to the expensive rituals performed at several places, when the Raja was in short of purse Lord Minto, the Governor-General, helped him with money when he met the latter at Calcutta. This was an opportunity for the Governor-General to confer with the Raja of Cachar regarding mutual relations. Subsequently Raja's younger brother, Govindachandra, also visited these shrines having been favoured with necessary passport and escort by the Government of Bengal.[22]

These pilgrimages, on the other hand, brought the ruler of Cachar more and more within the fold of the East India Company. In fact, the Raja was always in perpetual fear of attack by his neighbours and was not even free from the dread of internal rebels. To move from one part of the country to another he requested the Calcutta authorities to provide him with escort. On several occasions the Raja professed his complete dependence on the East India Company and repeatedly sent his *Vakeels* Hridaynath Dev, Kushalram Dutta, Durgacharan Dutta, Shyam Dutta, Kebalkrishna Das, Manikyaram Deb, Goursundar Chatterjee, Kalidas Banerjee and others to the

Governor-General praying help in many respects and offering the latter rich presents of ivory hat, fan and box, tusked elephants and bottles of honey.[23] He had even represented to the British Government, in 1809, soliciting that a guard of 25 sepoys might be stationed for the protection of Cachar during his absence on holy mission. Although this was not complied with, two years later a second and still more urgent application was made which was equally unheeded. However, the Raja was promised that every attention would be shown to him that was due to a friendly neighbour.[24] Inspite of this, the Raja carried on loud appeals for British protection thus exposing tactlessly the highly deplorable condition of his country. Such inclination towards an alien Government was nothing but the humiliation of the prestige and status of the sovereign State.

It may, however, be noted that the attachment of Krishna-chandra towards the British Government was not from any love or respect. This was essentially for his trading necessities with Sylhet and devotion towards the religious shrines that had fallen in the mainland. The Raja was also haunted by internal and external enemies, and, as such, needed a strong ally to support him against any upsurge. Otherwise, he was always suspicious about the conduct of the British, and was highly cautious in his contacts with them. As early in 1789, when one Marsh, a botanist, was deputed by the Home Government to study the vegetable products of North East India, J. Willies, Collector of Sylhet, requested the Raja of Cachar to allow Mr. Marsh to visit his country, but the Raja pertinaciously refused his entrance. To quote Willies : "The refusal probably originated in fear, the Raja imagining that Europeans are desirous of becoming acquainted with his country only with a view of reducing it under their subjection; and it is difficult to persuade savages that a European gentleman entered his country solely for the purpose of examining vegetable productions."[25] Realising that further request from the Collector would only tend to increase the Raja's jealousy, Willies advised Marsh to send a *Vakeel* to Cachar and endeavour as a private merchant to conciliate, if possible, the Raja to his admission.[26] When this too failed, Lord Cornwallis, the Governor-General in Council, ordered Marsh to proceed to the execution of his mission in

Tripura and Chittagong and to postpone his researches in Surma Valley.[27] The British Government, on the other hand, wanted to keep the Raja in good humour for their own interest, as has already been mentioned, and on several occasions gave the Raja many concesions.

The troubles were also not far to come from Manipur. Krishnachandra had allowed himself to be entangled in the web of intrigue that had encircled the throne of Manipur, with results that were fatal for his own principality. In 1798, Jai Singh abdicated in favour of his son Rabindrachandra who was murdered by his brother, Madhuchandra, after a brief reign of three years. But the usurper in his turn had been expelled from the throne by his brother Chourjit. Madhuchandra appealed to Krisnachandra for help which was extended. But his effort to recover the throne with aid from Cachar ended in discomfiture and death. However, another competitor for the crown of Manipur shortly appeared in the person of Marjit who turned his steps to the Raja of Cachar, but was refused any assistance. Baffled in his attempt to secure aid from Krishnachandra, Marjit left Cachar in anger and applied to the Court of Ava for help, and with Burmese aid made himself the master of Manipur. The two brothers, Chourjit and Gambhir Singh, with their followers took refuge in Cachar.[28]

In the midst of these troubles Krishnachandra passed away* in 1813, and was succeeded by his brother Govindachandra.[29] Evidently, the new Raja began his career in the face of a host of problems, both internal and external. He was, on the other hand, very unpopular amongst his subjects. By marrying Indraprabha, the widow of Krishnachandra, he incurred the displeasure of the nobles of the country. He promulgated a series of laws for the civil and criminal administration of the country which painted him as the most reactionary ruler. The people felt insecure under his rule, and the Raja was deprived of proper co-operation from indispensable quarters. Taking advantage of this anamalous situation, Kahi Das, the Revenue Collector in North Cachar, along with some officials revolted against the Raja. But the rebel Collector was arrested and

---

* He died on Tuesday, the 3 *Kartik*, 1735 *Sakabda*.

hanged under the orders of the Raja.[30]   The information of the
assassination of his father having reached him, Tularam, the
son of Kahi Das, who was the commander of a wing of foot
soldiers, escaped into the hills, and having taken the leadership
of the rebels continued to disturb Govindachandra through frequent raids and plunders.[31]   In collaboration with the officers
in various charge of the 'hill areas' in the north like Sanudram,
Ramjay and Demradeo, Tularam embezzled the revenue of the
state, fled to Jayantiapur and ensured the support of the Raja
of Jayantia, Ram Singh II.   Thereupon, the rebel leaders proceeded to Dharampur *pargana* in the northern frontier of the
kingdom and instigated the *Zamindars* in the locality to with-
hold the payment of revenue to the Government of Cachar.
They also allied themselves with the hillmen in North Cachar
and the dissatisfied *forty Sempungs*, which was a council of the
representatives of the forty Dimacha clans.[32]   The period of
confusion initiated by the Manipuri adventurers gave Tularam
an opportunity to extend his sway and to make a determined
bid to establish himself as the Raja of Cachar.   The extremely
disquieting situation in the country left no alternative for
Govindachandra but to seek help of the British.   The Cachar
Army being untrained, indisciplined and without sufficient
muskets, the Raja appealed to Lord Harding the Governor
General, to favour him with 25 sepoys, but the latter refused
to comply with this request. As a result, the Raja was systematically harrassed by his enemies.[33]

The fugitive Manipuri brothers were also not unharmful to
the Raja.   They expected to persuade him to help them in re-
covering the throne of Manipur.   But in view of the chaotic
condition of his own principality Govindachandra could hardly
be of any use to Chourjit against his rival seated on the throne
with the Burmese support.   Govindachandra further hinted
that both the contenders being equally related to him his siding
with either was never justifiable.   Enraged by the reluctance,
Chourjit repaired to Jayantia and in league with Ram Singh II
and Tularam commenced prolonged incursions in the Kalain
pargana as far as *mouza* Tarapur.[34]   But Gambhir Singh stayed
in Cachar with his host and assured the Raja of his best help.
As a result, Govindachandra appointed him as the Commander-

in-Chief of the Cachar Army at a monthly salary of Rs. 50.[35]

More serious threat was, however, waiting for Govinda-chandra. In December 1817, Marjit with a large number of Burmese in his army attacked Cachar. With his existence at stake, Govindachandra appealed to the British Government for help, but to no purpose. Consequently, the invaders had spectacular success in a short time. Starting from Lakhipur they rapidly advanced as far as the British frontier of Badarpur where one Carey, a British officer in the Company's fort at Badarpur, took the command of the Cachar Army. The Raja was hopeful that Carey would be able to save his country from total extinction but to his disappointment, the latter left Cachar in the midst of the war without even giving any information to the Raja. The success of Marjit over the Raja and his advance upto the Company's frontier alarmed J. French, the Magistrate of Sylhet, who immediately sent Captain David-son with troops to guard the British frontier. Marjit then dreaded an attack from the British Government and, although he had virtually made himself the master of Cachar, wrote a letter to the Magistrate of Sylhet requesting him to appoint an European officer to keep Govindachandra and Gambhir Singh in check so that they might not resort to any war against Manipur.[36] The Magistrate could not comply with the request, but assured Marjit that if he did not cause disturbance in the Company's frontier the British would have no occasion to dispute with him. Govindachandra and Gambhir Singh by the time had retired to a defensive position on the bank of Barak and then made a determined attack to expel the invaders from Cachar. Their endeavours were crowned with success, and Marjit and his men were gallantly repulsed and the country liberated.[37]

But no sooner had the invaders retired, a fresh spell of disturbance broke out in Cachar. Chourjit persuaded Gambhir Singh to part with Govindachandra, and the two, joining hands with Tularam, resumed atrocities in the Raja's territory. At the head of hill rebels, they set fire to the villages in the plains and looted or destroyed the properties.[38] In his letter of 10 April 1818, the Raja requested the Governor-General to grant him a passport for importing 200 Hindusthanis and an Englishman

for his protection and also to help him with some of the Company's sepoys for the supression of his enemies. The Raja agreed
to bear the expenses of the troops, and, in addition, to pay an
annual tribute to the Government.[39] To pursue the matter, he
sent two of his *Vakeels*—Kalidas Banerjee and Gaursundar
Chatterjee—to Calcutta.[40] The *Vakeels* submitted a petition to
the Governor-General soliciting immediate compliance of the
Raja's request. But the authorities in Calcutta still clung to
the policy of non-intervention and, therefore, no help was accorded.[41] As a result, the rebels were encouraged in their plunderous atrocities and by a night attack, in June 1818, compelled
the Raja to escape to Sylhet.[42] The Manipuri brothers took the
possession of the Cachar plains, while Tularam became the
master of the northern hills.[43] In the meantime, the Burmese
overran Assam and Manipur. Marjit being driven out of his
country came to Cachar, in 1819, carrying the sacred image of
Govinda with him. 'Brother-like', he was warmly received by
Chaourjit and Gambhir Singh. They parcelled out Cachar
amongst themselves, and thus the three Manipuri princes began
to reign over three different parts of the Cachar plains as perfectly independent of one another.[44]

Cachar thus remained a prey to the depredations of the fugitive Manipuri princes. These usurpers at the same time made
repeated attempts to expel the Burmese from Manipur causing
huge material drain from Cachar. Hirachandra, son of
Rabindrachandra, at the head of a small cavalry, continued to
annoy the Burmese garrison stationed in Manipur. In 1822,
Pitambar Singh, another nephew of Chourjit, was sent to Hirachandra's assistance. The brave young man defeated a Burmese
force, but had to retreat to Cachar owing to the shortage of
provisions and the Burmese ravaged Manipur. In 1823, Pitambar
Singh again invaded Manipur, deposed Shubal Singh who was
the Burmese nominee to the Manipuri throne, and himself
assumed the Royal dignity. Gambhir Singh at once infiltrated
into Manipur with a small levy and deposed Pitambar who then
fled to Burma and found a permanent asylum there. But
Gambhir too could not stay in Manipur as he fails to secure
supply and shortly returned to Cachar.[45]

Meanwhile, the presence of Govindachandra in Sylhet,

developments in Cachar and the esstablishment of the Burmese rule in Manipur could not but make the British authorities concerned about the defence of their eastern frontier. The Collector of Sylhet feared that Govindachandra might try to go back to his kingdom thereby giving rise to complications embarrassing to the Company. As a matter of fact, the poor Raja was anxious to return to his country and repeatedly appealed, in vain to the British Government for re-instatement.[46] He also prayed for the restoration of the Shirishpur *pargana* which previously belonged to Cachar, but was taken away by the authorities at Sylhet and attached to that district. The Company had promised to give him in exchange a similar tract of land elsewhere which the Raja had then refused to accept. He now reiterated his claim and even prayed to become the *Zamindar* of Shrispur under the Company. He wanted his kingdom to be attached to the British dominion for better security and government. The Raja had become so destitute that he could hardly maintain himself and begged to be allowed to live at Shirispur where essential commodities were comparatively cheaper. Unfortunately, however, none of his prayers could easily move the authorities at Fort Wiliam.[47] Any way, in early part of 1820, Govindachandra was permitted by the British Government to go back to his country. Along with his officials, the Raja reached Katgorah, but the Manipuri brothers soon forced his retreat to Sylhet.[48]

The lawlessness and misrule which had convulsed the unfortunate state, however, soon took a new turn. The Manipuri princes, who acted in unison in the beginning, now fell out with each other. In the contest that followed, Chourjit escaped to Sylhet, while Marjit and Gambhir Singh divided Cachar plains between themselves. Marjit Singh occupied Hailakandi, and Gambhir Singh possessed himself of the rest of South Cachar.[49] Chourjit proposed to make over his interests in Cachar to the British Government and requested the Magistrate of Sylhet to send an officer to take charge of his territory. Govindachandra now proposed the merger of Cachar with Sylhet. But the authorities in Calcutta did not find any inducement to accept either of these proposals. On the contrary, on a report from the British *Vakeel* at Jayantiapur that Govindachandra had applied for help to the Burmese in Assam the Raja was removed to Dacca from Sylhet.[50]

About the same time the stationing of the Burmese forces heading towards Cachar, in Assam and Manipur, reached the ears of the local officers, and centring the small principality of Cachar now began intensive diplomatic activities. Geographically Cachar occupied a commanding position and the British Government were determined from the very beginning not to allow the Burmese to use Cachar as the base of their future offensive. Naturally, the gradual advance of the Burmese from Nowgong towards Cachar compelled Lord Amherst, the Governor-General, to think seriously of the future of this ill-fated principality. The problem of Cachar was at once lifted into prominence and the case of its future settlement was thus at last taken up by the Council at Calcutta. The Council resolved to accept Cachar as a tributary kingdom, but, strangely enough, it instructed the local officers to open negotiations with the Manipuri usurpers.[51]

Accordingly, the Governor-General in Council, on 19 June 1823, instructed the Magistrate of Sylhet to avail himself of Chourjit's letter which offered to place his interest in Cachar under the protection of the Company to open up communication with him and eventually with other chiefs of Cachar to ascertain their sentiments and to furnish a full report of their relative power and influence and the actual condition of the country and its inhabitants.[52] On the basis of this report, it was proposed to determine how far it would be expedient to extend to Cachar the protection of the British Government on the usual terms of political dependency or the annexation of the country to the dominion of the Company.[53] But before the instructions of the Government of India had reached the Magistrate, Chourjit lost all footing in Cachar and Gambhir Singh obtained a solid ascendency in its affairs, though Marjit continued to hold a small tract. In his letter to Mr Moore, the Acting Magistrate of Sylhet, Gambhir Singh declared himself to be the sole ruler of Cachar, denied the right of Marjit as his subordinate to conclude a treaty with the British authorities, and winced on his own part a marked disinclination to enter into any new or specific engagements, though he professed

himself to be willing and anxious to be considered under the
protection of the British Government.[54] Whilst the authorities
at Fort William were thus deliberating to shape their policy
towards Cachar, troubles broke out with the Burmese in the
Chittagong frontier. The threat of invading the British
territory was clearly voiced by the Burmese and a private
communication from Scott, on 11 November 1823, informed
the Government that a force had already been despatched from
Assam to conquer Cachar. The Calcutta Council then opined
"that after the steps which had been already taken by the
British Government for effecting a connection of a tributary
and protective nature with the state of Cachar it would be a
culpable dereliction of their own interests if the Government
offered the Burmans to carry into execution their fresh purpose
of aggression."[55] Finally, the Council decided that Govindchandra should be reinstated on his ancestral throne and that the
Mainpuri brothers would be provided with pensions chargeable
from the revenue of Cachar provided they would agree to reside within the British territory, while Tularm was assured
of a place in the general arrangement that would subsequently
follow.[56]

Meanwhile, Farquand, the Acting Magistrate of Sylhet,
reported that a Burmese force under Tularam and Sanudram,
two hill-chiefs of North Cachar, had actually passed into
Cachar from Assam and had captured one of the forts at
Jaflong. Reacting to these movements and apprehending
hostilities against Sylhet, the Magistrate thought it necessary
to call upon the Officer commanding the Company's troops in
the eastern frontier to move with his whole force to the frontier, and likewise to apply to Dacca for reinforcements to place
the station in a sufficient state of defence.[57] On 24 November
1823, the Magistrate reported that Gambhir Singh was not only
disinclined in enter into any terms with the British but was actually holding communication in a secret and clandestine manner
with the Burmese Agent in Manipur to procure the presence of
a Burmese force in Cachar to help him in seizing the person of
his rivals. He was also discussing with the Burmese the terms
of his alliance which would enable that power to occupy Cachar
preparatory to an attack on the British possessions.[58] Soon

after the Magistrate again reported about a rumour that Govindachandra had invited the Burmese troops into his country and
that his *Vakeels* were actually in the enemy camp and, therefore,
deemed expedient to place the Raja under honourable arrest
until the orders of Government could be received.[59]   However,
the Governor-General treated Gambhir Singh only as a usurper,
while he attributed the conduct of Govindachandra, if true,
to the prolonged reluctance of the British Government to help
him to recover his ancestral kingdom.[60]   Scott suggested that
Govindachandra should be reestablished allowing him to remain
independent of both the British and the Burmese Governments
but under their mutual guarantee, so that Cachar would serve
as a buffer between the two rival dominions.[61]   But Amherst
described it as too late a measure in view of the altered situation
in the Eastern frontier, and desired that Govindachandra
should be reinstated as the Raja of Cachar under the protection
of the Government of Fort William and a treaty embodying
the terms of relations between the two should be executed.[62]

The Governor-General also asked the Magistrate of Sylhet
to enquire into the number and nature of the passes leading from
the Burmese possessions into Cachar and Jayantia and the
expediency, with reference to the climate and other considerations, of sending a detachment of the British troops to
occupy them. Precautionary measures were also at once
adopted for the protection of Assam and Chittagong frontiers;
troops were sent to Rangpur and Sylhet and the officers in
these districts were directed to collect reliable information
about the movement and intention of the Burmese.[63]   Towards
the close of November 1823, information poured in that about
900 Burmese soldiers were on the Cachar frontier, ready to
invade.[64]   Scott was immediately directed to ask the Burmese
commander in Assam in the name of the Governor-General in
Council to desist from invading Cachar on the ground that it
had already been taken under British protection. He was also authorised at his discretion to direct the troops in Sylhet to move
to Cachar and to occupy the passes through which the Burmese
would attempt to penetrate, and to proceed in person to Sylhet
to bring to a speedy conclusion all contemplated arrangements
regarding Cachar.[65]   Accordingly, a detachment of sixteen

hundred men was despatched to the Sylhet frontiers. On their arrival it was found that three columns of the Burmese forces were in the neighbourhood of Cachar : one of about four thousand men was advancing from Nowgong through North Cachar, another was marching through Jaintia Hills, while a third, from Manipur, had already arrived in South Cachar and inflicted a defeat on Gambhir Singh's local levy.[66] In pursuance of the Governor-General's instructions, on 1 January 1824, David Scott addressed a letter to the Burmese Governor in Assam. But the Burmese in reply pleaded that they had been sent by His Majesty, the King of Ava, to re-establish Govindachandra on the throne in response to his earnest appeal and to arrest the Manipuri chiefs who had dethroned him.[67]

The situation in North-East Frontier thus entered into a critical phase, and the East India Company's Government in India now had to reckon with one of the most typical challenges in its history. Lord Amherst, the Governor-General, rightly realised that the Burmese intrigue in the affairs of the frontier states was a dangerous threat to the very existence of the British in Bengal. But the expulsion of the Burmese was a formidable task. The latter had established their suzerainty in Manipur and laid a claim upon Jaintia on the ground that it was feudatory to the Ahom Government. It also claimed that as early as the reign of Hshin-byu-shin, the king of Ava, the Raja of Cachar had handed over to victorious Burmese general a tree with roots in their native clay as a recognition that his person and land were at the disposal of the Burmese king.[68] As a matter of fact, the policy of non-intervention followed by the British Government since the time of Sir John Shore was singularly responsible for encouraging the Burmese to overrun Assam and Manipur and to encroach upon Cachar. The same policy had given all indulgence to the Manipuri usurpers to exploit Cachar and to expel its legal chief from the country. However, so long the Burmese incursions were in the nature of burglary or gang robbery or oldfashioned border raids, but now it was a imperial tussle between the British and the Burmese.[69] Had the British Government listened to the appeals of Govindachandra before his expulsion from the Cachar, the Burmese menace might have been more easily and effectively dealt with. But now the whole situation was so

confusing that military action must precede any political settlement.

Lord Amherst took serious notice of the question of
extending British protection to Cachar. He discovered
several inducements for the British Government to establish its
direct authority, or at least a preponderent influence, in Cachar.
He also favoured the restoration of Govindachandra as the
Raja of Cachar under the protection of the East India Company's Government as an alternative to direct British rule.[70]
But the Burmese plea that Govindachandra had appealed to
the King of Ava for help reacted sharply among the local
officers who proposed to prosecute the Raja for inviting an
alien power while living within British territory. But the
Governor-General opined : "Even if these allegations against
Govindachandra proved to be true, he could only have sought
it when denied the assistance of the power to whom he had
for so many years appealed in vain."[71]

Amherst also had dialogue with the authorities in England.
In his letter to the Court of Directors on 9 January 1824, he
observed that Cachar did not appear to have ever been subject
or tributary to the Government of Ava. It is true that Marjit
Singh when in possession of Manipur, which he attained through
Burmese help, and held as their feudatory, did invade and for
a time possess himself of Cachar, but he was speadily repulsed
by Govindachandra and no trace was found in the correspondence of the Burmese at any time having laid claim to the
country or to any right of interference in its affairs.[72] The
British measures with regard to Cachar might, therefore, be
taken without any fear of infringing the rights or claims of the
Burmese. The only question for consideration was one of
policy as to whether they should extend authority or influence
over Cachar, which was bordering and having relations with
their Government. The British Government should, as the
Governor-General felt, run the risk of embroiling itself with
Manipur, because the measures proposed by the Government
of India was expedient on many grounds. It should not
deprive itself of the advantages of occupying Cachar from
an apprehension of giving umbrage where it could not with any
colour of justice be taken and where no opposition was likely
to be offered.[73] One of the easiest passes from Ava into the

Company's territory was through Manipur and Cachar and the occupation of the latter was essential for the defence of the pass, which it effectually secured. Ths occupation of Cachar would contribute to check the progress of the Burmese arms, their permanent occupation of Assam and the atrocities of the forces stationed there.[74]

These considerations were not deemed sufficient by the British Government on former occasions to avail itself of the opportunities that presented themselves of effecting this object, nor did they indeed possess the weight that subsequent occurences and further experience have given them. Cachar had long been a prey to internal dissensions, its weekness had more than once been the means of menacing the tranquility of Sylhet, and that the contentions of the parties struggling for superiority and their appeals for British assistance and support have been a frequent source of embarrassment to the authorities at Fort William. There seemed no other probable mode of appeasing these dissensions than employment of British influence for the purpose, and this could be rendered effectual, the Governor-General observed, only by taking the country openly and decidedly under British protection. Cachar was described for the most part to be an 'open country' of no great extent, forty or fifty square miles and partly hills, and similar in climate to the neighbouring parts of Sylhet. Its occupation could probably be attended with little additional charge, even if it was formally annexed to British dominion, and with still less if it continued to be governed by its traditional Chief under the general protection of the East India Company.[75]

But before anything could be done, on 15 January 1824, the Magistrate of Sylhet reported that the Burmese forces of a considerable strength had already invaded Cachar. The Officers who were commanding the detachments which had previously been detailed at Badarpur applied to Furquand to guide them in the emergency.[76] Meanwhile, Amherst had desired the advance of the British troops to the frontiers 'for the purpose of enforcing the declared intention of the British Government to protect Cachar from invasion', and hoped that it 'would not fail to induce the General of the King of Ava to halt.'[77] Should it be urged by them that they were acting under the 'orders received from the Court of Ammerapuram to reinstate Govind

Chunder in the possession of Cachar', Amherst desired Scott to apprise them that the British Government was itself disposed to favour the claims of that chief, but that adverting to the doubtful nature of the relations existing at present between the two states, and to the declaration of the Burmese in Arracan that the forces of the King of Ava would invade the British Territory along the whole line of its Eastern Frontier the Governor-General in Council could not under any circumstance permit them to establish themselves in Cachar and thus acquire a position the command of which would greatly facilitate the execution of that threat.[78] If the Burmese evinced a determination to establish themselves in Cachar inspite of this warning, the Agent was categorically authorised to take immediate measures for expelling the invaders by force.[79] At this moment, Raja of Jaytia also apprehended an invasion by the Burmese and offered to the Magistrate of Sylhet to enter into engagements with the Company. While communicating the offer to the Calcutta Council, the Magistrate explained the advantages of including this 'pettey state' in the general system of defensive arrangements for the frontier. The Government of India readily accepted, and instructed Scott to take advantage of the opening which that communication afforded for requiring the Raja to enter into engagements similar to those proposed for Cachar.[80]

The Burmese too were determined to execute their mission. The warning issued by Scott failed to induce them either 'to halt or retrace'. On the other hand, the Governor claimed, as mentioned above, that they had a special mandate from their Emperor to restore Cachar to its legal ruler. Robertson, the Magistrate of Chittagong, also reported that the dispute in Shahpuri was no longer a mere provincial issue as it had been taken away from the jurisdiction of the Governor of Arakan by the ministers. He suggested that military action was the means to keep the hostile Burmese at a distance. He also pointed out that considering the state of affairs in Cachar and the conduct of the Burmese the British Government must be regarded virtually at war with the Government of Ava.[81] Amherst naturally took a very serious view of the situation and determined to expel the intruders. He communicated the facts to the Home authorities and pending their approval asked Scott to take active measures for removing the Burmese from Cachar as the season was still favourable for military operations in the eastern frontier. Accordingly, Major Newton, Commandant of the British troops, was advised to launch the offensive before the rival forces had joined hands. Scott established his temporary headquarters at Badarpur to keep himself available for Newton's guidence.[82]

On 17 January 1824, Newton marched against Nowgong column which had stockaded itself at Bikrampur and easily put them to flight. The Burmese escaped into the hills and subsequently effected a junction with the Manipur force. The British detachment was then withdrawn to Badarpur, whereupon the Burmese advanced to Jatrapur, erected stockades on both banks of Barak and bridged the river. The forces in this camp amounted to about six thousand men, of whom two thousand were Burmese and the rest 'Assamese and the Cacharis'. Another detachment of about two thousand Burmese was stationed in Hailakandi. The invaders gradually pushed forward their stockades on the north bank of Barak; but when within a thousand yards of the British, they were attacked and put to flight. The Nowgong contingents were attacked at the foot of the Bhetika pass, on the bank of Jatinga river; driven from the stockades they fled into the hills and made their way back to Nowgong. The British troops then marched against the Manipur column which had taken up a very strong position at Dudpatil. On 13 February, the most remarkable battle was fought at Badarpur on the Bank of the Surma which considerably cracked the morale of the invaders. The Burmese suffered heavy losses in the encounters and the scarcity of supplies in Cachar rendered it extremely difficult to maintain a large force there. The contingent, therefore, ultimately fell back to Manipur.[83] Cachar was thus liberated from the Burmese occupation forces. There seemed little reason to apprehend their speedy return to force and, therefore, a small detachment was left in Cachar, while the main body went into cantonments in Sylhet.[84]

The success of the British troops in expelling the Brumese from Cachar cleared the ground for a political setlement of the country. Lord Amherst was sanguine to establish preponderent influence of the British in this strategic state and reinstate Govindachandra on the vacant throne. His arguments found favour with the Council at Fort William and the Agent to the

Governor-General was, accordingly, instructed to settle the terms
of future relations with the Raja. True to the instructions from
Calcutta, a treaty[85] was concluded, on 6 March 1824, at Badarpur between David Scott and Govindachandra under which the
Raja, for himself and his successors, acknowledged allegiance
to the East India Company and placed his country under the Company's protection. The Company, in its turn, undertook to protect Cachar from external agressions and to arbitrate any difference that may arise between the Raja and other states. The Raja
also agreed to abide by such arbitration and to hold no
correspondence or communication with the foreign powers,
except through the channel of the British Government. It was
also agreed that the internal administration of the country shall
be conducted by the Raja, and the jurisdiction of the British
Court of Justice shall not extend there. But the Raja agreed
to attend at all times to the advice offered for the welfare of his
subjects by the Governor-General in Council and to rectify any
abuse that may arise in the administration of the country. He
also agreed to adopt, whenever necessary, all arrangements that
were in force in Sylhet in the Police, Opium and Salt Departments. In consideration of the promised aid, Govindachandra
agreed to pay to the Company an annual tribute of rupees ten
thousand, while the Company undertook to provide maintenance for the Manipuri Princes who lately occupied Cachar. In
case the Raja was a defaulter, the Company was placed "at
liberty to occupy and attach, in perpetuity, to their possessions,
a sufficient tract of Cachar country, to provide for the future
realisation of the tribute."[86]

Govindachandra thus sacrificed the independence of Cachar
in consideration for British protection. The Treaty of Badarpur virtually made the East India Company the lord-paramount
of Cachar and provided a window towards the west for interference even in internal administration. It categorically empowered the Company to attach any part of the country, in perpetuity
if the Raja failed to pay the tribute regularly. Once sovereign,
the kingdom of Heramba was thus reduced to the status of a
vassal state and even the welfare of the people was subjected
to the advice of the Governor-General in Council. As a matter
of fact, the long hands of Fort William had so much been
expanded over Khaspur that the annexation of Cachar to the

British Dominion in India was a matter of time only.

Be that as it may, the internal condition of the country was so chaotic and the Government so feeble that the sovereignty had become a myth. May be it was fortunate for the people that they were subjected to the British, and not the Burmese. Despite its seperate political entity, Cachar was socially, linguistically, geographically and demographically an integral part of greater Bengal and for the majority of its people, like any Indian, the ecclesiastical centres were at Varanasi, Hardwar, Dakshinesvar and others in the mainland. Had Cachar been occupied by the Burmese, the people would have been cut off from the main stream of Indianism and Bengali language and culture. At least, they were rescued from the Burmese menace.

In the meantime, the vulnerability of the eastern frontier of Bengal had compelled the authorities in Calcutta to abandon the policy of non-intervention.[87] A similar treaty was concluded, on 10 March 1824, with Ram Singh, Raja of Jayantia, who also acknowledged the British suzerainty and undertook to assist with all his forces and to afford every facility in his power in case the Company is engaged in any war to the eastward of Brahmaputra.[88] Jayantia thus followed the example of Cachar and both the kingdoms of *Mahabharata* fame became partners to the 'general system of defensive arrangements for the frontier' engineered by the Government of Fort William. Consequently, both the states, in no time, became an arena of Anglo-Burmese encounters.

On the declaration of the war against Burma, on 5 March 1824, British troops moved from Goalpara both by land and water. Scott himself commanded the Company's forces in Surma Valley where a battalion of the Sylhet Light Infantry marched from Sylhet to Nowgong through the territory of Jayantia. On the advance of the British the Burmese retreated, and their stockades at Raha, Nowgong and Kaliabor fell in rapid succession. But with the advent of the rains the advancing columns had to roll back which enabled the Burmese to reoccupy the lost possessions. The operations were resumed after the rainy season and the Burmese once again made hasty retreat. They withdrew from the various cantonments and entrenched themselves at Rangpur, the capital of the Ahom Government. Lack of reinforcement and division in their own

camp enfeebled the Burmese so much that they had no alternative but to appeal for peace.[89]

In Cachar, the Burmese were encouraged by the withdrawal
of the main body of the British troops to resume the offensive,
and occupied the stockades at Kalain, Dudpatil and Jatrapur.
This had rendered fresh operations in Surma Valley necessary.
The British had tried to make Manipur unfavourable for the
Burmese by utilising the services of the Manipuri brothers.
Gambhir and Marjit were detained at Sylhet, and it had been
proposed to make some provision for them out of the revenue
of Cachar. Realising that Gambhir Singh was a bold and
aspiring soldier, Scott induced him to lead an expedition for
the conquest of Manipur. He was told that Manipur would
be placed under him if he could liberate it and that the British
Government would not insist on Chourjit's admission to any
share in the Government. Frustrated, Chourjit attempted to
excite a revolt amongst the Manipuri recruits of a British
battalion, but was detected and removed to Nadia on a monthly
pension of rupees one hundred. Gambhir Singh proceeded to
Badarpur, in April 1824, and joined the Company's detachment
stationed there.[90]

The renewal of the hostility in Cachar enabled the Government to utilise the services of Gambhir Singh, and for the latter
to recover his ancestral state from the Burmese yoke. In June
1824, Colonel William Innes with twelve hundred men proceeded to Cachar to expel the invaders. He arrived at Badarpur
on 20 June and then moved to Jatrapur by water, along Barak,
where he arrived on 27 June. But his progress was rendered
extremely difficult by incessant rains and consequent innunda-
tion of the country. He took possession of Jatrapur, but failed
to occupy Kalain where the Burmese were stockaded. Assisted
by Gambhir, the British troops fired on the stockade for three
days, July 6 to 8. On the second day the position was so
difficult that Colonel Innes retired to Jatrapur where he took
up a strong position. This retreat was mainly due to the sickness among his soldiers, exposed to heavy rains, while the
Burmese were confined in their entrenchments by the rise of
the rivers. No further movement could take place on either
side during the continuance of the rains.[91]

A force of seven hundred men was then collected with the

object of freeing Cachar and Manipur from the enemy and also for making a demonstration against Ava. Towards the close of October 1824, the Burmese army in Cachar retired to Manipur having suffered from disease. The British troops could not pursue them as Manipur was still under water, but they occupied Kalain and Dudpatil and destroyed the stockades built by the Burmese.[92]

The invaders had now finally retreated from Cachar and Assam, and hence the Government could devote itself to the occupation of Manipur. The Burmese were fully occupied with the operations in Arakan and the Delta, and no significant opposition was apprehended. Brigadier-General Shuldham, Commanding Eastern Frontier, decided to march into Manipur, and Cachar was, obviously, made the base of offensive. Arrangements were made for the construction of a road from Dudpatil to Manipur, and on 24 February 1825, Shuldham arrived at Banskandi. But the geographical features of the country and incessant rains made it impossible for him to complete the road or to advance towards Manipur. The mountainous tract from Banskandi towards Manipur was highly difficult and with the commencement of rain assumed so turbulent a character that the idea of conquering Manipur had to be abandoned for the time being. However, in December 1825, campaign against the occupation forces was renewed. This time Gambhir Singh, accompanied by British troops under Captain Grant, with an irregular levy of five hundred Manipuris and 'Kacharis', successfully expelled the Burmese from the state altogether.[93] Meanwhile, the operations of the British arms, under Sir Archibald Campbell, in Burma itself was so successful that the Burmese had to make overtures for peace.[94]

The defeat of the Burmese in the First Anglo-Burmese War ushered in a new era in the history of the eastern frontier of India. At the Treaty of Yandabo, on 24 February 1826, the king of Ava agreed, amongst other things, to abstain from all interference in the affairs of Assam, Cachar, and Jayantia and Manipur.[95] Assam was annexed to the British Dominion, Manipur was placed under Gambhir Singh, Ram Singh was confirmed as the Raja of Jayantia, and Govindachandra was reinstated as the Raja of Cachar under the terms of the treaty of Badarpur and his ancestral territory, except North Cachar,

Hills, was formally handed over to him.[96]

Treaty of Badarpur

Treaty concluded between David Scott, Esquire, Agent to the Governor General on the part of the Honorable East India Company, and Rajah Govind Chunder Narayana, of Herumba

Article I

Rajah Govind Chunder, for himself and his successors, acknowledges allegiance to the Honorable Company, and places his territory of Cachar, or Herumba, under their protection.

Article II

The internal government of the country shall be conducted by the Rajah, and the jurisdiction of the British courts of justice shall not extend there; but the Rajah agrees to attend at all times to the advice offered for the welfare of his subjects by the Governor General in Council, and agreeably there to rectify any abuses that may arise in the administration of affairs.

Article III

The Honorable Company engages to protect the territories of Cachar from external enemies, and to arbitrate any differences that may arise between the Rajah and other states. The Rajah agrees to abide by such arbitration and to hold no correspondence or communication with foreign powers, except through the channel of the British Government.

Article IV

In consideration of the aid promised by the above article, and other circumstances, the Rajah agrees to pay to the Honorable Company, from the beginning of the year 1232 B.S., an annual tribute of ten thousand sicca rupees, and the Honorable Company engages to provide for the maintenance of the Munnipoorean chiefs lately occupying Cachar.

Article V

If the Rajah should fail in the performance of the above article, the Honorable Company will be at liberty to occupy and attach, in perpetuity, to their possessions, a sufficient tract of the Cachar country to provide for the future realisation of the tribute.

Article VI

The Rajah agrees, in concert with the British local authorities, to adopt all measures that may be necessary for the maintenance, in the district of Sylhet, of the arrangements in force in the Police, Opium, and Salt Departments.

Executed at Budderpore, this 6th day of May 1824, corresponding with the 24th of Fagoon 1230 B.S.

CHAPTER III

Paramountcy

On his accession to the throne for the second time Govindachandra discovered himself in a sea of problems, internal as
well as external. Despite the Treaty of Badarpur, the Government of Fort William doubted the capacity of the Raja to pay
the tribute and to maintain authority over his subjects. The
Commissioner of Sylhet was, therefore, instructed to keep a
keen watch on the conduct of the Raja and to ascertain whether
he will be willing to cede the territory to the British.[1] Thus
Govindachandra began his administration with the protecting
power keeping a grabbing eye over his possession.

As a matter of fact, Cachar by the time had been an imbe-
cile country. Although during the time of Krishnachandra the
state yielded a revenue of rupees one lakh per year, after his
death the amount fell off.[2] The condition of the country began
to deteriorate owing to prolonged incursions made by rebel
Tularam and the Manipuri brothers, while the pace of destruc-
tion was aggravated by the Burmese invasion. Due to the
uncertainty caused by the external aggressions and civil war,
the whole tract of land east of Bikrampur and Panchgram was
thrown out of plough and a large number of cultivators were
either killed or carried into captivity. After the restoration of
normalcy only a few of the *parganas* were reoccupied, and most
of them were still empty; none yielded revenue.[3] Despite such
a state of affairs the Commissioner of Sylhet reported that cultivation was making a rapid progress and that the Raja would
experience no difficulty to pay the dues regularly. Accordingly,

the tribute was fixed at Rs. 10,000 on a mere guess-work that the revenue of the state would be about rupees three lakhs.[4] Evidently, the Commissioner overestimated the situation, and the tribute fell into arrear.[5] In 1827, Govindachandra applied to the British Government for the exemption of tributes for two preceeding years.[6] Scott, the Agent to the Governor-General, supported the petition of the Raja endorsing that the amount of revenue conjectured was overated. Due to the strong recommendations[7] of the sympathetic Agent, remission was granted by the Government of India.[8] But he was required to construct a good road between Sylhet and Manipur across his country.[9] The Government, at the same time, again called upon the Commissioner of Sylhet to ascertain from the Raja if he was willing to hand over the kingdom to the British as he was advanced in years, bodily infirm and had no natural heir to succeed.[10] Apparently, the attitude of the Government towards Cachar was unfavourable and thus coloured the subsquent developments in the valley leading to ultimate annexation of Cachar to the British empire in India.

Realising fully that remission once granted might not be repeated in future, Govindrchandra had to resort to all possible means to improve his finance by effecting economy in expenditure and by raising additional revenue. Immediately he reduced the number of ministers from four to one. The Justice in Cachar had hitherto been administered by fifty judges, but the whole business would now be conducted by a few specially recruited for the purpose. The administration of revenue was entrusted, as before, to the *Barbhandari* but the services of revenue officials attached to each queen and members of the royal family were dispensed with. The immunities and rent-free grants allotted to the state officials and other dignitaries were discontinued. Such dignitaries, including the *Ranees*, were assigned fixed cash allowances. To increase the revenue the Raja commenced a series of unsparing exactions on the people. Although no change was made in the land tax, which was generally rupees five per *hal*, the amount due from the defaulters were realised by destraint of property, confinement and in cases, where land was laid waste, by a collective fine on the concerned *pargana*. Additional taxes were to be paid for the cultivation of poppy, fruit and vegetables, for manufacturing salt, and for the privileges of holding titles, riding on *dola*, wearing of gold ornaments and for playing music at marriage and other festive occasions. The custom duties were levied at the river *ghats** on all articles of export and they were invariably farmed out to the highest bidder. The Raja was also reported to have exercised a monopoly of trade in certain commodities, particularly grains, which could be sold by the merchants to the Government at an assessed rate, to be resold by the State with a margin.[11]

Govindchandra thus endeavoured hard to extricate himself of the financial tangle, by means fair or foul. But he was confronted with external peril of a very grievous nature which totally handicapped his requipment measures. Haunted by the fear of the repetition of the Burmese catastrophe, the British Government had not only raised Gambhir Singh as the sovereign ruler of Manipur but allowed him to maintain an army 3,000 strong to be trained and equipped by the Company.[12] Gambhir, as has already been mentioned, aimed at the acquisition of Cachar. Since 1827 he followed a policy of slow but steady penetration into Cachar west of the river Barak, and compelled the Naga tribes that occupied the tract to pay tribute and gratuitous services. This region abounded in excellent timber besides valuable ivory, wax, grass and bamboo which could be speedily exported by the river to the profitable markets† in Sylhet and earn revenue for the state and wages to the working population. Govindachandra lodged a complaint, in 1828, with Tucker, the Commissioner of Sylhet, who called upon Gambhir Singh to explain his conduct. The latter denied the tract in question as ever forming part of Cachar,[13] and the Government did not pursue the matter any more. Emboldened by the British indulgence, Gambhir Singh forcibly occupied Chandrapur wherein he constructed a house of his own and quartered a large number of Manipuris.[14] Although he claimed the *ilaka* as his paternal property which his father received, as he stated, as a gift from Krishnachandra, when asked by the Commissioner he failed to produce any documentary evidence to prove that he had any valid claim to the disputed possession.[15] As advised by the Government of India, Scott dismissed

* Sealtekh, Gumra, Jiri, Madhura, Catakhal, Sonai etc.
† Sylhet, Chatak and Nabiganj.

the claim of Gambhir Singh over the territory, but to conciliate him the Agent requested Govindachandra to assign the
Raja of Manipur fifty *Kulbahs* or *hals** of land in the same tract
for the establishment of a magazine and to quarter some
labourers for carrying the military stores to Manipur.[16] Although
initially Govindachandra strongly objected to the proposal,[17]
Scott ultimately prevailed upon the Raja to cede a plot of land
to the British Company. Accordingly, by a document executed
on 30 *Asarh*, 1236 *Bangabda* the Raja granted 50 *Kulbahs* of
land to the east of Banskandi for the construction of a Government Magazine in his territory for fifteen years.[18] The arrangement received the approval of the Governor-General in Council
and the tract was eventually assigned to Gambhir Singh.[19] But
this concession simply multiplied the aggressiveness of the Manipuri ruler who detailed sepoys to the frontier villages of Cachar
and exacted forced labour from the Naga subjects of the Raja.[20]
He encouraged the Manipuris in their habitual evasion of the
transit duties in the established *ghats* in Cachar and levied unauthorised tolls at Chandrapur on cutting grass, timber and bamboo
on the other bank of Barak.[21] He also prevented the hillmen of
the region from coming down to the plains and compelled them
to dispose of their cotton, ginger, pepper and other products
of the hills at an arbitrary value fixed by his agents. The merchants were prevented from having direct traffic with Manipur
and were forced to sell all their commodities to him at Chandrapur, wherefrom these were transported to his country. Thus the
extreme indulgence given to the Raja of Manipur fell too
injuriously upon Govindachandra and could not but produce
the wrath of Scott who asked Gambhir Singh to desist from
further acts of aggression with the severe warning that otherwise he and all other Manipuri settlers would be forced to
quit Cachar altogether.[22] But these could hardly effect any
change in the attitude of Gambhir who was bent upon grabbing
Cachar and greedily waited for an opportunity.[23]

Apart from the gradual encroachement upon his ancestral
territory by the aspiring and unscrupulous Manipuri Prince
Gambhir Singh, Govindrachandra had to reckon with many
other troubles. In the north-east while Tularam resumed hosti-

* One *kulbah* or *hal* was equivalent to 4.82 acres.

lities,[24] the entire Dimacha tribes dwelling in the hills backed up the pretentions and claim of Tularam.[25] The *Forty Sempungs* or the nobles of the state were highly dissatisfied with the Raja and at the instigation of Tularam challenged the authority of Govindachandra,[26] while in the south-west the Kukis repeated their occasional marauding practices with impunity, so also the north-east.[27]

In any case the prime threat to the *Raj* was posed by Tularam who in addition to his hostilities aligned with the *Forty Sempungs*, a Council of the Forty Dimacha tribes, issued a legal injunction questioning the authority of Govindachandra as the lawful Raja of Cachar.

In a memorial to the East India Company the *Forty Sempungs* claimed that it was the long established custom of the Heramba Kingdom that the Raja as well as the ministers should be chosen by the Council known as *Forty Sempungs* and that under no circumstances he could marry a princess other than from the tribe originating from *Hassoncha*.[28] They charged Govindachandra, with direct contravention of the established usage of the country by being a nominee of the British and having married a Manipuri princess. Backed by these nobles, Tularam publicly declared that Govindachandra had forfeited all claims to Cachar by his tyranny and disregard of the established customs and it was now upto the *Forty Sempungs* to elect a new ruler. But on enquiry it was found that the *Forty Sempungs* had no right to elect the Raja, and that the Manipuri princess married by Govindachandra was in fact the widow of Krishnachandra; such marriage being permitted by local custom.[29] The orthodox section of the Dimachas, however, had objection to the ceremony which should have been according to *Goondaboo* rites. Many of them, therefore, joined hands with Tularam, while many migrated to Jayantia and Tripura.[30]

As a matter of fact, the rivalries of Tularam went unabated. Towards the end of 1828 he made a swift descent to Dharampur and committed numerous outrages and murders.[31] However, due to old age he relinquished command of his army to his cousins, Govindaram and Durgacharan. The latter in March 1829 again swooped down upon Dharampur and prevented the officers of the Government of Cachar from collecting revenue. By *arzee* to the Commissioner of Sylhet, on 13 *Agrahayan*, 1235

Bangabda, Radhakrishna Aditya, a *Mukhtar* of Cachar, complained that Tularam had appropriated to his use the resources of the major parts of Cachar including twelve dependent states in the north. In *Chaitra*, previous year, he not only put the *ryots* of Warigram under heavy pressure but also established a *thanah* there. The *Mukhtar* was ordered by rhe Raja to collect revenue from the inhabitants of Dharampur, Meekeer, Tyooagariya and Hojai, all plains-villages in the Assam side of the kingdom. An advance military troop was sent from Narikuli *thanah* and posted at Warigram. the *Mukhtar* himself followed the troops and on the way received the deposition of the *Koork Sezwal*. On 12 *Chaitra*, Govindram and Durgacharan with a body of mountaineers interposed the royal *fouz* in a hostile manner and refused to allow them to proceed any further. The aggressors were, however, put to flight by the Raja's *paiks*. Thereupon the *Mukhtar* made revenue settlement in Hojai and Warigram. The *Amlas* were sent to Dharampur and to the Mikir areas of Cachar. But on 16th, Govidaram and Durgacharan with a thousand armed men surrounded the revenue party ; confined 15 *paiks* and killed 15 others on the spot. The rest of the contingent escaped to Narikuli. On 20th, Govindaram took up a post at Jonsukee with 500 *Barkandazes*. Being alarmed at the concentration of the gun-men, the inhabitants on the south bank of Kapili fled to the other side of the river where also they were threatened with attack. The *Mukhtar*, therefore, requested the Commissioner of Sylhet, on behalf of the Government of Cachar, to afford military assistance to enable them to realize revenue from the border areas, subdue the rebels and tranquilize the country.[32] Within a few day the *Amla* of Dharampur also submitted a *arzee* to the Commissioner of Sylhet informing the large scale depredations committed in his *ilaka* by Tularam's lieutenants, and requested the Company's Government to interfere on behalf of the Raja of Cachar who was being systematically harassed by the rebel leaders.[33] On 9 *Paus*, 1235, Govindachandra himself wrote to the Commissioner that Govindaram and his brother had twice failed to occupy Narikuli *thanah*, but took possession of Warigram and erecting a fort there, commenced oppressing the *ryots*. Although the Cachar Army was successful in compelling the enemy to decamp from Warigram, the rival forces took a strong post at Alunka and also fortified

themselves at Chang Choukey. By forcible eviction of the Raja's
people they caused a total depopoulation of the fertile Kapili
valley. Claiming that the British Government had stipulated to
protect the Raja and his country, Govindachandra urged upon
the Commissioner for military help to overcome his rivals.[34]
But inspite of these repeated appeals the British Government
took their own time to respond. Interesting enough, the report
from the British *Vakeel* in Cachar *Darbar* that the Raja was
contemplating to adopt a son, at once rocked Sylhet and Calcutta. The authorities took a serious exception to issue, perhaps
realising that the presence of a new incumbent would go against
the British motive to annex Cachar at any opportune moment.
Charles Tucker, the Commissioner of Sylhet, as advised by
Calcutta, wrote several letters categorically asking the Raja
that he should not adopt a son to succeed him in the *Raj* of
Cachar without prior sanction of the British Government and
that if he would select a successor contrary to the Government,
he could not expect any help from the latter for the maintenance
of peace and tranquility in his country.[35]

On the other hand, the people in central and northern valleys
of Cachar were constantly harassed by these internecine warfare. The collection of revenue was stopped, and a large
number of inhabitants fled in confusion.[36] In the meantime,
fortunately for Govindachandra, Govindaram turned against
his brother Tularam and, as a result, the latter was compelled
to flee to Jayantia. A few months later with the help of Manipuri detachment sent by Gambhir Singh, Tularam recovered
his lost possession. Govindaram then rushed with his brother
for life to Dharampur where they were warmly received by
Govindachandra.[37] He promised to forgive all their past mis-
chiefs they had committed in conjunction with Tularam, and in
return called upon them to dispossess the rebel hill chief. The
brothers readily agreed, a secret agreement was drawn up in
November 1829 and Govindachandra supplied them with
muskets, ball and powder. To defray the expenses of the expeditions, the Raja authorised Govindaram to collect and draw
on the custom duties of Dharampur.[38]

The situation now became too dramatic as Govindachandra
endeavoured to use Govindaram as a tool against Tularam,
while Gambhir Singh gave all possible fuel to the latter.[39]

Before long, the incursions of the North Cacharis in the plains became frequent and highly oppressive for the plain landers. Baffled in his attempt to repel the miscreants, Govindachandra appealed to the British Government for help. The Government of India called upon David Scott to effect a compromise between the two chiefs. Accordingly, the Agent arrived at Sylhet in June 1829, and induced Govindachandra to acknowledge Tularam as his *Senapati* or general with formal charge of the hills in the north which were under his *de facto* control. By an agreement signed on 28 July, 1829, Govindachandra, of course reluctantly, undertook not to send any force to the territory of Tularam Senapati, in defiance of which he would forfeit claims of protection from the British Government. Tularam was confirmed in this possession on the condition that he would refrain from further encroachment on the territory of Cachar, on the violation of which he was threatened with expulsion from his own territory.[40]

Although a compromise was thus effected, every one knew that a scramble for power would ensue after the death of Govindachandra as he, like his late elder brother, had no issue. In that event, Tularam was sure to assert his claim vigorously. Gambhir Singh would also not leave the chance to occupy the whole of Cachar. The *Forty Sempungs* and other nobles might also come forward to fish in the troubled water. Above all, the interest of the British Government in the affairs of the petty state was also significant. From the defence point of view, the territory offered no insurmountable difficulty to an invading power, while it effectively prevented operations of the British forces during the Anglo-Burmese War. The economic potentialities of the kingdom was sufficiently lucrative. Under better management Cachar would have become the granary of the surrounding regions. It would thus afford adequate supplies to Manipur which had frequently extended noble resistance to the Burmese invaders, and thereby would ensure security and tranquility of the North-East Frontier [41] All these considerations prompted the authorities in Calcutta to make a settlement with Raja Govindachandra who was growing old and bodily infirm. A proposal was, therefore, made through Tucker requesting the Raja to sign a deed making over the territory to the East India Company after his death.[42] In return, he was offered the bait

that the Government would relinquish the amount of tribute
for the rest of his life. But the Raja was encircled by a host of
enemies and did not dare even to discuss such a proposal. He
was also not willing to stop the payment of tribute as he considered it as the only security for the retention of his authority.[43]
The Raja, however, desired to adopt a child from amongst the
royal families of Cachar for continuation of the line of succession.[44] Although the Commissioner of Sylhet was deeply
impressed by the difficulties faced by the unfortunate Raja, he
rightly realised that the succession question may lead to civil
war in Cachar. Therefore, in his report to the Governor-General, the Commissioner observed : "It appears that as long as
the succession remained unsettled and in a manner open to all
claimants, many terbulent characters were restrained and kept
quiet who might disturb the tranquility of the country,
if the doors to their future hopes were finally closed against
them."[45] The Governor-General in Council also felt it inexpedient to carry on the negotiations any further, but they
desired Scott to give his sentiment on the whole subject. Accordingly, the Agent held an interview with the Raja and reported
that the British Government could not prevent the Raja from
adopting a child as he had the sanction of the Hindu Law in his
favour, nor could they succeed to the *Raj* without having a
specified agreement to the effect. But the Agent was led to
believe that there would not be much difficulty in obtaining
from the Raja the cession of Cachar in consideration of an adequate money payment and the assignment to him of a *Jagir*
where he might reside with security.[46] About the valuation of
Cachar, Scott fixed it at twenty times the amount of the existing
revenues.[47]

But the act was fast drawing to a close, and Raja Govindachandra soon fell a victim to the assailants.[48] The murder which
was the outcome of a deliberate plan, occured on the night of 24
April, 1830, when a band of Manipuris in league with the
Manipuri members of the Raja's body guards entered the Haritikar palace, hacked the Raja into pieces and set fire to the
capital-complex.[49] The incident created a great terror, and most
of the members of the household fled with the family deity across
the Barak to Katigorah.[50] Furquard, the Commissioner of Sylhet,
immediately posted a military detachment in Cachar and report-

ed the matter to the Government of Bengal.[51]   Commenting on the report, Scott observed that the incident should afford a justifiable ground and a desirable opportunity for the Government to interfere effectually for the suppression of the disturbances which had so long prevailed in Cachar ![52]   In June 1830 the state was placed under Lieutenant Fisher, who was then on survey duties in Sylhet, with powers of a Magistrate and Collector on a monthly salary of Rs. 1000 chargeable upon the revenue of 'Cachar country'.[53]

In the meantime, Scott, under the instructions of the Government of India, commenced an enquiry into the murder.   He suspected that the murder had been committed under the orders of Gambhir Singh.[54]   Such a presumption was quite obvious, since there had been repeated disputes between the two chiefs over several issues and only a fortnight before the tragedy Govindachandra had requested the Agent for military aid against Gambhir Singh who had despatched a special brigade to seize Cachar in concert with Tularam.[55]   The suspicion of the local officers also fell upon Tularam on the ground of his long feud with the slain.[56]   Even the *Forty Sempungs* could not escape the list of probable culprits, as their previous conspiracies against the Raja were well known to the authorities.[57]

The enquiries revealed that in the early part of 1830 Govindachandra had prepared to adopt a child. Gambhir Singh feared that the proposed adoption would foil his long cherished ambition over Cachar. He then entered into league with Vidyananda Sen, the Company's *Vakeel* at the Cachar *Darbar*, Ramgovind, a *Mukhtar* under Vidyananda, Gourshyam, a confidential agent of Gambhir Singh, and Balaram Singh, a Manipuri *Havildar* in the Cachar Army, and thus put an end to the life of the last Raja of Cachar.   Scott in his report observed : "The murder had been planned and executed with the knowledge and under the direction of Raja Gambhir Singh to secure him the benefit of crime."[58]   Finally, Vidyananda, Ramgovinda and Balaram were apprehended and sent up before Thomas Fisher, the officiating Magistrate of Cachar, to stand the trial.[59]   The Magistrate, in concurrence with the Jury, passed the verdict of guilt and sentenced them all to death.[60]   The Government of India, however, commuted the sentence to imprisonment and transportation for life.   Accordingly, the convicts were transported to Tenasserin to undergo the term of imprisonment.[61] Strangely enough, although it was clear that Gambhir Singh was the real villain and the prime perpertrator of the crime nothing was done against him. Even no verbal remonstrance was administered to him. There was direct evidence against Gourshyam· but he was not required to be examined as it would have been tantamount to the public accusation of his own master Gambhir Singh.[62] The British Government thus continued to extend extreme indulgence to the Raja of Manipur even after he was known to be guilty of an universally condemnable crime. It is believed by some historians that had the Government of India adopted strong measures against their pampered ally in February 1830, when the Cachar-Manipur dispute was heading to a crisis, Gambhir Singh would not have dared to take this extreme and fatal step.[63]

Meanwhile, the Government of India published a proclamation inviting the aspirants to the Cachar *Raj* to present their cases within six weeks.[64] Naturally, there appeared several claimants to the vacant throne. Indraprabha, the eldest queen of the Raja, prayed to the East India Company to be confirmed in her hereditary possessions. Tularam, the rebel chief, claimed the Crown of Cachar as a descendant from the ruling family. The *Forty Sempungs* also submitted an *arzee* pleading their right to elect the Raja from amongst their own rank. Even Gambhir Singh was not out of the scene ; he, however, submitted an alternative proposal—to farm out Cachar for a period of twenty years in return for an annual revenue of rupees fifteen thousand and promised to provide his niece, the widow of the late Raja, with sufficient means of subsistence.[65] Although Govindaram did not prefer any claim in person, a few of the Dimacha chiefs advocated his right to the throne alleging that he was the natural son of Raja Krishnachandra by a slave girl who was married to one Anandaram with royal blessing to save her face a few months before the birth of the child, Govindaram.[66]

The Calcutta Council then instructed the local authorities to enquire into each of these claims and to give their sentiments on how best Cachar could be disposed[67] off. Scott supported the case of the *Ranee* and recommended to the Government of Bengal to confirm her in the possession of Cachar on a *Zamindari* basis anticipating that in no distant future the estate would escheat to the British Government as Indraprabha was already advanced in years.[68] But Mr. Cracroft, who soon after officiated as Agent to the Governor-General, opposed the proposal, feeling that such an agreement would simply prolong the misrule in Cachar. From Fisher's report, he doubted whether the *Ranee* would be acceptable to the people, because a substantial section of them had questioned the validity of her marriage. The Dimachas alleged that the wedding was not according to *Goodaboo* rites, while oxthodox Hindus, particularly the Bengalees, condemned such union as she was once betrothed to Krishnachandra and the widow marriage was not recognised by Hindu ethic. Cracroft also dismissed the pretensions of Tularam since he was looked down upon as of low origin by the people of the plains.[69] He had not even a shadow of title to the throne and that his claim to be a descendant of Raja Tamradwaja was totally denied by the nobles of the state. On the contrary, he was reported to be the son of a Manipuri slave girl by a *Khitmatgar* in the service of the Raja of Cachar.[70] About other claimants, Fisher had already set aside their cases. Nothing was known of the relationship of Govindaram with Krishnachandra during the life time of Govindachandra and, in fact, Govindaram by himself was not a candidate to the throne.[71] After a searching enquiry into the past records, the Magistrate doubted if there was any instance of actual election of the Raja by the *Sempungs*. The only precedent, he could gather, was about 150 years ago when Chandraprabha, the widow of Tamradwaja, in conjunction with the *Mantris* and the *Sempungs* was reported to have elected Raja Kirtichandra to the vacant throne. This was necessitated by the fact that Raja Suradasanarayana. son of Tamradhwaja, died young and without any heir. Although the witnesses examined by Fisher established that the succession to the Heramba throne must be from the *Hassoncha* clan, none disputed the fact that, in the former case, the *Ranee* could exercise her veto against the decision of the assembly and that the right of choice lay in the widow alone. Ranee Chandraprabha is known in the history of Cachar for her noble character, patronage of scholars, her personal scholarship and works of public utility. It is not unlikely that she consulted an assembly of nobles and officials to select a Prince from amongst her son's kins so that the new Raja would be popular in the state.

But even if it was the custom of ancient time to procure the confirmations to the title of the Raja at a high-power assembly it had long been discontinued. Fisher, therefore, remarked : "If it ever existed, it is now obsolete; the revival of it is unlikely to be attended with any benefit ; on the contrary, likely to be the source of interminable civil war".[72]   His sentiments were shared by Cracroft, and the pretensions of the *Forty Sempungs* failed to receive any sympathy from the Agent.[73]

On the otherhand, the claims of Gambhir Singh was strongly advocated by Major Grant, the British Resident at Manipur who was under the impression that the acquisition of Cachar would provide the Raja of Manipur with sufficient means to build up a stable and efficient Government so indispensably necessary for the security of the North-East Frontier. Grant saw in the measure the chances of assimilation of the people of Cachar and Manipur who had been warring all these years with each other. Apprehending the probable objections to the proposal, he desired that if it were not possible to transfer the whole of Cachar, Gambhir Singh should at least be favoured with the cession of the tract between the Jiri river and the western bank of Barak over which he had already extended his sphere of influence.[74] But local authorities were apprehensive of the fact that such an arrangement would place the helpless people of Cachar at the tender mercies of a cruel chieftain. Sharing the sentiment, Cracroft wanted to assume the territory 'openly and immediately' instead of waiting till it was further reduced by letting Gambhir Singh to rack it for a sum of rupees fifteen thousand per annum.[75] On the contrary, the Agent considered it wiser to make Gambhir Singh a present of Rs. 15000 than to admit him to Cachar.

The role of Gambhir Singh behind the murder of Raja Govindachandra was well known to the Government from the proceedings of the case. It was, therefore, considered mischievious to allow him to profit by the crime which was believed to have been committed at his instigation. Despite, the authorities at Calcutta desired to get views of Lieutenant Pemberton and Captain Jenkins, who had recently visited this region in connection with the survey of the Eastern Frontier, about the alternative proposal submitted by Major Grant.[76] Pemberton strongly advocated the cession of the tract east of Jiri to Gambhir

Singh on the ground that it would provide the Government with an authority sufficiently strong to control the various Naga clans that inhabited the area.[77] But Jenkins held completely opposite views. He found the tribals highly disaffected under the rule of Gambhir Singh, and looked upon a command over them essential only to trap the valuable resources of the region. The tribes were restrained from open rebellion by the feeling that they would not be surrendered to Manipur. Jenkins also argued that the British Government had no right to impose a rule against the 'understood wishes of the people'.[78] But so far as Cachar was concerned both the officers strongly recommended its annexation to the British dominion as it was likely to produce in course of a few years a revenue nearly equal to that of Sylhet and would become a granary capable of supporting any number of troops to be stationed in Cachar in case of the renewal of wars with Ava.[79]

Considering that there was no legitimate heir to Raja Govindachandra, that all the local officers were in favour of annexation and that the proposal was re-inforced by the wishes of the local people 'to be placed under the rule and protection of the British Government in preference to being made over to Raja Gambhir Singh', the Government of Bengal recommended the plains of Cachar be annexed to the British dominion making suitable provisions for the widowed *Ranees* and confirming Tularam in his hill possessions.[80] It was further observed that Gambhir Singh be allowed to retain the areas east of the river Jiri, but he must retire from Chandrapur and the surrounding plains over which he had been gradually establishing his unauthorised control.[81] On 9 July, 1832, the Governor-General in Council accorded their approval to the recommendations regarding the annexation of Cachar, but entertained great doubts about the propriety of ceding Gambir Singh a portion of Cachar in the face of the objections raised by Jenkins which appeared to them more weighty than the reasons argued by Pemberton.[82] Therefore, without having further details from the local authorities the Governor-General in Council declined to pass their final verdict on the subject and postponed the decision pending further report from Pemberton.[83]

Accordingly, by a proclamation, issued on 14 August 1832,

the plains of south Cachar* was annexed to the British dominion. Tularam, the rebel chief, was confirmed in the possession
of the hill tract that had been assigned to him by Govindachandra through the mediation of Scott in 1829. A suitable
provision was made for the widows† of the deceased Raja with
rent-free grants and monthly cash allowance of the total value
of Rs 3,875 per annum out of the revenue of Cachar.[84]

The 'open question' of the eastern boundary of Cachar was
also immediately taken up. Fisher, Robertson and Pemberton
were required by the Government of India to give further
report on the subject. The detailed enquiries conducted by Fisher
revealed that the tract beyond Jiri proposed to be 'presented'
to Gambhir Singh, was sixty miles in lengh and eighty miles in
breadth, contained a population of 10,000 and yielded an annual
revenue of Rs. 1000.[85] Fisher was, therefore, thoroughly convinced that this potent and strategic part of Cachar should in no
way be ceded to an alien ruler. He also brought home to the
Government of India that the various Naga tribes of the region
had strongly resented the proposed measure and many of them
were then fleeing to the plains of Cachar in anticipation of their
land being transferred to the rule of Gambhir Singh. Some of
them presented a petition, to Fisher, protesting against the
transfer and prayed that "they might be permitted as before, to
bring away timber and other articles of trade from the hills
without interruption from the officers of Gambhir Singh".[86]
These tribes, he added, had rendered valuable services during
the Anglo-Burmese War and the loss of them would be severely
felt in the event of another conflict ; while their presence on
the otherside of the frontier would be a source of constant
embarrassment in consequence of the measure being carried out.
The inhabitants of the plains, too, would be no less sufferers ;
for it would ruin their timber trade in that quarter which had

---

* Silchar and Hailkandi subdivisions of the modern district.
† Govindrachandra left behind five widows. Of them, *Maharani*
Indraprabha was the eldest and most formal under Hindu rites. She was
given a life pension of Rs. 100 per month and some *baksha* (rent-free)
grants for her establishment. Chandraprabha was granted an allowance of
Rs. 30 per month. No consideration was shown to the other queens as there
war no proof of their marriage according to the Hindu system. However,
Parbati Singh, Mahadebi and Bhabanipriya, the brother-in-law, mother-in-
law and sister-in-law of the deceased Raja were provided with certain
grants and allowances.

enabled many to subsist and repair the severe losses sustained during the last invasion.[87] Agreeing entirely with the opinion expressed by Fisher, and Robertson, the Agent to the Governor-General, desired that the Jiri frontier should be retained in Cachar and Gambhir Singh should be removed beyond Barak, as his principal motive in extending his territory to this side was a step forward to that of appropriating the whole of Cachar. Therefore, the Agent observed, "nothing can be more objectionable than the vicinity of a pretender whose agents would keep our subjects in a state of continued alarm".[88]

Unfortunately, Lieutenant Pemberton, who was specially deputed to interview the Raja of Manipur, gave an altogether different verdict reiterating his old argument in favour of the disposal of the eastern portion of Cachar to Gambhir Singh. He feared that the expulsion of Gambhir Singh from Cachar would be attached with disgrace and so to counteract, he advocated the grant of the tract east of the river Jiri to him.[89] Pemberton believed that this act of charity appeared to be one of mutual convenience and would establish an additional claim to the attachment and gratitude of the Raja. The Government of Bengal too invoked their earlier recommendations to establish the river Jiri and the western branch of Barak as the line of demarcation between Cachar and Manipur. Finally, the Government of India were also influenced by a feeling that Gambhir Singh might be required to make sacrifices in the Kabbow Valley which was also under his occupation ever since the Treaty of Yandabo and on which a decision was still awaited.[90] Concurring with Pemberton, they resolved on 5 November, 1832, to relinquish the tract in question, to the Raja of Manipur on the condition that he should immediately withdraw his *thanah* from Chandrapur ; that he should not obstruct the trade between Manipur and Cachar : that the Nagas occupying the hills ceded to him should have free access to the plains for trading purposes; that he should keep the communication from the Jiri to Manipur in good order for transit throughout the year ; that he should readily afford the assistance of a portion of the Manipur Levy and also to furnish porters and labourers whenever required by the British Government.[91]

The cession of the tract thus marked the climax of the policy of appeasement persistently followed by the British

Government towards Manipur. The policy that was shaped by a mistaken fear of Burmese invasion and had occasioned the assassination of Raja Govindachandra and oppressions of the people of Cachar by rulers of Manipur, was also responsible for the surrender of a valuable part of Cachar to Gambhir Singh which he had acquired by unfair means. The forcible occupation by sheer usurpation under the very nose of the protecting power was certainly not a genuine claim to be advanced in favour of the Raja of Manipur and the local officers were definitely judicious to plead against the measure. Even the Board of Directors concurred with the view expressed by Jekins, Fisher and Robertson regarding the disposal of the eastern division of Cachar.[92] They felt that the transfer of the tract accomplished the very object for which Raja Govindachandra was murdered and the authorities in Calcutta had erroneously allowed Gambhir Singh to reap the fruits of his own crime. They strongly condemned the acts of exactions and usurpation committed by the men of Gambhir Singh on the people of Cachar and wondered how a tract of country unquestionably belonging to Cachar could be ceded to a prince whose rule was regarded with aversion and terror by its people'.[93] But Gambhir Singh being already confirmed in his new acquisition, their disapproval was too late a sermon to have any effect. Any way, Gambhir Singh too could hardly make his rule effective over the tribesmen in the frontier who took a long time to cease to consider themselves as belonging to Cachar.[94] No wonder, therefore, the Kachha Naga areas continued to be a disturbed spot both for the Government of Manipur and the British authorities for at least another half a century.

Meanwhile, the question of the *Pargana* of Dharampur which was hitherto an integral part of Cachar and held by Govindaram and Durgacharan also came up for disposal. It may be recalled that by a secret agreement with Govindachandra, Govindaram had undertaken to disposses Tularam.[95] True to his words, the latter was never negligent to the task entrusted to him. After the death of Govindachandra when Tularam went to the plains to present his claim to the throne of Cachar, Govindaram made fresh inroads in to the hills. With Dharampur as the base of operation, he occupied, by October 1831, the western part of Tularam's territory. In his offensive

Govindaram was materially suported by the widowed *Ranee* of Cachar who on the counsel of Brajaram Burman, the *Barbhandari*, and officials of the household like Dhananjay and Kiritiram supplied him with arms and money which were then in their custody.[96] Fisher perceived that unless these hostile conflicts were stopped, law and order could not be maintained in central Cachar.[97] Although Tularam and Govindaram, both products of Palace revolution, were much alike in their personal character being tyrannical, oppressive and treacherous, the former appeared to Fisher to be 'lesser evil' and prepared to acquiesce in any arrangement that would give him a respectable settlement. The British Government, Fisher felt, had also a moral obligation to support him to retain his possession. Accordingly, on 7 July 1ʼ32, he proposed to the Agent to the Governor-General to remove Dhananjay and others from the service of the *Ranee* and place the latter under Parbati Singh, the brother of Chadraprabha ; while *Barbhandari* and Govindaram should be kept under restraint at least till Tularam was fairly established in his territory. To effect these, the Magistrate sought to employ a detachment in the ensuing cold season and in the event the Government considered the employment of troops inexpedient, Tularam might be asked to undertake the operation himself and provided with money, muskets and ammunitions.[98] Robertson had doubt about the propriety of interfering in the private life of the ex-queens and persons of rank and influence[99] but the Government of India approved of the measures proposed by Fisher with regard to Govindaram and the *Ranees,* on the ground that as the successors to the late Raja of Cachar the Government had pledged not to allow the subjects to be molested, but they also questioned Fisher's right of interference on behalf of Tularam. They pointed out that under the treaty of 1829 the British Government offered Tularam the only guarantee that he should not be harassed by Govindachandra in his hill territory. The authorities at Calcutta further held that the *Senapati* had no claim on the British Government for protection and support against any other individual who might dispute his right over that tract.[100]

But Govindaram and Durgacharan were fairly seated in the Dharampur region and Tularam had lost all his control there. Earlier, on 25 May, 1832, Jenkins wrote to the Chief Secretary to the Government of India advocating the annexation of this division, popularly called Central Cachar, to the British territory, but had desired that the Officer-in-charge of Cachar plains should take over its administration on the ground that this fertile area was peopled by the 'Cacharees' and historically was an integral part of Cachar.[101] But Fisher, on 31 August, 1832, pointing out the difficulty of communication from Dudpatil through the hills, proposed that Dharampur should be attached to Assam.[102] Subsequently, however, he revised his previous recommendations and suggested that the area might more conveniently be leased out to Govindaram and Durgacharan who held it since the death of the Raja of Cachar.[103] He was also bent upon helping Tularam and proposed the conclusion of a new treaty with the *Senapati* by which the latter would become a direct tributary of the British Government and also recommended the assignment of a small force to him for the protection of himself and his country against aggressions by his neighbours.[104] This proposal was strongly supported by the Agent,[105] but Lord William Bentinck, the Governor-General, turned it down finding no valid ground for incurring additional expenditure for supporting the authority of a petty chief like Tularam and considered it unnecessary to enter into any fresh engagement with him.[106] The local officers in Cachar and Assam, however, adopted all possible means under the old treaty to protect Tularam from frontier troubles. But at this stage Tularam himself committed some highhanded atrocities which not only cost him the good will of the paramount power but also deprived him of a significant part of his territory.[107]

In September 1832, Tularam made a swift descent upon Dharampur, burnt some villages, captivised several individuals of whom two were butchered in the jungles, reportedly, under the immediate and personal direction of the *Senapati*. The victims were also reported to be British subjects and, as such, Robertson issued orders for the immediate apprehension of Tularam whom he declared to be the leader of the gang of lawless marauders liable to severe punishment. On 3 October, Tularam was arrested by Fisher and sent to the Magistrate of Sylhet for trial. But the Government of India instructed the Agent to withdraw all proceedings against Tularam as he was an independent chief and as such not liable to be tried by a

British Magistrate.[108] However, the Agent was asked to hold an enquiry into the matter in his political capacity.[109] In the process, the question of the disposal of the Dharampur areas received serious attention of the Government. Fisher's suggestion of leasing out the tract to Govindaram and Durgacharan was not supported by the Agent who doubted the fitness of the persons, while the Governor-General in Council ignored their claims altogether. Ultimately, the region between the rivers Kapili and Jamuna and extending from Jamunamukh to Dharampur including Hojai and Davaka was attached to the British territory and placed under the jurisdiction of the authorities of Assam.[110] Lieutenant Vetch, an officer of the Assam Light Infantry, was to supervise the affairs of Nowgong and Raha including the tract annexed from Cachar.[111] Govindaram and Durgacharan were granted life pension of Rs 50/- each. besides some rent-free grants in Cachar.[112]

On the other hand, the enquiry into Tularam's case revealed that the two persons murdered in September, 1832, were the subjects of the *Senapati* and were guilty of gross and unprovoked outrages against him.[113] But, although acquitted of murder charge, the aggressions committed by him in the Dharampur areas were in violation of the treaty of 1829 and punishable by forfeiture of his possessions. Nevertheless, the Government of India had no intention to resume the whole of his territory and resolved to occupy the western part of his dominion. This division being the meeting ground of four principalities, namely, Assam, Bengal (Sylhet), Khasi- Jaintia Hills and Manipur, was useful to the Government for defence and commerce.[114] Jenkins and Fisher were sent on a tour to ascertain the wishes of the inhabitants of the area regarding the proposed transfer. The people were found decidedly averse to the rule of Tularam and expressed their desire to be under the British administration.[115] Accordingly, on 3 November, 1834, a new treaty was concluded with Tularam, under which the *Senapati* surrendered to the British Government his claim to the territory between the rivers Mahur and Dayang on the one side, Dayang and Kapili on the other, and was allowed to retain only the eastern part of Hill Cachar. His territory would now be bounded by Dayang on the west, Dhansiri on the east, Jamuna and Dayang on the north and by Naga Hills and Mahur river on the south and south west. He also agreed to pay an annual tribute of four pairs of elephant tusks, which was later on commuted for a cash payment of Rs. 490. The British Government obtained right of placing military posts in any part of his territory and in the event of British troops marching through it, Tularam undertook to furnish them with provisions and labour. He also agreed not to commence any military operation against the neighbouring chiefs without prior permission from the Government of India. Further, he undertook not to establish any custom *chouk* on the river forming the boundaries of his territory. He would try all petty offences committed within his jurisdiction, take cognizance of and do justice according to the established custom, but all heinous offenders must be transferred to the nearest British court.[116]

Reduced to the position of no better than a *Sardar*, Tularam *Senapati* was not undisturbed even in the hilly remnant of Cachar. Although freed from the intrigues of his ungrateful cousins, he had now to reckon with the incursions of the Angami Nagas in the south-east.[117] The Angamis like other hill tribes of the north-east frontier were economically hard pressed, and used to come down to the plains of Cachar collect food, salt, dried fish and other provisions. If they could collect their requirements unopposed no harm was done to any one; otherwise, they carried off forcibly whatever they could.[118] The people had long yielded to such demands, but emboldened by the prospect of the British protection they now resisted such exactions and, therefore, had been subjected to the frequent reprisal by the Nagas. Troubles also errupted from the old disputes over the salt-springs near Semkhar, which were situated within Tularam's territory. The inability of Tularam to repel these attacks and the early indifference of the British authorities engendered by a false sense of security fell too injuriously upon the Kacharis and Mikirs. The repeated raids and plunders by the turbulent Nagas* made the lives of the innocent tribes of

---

* To quote Robinson : "In 1836-37, the Nagas having grievously oppressed the inhabitants of Northern Cachar, and the Superintendent being unable to afford them efficient protection, that division was transferred to the jurisdiction of Assam. The territory thus attached, may be divided into three portions : the valley of the Jamuna and Kapili rivers, heretofore known by the designation of Dharampore, and now called the district of Jamuna Mukh; second, that portion of the country between the

the area extremely miserable. Many of them were massacred,. while several others fled into Cachar plains. In January 1839, the marauding raids reached the British frontier which com-- pelled the Government to take a serious note of the situation. A series of punitive expenditions were despatched against the Nagas under Grange, the Sub-Assistant, and Lieutenant Bigge,. the Principal Assistant, Nowgong.[119] Tularam himself accom- panied the officers, his people cleared the passage for the troops, provided supplies and errected sheds for their encamp- ment.[120]

Inspite of all attempts on the part of the Government, the Angami distrurbances continued. Worn out by old age and these internecine strife, the *Senapati* relinquished, in 1844,. the charge of his Government in favour of his sons-Nakulram Barman and Brajanath Barman with permission from the authorities at Fort William.[121] The sons too made all endea- vours to win over the Angamis, but without success. The Naga depredations desolated many Dimacha villages, and in 1851, the whole territory of Tularam covering an area of about 2000 square miles had only a population of 5000. The brothers were utterly incompetent to restore confidence among the people. On the other hand, the relations between the two brothers became far from friendly when Brajanath became guilty of abducting the wife of Nakulram and the latter made an attempt over the life of his younger brother. However, an imminent catastrophe was averted by the timely mediation of the aged father, Tularam.[122]

Tularam also failed to meet the requirements of the British officers operating the forces due to internal disturbances This often led to frictions and forcible seizure of men and provi- sions in Tularam's territory by the said officers. In July 1850 Nakulram protested against such exactions and the Government of Bengal directed an enquiry into the matter. In his explanation, Captain J. Butler, the principal Assistant at Nowgong, assured that he would be vigilant, in future, about such unauthorised and irresponsible action on the part of the

upper parts of the Jamuna and Myung rivers, retained by Tularam; and third, the hilly tract between the Myung and Kapili, which was resigned by that chieftain". See W. Robinson, *A Descriptive Account of Assam,.* pp. 402-3.

officers on duty.[123] Availing the opportunity, Butler urged upon the Government to resume the territoty of Tularam since the conduct of the Chief and his sons had already amounted to a breach of the agreement. It was pointed out that the chief had not only opposed the quartering of the British troops in his principality and refused the supply of coolies and provisions as specified in article 5 of the said treaty. They were also charged with oppressing their subjects and making exactions from the people contrary to article 9. When called upon to explain their conduct, the sons of Tularam not only defended their actions the validity of which in some degrees were admitted by the Agent, but also brought some counter charges against the local authorities which were, however, dismissed by the Court.[124] All these naturally embittered the relationship between the Chief and the British Government. The proposals were also made to stop the payment of pensions to Tularam, but no action was taken during his life time.[125]

As stated above, the charges against Tularam could not be substantially proved by the complaining local officers. There was hardly any evidence of oppression. The fact of deliberately harbouring the criminals, who might have managed their own shelter in the jungles, also lacked sufficient testimony. Some have attributed the failure to meet the demands of the British officers, to the inherent weakness of the *Senapati's* nominees and to the excesses of the sepoys or some irresponsible British officials. Even Jenkins remarked : "I can well imagine that the conduct of our police and other officers may have been very galling to these rude chiefs."[126] He also felt that their repeated forcible exactions without any payment scared the inhabitants away. Although the Agent ultimately forwarded the report of Captain Butler for the considerations of the Government of Bengal, the Deputy Governor of Bengal did not agree to the proposal. In his opinion, nothing serious had occured to affect British relations with Tularam as to warrant such a severe measure as recommended by the local authorities.[127]

Nevertheless, the death of Tularam in October, 1851, offered Captain Butler a fresh opportunity to reiterate his recommendation for the resumption of the territory on the ground that the arrangement entered into with Tularam, was a life tenure and, therefore, it lapsed to the British Government with the death of the *Senapati*. But the Agent rejected the proposal, and even Lord Dalhousie, the Governor-General, was not convinced of Butler's arguments. In his Minute on 6 March 1852, the Governor-General pointed out that "the agreement of 1834 did not limit the tenure of the country to Tularam Senapati during his life time only, nor that alleged violation of that agreement would justify the Government of India in assuming the territory and that something more than that consideration was necessary to justify the action."[128] The Governor General, therefore, instructed the local authorities to confirm the sons of Tularam Senapati in their possessions subject to the conditions that the tribute should be paid regularly, that the British troops should be assisted in their territory, heinous offenders given up and all custom exactions abolished.[129]

Accordingly, Butler had no other alternative but to confirm the sons of Tularam in their possessions. But before long the latter was subjected to more frequent raids of the Angamis whose excesses had made even the adjoining British districts wholly insecure.[130] To enquire into these atrocities, the Agent to the Governor-General, North-East Frontier, deputed in December 1851, Lieutenant Vincent, Junior Assistant at Nowgong, who learnt on arrival that since December 1847 twenty-four outrages had been committed. In 1851 alone, 55 persons were killed, 10 wounded and 113 carried off into captivity. At the suggestion of Vincent, the Government of Bengal affected some strong measures for the security of North Cachar. The frontier outposts were strengthened and an office of the Junior Assistant for North Cachar was created with headquarters at the strategic position of Asalu and one Lieutenant H.S. Bivar was posted there.[131]

Meanwhile, the situation in North Cachar drifted from bad to worse. On 3 April 1853, a considerable number of armed Nagas attacked the village of Semkar. The marauders killed 86 persons, wounded many, carried off about 115 persons and burnt and plundered five villages.[132] In retaliation, Nakulram proceeded against the Nagas at the head of 300 armed followers consisting of the Nagas and the Kacharis. But when he was within a few miles of the offending village, Nakulram espoused the cause of a Naga clan in their inter-clanish feuds. A bloody encounter took place in which Nakulram was trapped and hacked to pieces.

His followers then made a hasty retreat towards Cachar while many lost their lives. On receipt of the intelligence of the incident, Major Jenkins directed the Principal Assistant, Nowgong, to detach immediately a company of sepoys to the site of the occurence and take such measures as might be necessary to prevent the repetition of the Naga menace.[133]

The incident, on the other hand, afforded the local authorities the much awaited pretext to press for the annexation of the North Cachar. The unprovoked attack launched by Nakulram against the independent tribe, not in any way guilty of offence against him, without the sanction from the Paramount power was treated as a gross violation of the terms of the agreement recently renewed. At the same time, the worst passions of the hill tribes were inflamed and it was apprehended that a series of reprisals and counter-reprisals would follow entailing heavy bloodshed.[134] Bivar reported that nothing short of resumption would effectively prevent the recurrence of atrocities since Brajanath Burman, brother of the deceased, had neither the means nor the ability to repel the tribes who intoxicated by the recent success would surely follow up their victory and lay the country waste unless strong measures were adopted for their counteraction.[135] Jenkins was impressed by the arguments of the local officers and changed his earlier attitude. He also advocated to the Government in favour of resumption of the territory proposing, however, compensation to the remaining heirs of Tularam to the extent of Rs. 3,000 annually, with rent-free grants for life.[136]

As a matter, of fact, the early British relations with the Chief of this hill tract was expected to be a source of strength in the event of another war with Ava or any collusion with the predatory tribes in the neighbourhood. He was, therefore, allowed to have undisturbed possession of his hill tract, the resources of which were then little known. But the operations of 1842 under Lieutenant Bigge had revealed that this area was immensely potent. It abounded in coal, limestone, iron-ore, salt, ivory, lac and wax.[137] Contrary to earlier expectations, of being a solid strength and a bulwark against the Nagas, the local arrangement had become a source of danger and constant embarrassment to the Government. To maintain law and order in North Cachar and to reduce the Angami Nagas to submission, the frontier outposts from Goomy Goonjo to Dimapur were required to be brought under the effective and direct control of the Government.[138]

The recommendations of the Agent was seriously considered by the Government of Bengal. A.J. Moffatt Mills, a Judge of the *Sadar Dewani Adalat*, who was then touring the districts of Assam, was called upon to give his sentiment on the subject. After a careful study of the whole problem, Mills concurred in Jenkins proposal for resumption and recommended that a sum of Rs. 1,560 be bestowed annually as pensions to the three prominent members of the *Senapati* family, observing "that the country under its present management is a serious obstacle to the settlement of the Naga territory."[139]

Finally, Lord Dalhousie, the annexationist Governor-General too shared the sentiment of the local authorities and accorded his approval to the annexation of North Cachar Hills, on the ground that the occupation of the territory was "a less objectionable alternative than letting it alone."[140] Accordingly, in early 1854, the territory of Tularam Senapati was formally annexed to the British dominion under a proclamation issued by the Government of India and was merged with the Nowgong district of Assam with the status of a sub-division. Under the direction of the Government of Bengal, Lieutenant Bivar immediately resumed the administration of the tract and granted pensions to several members of the *Senapati's* family aggregating to Rs. 1002 annually, besides rent-free grants in the village of Mohungdijua on the understanding that these would be resumed upon the death of the respecyive holders.[141] Thus the whole of the Heramba Kingdom came under the Government of the East India Company and the British paramountcy in Cachar became a *fait accompli*.

Agreement with Tularam Senapati

*Terms of Agreement concluded with Toolaram Senaputtee
on the 3rd November under the Orders of Government,
dated 16th October 1834*

First : Toolaram forgoes all claims to the country between the Morihur and Dyung and the Dyung and Keopoli rivers, from which he was dispossessed by Govind Ram and Doorga Ram.

Second : Toolaram is to hold the remainder of the country formerly in his possession, or the tract of country bounded on the west by the Dyung river, and a line to be determine here after, drawn from the Barce ford or the Dyung to a point on the Jamoona river, between the cultivation of Seil Dhurmpur and of Duboka and the Hajaee (excluding the two latter) ; by the Jamoona and Dyung rivers north, by the Dunsira river east, and to the south and south-west the Naga Hills and Mowheir river, and he agrees to hold the above tract in dependence on the British Government, and to pay a yearly tribute, for their protection, of four pairs of elephants' teeth, each pair to weigh thirty-five seers.

Third : Toolaram, during his life, shall receive from the British Government a stipend of fifty Rupees a month in consideration of the foregoing cessions and the Agreements.

Fourth : The British Government shall have the right of placing Military Posts in any part of Toolaram's country, and should there be occasion to march troops through it, Toolaram engages to furnish them with all the requisites of carriage and provisions in his power, he being paid for the same.

Fifth : All petty offences committed within Toolaram's country, he shall take cognizance of, and do justice according to the custom of the country, but all heinous crimes shall be transferred to the nearest British court, and Toolaram engages to bring such to notice, and endeavour to apprehend the offenders.

Sixth : Toolaram shall not establish any custom chowkies on the rivers forming the boundaries of his country.

Seventh : Toolaram will not commence any military operation against neighbouring chiefs without permission of the British Government, and in case of being attacked, he shall report the same and be protected by British troops, provided the British Authorities are satisfied that the aggression has been unprovoked on his part.

Eighth : *Ryots* shall not be prevented from emigrating to, and settling on, either side of the boundary they may prefer.

Ninth : In case of failing to abide by these conditions, the British Government shall be at liberty to take possession of my country.

(Sd.) TOOLARAM SENAPUTTE
F. JENINS

CHAPTER IV

New Regime

Immediately after the assassination of Raja Govindachandra, in 1830, Thomas Fisher, the Superintendent of Survey in Sylhet, was posted 'in charge of the Cachar affairs'.[1] Since the formal annexation of South Cachar,* in August 1832, the administration of the tract was entrusted to the Agent to the Governor-General, North-East Frontier, whose jurisdiction extended to Assam, Cachar, Jayantia, Manipur, Cooch Bihar, Hill tracts and Bhutan, while Lieutenant Fisher continued in the immediate charge of Cachar.[2] But in view of the difficulties for the Agent to supervise effectively, the affairs of Cachar from Cherapunji, the Government of India appointed, in early 1933, Fisher permanently, as the Superintendent of Cachar on a consolidated salary of Rs. 1000 chargeable on the revenue of the province, with headquarters at Dudpatill.[3] The Superintendent was to exercise the powers of a Magistrate, Collector and a Civil Judge under the supervision of the Agent to the Governor-General. In addition, he was to exercise political authority over the hill tribes on the Cachar frontiers on behalf of the Government of India.[4]

Cachar, like Assam, was declared to be a Non-Regulated Province under the Regulation X of 1822 which had its origin in the civil commissionership of North East Rangpur[5] and gradually crept into many other areas of the British dominion in India. It exempted the operation of the normal rules and

* Silchar and Hailakandi Subdivisions.

provided for the administration by an executive upon a mixed system into which the spirit of the Regulation was to be harmonised with the native institutions. Thus the head of a Non-Regulated Province was to administer civil and criminal justice, to supervise the collection of revenue and the superintendence of police and all other branches of the Government by the principles and spirit of the existing Regulations. Evidently, a great task had fallen upon Fisher as the first Superintendent of Cachar. Born in 1772, Thomas Fisher began his career as a clerk in East India House and by dint of his calibre and sincerity was elevated to the position of a Researcher there in 1816. An F.S.A. of Perth and London in later life, he had shown considerable talent for drawing and distinguished himself by drawing some monumental remains and antiquities. In 1821, he was deputed by the Government of India to enquire into the early history of Cachar and the report he submitted to the Government and his articles which appeared in subsequent issues of the Journal of the Asiatic Society of Bengal, bear eloquent testimony to scholarly zeal and spirit of research. Shortly afterwards, he was appointed as the Superintendent of Survey, Sylhet, which position he held till his posting 'Incharge of Cachar Affairs.'[6] The intimate knowledge of the country which Fisher had already acquired eminently fitted him to the new assignment.

Meanwhile, the attention of the Government was drawn by the fact that socially, linguistically and geographically, Cachar was a part of Bengal. Lord William Bentinck the Governor-General, in his Minute of 18 January 1834, observed that as the Province of Cachar was in the plains and was distinct from the hill tract of the north-east frontier it should ''be placed under the control of the Dacca commissionership and managed under the same regulations as exist for the neighbouring district of Sylhet.[7] Accordingly, in 1836, Cachar was included in the Dacca Division and the Superintendent's headquarters shifted to Silchar. This was a judicious arrangement as the various innovations in Cachar could be compared with other districts of Eastern Bengal in a common Platform and the people in Cachar Valley, so long under feudal rule, now found a larger field and better contact with their kith and kins in Bengal.

Anyway, it was a problem before Fisher ever since the

de facto occupation, in 1830, to engineer an administrative machinery in a province like Cachar which till then had known nothing but medieval despotism and for the previous decades, misrule, chaos and confusion, under its hereditary rulers as well as usurpers. Traditional to the British pattern, he had to enquire into the local system, customs and usages, and set up a government befitting to the geo-political circumstances and temperament of the people. But most of the offical papers were burnt or otherwise destroyed at the time of the assassination of the late Raja. From a few available papers and men of age and experience, Fisher, however, collected some information regarding the past history, tradition and institutions which were referred to in the reports he submitted to the Government.[8]

It may not be out of place to give here a short account of the system of administration and the history, its evolution, that preceded the British rule in Cachar.[9] Although held in succession by the Tipperahs and the Dimachas on the eve of the British annexation, the fertile valley of Barak, being a continuation of Bengal, had a sizable Bengalee population from an unknown date of their history. There were numerous Bengalee villages on the northern side of the Barak bordering Sylhet, while major part of the tract was even recently uninhabited. On the invitation of Suradarpa Narayana, the Raja of Cachar, many more Bengalees had immigrated into the 'country' during the early years of Heramba rule in the Cachar plains. The immigrants occupied the fallow lands and brought them under cultivation. The Raja allowed them to practise their own customs, usages and institutions like other inhabitants and enjoyed much autonomy in their respective *Parganas*.[10] These autonomous units, on the other hand, automatically influenced the Dimacha settlers, including the members of the royal family, to embrace the Hindu way of life accepting many of the Bengalee ethics. Although the orthodox section of the Dimachas were indifferent to the occulturation, they were concentrated in the hills in the north and the Cachar plains and continued to be a Bengalee state ruled by a pro-Bengalee tribal Chief, the important offices of whose Government were mainly held by the Bengalees.[11]

Evidently, on the eve of the British occupation two types of

political institutions existed in Cachar, one following the traditional system of the Dimacha Government with its hierarchy
of officials and the other as the socio-economic units of the
plainsmen who were ever growing in number and importance.
The first consisted of the *Barbhandari* or Prime Minister, *Patras*
or Minister, *Senapati* or Commander-in-Chief and *Raj Pandit*
or Royal Priest, besides several others. The jurisdiction of
these officers was mostly confined to the hill-Kacharis i.e.
Dimachas, Kukis and the Nagas. The Bengalees were almost
independent of their control. They sought a very limited
influence at the *Darbar*, only to secure them from the interference of the royal officers, and had a constitution of their
own, based on the land-revenue system, peculiar in Cachar,
under which the agricultural units were known as *Khels*.[12] The
fundamental principle of the system was the holding of land in
guild by a number of persons by voluntary association. 'Just
as in the Hindu communities the village forms the basis of the
agricultural commonwealth, which is bound together theoretically, by the ties of kindred in caste, so *khel* formed the unit
of the agricultural community of Cachar, but its members were
not connected by any ties of kindred, caste, nationality or
creed.[13] At first only the Bengalee Hindus and Muslims were
found side by side in the same *khel*, but gradually the scope
for voluntary association was extended to the Naga, Kuki and
other settlers. The guilds were even formed for leasing fisheries
or catching elephants. The constituent members were obliged
to pay collective revenue and to discharge services including
the supply of labour for state enterprise. Such payment or
supply were made through a *Mukhtar* elected by the members
and confirmed by the Raja. He was generally the leading
personality in the corporation and responsible to the Raja for
the dues of the unit. Obviously, this officer was the liaison
between the Raja and the *khel*. He carried into execution all
orders of the Government in respect of his *khel*, took charge of
the abandoned *taluks* and collected the state revenue, and, in
return, held rent-free grants, enjoyed honorary titles and had
the authority to confine and punish defaulters. In course of
time, as the number of *khels* increased, adjacent *khels* were
grouped together into larger unions, called *Raj* or *Pargana*. The
Mukhtars of the constituent *khels* elected a *Raj Mukhtar*, with

various titles like *Choudhury, Mazumdar, Bara Laskar, Bara-bhuiya, Major Bhuiya, Chota Bhuiya* etc. all according to the status and importance of the unit. These titles are of Bengalee origin and are still in use in different parts of the greater valley; one of them, namely, *Laskar*, extends far up into the Garo hills. Initially, they clung to the land and its repre-sentatives, but,curiously enough, in course of time they became transferable at fixed prices. In the early days of the Company, the title of *Choudhry* fetched Rs. 100 that of *Mazumdar* Rs. 75, *Laskar* Rs. 60, *Bara Bhuiya* Rs. 50, *Major Bhuiya* Rs. 45 and *Chota Bhuiya* Rs. 40. The titles became hereditary and by degrees the unions began to seperate into classes.[14] The members of the *khel* paid their portion of the revenue of the *Khel-Mukhtar* while the latter paid the total dues of his *khel* to the *Raj-Mukhtar* who in his turn deposited the entire colle-ction to the Royal Treasury. The office of the *Mukhtar* was originally elective, but gradually became hereditary, either the eldest son or the next of his kin succeeding only with a show of election.[15] There were also some *debottara khels* whose income were appropriated to meet the expenditure of some important temples, *viz.* income of *Paikan* towards *Ranachandi,* that of *Bishnugarh* towards *Laksmi-Narayan, Bhisings* towards *Shyama Kali.* The *Lakhiraj* estates were ear-marked for the mainte-nance of the members of the royal family, who had accepted vedic Hinduism and always endeavoued to imitate the Benga-lees, and were, in fact, thoroughly Bengaleeised on the eve of the British annexation.[16]

Fisher was not in favour of interference with the system of revenue in view of the fact that this might injure the sentiment of the people in addition to incurring huge work load for the Government. The financial difficulties, on the other hand, stood in the way of altering the existing institutions. Fisher, therefore, introduced only such changes as were considered absolutely necessary confirming the former officials in their respective positions with customary powers and privileges. The Superintendent had great hopes about the revenue prospect of Cachar, and estimated the cultivable lands in the province at 120, 160 *kulbahs*, roughly 480, 640 acres, assessable at the average of Rs. 2-8-0 per *kulbah*, yielding a revenue of Rs. 300,400 a year. But to his disappointment, Fisher found in the first

year of occupation that the receipt could barely meet the charges
on the establishment and the years following it the collections
were far from satisfactory; the total revenue for the Bengalee
year 1238 (1831 A.D.) was Rs. 30,595[17] against Rs. 32,679-3-0
in the previous year.[18] Fisher, therefore, realised that without
the increase of population there could not be any improvement
in the country or revenue of Cachar as the indigenous people
were only microscopic and miserably poor to trap the vast
natural resources of the province. To achieve his object, the
Superintendent wanted to introduce a fresh settlement and
undertook a general survey of the land to arrive at an accurate
assessment.[19] Meanwhile, he had abolished the river *ghats*
excepting a few on the Surma, at which duties were levied on
exportable commodities at moderate rates; the agricultural
products being totally exempted. The state monopolies on
betel-nut, timber, salt, cotton, grass etc. were done away with,
retaining the hill *ghats* which offered the only means of raising
state dues from the dwellers of the adjoining hills.[20] With the
approval of the Government of India, Fisher introduced towards
the close of 1832 the same rent as was prevalent in Sylhet i.e.
Rs. 5-2-0 per *kulbah or hal* of cultivable lands, but the *bari* and
chara lands and tanks were exempted from the assessment. To
attract settlers from Sylhet, Dacca, Tripura and Mymensing,
circular letters were issusd through their respective district
officers to the effect that the country of Cachar has been permanently annexed to the British dominion, that the tax there
will be levied at the rates analogous to such as have been adopted in recent assessment, that they may get good jungle lands
rent-free for 1,000 days, at the end of which a settlement will
be concluded for the portion brought under cultivation to which
the holder will acquire a proprietory right as a *Talukdar* or
Zamindar and that were an outlay was made for draining or
filling marshes, clearing forests, the period during which the
land will be allowed to remain rent-free would be extended to
five years..." etc. etc.[21] In response, many more newcomers
poured into the province, but the revenue fell too pressingly on
the people of Cachar who were not so much resourceful as
those in Sylhet and new immigrants were generally from the
poorer section of their former districts. To make matters worse,
there were three consecutive unusually wet seasons, added with

terrible innundations in 1834 which caused great miseries to the people and huge arrears in revenue.[22]

In 1836, the *Mukhtar* system having been found expensive and inefficient was substituted by three salaried *Tahsildars* at Silchar, Hailakandi and Katigorah. Towards the close of the same year, E.W. Gordon, the Commissioner of Dacca, reported to the Government of Bengal that the people who had settled in Cachar from Sylhet, with a view to speculate on lands, were obliged to return on account of high rates of taxation, that many had absconded to evade the arrears, while many of the Collectors had tendered their resignation or were prepared to do so.[23] On the recommendations of the Commissioner, the Government decided to make a new settlement of Cachar on easier terms for the *Mirasdars*. Accordingly, under the direction of the Board of Revenue, in 1838, Major J.G. Burns, who had succeeded P. Mainwarring as Superintendent of Cachar[24] on 13 April, 1836, effected a new settlement for a term of five years. The highest rate, imposed on the cultivable land, was Rs. 3 per *hal*, but the *chara* lands were brought under cultivation and assessed at Rs. 2-8 per *hal*. The *bari, baksha,* and *lakhiraj* holdings remained rent-free as before, and jungle lands were settled rent-free for 1,000 days and at the above rates. The total area settled by Burns returned 11,132 *hals*, of which 7,563 were paying and the rest rent-free; while the total revenue amounted to Rs. 24,974-11-9 annually. The settlement was very favourable to the *Mirasdars* who, with few exceptions, had cleared and cultivated the jungle lands bordering on their holdings in excess to that for what they paid revenue.[25]

Meanwhile, even the land measurement conducted under Fisher was found to be inaccurate and, infact, Burn's settlement was made only for five years as an interim arrangement sufficient to undertake a fresh survey as a pretext to the future settlement. Therefore, a survey was conducted under Lieutenant Thuillier, Superintendent of Survey, in 1842, which brought more lands under assessment.[26] In October, 1842, Rai Bahadur Gulak Chandra Bole, Deputy Collector of Sylhet, was specially deputed by the Government of Bengal to make a fresh settlement for fifteen years. The rates fixed by the temporary settlement on the rice lands were retained, but the *chara* and *bari* lands were reassessed at rates varying from Rs. 3 to 2 per *hal*.

The jungle lands were left revenue-free for first five years, and for the next five years assessed at Rs. 1-8-per *hal,* while for the last five years at full rates. The *Lakhiraj* claims were left to be decided by the Superintendent of Cachar.[27]

In this settlement more lands were taken up than could be cultivated. There were 6,742 estates with an area of 20,325 *hals* of which 14,088 *hals* were under cultivation and 6,237 jungle. The *Jumma* for the first five years was Rs. 43,146, next five years Rs. 50,831 and the last Rs. 58,518. For the first term the revenue was paid regularly and there remained but little outstanding balance, but when the jungle land began to involve rent, in 1849-50, the *Mirasdars* found that they had taken more land than they could possibly reclaim. They now offered to give up the whole of the jungle land rather than pay the revenve.[28] As a result, in 1850, the Board of Revenue allowed them to relinquish the surplus portion of their lands paying for the remainder at the rate of Rs. 3 per *hal.* The holders of 481 *pattas* took advantage of the concession and gave up 2,971 *hals,* the decrease of revenue being Rs. 4,227-15-9. This was nearly made up by fresh settlements made from time to time to expire contemporareously with the fifteen years settlement. The number of *mahals* settled on this principle was 1,458 covering an area of 7,326 *hals* with a *jumma* of Rs. 20,302-12-11. The demand on account of land revenue including the increase effected by these coterminous settlements amounted to Rs. 67,660 in 1854, the number of *mahals* being 7,773.[29]

For the collection of revenue, Fisher followed the system that was prevalent under the native government when the *Mukhtars* were appointed to collect the state dues. The *Mukhtars* had establishments allowed to them but conducted the business and accounts themselves. On the *kist* becoming arrears, notices were given by beating drums throughout the *khel* that on a certain day they could pay their revenue to the *Mukhtars* at an appointed place. Formerly, the *Mukhtars* had the authority to confine the defaulters, but the rules introduced by Fisher prohibited any ill-treatment and strictly confined the punishment to the personal restraint of the defaulters who were detained in the *Mukhtars,* houses. If the *Mukhtar* reported his efforts to collect the arrears unavailing, the defaulter's property was attached in the usual manner by the Government *Nazir* with orders from the Superintendent. But the *Mukhtar System* was abolished, in 1836, on the recommendations of P. Mainwarring, who succeeded Captain Fisher in 1835, having found 'expensive and inefficient'. There were also charges of high-handedness and lack of confidence of the Government in the integrity of the *Mukhtars*. Also, it was felt necessary to extend the jurisdiction of the Government over the *ryots* through the *Nazirs* to make the people realise the presence of the British Government. The result was the introduction of the *Tahsildari System*, when Cachar was divided into Silchar, Katigorah and Hailakandi *Tahsils*. But the collection fell down from the very beginning of the innovation and the arrears made a mounting increase because of the lack of acquaintance of the *Tahsildars* with the *Mirasdars*. Accordingly, on 16 May 1837, J.G. Burns, Superintendent of Cachar, in his letter to E.M. Gordon, Commissioner of Dacca Division, proposed the restoration of the *Muhkhtar System* and adherence to a scheme for the collection of revenue in three instalments—the first becoming due on 1 *Shravan*, 2nd on 1 *Kartick*, and the 3rd on 1 *Falgun* of the BengaliCalender.[30] Some *Mirasdars* of Cachar, too, made representations protesting against the exclusion of the *Mukhtars* from the Collectorate as well as the Courts which was rather customary in the province. The Government *Peadahs* were held guilty of unwanted excesses and oppressions and, hence, the Mirasdars prayed before the Superintendent to restrict the conduct of these unscrupulous officials by bringing in the former *Mukhtars* to their services.[31]

Ultimately, the Commissioner agreed to the revival of the *Mukhtar System* and, in November 1837, the Superintendent reappointed the *Mukhtars*.[32] On 22 August 1838, Burns reported with pleasure that the system was working more satisfactorily and that by the end of July the collections had amounted to Rs. 22,626-6-0, the cost of collection being Rs. 1537-8-0. The sum collected, according to the Superintendent, was much greater than could have been realised under the former system, and what was more commendable, the achievement was without restraint and sale of cattle and implements of husbandry or any oppression which was a common feature under the *Nazir System*. Burns also reported that, not a single case of speculation had occurred on the part of the *Mukhtars* and the people had derived immense advantage being freed from the alarming oppressions and fraud under the former *Peadah System*. Recommending the continuation of the *Mukhtar System* for two years more, the Superintendent suggested a more simple mode of meeting the cost of collection wherein the establishment of the *Mukhtar* would include a Writer at Rs.15 and two *Mohurirs*, one at Rs. 8 and the other at Rs. 7 per month. He recommended that this monthly expense of Rs. 30 and 6 per cent on the bonafide collection, as commission for the *Mukhtars*, be allowed from the revenue.[33] The recommendations found favour with the Government of Bengal and the experimental native agency was extended till 1 May 1840.[34]

But E.R. Lyons, the next Superintendent, who succeeded Burns on 15 June 1839, in his letter to the Commissioner on 4 April 1840, termed their working as 'decidedly bad'.[35] His chief objection to the system was the small amount of revenue forwarded by the *Mukhtars* to the *Tahsils* at stated periods and the inadequate assistance afforded to him by the native agents. Of the total revenue of Rs. 25,481 for 1246 B.S., Rs. 9,509-7-8 remained unrealised on 1 March 1840, thus leaving more than one-third of the annual revenue to be collected in two months, while the commission was due to be paid on the total revenue. The agents' fees in most instances were not sufficient to defray the expense of *Mohurir* and *Peadahs* which they must keep up throughout the year and to meet this expenditure many appropriated a part of their collection to personal use for a time and invested the money in some profitable enterprise before crediting it into the treasury. The *Mukhtars* also most artfully exhibited a small balance against each estate-holder in their accounts which rendered it perplexing to determine whose estate ought to be attached. Notwithstanding, some estates were of course attached by the Government, but not proportionate to the unrealised revenue-demand. The estates in Cachar were for the most part very small and numerous, there being 3,721 concerning which Lyons had incessantly to send orders to the *Mukhtars*, who were 45 in number, to collect the revenue. This large number of *Mukhtars*, according to him, was very objectionable, since separate account of the collections of each had to be maintained. Besides, their accounts were generally full of mistakes and alterations, because they were unable to write them-

selves and employed the cheapest clerks. As a natural consequence, extra labour was charged on the Superintendent's
office which itself had skeleton staff to work properly. Lyons
also felt that the system of collecting the revenue of the province through the medium of some land-holders was undesira-
ble, All of them being moved by a common feeling and even
suspicious, one might think that punctual payment would lead
the Government to suppose that taxation was too light and
that their zeal would ultimately prove injurious for them. A
Mukhtar hardly cared for the fees, but valued the situation
which gave him authority to regulate the payment of land-dues
with weight. The Superintendent believed that these abuses
and irregular payments would continue as long the *Mukhtar
System* lasted. The *Mukhtars* had also already failed in an
important part of their agreement which stipulated for the
recovery of the balance of the former years and bore the sem-
blance of collusion among them and with other landholders.
The *Mukhtar System* was merely experimental and, therefore,
Lyons submitted another scheme suggesting appointment of
the *Tahsildars*. Under this plan, according to his estimate, the
expenditure would be less and fixed whereas the amount of
Mukhtars' fees would be enhanced every year at par with the
increase of revenue and thus would exceed Rs. 2160 in 1247
B. S. Being paid Government servants, the *Tahsildars* would
naturally exert themselves to make full collections in the hope
of being confirmed to their posts and there would be no reason
for fraud to enable them to pay for an establishment. Their
accounts would also be clear, uniform and valuable records.
Whereas it was to the interest of the *Mukhtars* to retard the
payment of revenue on various pleas, the reverse would be the
object of the *Tahsildars* to ensure permanent employment. The
Tahsildars would be more immediately under the control of
the Superintendent and latter could exercise a better command
over them and might reasonably expect assistance and co-operation from them in official matters.[36]

The proposal received the approval of the Government, and
in May 1843 *Tahsildari System* was re-introduced. Cachar was
again divided into three such *Tahsils*, namely, Silchar, Hailakandi
and Katigorah.[37] The actual collection was made by the *Tahsil
Mohurirs*. In case, the simple demand had failed in realising

the due tax, the defaulters were detained in the *Tahsil* and urged
upon to pay up before proceeding to attach their property for
arrears.[38] No objection had ever been raised by the *Mirasdars*
to such detention and there was no complaint of torture or coercion. On the contrary, after confinement for a few hours or
days the dues were paid up by the detenue himself or through
someone on his behalf to escape attachment.[39] The regularity
with which the collections had since then been made proved the
vast superiority of the system of salaried *Tahsildars* with a small
establishment over the former mode of collection and a saving
of about Rs. 1200 in respect of collection charges was done
annually. The whole revenue demand for 1852-53 (1258 B.S.)
amounted to Rs. 65259-10-4 ; of this 7554 *mahals* yielded a land
revenue of Rs. 56737-0-8, 113 tribal villages inhabited by the
Dimacha, Naga and Kuki tribes, who were required to pay at
the rate of Re. 1 per house per annum, credited Rs. 2324, 42
Fishery *mahals* paid Rs. 619-8-0, and the rest realised from the
salt-wells and the *ghats* where transit duties were levied on
timber, bamboo, cane, grass, cotton, wax, ivory etc.[40] Next year,
1853-54, the total revenue of Cachar amounted to over
Rs. 80,000 including the miscellaneous revenue and *Abkaree*,
while the cost of collection was reduced by 3 per cent.[41]

During the Heramba regime, a number of *Patras* or Ministers formed a Court of Justice. There were 54 of them at the
time dynasty was at the zenith of its powers, 18 of them were
retained during the reign of Krishnachandra, but the number
was reduced to 4 by Govindachandra. The proceedings of
the Court were reduced to writing, but the more common
procedure was the *viva voce*. The findings of the Court were
reported to the Raja who was the Chief Administrator of
Justice, had full jurisdiction either to punish or to pardon the
accused. In Civil suits there was no specified Code of Laws,
and the Raja on the advice of the Court pronounced such judgement or sentence as he deemed necessary. The guilt or inno-
cence of the party was frequently determined by an ordeal and
punishments were recommended at the discretion of the Judges.[42]
There was no sharp distinction between the administration of
civil and criminal justice. All suits were decided in a summary
way under the direction of the Raja and the losing party was
often punishable by a fine or a term of imprisonment. How-

ever, during the reign of Govindachandra the criminal laws
were tightened by a series of royal statutes, which provided
severe punishment for different crimes including the mutilation
of limbs. The statutes were necessitated by the increased crimes
during the weak rule of the Raja and the misrule foistered by
the rebel-conspirators including the Manipuri usurpers. A study
of the statutes, issued in Bengali, makes it clear that they were
drafted under the influence of the Brahmins and that the offences of the time were mainly against the Raja, Brahmins and
other high caste people, and upon the chastity of the women.[43]

After the British occupation, in 1830, the common people
in Cachar were found to be easily amenable to the Judiciary,
and the Officiating Magistrate exercised the powers of a District
Magistrate.[44] He was empowered, with the concurrence of the
Jury, to execute punishment not involving a sentence of three
years, while offences of a heinous character, after having been
tried by a Jury, were referred to the Court of the Agent to the
Governor-General for final adjudication. The spirit and practices of the Regulations in force in the Company's territory
were generally followed in determining the character of the
offence and in awarding the punishment. Fisher recommended
the continuation of the existing procedure with necessary
modification in deciding cases regarding the Dimachas, Kukis,
Manipuris and the Nagas. In addition, he suggested that the
Jury should be taken from as large a number of intelligent
men as could be assembled and it should include some persons
of the same tribe of the accused and should never consist of
less than five individuals. But the Government of India felt
that it might prove inconvenient to have the Jurors constantly
sitting at least for some years to come, because the persons
eligible for such services might not be numerous in Cachar and,
therefore, vested the Superintendent with discretion to dispense
with the Jury, if and when necessary. The Superintendent was
further advised that no Jury was to be summoned except in
cases which might call for a severe punishment of rigorous imprisonment for more than two years in the event of conviction.[45]

But the system of judiciary for the plainsmen was different
from that of the tribal inhabitants. In their case, the royal prerogatives were thoroughly relaxed, particularly in civil disputes.
The guilds were unpaid magistracies with certain fisca¹ and

criminal powers. In case of a dispute between the sharers in
the *khel* the matter was decided by the *khel-Mukhtar* with the
counsel of the elders in the *khel*, and in case of his inability to
arrive at a settlement the matter was referred to the *Raj Mukhtar*. The fiscal and criminal powers of the *Raj Mukhtar* gave
him a large and loose authority and, as a matter of fact, his
decree was enforced by detention of the person who delayed to
obey. In case of disputes between *khels* belonging to different
rajs, the matter was referred to the *League*, a union of a number of *rajs*, whose members were all the constituent *Raj Mukhtars*. The most influential member was elected to be the Chief
of the *League* and was known as *Mazumdar*. The *Mazumdars*
or the representatives of all the *Leagues* in the kingdom formed
a *Council of Leagues* headed by the *Mazumdar* of Bikrampur
who was known as *Bar Mazumdar*. The importance of the
Bikrampur estate lay in the fact that Bikram Roy, the founder
of the *Pargana*, obtained the first lease from Suradarpa
Narayana, the Raja of Cachar, after the Heramba Government
had invited more number of Bengalees from Bengal to immi-
grate into Cachar and receive land on liberal terms. The *Bar
Mazumdar*, therefore, exercised a sort of primacy among the
Mirasdars, headed the Council of the Agricultural Leagues, and
decided *inter-raj* or *inter-League* disputes. The *Bar Mazumdar's
Council** was, thus, the *Chief Court of Justice* in the Cachar
plains. Only in difficult or keenly contested cases an appeal or
a reference could be made to the Raja. The Raja retained his
judicial prerogatives in all heinous offences. The *Bar Bhandari,
Raj Pandit* and the *Bar Mazumdar* formed a sort of Judicial
committee to advice the Raja in complicated cases. The Hindu
Civil Code was based on the *Shastras* and the Mohammedan
Code on *Quran*, but the Raja of Heramba had poor or no
knowledge in either. As a result, the Bengalees had to depend

---

*Khel was the lowest self-governing agricultural unit headed by a
Mukhtar. A group of *Khels* formed a *Raj* headed by a *Raj-Mukhtar*,
known variously as *Chaudhury, Barbhuiya, Major Bhuiya, Chota Bhuiya* etc.
A number of *Rajs*, also known as *Parganas* formed a *Leaguer* or *Union* in
which the constituent *Raj-Mukhtars* were the members, while the most
powerful of them was the *Head* of the *League* and was called *Mazumdar*.
The *Mazumdar* or the *Heads* of all the *Leagues* in the state formed the
Council of Leagues headed by the *Bar Mazumdar*. The *Bar Mazumdar's
Council*, i.e. the *Council of Leagues*, was thus the *genus-politik* in which
all other agricultural *Communes* of Cachar Valley were the *species*.

upon some voluntary organisation to settle their internal feuds
or grievances and the chiefs were entrusted with certain judicial
powers.[46]   They ran the criminal and fiscal administration with
nominal royal interference, while the civil suits were decided
without any interference.   Even in the cases that went before
the Raja, latter sought the advice of the *Raj Pandit* if the parties
were Hindus, and in case of Muslim he consulted an acknowledged expert in the Law of *Quran*.[47]

Fisher, therefore, had no other alternative but to decide
such cases according to the existing practice of the country
as could be ascertained from the former officials and no-
tables of the state together with such information as could
be gathered from legal documents.   But for the future, he
felt that the basic principles for the administration of Justice
should be analogous to that of Sylhet, finding a significant section of the people had already accepted them.   Further, it was
anticipated that in no distant future the bulk of the people of
Cachar would consist of settlers from Bengal. Fisher, therefore,
recommended that the administration of justice should be conducted in the same manner as was done in the *Zilla Courts* of the
Presidency. The proceedings would be based on the Hindu and
Mohammedan Laws, but these were to be modified by such local
usages and customs which might be found well established and
deserved respect.   To ensure speedy justice, he suggested
the establishment of a native court for the trial of petty
cases, both civil and criminal, consisting of a few assessors of
intelligence and acquainted with local usages. This court was to
be aided by some *Mohurirs*, in taking evidence, having knowledge of the Mohammedan law and also of Bengalee in which the
proceedings were recorded. To hear appeals from these courts,
particularly in cases involving local customs, Fisher further desired to appoint a Jury of not less than three members. But
Robertson, the Agent to the Governor-General, felt that it
would be a problem to ensure whether a Jury had the compe-
tence to decide civil cases, and observed that two well-qualified
Sadar Amins would be more useful than a court consisting of
several Assessors ; one of whom might be a native of Cachar
and the other any intelligent Muslim, and the people might be
left to whichever Court they prefer.[48]   Nevertheless, the Vice-
President in Council overlooked these objections and by way

of experiment authorised the Superintendent to carry on the measures proposed by him as he was supposed to have known more of local conditions. The Superintendent was, of course, advised to exercise his discretion to do away with them in the event of their proving 'objectionable or impracticable'.[49]

As stated already, the Superintendent was vested with the powers of a Judge, Magistrate and a Collector. The appeals from his court were made to the Agent, to the Governor-General, North-East Frontier. But the Act V of 1835 placed Cachar under the jurisdiction of the High Court of Bengal at Calcutta in Civil and Criminal matters and that of the Board of Revenue for fiscal administration. Since then, all appeals in criminal cases were referred to the *Sadar Nizamat Adalat* and in civil cases to the *Sadar Dewani Adalat*, while the jurisdiction of the Sessions Judge at Sylhet was extended to Cachar. With the transfer of Cachar to the 15th Division, in 1836, the Commissioner of Dacca heard the Revenue Appeals.[50]

The Judiciary in Cachar consisted of one Superintendent's Court and a *Panchayat Court*. One *Munshi*, one *Mohurir* and one *Nazir* were attached to the former, while the latter consisted of 3 Native Judges—1 *Bar Bhandari* and 2 *Bitra Dalois**—and 1 *Mohurir*. These three Native Judges were in service of the former Government of Cachar, and were chosen by Captain Fisher for their past judicial experience, knowledge of customs and usages of the country and Bengalee language. Fisher further had arranged that, they would sit together in the manner of a traditional *Panchayat* in Bengal. If one or both of the Junior members subscribed to the views of the Senior the judgement was at once pronounced, but in case of division the case was referred to the Superintendent's Court. The *Panchayat Court* took cognisance of suits for private property to the amount of Rs. 100/-, and the suits above the sum were seldom filed.[51] The cases in the Superintendent's Court were mainly confined to land disputes, appeals and suits where any of the *Amlas* might be a party. The *Vakeels*, without any legal qualification, were engaged by the parties in all the courts.[52]

---

* The salary of the *Bar Bhandari* was Rs. 10 and of the *Bitra Dalois* Rs. 5 each per month. Brajaram Barman was the first *Bar Bhandari*, and the *Bitra Dalois* were Krishnaram Deb and Krishnanath Dutta. C.R., No. 51 of 1839.

The Stamps were not used in the Non-Regulated Provinces and in lieu of that a commission of Rs. 6—4 per cent was levied on all regular cases. But in Civil cases no commission was even required. As a result, numerous frivolous or vexatious petitions were presented, thus increasing the work-load of the courts. The *Vakeels*, to increase their practice, encouraged the people to rush to the courts. The title suits also began to pour in with the gradual leasing out of the fallow lands and fixation of ownership. The crimes also increased ; tresspass, fraud, perjury, theft, bribery, abduction and others. Therefore, Burns suggested, on 6 May 1838, to introduce Stamp Law in Cachar as a check to the frivolous and vexatious cases. He also wanted to forbid the practice of the *Vakeels* in the *Fauzdari* and *Jumma* cases, as these people were the instigators of every litigations and fanned the flame of discord among the ignorant inhabitants on whose very vitals they subsisted and exhibited systematic turbulent and disrespectful conduct in the *Kutchery*. Recommending higher salaries for the officers and government employees, the Superintendent advocated the introduction of the Stamp Laws in Cachar to secure the additional benefit of more revenue for the Government.[53] E.R. Lyons, the next Superintendent, also repeated the suggestions made by Burns.[54] Acknowledging the efficiency and sincerity of the *Panchayat Court*, he observed that the business of the court was so fast increasing that it was necessary to establish three *Munsiff Courts*, one each in the neighbourhood of the three *thanas* and also to appoint a few more *Mohurirs*. The Superintendent also advocated the immediate introduction of Stamp Laws in Cachar to meet expenses accrued by the additional appointments and also to prevent the greedy *Vakeels* from inducing their innocent clients to institute fictitious suits.[55]

Realising the volume of works that the judiciary in Cachar had to discharge, the Government of Bengal appointed on 1 April 1841, a Munsiff to deal with the *Dewani* cases. Further, the number of *Mohurirs* was increased, and pay and honoraria of the officers including the Native Judges were enhanced.[56] Since this appointment, the Munsiff's works had been performed with greater regularity and the court procedures were better observed. On 27 January 1842, Lyons reported[57] that he was satisfied with the Munsiff Court; that 250 pending cases in the *Panchayat Court* were all disposed of, that in other courts also the pending cases were not older than few months ; and that the people of Cachar have appreciated the improvement over the old system. Being fully satisfied with the efficiency of the Munsiff's Court, the Superintendent recommended that the *Panchayat Court*, then consisted of three native members be broken up and the acting Junior Judge, Krishnanath Dutta, who was considered in every respect competent of responsible duties, be appointed as 2nd Munsiff on the same salary then paid to the other Munsiff. This would effect a pecuniary savings of Rs. 80 *per mensem* then required to meet the expense of the native court. On the otherhand, both the senior members of the *Panchayat Court* were too old and infirm and their servi- ces, by reason of being old-servants of the Raja and acquainted with the various customs and usages of Cachar under native rule, was no longer necessary to the British Government. They were officers of the Heramba Government and, upon the country being taken under the British rule, were retained by the Government to make use of their local know- ledge. The gradual introduction of the regulations into the province and the increased acquaintance of the officials with the local language, customs and usages had lessened their utility and they were too old for their duties, while there was no other situation in which they could be employed. Upon the administration of the country being assumed by the British Government, the employees of the Raja except these two were pensioned off, and as these two officers were now to be thrown out of employment, not from any fault of their own, W.M. MacCulloch, the Officiating Superintendent, who took over temporarily from Lyons on 10 February 1842,[58] in a subsequent letter on 22 August 1842, having asked by the Government to give his comment, believed that they had a fair claim to pen- sions. The Officiating Superintendent further observed that as the average salary during the previous five years of the senior member had been Rs. 44 and of the junior Rs. 28 *per mensem* and the general conduct of both appeared to have been satis- factory, if one-third of their respective salaries were granted to them as pensions, a pecuniary savings of about fifty rupees per month would still result.[59] But Lyons had not considered the two Judges entitled to pension, as the officers were too old to perform the duties required of them in efficient manner and, in fact, they had been in the Government employment for few years only. Moreover, during this period they held rent-free lands which were granted to them by the late Raja of Cachar.[60]

Meanwhile, the cases in the *Panchayat Court* increased alarmingly, the *Mahajans* having instituted 96 more suits on *Tamasuks* and *Dastavezs* in 1842 than in the previous year. These were mostly out of the timber trade, which was the chief export from Cachar, and the leading merchants resided in the towns or large *bazars* within the jurisdiction of the *Panchayat Court* which were situated not more than 200 yards from the *Kutchery* where the cases were disposed of in a more summary manner than in the Munsiff's Court. The suits tried in the latter had been almost exclusively land disputes and disposed of in strict accordance with the Regulations and, therefore, required more time and attention than the cases in the *Panchayat Court*. Despite, the cases pending in this court were of a very recent date. The number of regular suits and appeals instituted before the Superintendent during year 1842 numbered 210 against 133 in 1841, while in the *Panchayat Court* reached 418 against 308 in the previous year, showing a total increase of 187 suits.[61] In view of this, the Registrar of the Presidency Court, *Sadar Nizamat Adalat*, asked for some suggestions from the Superintendent of Cachar for simplifying the proceedings of the Magistrates and of police. In his long report[62] on 18 April 1845, the Superintendent observed that the delay in the proceedings were caused by the defendents' witnesses who invariably schooled to ensure the accused the best chance to escape. The proceedings would then take a long time and the party would obtain acquital through the Court *Peadahs* and *Thana Barkandazes* "whose chief source of gain was to give false returns showing the absence of persons summoned to attend the Court." The Superintendent, therefore, opined that no plan could be devised to ensure the attendance of all parties at once in the absence of a Record of Cases to refer. The existing system of recording cases in Bengalee could not be abolished altogether, but it would admit of curtailment. Thus, written petitions and answers with the names of witnesses might be given in and no supplementary petitions allowed. The evidence of witnesses might be briefly taken down by the *Mohurirs* in the manner of Press reporters.

The Superintendent further observed that if some officers, to be appointed by the court, retained a sufficient time to admit of their gaining a knowledge of the most litigious and quarrelsome characters within their jurisdiction and possessed such an acquaintance with the vernacular as would enable them to put their own searching questions and note down the answers of the parties without the aid of a third person and punished the delinquents when a case was satisfactorily proved to be unfounded and vexatious and no *Vakeels* or *Mukhtars* were allowed to interrupt the business of the courts with their pertinacity and loquacity and strict jail discipline was maintained, a decrease in the number of suits would soon be evident from the periodical statements. As the *Vakeels* and *Mukhtars* were allowed, instead of the Principal, to have the entire management in the cases, the interruption and delay caused by them was excessive and their clients were mere objects of plunder. These people fearfully exaggerated facts, prepared a long list of witnesses all of whom clubbed to make a slight variation in their statements so as to cause a doubt in the Magistrate's mind about the decision. The *Vakeels* of both plaintiff and defendent endeavoured to balance evidence so nicely that there could be always an opening for appeal without its appearing vexatious and thus contrived to get their fees or presents over again. There was always an understanding between the *Vakeels*, when those of the original Court and the appellate Court were not the same. This was really the chief reason behind numerous appeals. A vast proportion of the cases tried in the court were unfounded ; they were out of an old grudge or enmity existing between *Zamindars* who put their cases in the hands of *Vakeels* and whose sole aim was the gratification of gaining a case at the expense of their antagonist, for the loss of a case amongst natives of respectability was considered to reflect highest disgrace on the losers. So to attain their object they gave money without compunction to the *Amlah* who could not withstand the temptation and always received bribes and presents through the *Vakeels* of the litigants, who again not only received a portion of the money but rendered this detection next to impossible. With such a powerful motive, they would of course continue by every means in their power to flare up both ordinary cases and appeals until some kind of reform was introduced. Lyons, therefore, believed that a definite way of reducing the frightful number of appeals was to limit the functions of *Vakeels* in criminal prosecutions to writing petitions and giving advise to those who chose to consult them outside the Court. But a more effectual plan, according to the Superintendent, would be to confine the liberty of appeal to questions of law and justice would certainly not suffer by such wholesome reform.[63]

Be that as it may, in the following years the judiciary in Cachar underwent several changes. The *Panchayat Court* was replaced by Second Munsiff's Court. Krishnanath Dutta, the Junior Judge of the former native court, was appointed as Second Munsiff in 1848, while with the retirement of the first Munsiff in 1859, Dutta was promoted as the First Munsiff, now called *Sadar Munsiff* and one Baidyanath Deb was appointed as Second Munsiff. The interruptions of the *Vakeels* were reduced with the gradual joining of the Pleaders with required know-ledge and specialisation in law as in other Courts of Bengal. Most of the Bengal Regulations were also gradually enforced in the district. In January 1851, the Superintendent of Cachar was sworn in as the Justice of Peace,[64] and in 1852 the office of the Marriage Registrar was created and the Superintendent was authorised to exercise the functions in his capacity of Magistrate and on the same terms and salary attached to the office. The changes undoubtedly increased the efficiency of the judiciary and speedy justice was ensured to the people. On 1 January 1852, there was not a single case pending in the Court of the Superintendent ; while 25 suits were in file of the Sadar Munsiff and 13 before Second Munsiff, but all of very recent dates.[65]

In 1853, a Munsiff's Court was established at Sealtekh to deal with numerous cases originating from trade through this most important transit station of Cachar.   During the time of Mill's visit in 1854, Babu Baidyanath Deb was the Munsiff at Sealtekh while Babu Ram Govinda Deb was the Sadar Munsiff.[66] But, although G. Verner, who took over as Superin-tendent from Lyons on 3 May 1849,[67] repeating the arguments of his predecessor, advocated the introduction of Stamp Laws in Cachar at lower rate than in the regulation Provinces,[68] the Government did not enforce the law till 1860.

In the matter of Police administration too, every endeavour was made to follow the system that would be at par with the native system. Under the former Government there was no regular police in the country. A certain number of able bodied people used to serve the country as *Barkandazes* to prevent crime, apprehend the recalcitrants and serve the royal summons. They did not receive any cash-payment, but were allowed rent-free land, according to rank, for which they would be obliged to serve as police for three months during the year. There were four such batches to act in rotation for different calendar quarters.[69] With British annexation, the country was divided into three *thanas* viz., Silchar, Hailakandi and Katigorah—each under a *Daroga* at a monthly salary of rupees seven. Each *thana* had 16 *Barkandazes* attached to it and divided into parties of four members each who took the duties by rotation for three consecutive months. In addition, there were four *Jammadars* to captain the *Barkandazes*, one for each quarter of the year. The *Jammadars* and *Barkandazes* were remunerated, as previously, through some rent-free lands ; the former 3 and the latter $2\frac{1}{2}$ *kulbahs*.[70] Captain Fisher considered the salary of the *Daroga* to be too poor and, therefore, authorised a monthly levy on the *Mirasdars* under jurisdictions of the respective *thanas* in terms of oil and stationery for official use.[71]

Numerous instances of crime in Cachar at the time of the British occupation and the transfer of about three hundred convicts from other districts led to the establishment of a Jail *Daroga* at Silchar. The *Barkandazes*, in-charge of the Jail, received Rs. 4 *per mensem*. While the police-men were unhappy with their poor salary, the taxes levied were considered by the *Mirasdars* to be most unwanted hardships. The collection was attended with constant quarrels and litigations and the short sighted obstinacy of the people themselves, in not paying promptly, was considerably augmented subsequently by the unavoidable employment of the *Peadahs* who were, on the other hand, suspected of not confining their exactions to the original demand. In addition, the *Mirasdars* were obliged to pay the expense of repair and renovations of the *thana* houses, which was also attended with the same train of evils. In Hailakandi, during the rains and minor inundations, the *Mirasdars* were required to furnish boats for transhipping the *thana* records and were allowed for this service two *kulbahs* of *Buksha* lands.

However, in 1837 on the proposal of Major Burns the salary of the *Daroga* was enhanced to Rs. 15 *per mensem* with an allowance of Rs. 2 for oil and stationery. Three regular *Jammadars* were appointed at Rs. 5 each and 18 regular *Barkandazes* at Rs. 2½ each *per mensem*, while a group of 6 *Barkandazes* headed by a *Jammadar* was attached to each *thana*. The lands so long enjoyed by the *Barkandazes* were ordered to be assessed and the police establishment, stated above, was entertained at no extra expense to the Government, for it was calculated that the rent of the resumed lands would pay for the establishment. The *Darogas* were now at par with their counterpart in other districts of Bengal.[72] In 1842, the number of *Barkandazes* attached to each *thana* was raised to seven and their salary was increased to Rs. 4 *per mensem*. Although the *Darogas* were under the physical control of the Superintendent of Cachar, the Superintendent of Police at Sylhet exercised his jurisdiction over the police affairs in Cachar. However, since 1850, an Assistant Superintendent of Police was posted at Silchar in direct command of the Cachar Police.[73]

The police department, in view of its skeleton structure, was not sufficient to watch over the extensive rural areas where the system of communication was extremely backward. During the Heramba Regime, an establishment of *paiks*, called *Dakuahs*, was maintained by the Raja in the villages. These *Dakuahs* were remunerated, like most other officials, by assignment of lands which were estimated to bring in about Rs. 5 *per annum* per incumbent. With the beginning of the British administration, these grants were resumed and a *Chaukidar* was appointed in every village generally covering 64 houses, each of which contributed one *pie*, monthly, for his support. His duty was to report all heinous offences to the Officer-in-Charge of the Police Station and to arrest persons committing such crimes in his presence, to collect vital statistics, to observe the movements of bad characters and to inform his official superiors of anything likely to affect the peace and tranquility of the area. He was, of course, not required to patrol at night since the fear of wild elephants kept the people at home after dusk. In course of time, the pay of the *Chaukidar* was felt to be very inadequate for their maintenance and, in consequence, they became gradually indifferent to their duties. To save the situation, Regulation I of 1833 was extended to Cachar in fifties of the last century, but this was not fully suited to the local circumstances. As a result, the *Chaukidars* were authorised to make their own arrangement with the villagers for their remuneration which they never received punctually or fully. Anyway, the lot of these poor officials was, to some extent, improved by the introduction of the *Chaukidari* tax.[74]

Apart from the general policing of the Province, the defence of the Cachar frontier from the predatory tribes in the neighbouring hills posed to be a formidable problem to the British authorities ever since the military occupation of the Barak Valley. The hostilities of the North Cacharis including marauding in roads in the plains under the instigation of the rebel chiefs endured for a long time. Encouraged by Gambhir Singh, the Nagas carried their onslaughts in South Cachar to an alarming height. But most dreadable were the raids of the Lushais and the Kukis who indulged in frequent incursions in the plain to obtain their essential commodities from the villagers in the Southern frontier. The fear of the Burmese invasion had also never ceased to occupy the authorities at Fort William who were highly concerned about this vulnerable frontier to avoid the repetition of the imperialistic encounter.

All these demanded a strong military detachment to watch over the extreme North-East Frontier of the country. In fact, since the Burmese War, a Military Battalion belonging to Bengal Army continued to be stationed at Silchar with a large number of out-posts.[75] On the otherhand, the Government of Bengal, in 1830, decided to raise a semi-military body, clothed like the civil police and armed with the old Brown Bess, to carry out arduous duties often involving fights and mortal danger in the most unhealthy jungles, and recruited from the Bengal Civil Police. The first unit of this force was organised by Lieutenant Gregory, Principal Assistant at Nowgong and called Cachar Levy, which in course of time became the nucleus of modern Assam Rifles. The unit had a strength of 750 men of all ranks, *viz.*, Inspectors, Head Constables and Constables.[76] Three years later a similar body, of course of lesser strength, was raised at Jorhat, mostly from the Shans settled in that area, and was known as Jorhat Militia. After a few years, however, this Militia became amalgamated with the Cachar Levy. The duty of this Levy was to guard the then eastern frontier, from Brahmaputra Valley to Cachar, supported by strong detachment of troops at Silchar and Nowgong. Along the stretch which ran for several miles through the Nambar forest at the foot of the Naga Hills and through North Cachar Hills to the plains of Surma Valley east of Silchar, the Cachar Levy held posts at Barpathar, Dimapur, Mohong-Dijoa, Mahur, Maibong, Hosang Hajoo, Guilon, Gumaigajoo, Asalu, Hangrun, Baladhan and Jirighat. All the posts were in the heart of dense forests and the paths were kept clear for constant patrolling. Dimapur, Mahur, Maibong and Asalu were the most important posts, being on the route used by the predatory Nagas for both trade and raid. The other portions of the north and north-eastern borders were guarded by the troops and armed civil police of Bengal.[77]

Meanwhile, the regular troops were gradually removed to the nearest posts of Bengal, but the Khamti-Singpho rising of 1839, compelled the Government to augment the defence machinery in Upper Assam from Dhansiri to Sadiya. For the defence of the extensive frontier, the troops were brought down, in 1840, to four regiments, *viz.*, the 1st Assam Light Infantry at Gauhati, 2nd Assam Light Infantry at Sadiya, Sylhet Light Infantry at Sylhet and Bengal Infantry Battalion at Silchar.[78] Inspite of all these arrangements, the tribal inroads along the whole north-eastern borders continued to be a living menace. The Nagas, in particular, made challenging tirades in Cachar and Nowgong. Their attack on the post at Hosang Hajoo, in 1844, was extremely mortal, in which several members of the Cachar Levy lost their lives. Captain Eld, the Principal Assistant at Nowgong, immediately deputed Lieutenant Woods, the Sub-Assistant at Nowgong, to the Border with 50 men of the Assam Light Infantry and 70 of the Cachar Levy. After several encounters, Woods chased the enemies upto Asalu, 15 miles east of Haflong, and then burnt the offending villages. This was followed by the hostilities of several Naga clans under the instigation of Tularam involving desultory fighting in different parts of North and South Cachar. Captain J. Butler, the next Principal Assistant at Nowgong, took a serious view of the situation. He realised that the administration of North Cachar from Nowgong was too difficult a task. Under his strong recommendations, a small civil staff was located, in 1853, at Asalu under a Sub-Assistant together with a strong detachment of the Cachar Levy. Attempts were made to connect Asalu with the neighbouring Civil stations through road, and this was in fact, the beginning of civil administration in North Cachar that became a *fait accompli* in 1854.[79]

In the meantime, the Kukis and the Lushais increased their disturbances on the other frontier of Cachar. In 1844, thirty Kukis, headed by a Chief, from the villages of Thadoi and Kyong, subject to the Manipur state and about five days' journey in the hills, resorted to onslaught. They murdered eight Kuki women of a village south of Banraj *Pargana* in Cachar, where a few Kuki families had recently settled, and carried off their heads.[80] One of the marauders was apprehended, who confessed that he accompanied others by the desire of their Raja for the expressed purpose of carrying off skulls, and though he denied any hand in the actual crime, according to Lyons, he was an assessory before and after the incident. When the village was attacked by the British troops, the inhabitants, save one, absconded. Thus, there appeared no likelihood of obtaining further evidence.[81] The Political Agent of Manipur was requested by the Commissioner of Dacca to take measures to prevent the recurrence of these violent inroads[82] and a police out-post was introduced at Banraj.[83] But, before long, the situation in Hailakandi Valley became extremely disquieting. The sufferings of the people within Cachar borders from the Lushai raiders knew no bounds. These frequent depredations compelled the Government to place detachments of the Sylhet Light Infantry at two strategic points in Hailakandi area for protective purposes.[84] Failing to ensure good conduct of the tribesmen, the first expedition across the Cachar-Lushai borders, in a small scale, was despatched under Captain Blackwood with a section of the Sylhet Light Infantry and the armed civil police in December 1844. Proceeding through Kailasahar, on the north-east border of Tripura, Blackwood managed to surround one of the offending villages and captured its Chief, Lalchokla. Despite this, the Kukis in south and Lushais in south-eastern borders of Cachar carried on repeated incursions. Many people lost their lives and their skulls were carried away for superstitious purposes.[85] The people in the border areas were compelled to abandon their villages, and during the period from 1845 to 1847 a large number of villages were deserted. But in 1847, the situation reached at an alarming end when in addition to the Khasi incursions in Sylhet, the tribes from the Tipperah hills also commenced a series of violent raids in Cachar. To make matters worse, the Lushais and the Kukis multiplied their aggressions and, before long, they were joined by the Nagas.[86]

Evidently, the situation in the Surma Valley posed a serious threat to the security of the British Frontier. The detachment of the Sylhet Light Infantry and Civil police were pushed along the borders. A serious conflict took place with a large number of tribesmen in the Sylhet-Tripura border in which, although the invaders were driven back, Major Lister, Officer-Commanding, Sylhet Light Infantry, was wounded. However, the operations in all the sectors were successful and the situation gradually moved towards normalcy.[87] But, in 1849, the Lushais again attacked a Kuki village, 10 miles south of Silchar, with greater injuries ; 29 persons were killed and 42 carried off captive. In the following year, Lister conducted a strong punitive expedition, consisting of the S.L.I. and 150 armed civil police. By 4 January 1850, Lister surprised and destroyed a large and troublesome village of Mora with 800 houses and granaries and relieved the captive British subjects. The force suffered a few casualties and Lister was again seriously injured. The return journey was considerably harrassed by the Lushais, obliging Lister at one point to destroy a large quantity of stores which could not be carried away.[88]

Anyway, it was now realised that the Civil police or S.L.I., mostly consisted of the Bengalees or other plainsmen were unfit for encounters with the tribesmen. It may be noted that, the local officers, in thirties, were astonished at the martial bravery of the Bengalees of Cachar. Lieutenant Fisher spoke well of the bravery of Bengalees of this frontier in his repeated despatches to the Government of Bengal. Immediately after his appointment in-charge of Cachar affairs, he had handsome offer from the people in Badarpur to assist the Government in apprehending the murderers of Govindachandra with 200 Musketeers and 200 *Paiks*. Following the incidence of dacoities, Regulations were introduced prohibiting use of arms by private individuals. Thus, an inoffensive and bold peasantry were disarmed for Government's fancies and fears. The bad effects of this system were seen during the Gurkha War, and, ultimately, the *Zamindars* were encouraged to arm their retainers.[89] Major Lister, Officer-Commanding, Sylhet Light Infantry, also corroborated this evidence to the bravery of Bengalees in his Corps.[90] Captain Jenkins, who extensively toured Cachar in 1831, highly appreciated the war-like genius of the Bengalees in the local Corps and Militia.[91] Commenting on his Journal of Cachar, G. Suinton, Chief Secretary to the Government of Bengal, wrote : "We have been accustomed to consider the people of Cachar a cowardly race of people, but Captain Jenkins, it will be observed, thinks better of them."[92]

True to the expectation of the officials, the local people of Cachar had rendered commendable services to the Government through various local Levies, Infantries and Corps. But the Lushai expeditions reflected that the climate of the hills were unsuited to the plainsmen. Along the frontier there were several Kuki Villages, called *Punji*, and the recent attacks were mostly on these villages. The Kukis were racially identical with the Lushais, and, to some extent, with the Nagas. They were, naturally, considered to be more suited to prevent the Lushai raiders. Further, the *Punjis* being on the foot-hills the upland climate was not supposed to be difficult for them to stand. Therefore, in 1850, a Kuki Levy, of 200 strength, was raised from the local Kukis of Cachar, at the suggestion of Major Lister, to assist the armed Civil Police Battalion in controlling and protecting the borders. Several check-posts, manned by these Levymen, were established along the Cachar frontiers, and the Nagas and Lushais were forbidden from trading at the *ghats* of Cachar.[93]

The new system, particularly the Economic blockade, worked well, and in 1852 the number of Levymen was increased through fresh recruitment to strengthen the defence structure and also to provide employment to the Kukis, otherwise economically helpless, living within the British territory.[94] Sealed to the hills, the predatory tribesmen were deprived of all sources of supply of the most essential commodities, and thus were forced to make rapture for peace. Sukhpilal, a prominent Lushai Chief, sent an embassy to G. Verner, Superintendent of Cachar, for permission to visit and establish friendly relations with the British officials at Silchar. The interview was granted, and this affected peaceful situation in the frontiers for some years.[95]

The period from 1832 to 1854, thus, marked the gradual evolution of the British Regime in Cachar. In addition to the Revenue, Judicial, Police and Defence measures, stated above, attempts were made to bring all the fallow lands under the Government and lease them out. The lease-holders were direct tenants of the Government and, in course of time, they also came to be known as *Mirasdars* or *Zamindars.* Abundance of land and other resources of the Province, together with the increase of employment facilities under the new regime, attracted new comers from the adjacent districts of Bengal, who permanently settled themselves down in Cachar. A Settlement Officer, also known as Deputy Collector, was appointed in 1850 to deal with rehabilitation of the immigrants. The *khel* System was gradually abandoned and all lands brought under assessment. Attention was given to improve the lines of communication and to provide educational facilities to the native children. Post Offices were established and a Post Master was posted at Silchar with necessary establishment. Medical Centres were opened, and a Civil Surgeon was placed in-charge of the Silchar Civil Hospital, while an Assistant Surgeon was in-charge of the Cachar Jail Hospital at Silchar. Endeavours were set on foot to explore the natural resources of the new province. The details of all these may be found in the appropriate pages.

APPENDIX 3

Memorandum on the Extent and Revenue of Cachar (*June 1830*)

The only measurement ever made in this country on which to ground any estimates of its extent were partly effected in 1824, but being intended only for Geographical and Military purposes were not made with that degree of exactness which is usual in Revenue surveys, neither were they so numerous as for Revenue purposes it could be wished they were. However, as the triangulation which was effected proceeded from the extremities of a well measured traverse line (for a Base) and was verified whenever opportunities offered, it is probable that as far as defends on the measurements no material erroute (sic) has been involved though the want boundary lines leaves the estimate necessarily subject to a certain degree of vagueness.

This inconvenience may by obviated partly by a reference to the map on which it will be easy to trace the outline of those tracts the superficial contents of which has been computed.

1.   The tracts bounded on the East by the Sonaie N. and the forest or the south by a line drawn from the Sonaie to the Delaserree N. on the West by the Delaserree N. and the small Nullas running between Panchgaon and Bickrampoor and on the North by the mountains contains 645.9 British Square Miles.

2.   West of the above the tract bounded on the South by the Soorma R. on the East by the Nullas running between Panchgaon and Bikrampoor on the North by the Mountains, and on the West by the Keroowah Nullah contains 212 Do. Total B. Sq. Miles 858.3.

This computation it will be observed does not include either Dhurmpoor, the mountains lying between it and Cachar or the great forest to the Eastward towards the Naga Mountains (the extent of the Raja's claims or possessions in those directions not being well ascertained) but is limited strictly to the plain and the low hillocks by which it is diversified.

By far the greater part of the two tracts before mentioned is waste land covered with grass jungle but capable of culture, however, it is probable that about one-eighth of the whole may be unfit for the purposes of the agriculturist, after making which deduction there will remain 751 square miles, equal to 1,20160 Koolbahs (nearly 4,80,640 acres) of land which assessed at the average rate sanctioned for new settled lands in Sylhet $2\frac{1}{2}$ per Koolbah would yield a revenue of Sa. Rupees (3,00,400) three lackhs four hundred per annum.

Under its present management however there is not any prospect whatever of bringing even a material portion of the country under cultivation for the measures pursued are calculated to retard the improvement of the country rather than to forward it. The rate of assessment from five to six Rupees per Koolbah is not high in comparison with that taken by Zemindars in Sylhet but in addition to it the Ryuts have to meet other vexatious demands upon their gains, as fruits and cattle for sacrifices whenever called for by the Rajah, customs upon the transport of grain, fees upon titled etc. etc., which last are forced upon all supposed capable of paying for them.

Cachar is said to have yielded a Revenue of about one Lackh (S. Rs. 1,00,000) per annum to Rajah Kissen Chundra but after his death it fell off and the second invasion of the Burmese in 1824 completed the ruin of the country all the land east of Bikrampoor and Panchgaon was thrown out of cultivation and numbers of inhabitants were destroyed or carried into captivity. Since the peace a few Purgunnahs have been reoccupied but still most of the villages east of Filyn are nearly empty.

The want of people is obviously the difficulty to be overcome in improving the Revenue here, and with this view ample encouragement should be given to settlers possessed of capital from other districts. Few however are to be found in the neighbourhood as the people of Sylhet (the only contiguous district) evince no disposition to emigrate and the hill tribes are too poor and savage for the purpose in view. Perhaps proclamations distributed in the more populous districts as Burdwan etc. holding out the prospect of adequate remuneration and security would induce native capitalist to try their fortunes in a country which as it is eminently fertile would not fail in a few years to realise their most sanguine expectations.

(Sd.) T. Fisher

CHAPTER V

Transition

The boundaries of Cachar underwent radical changes during the early years of British Rule. The first casualty upon the integrity of the 'state' was the annexation of the *Pargana of Sirispur*, in 1813, to Sylhet by the Collector of the latter. Throughout his life, the unfortunate Raja had made several futile appeals to the authorities at Sylhet and Calcutta for the restoration of the *Pargana*. During his enforced exile in Sylhet, at a time when the Raja had lost all hopes of his reinstatement to the throne of Cachar, Govindachandra had even offered to be recognised as the *Zamindar* of Sirispur under the East India Company.[1] However, soon after Cachar was formally annexed to the British Dominion, Thomas Fisher, Superintendent of Cachar, held an enquiry into the matter and was thoroughly convinced that Sirispur was really a *pargana* of the former Heramba State. Accordingly, the Superintendent recommended, in 1833, that Sirispur should be restored to Cachar.[2] J.C. Robertson, Agent to the Governor-General, then held a discussion with the Collector of Sylhet on the subject, but could not find any reasonable objection to be raised against Fisher's recommendation.[3] Ultimately, the Governor-General in Council, on 16 May 1833, resolved that 'the *Pargana* of Sirispur be retransferred to Cachar',[4] which was actually done shortly after.[5] Thus in 1839, when the prosecutrix in an abduction case lodged her complaint at the *Thana* at Latoo, in Sylhet District, the *Thanadar* forwarded the proceedings to the Superintendent of Cachar as the place of occurrence was in the

Sirispur *Pargana*, although the perpetrators resided in the district of Sylhet, and the case was tried at the Superintendent's Court at Silchar.[6] About the Cachar-Sylhet Boundary, R. Stewart, Superintendent of Cachar, reported on 7 September, 1858, that the boundary between these two districts was not accurately laid down but was 'indefinitely known as the watershed of the range of the hills which separated the *Pargana* of Chapghat in Sylhet from that of Serespur in Cachar—all the eastern slopes being Cachar and the western Sylhet.'[7]

On the other hand, in November 1832, Central Cachar, consisting of a vast chunk of territory extending from Jamunamukh to Dharampur including Hojai-Davaka areas, was finally separated from Cachar and attached to Assam.[8] This fertile Kapili-Jamuna Valley, described by Captain Jenkins as the most flourishing spot in the frontier,[9] was notable for the luxurious growth of paddy and jute. Mahung-Dijua, in the valley-end, was a strategic corner as well as a commercial centre. Situated in Latitude 25.59″ and Longitude 23.30″ and on the bank of Jamuna, Mahung was the meeting point of Cachar, Assam, Manipur and 'Naga Country'. Besides the traditional lines of communication with Cachar, Manipur and Naga Hills, it had water route with Gauhati and Jorhat and a regiment of Assam or Sylhet Light Infantry could well check the predatory tribes from this advantageous base. The cultivation of rice, cotton, poppy, and mustard was considerable in the area, while the plantation of silk-worms was also extensive. The capability of the place for agriculture, commerce and traffic was highly admired by Jenkins, Pemberton and Gordon. While in a survey mission in March 1832, these officers noticed a big market in the area with about 500 huts.[10] The separation of such a potent tract was indeed a great loss to the economic life of Cachar. Traditionally, the river Kapili occupied a prominent position in the Cachar culture. There is a legend that in a remote period of their civilisation the river had confluenced with Barak at Sidheswar, Badarpur, which is associated with the name of *Kapil Muni*, the celebrated author of *Sankhya* Philosophy. The people had, therefore, inherited a long tradition of performing certain customary rites in the Holy water of Kapili. The separation of Dharampur (Dharmpur) thus deprived the Cacharis of their pilgrim-spot and was a severe injury to the religious sentiment of the people. History repeated one of its most cruel ironies in January 1839, when the *ex-Rani* of Cachar had to apply to J.G. Burns, the Superintendent of Cachar, for permission to visit and bathe in the *Kapili-Ganga* in Dharampur.[11] The Superintendent, on his turn had to request F. Jenkins, Commissioner of Assam, to allow the *Rani* to proceed to Dharampur, but the Commissioner turned down the request on political ground.[12]

Similarly, on 5 November 1832, Jiri Frontier was ceded to Manipur.[13] This extensive tract beyond the river Jiri, sixty miles in length and eight miles in breadth, had a population of 10,000 souls and formerly yielded an annual revenue of Rs. 1,000 to Cachar. The Naga and Kuki inhabitants of the area had rendered magnificent service to the Government during Burmese intrusion, and the merchants in Cachar had a long trading tradition with them. From time immemorable, the tribesmen used to barter timber, grass, cane, ivory, wax and other jungle products at the hill *ghats* for their daily necessaries like rice, salt, oil and cloth. The transfer of such a valuable territory thus proved a heavy drain upon the Cachar treasury and legalised the monopoly of the border trade earlier usurped by Gambhir Singh who had now an easy recourse to systematic exploitation of the innocent dwellers. No wonder, therefore, the tribesmen too embarked upon a series of retaliatory inroads and kept the vulnerable region in a state of continued alarm.[14]

A splendid territorial acquisition, however temporarily, eventually accrued from the neighbouring kingdom of Jayantia. This state of great ancient heritage had escaped the imperial design of the Mughals, but Raja Ram Singh, as has already been mentioned, placed himself under the British protection on the eve of the First Anglo-Burmese War. The things having passed very fast in the eastern frontier, the authorities at Fort William could hardly justify for long this status of Jayantia when the surrounding territories were all under the direct administration of the British Government. Raja Rajendra Singh, who succeeded Ram Singh in 1832, also ran into disputes with the British officers over the establishment of an outpost on the Nowgong border resulting in frequent conflicts in the frontier. To make matters worse, Raja of Goba, a vassal of Jayantia, immolated three British subjects, captured by him on the ground of tresspass, at the Shrine of *Kali*.[15] On the refusal of Rajendra Singh to surrender the perpetrators of the crime, it was decided by the authorities at Fort William to resume the more valuable part of his territory in the plains as a penalty. Ultimately, in March 1835, the Jayantia kingdom was annexed to the British Dominion by a proclamation issued by the British authorities; the Jayantia *Parganas* on the southern plains were attached to Sylhet, and Goba to Nowgong.[16] During the survey and demarcation of the boundary between Sylhet and Cachar, a small portion of the Jayantia plains was merged with Cachar on the ground of proximity and geographical continuity. This tract consisted of 30,000 *kulbahs* of cultivated land, 1,300 *kulbahs* of *Jheel* and *Nalla*, and 46,700 *kulbahs* of waste and jungle lands, and was assessed under the revenue rules of Cachar.[17] However, on 21 March, 1837, this tract was transferred to Sylhet.[18]

Nevertheless, this could hardly make good the territorial losses suffered by Cachar, being thoroughly truncated at the will of the British Rulers. Anyway, the most significant partition of Cachar was between the North and South. The North Cachar Hills got their identity as an administrative unit in 1829 when the Raja of Cachar was persuaded by David Scott to recognise Tularam as the Chief of the hills in the north. With the passing of the rest of Govindachandra's territory under the British, in 1830, the separation between the two wings became a *fait accompli*. As the Partition of Bengal in 1905, (although withdrawn in 1911), had moulded the political situation in Bengal in favour of a final whistle in 1947, the separation of the northern region from the mainland of Heramba acted as the pretext for the creation of two different districts predominated by the Dimachas and the Bengalees, hitherto all known as 'Cacharis'. The political opening, once given, is difficult to cover up and history has couple of instances to justify the plea. As a matter of fact, after the assassination of Govindachandra, Tularam offered his candidature to the vacant throne of Cachar but failed to establish his claim. Although the rule of this weak chieftain would have done no material help to the state, particularly in face of the grabbing attitude of Gambhir Singh, the last hope for the unification of Cachar finally belied. What was worse, even the North Cacharis were not allowed to live together. In 1834, the *Senapati* had to enter into an agreement with the British Government foregoing all claims to the western part of his territory bounded by the rivers Dayang, Mahur,. Kapili and Jatinga, and retaining the tract in the east bounded on the south by the Mahur river and Naga Hills, on the west by Dayang, on the east by Dhansiri and on the north by Jamuna and Dayang rivers. For this, he was required to pay an annual tribute of four elephant tusks, and received in return a pension of Rs. 50 per month.[19] The tract so resumed, was annexed to the *Pargana* of Dharampur and placed under the Principal Assistant at Nowgong.

The increased Naga disturbances, however, made it difficult for the P.A. to effectively supervise the frontier from the headquarters at Nowgong. Consequently, in 1853, North Cachar was constituted into a subdivision with Asalu as the headquarters. Lieutenant H.S. Bivar was appointed as the first Sub-Assistant. In 1854, the rest of Tularam's territory was also added to this unit. Since then, administration of North Cachar was vested, in all departments, in a Junior Assistant Commissioner, as defined in the Assam Code, under the control of the Commissioner of Assam, while all civil and criminal appeals would go to the Deputy Commissioner* of Assam.[20]

The North Cachar, as stated above, was bounded on the north by the Jamuna river, Mikir and Rengma Naga Hills, on the south by Barail Hills and Cachar District, on the east by 'Kachha' and Angami Naga Hills, on the west by the Kapili and Ompung rivers and Jaintia Hills. The only practicable communication with the tract from Assam side was through the river Dhansiri which was navigable as far as Dharampur, while almost from all sides the hills and dense jungles had cut off the unit from the outer world. The villages, in most cases, were mere clearances in the jungles, scattered and isolated. There was no road in the true sense of the term, and elephant traps were used as paths. The labour was scarce and dear to the extreme. The inhabitants raised little beyond what was sufficient for their own sustenance. The climate, except in the hills towards the south, was difficult for any

---

*In 1861, the Deputy Commissioner was recognized as the Judicial Commissioner with almost all the functions of a Civil and Sessions Judge of Bengal.

stranger. No wonder, therefore, the region was exposed to the predatory Naga raids.[21]

The foremost task before the Junior Assistant was to reckon with these hostile Naga clans for which the North Cachar Unit was actually created. The police forces stationed at Asalu failed to prevent the atrocities. Several punitive expeditions led against the rebels were foiled by difficult communication and unfavourable climate. The British military organisation, the quality of the troops, the conditions of their recruitment, their drill, their discipline proved inappropriate to the exigencies of hill-warfare. Consequently, the defence of the frontier was suggested, by the local officers, to be entrusted to a local corps under the control of the Chief Civil Authority.[22] On the otherhand, the administration having failed to protect the life and property of the inhabitants, the Cacharis in the disturbed areas gradually deserted their villages. Lieutenant Bivar, the Junior Assistant, North Cachar, submitted a plan to the Government of Bengal envisaging the establishment of a Kuki colony in the deserted areas to the east of the Lunting river, in a direction of about thirty miles north-east of Asalu, with a view to holding the Naga intruders in check. The plan was strongly supported by Colonel Jenkins, Commissioner of Assam, and was in turn approved of by the Lieutenant Governor of Bengal.[23]

Accordingly, the Kuki immigration was encouraged, and Bivar conducted the settlement of the Kukis. The Kukis had left their original home in Lushai hills being hard-hit by the frequent famines there, and settled themselves in Manipur, some in Cachar, while bulk of them moved to the North Cachar Hills. The immigrants showed a good deal of enthusiasm to develop their new home, and shortly many Kuki colonies emerged in the district, the tract adjoining the Angami Hills being thoroughly colonised by them. These clan-colonies had their chiefs, called *Rajas*, through whom the jurisdiction of the Government extended to the people. The lands were assigned revenue-free for twenty-five years and soil proved fertile for agriculture. The facilities offered by the Government attracted more chiefs from the adjacent districts to settle in North Cachar, while others sent their emissaries to collect information about the 'country'.[24] Bivar expected, therefore, that the size of the colonists will gradually increase and thereby would contribute to the peace and prosperity of the district. The Kukis were provided with fire-arms for self-defence and to form themselves into a buffer between the North Cacharis and the Angamis.[25]

Unfortunately, however, the plan was not attended with any great measure of success. The villages of the Kukis were, no doubt, respected by the Nagas, but the other tribes were, as before, exposed to depredations. The total population of North Cachar that was 24,369 in 1856 rose to 29,428 in 1857, showing an increase of 5,059 in one year. Ultimately, the population in Kuki colonies reached about 16,000 souls, but only a few years after, it became restless and anxious to migrate elsewhere. The Kukis were wretched agriculturists, and used to shifting cultivation which exhaust all land in the vicinity of their settlement and then make the people move off to escape starvation.[26]

The local authorities now advocated that the British Government should break the isolation of the Nagas and exercise their sovereign power by giving the people the benefit of settled administration.[27] Sir Cecil Beadon, Lieutenant-Governor of Bengal, agreed to place a British officer among the Nagas who would adjust their internal disputes, protect the well-disposed members of the tribes from the consequences of the crimes of others, introduce peace and order in their villages, and bring them into free and friendly communication with the inhabitants of the plains.[28] Accordingly, in 1867, the Naga areas of North Cachar, lying on the bank of the Dhansiri, together with the Angami Naga Hills and territories on the both banks of Dayang were formed into a separate district with headquarters at Semaguting. Lieutenant Gregory, Junior Assistant Commissioner of North Cachar, was appointed as the first Deputy Commissioner under the direct control of the Commissioner of Assam. The civil establishment at Asalu was shifted to Semaguting. On the other hand, the North Cachar Unit was abolished and its territories apportioned among the neighbouring districts of Cachar, Khasi-Jaintia and Nowgong. The North Cachar Hills were thus again fractioned-out into alien units.[29] However, a significant part of the subdivision including Asalu was transferred to Cachar.[30]

As required by the Government of Bengal, Edgar, Deputy Commissioner of Cachar, visited Asalu, in early 1868, and

submitted a report[31] which envisaged a scheme for the administration and development of North Cachar Hills. He proposed that the route between Katigorah and Asalu be made
passable at an expense of Rs. 7,500, and to keep this and the
Baladhan route open with an annual grant of Rs 3,000.
The regular Postal Service between Asalu and Silchar was not
found necessary, as the Deputy Commissioner thought that the
advantage to be gained would not be worth the cost of maintaining a postal establishment. But arrangements were proposed to be made to collect emergent reports from the Police
Stations at Asalu and Semkhar, while the formal reports could
be brought down to the District Headquarters at Silchar by
the constables sent for the purpose to make payments to the
policemen stationed there at the hill-guards. Regarding revenue,
the scheme envisaged as in other hill districts of this frontier,
that a house-tax of Re. 1 be levied on each house. To ensure
proper assessment, Edgar wanted that the whole of North
Cachar must have a uniform system of taxation and, to
ensure proper assessment, a detail census of the people and the
houses was proposed to be taken in the next cold season. He
believed that with a proper system of administration the
revenue would increase to Rs. 10,000 within few years. An
establishment[32] was also proposed for collecting the house-tax
and numbering the houses. The total expenditure of the establishment would be Rs. 1,344 yearly and, including Rs. 3,000
for the repair of the road, the entire annual expenditure would
be Rs. 4,344 for the administration of the hills and for keeping
open the roads, exclusive of the cost of police guards. Each
village would be required to be brought to a certain proportion
of their house-tax in grain to Asalu, whose value together with
a fair allowance for coolie charge according to the distance of
the village from Asalu could be deducted from the total amount
of revenue payable by it. These grains would be stored at the
police posts and rationed off to the constables at prices
recoverable from their pay. The value of the rice might be paid
to the Deputy Commissioner by the Police Department, either
on delivery or after the amount had been realised from the
consumers.[33]

Edgar was of the opinion that there was no need of the retaining a Police Station at Asalu. He thought that it would be well if

the police were not to enquire into the cases occuring among the hillmen. They should merely report to the Magistrate who might summarily investigate into the complaint. The Deputy Commissioner's authority over the tribals was to be defined and he should, in his political capacity, have powers to sentence to imprisonment for one year and fine. In cases demanding higher punishment, the trial should take place according to the provision of the Code of Criminal Procedure. Edgar also proposed that all matters connected with these hill people should be managed by European Officers and that the agency of *Amlah* or *Vakeel*, as much as practicable, be avoided ; for this purpose the Deputy Commissioner or his Assistant should annually visit Asalu.[34]

The Government of Bengal, in November 1868, approved the Proposals submitted by Edgar with certain reservations.[35] The suggestions regarding the Silchar-Asalu Postal Service and the collection of a part of the revenue in kind found favour with the Government. But the proposals of taking a correct census of the hills, uniformity of tax, appointment of a native establishment for the collection of revenue and the system of civil and criminal administration remained as a matter of future consideration. The Government asked Edgar to report after visiting Asalu in the cold weather of 1869 and after enquiry and discussion with the local people about the details of the pattern of administration best suited to the local circumstances of North Cachar. In other words, he was asked to suggest a system of Local Self-Government by means of Headmen and *Panchayats* under the supervision of the Deputy Commissioner of Cachar. The Government felt that the concentration of fiscal and petty judicial powers in the hands of the village headman, assisted by a *Panchayat*, would render any extraneous collectorate or Police agency completely unnecessary. A percentage of the revenue by way of remuneration for collection and performance of police duties might be given to the headmen, selected or appointed by the Deputy Commissioner. The heinous offenders would be sent down to the plains for trial, and the important civil disputes might be reserved for Deputy Commissioner's disposal during annual visits. Edgar was also asked by the Government to submit an estimate of the annual outlay for keeping the Asalu and Baladhan Routes open, throughout the year.[36]

In his reply, on 26 November 1868, the Deputy Commissioner fully explained the nature of the two routes and insisted on the sanction of the amount, he originally proposed, soliciting at the same time only half of the annual grant of Rs. 3,000 for the Baladhan Route for that year. On 17 December 1868, the Secretary to the Government of Bengal telegraphically informed the D.C. of the Goverment's sanction of Rs. 7,500 for the Asalu Road and Rs. 1,500 for the Baladhan Road.[37] The decisions on the other aspects of the scheme were kept pending for the next year as the Deputy Commissioner failed to report on the point raised by the Government. The Lushai raids and the repeated expeditions against the eastern tribes had prevented the Deputy Commissioner and the Assistant Commissioner from visiting Asalu. In 1871, MacWilliam, next Deputy Commissioner, was for about a week in the hills, but this was not sufficient to acquire informations required for the report as he was called to the station by the message of a Lushai attack on Alexanderpur.[38] The existing system of administration had, therefore, to continue for next few years. However, the Deputy Commissioner, in 1877, reported that the transfer of North Cachar under the Cachar Administration had produced a peaceful situation in the hills. The inhabitants behaved remarkably well and there had been very few complaints of any kind.[39]

In 1880, the sub-division of North Cachar was re-constituted with headquarters first at Gunjong and afterwards at Haflong. This was done to give more direct attention to the development of the territory and improvement of the general condition of the people. Since then North Cachar had continued as part of Cachar throughout the rest of the British Period, and in a peaceful condition.[40] But, in 1882, a curious outbreak took place in North Cachar resulting in the death of the Deputy Commissioner. A Dimacha, named Sambhudan, who had set himself up as a performer of miraculous cures, claiming Divine inspiration, took the title of *Deo* and attracted sizable followers from the hillmen. He pitched *Ashram* at Maibong and lived on the contributions of the neighbours. At length one person sued him in the Court of the Sub-divisional Officer, Haflong, accusing Sambhudan of assaulting him. The proceedings brought to light the prolonged exaction done by the 'Holy Man' and the gang behind him. Major Boyd, Deputy Commissioner of Cachar, proceeded with a party of armed police to apprehend the miscreants. During the skirmishes that followed many of the disciples of Sambhudan were massacred, but Boyd received a mortal wound to which he succumbed. Although Sambhudan managed his escape on that occasion, a few days later he was surrounded by a police cordon. In his attempt to escape again, Sambhudan sustained an injury in the leg and bled to death. Man Singh, the high priest of Sambhudan, was transported for life.[41]

But the Lushais and the Kukis, who occupied the hills in south-east of Cachar, indulged in incessant* raids upon the Plains; massacred the villagers and plundered their property. The head-hunting, amongst these tribes, was an art of chivalry affording them the greatest delight and social distinction as a man's importance was calculated by the number of skulls decorating his house and according to their custom the funeral of the chiefs required a certain number of skulls. Many Nagas and Kukis were arrested in Cachar for this heinous crime since the beginning of the British administration in the 'province' and were committed to Sessions and held up in Sylhet Jail. The inter-clanish feuds and scarcity of food-staff and domestic servants were among the other causes of the tribal incursions. In June 1844, thirty Kukis from Thadoi and Kyong villages of Manipur attacked a Kuki settlement in Banraj *Pargana* in Cachar and murdered and carried off the skulls of eight Kuki women. One of the perpetrators was later apprehended, who confessed that he accompanied the party by the desire of their Chief for the express purpose of carrying off human heads, but denied having any hand in the actual crime of murder. E.R. Lyons, Superintendent of Cachar, then requested the Political Agent in Manipur to induce the Raja of Manipur to take measures to prevent the recurrence of the inroads and committed the arrested person to Sessions as an assessory.[42] But the Kukis inhabiting the southern hill tract of Cachar, through repeated

---

*"A private quarrel with a neighbouring clan, a scarcity of women and domestic servants, and the consequent necessity of procuring a requisite number of captives to supply the wants of the tribes, the simple desire of plunder, or of obtaining heads to grace the obsequies of some departed chieftain, were the principal causes of these raids." See C.E. Bucklands, Bengal under the Lieutenant Governors, Vol. I, p. 180.

raids and plunders had completely depopulated many Bengalee villages in the plains. The Government despatched a series of punitive expeditions and imposed a rigid economic blockade. As the Kukis subsisted on the border *hats* where they traded with the Bengalees, the blockade resulted in a serious economic crisis in the Kuki hills. Ultimately, the Kuki Raja sent three elephants' teeth and a copper gong, which together fetched Rs. 121-4-0 at public auction, to the Superintendent of Cachar as *nazzar* and promised to maintain peaceful situation in the border, while the latter sent a pony as a return present. Lyons also sent four Bengalee residents of Cachar with an invitation to the Kuki Raja and successfully induced him to hold an interview with the Superintendent at Silchar. The Chief paid a visit to Lyons and evinced a considerable desire to resume the trade with the Bengalees. They subsisted by exchanging the produce of the hills for essential commodities obtainable at the *hats* and also secured full value of their elephants' teeth and purchased clothes from the traders in cash. The trade between the Kukis and the Bengalees were soon fairly established and the villages earlier deserted by the inhabitants, were again inhabited and the cultivation revived. Lyons felt it to be of much utility if the atrocious propensities of these people could be restrained by conciliatory measures. He endeavoured hard to keep the predatory tribes, in good humour, but only temporarily.[43]

Meanwhile, a large number of Kukis from Manipur immigrated into Cachar deserting their villages *en masse* and settled in the vicinity of Lakhipur *Bazar* forcibly occupying lands hitherto owned by the local people. This created a great commotion in the area, and Lyons took up the matter with the Political Agent of Manipur, who put pressure upon the Raja of Manipur to call back his Kuki subjects from Cachar. The Raja then sent a *Subahdar* to induce the Kukis to return to their hills, but the mission failed to impress upon the refugees to change their minds. The Raja then deputed a *Dewan* to visit the Kuki evacuees at Lakhipur and induce them to accompany him back to their homes. The Superintendent of Cachar also sent some *Chaprasis* to assist the *Dewan* in his mission, but to no purpose.[44] On the other hand, on 6 November 1849, about two hundred Lushai-Kukis, an independent tribe residing at about ten days' journey from the southern border of Cachar, armed with muskets, spears and daos, appeared in the Bhowaljoor Kuki *Punji* in *Pargana* Sunapur in Cachar in broad daylight and massacred several people and then set fire to the village. The invaders then proceeded towards Sahbajpur and burnt two other Kuki *Punjis* of Lulong and Augum, both in the same *Pargana*, and then left Cachar. The inhabitants of the *Punjis* came down into the plains as refugees. On 8th, about 400 hundred Kukis from the three affected villages came to G. Verner, Superintendent of Cachar, and prayed for redress. The Police party despatched by the Superintendent discovered in Bhowaljoor alone 29 bodies without head (15 men and 14 women), while 42 others were missing and were supposed to have been taken away as prisoners. The Government then sent a contingent of *Barkandazes* headed by a *Havildar* to guard the villages and to restore confidence among the Kuki settlers.[45] But the Kuki chiefs had the information that the invaders were preparing for the onslaught and, therefore, fled from southern Cachar and settled themselves in northern and eastern hills. Terrified at the Kuki influx, the plainsmen in the neighbourhood also deserted their villages and sought refuge elsewhere. Ultimately, sections of the Sylhet Light Infantry were posted at Sunabarighat in Sonai *Pargana* and Nagdirgram in Banraj *Pargana* to protect the people of the plains from depredations.[46]

As a matter of fact, the Kukis were allied tribes of the Lushais originating from the same racial stock. They had several sub-tribes, like Chasad, Sooti, Howlong, Thadoi etc., and were scattered over the hill areas of Manipur, Cachar, Tripura, Chittagong and Lushai Hills during the period under review. The refractory tribes referred to as Lushai-Kuki in the official records of Cachar were a Kuki tribe who might have been so called because of their situation in the Lushai range. They were a large and warlike tribe whose territory occupied about eight or ten days' journey from the southern border of Cachar. They were related to the Kukis who were settled in Cachar and were formerly living together in Lushai-Tripura Hills, the tract between 92 and 93 degrees East Longitude and some miles to the north and south of 23 degree North Latitude, but the fact that the Cachar Kukis had deserted them and set-

tled in a new country supported by prosperous *Jhum* fields and
thereby enraged their counterparts who retaliated through
systematic massacres.[47] They never remained in Cachar for more
than a day, and collected grains and heads of the slain and then
walked off.[48] Their village was nearer to Chittagong, being
about four days' journey, and they used the markets in Chittagong, Tripura and Comilla. Realising that any economic
blockade in the Cachar frontier will not affect them and would
rather harm the loyal tribes in the frontier, the Government
contemplated to send a punitive expedition against the Lushai-
Kukis in their own hills. But Verner felt that it would be
attended with great difficulty as there was no road and the
troops would be required to follow Passes through dense jungle,
swamp and uninhabited hills. The Bhowaljoor *Punji* was
already deserted, every hut was burnt and there remained
nothing but the dead bodies which having been lightly covered
with earth made them unhygienic and offensive for superstitious
security guards from Bengal and upcountry. The path beyond
Bhowaljoor river was so wretched and fatiguing that the passers
were obliged to go the greater part of the way along a single
stick raised from two or three feet from the ground to avoid
the marshes. Evidently, the armed force would be of no service
beyond protecting the people in the plains as the troops could
not be despatched into those dense jungles to follow-up or overtake the invaders without running great risks, the passes being
known to the Kukis alone. Even this would be a difficult task
according to the Superintendent, 'till such time as the Kookie
race will have been exterminated.'[49] Therefore, he contemplated only to endeavour to protect the people in the plains for
which two guards were already encamped and proposal for a
third was sanctioned. But the local people unequivocally expressed their dislike for militarisation as they were obliged to
supply ration for the sepoys which only added to their hardship
caused by the severe damages to harvest in the previous
season. Further, several villagers were supplied with muskets
by the Superintendent and if few more were provided with the
same, the local people, Verner felt, would be able to defend
themselves against the Kukis.[50]

But the Government of Bengal considered it necessary to
punish the invaders by beating them in their own territory so

that they would not dare in future to indulge in incursions within the British territory, as there was a strong rumour that the invaders intended to raid upon South Cachar again and to liberate, if possible, the captives of Bhowaljoor. Accordingly, in December 1849, Col. Lister with a detachment of the Sylhet Light Infantry proceeded against the recalcitrants, but upon approaching their villages realised that the Lushai-Kukis were a much powerful tribe than estimated by the local officers and the difficulties of getting at them increased terribly with every step. Finding that the retreat would be more dangerous as the Kukis might easily block the path, Lister thought it most prudent to retire and actually returned to Silchar on 4 January 1850. These tribes were well known to be of the most vindictive nature and the officials guessed some possibilities of their being emboldened by the expedition. Therefore, four companies of the Sylhet Light Infantry were left in Cachar besides establishing military posts and creating stockades at the most exposed spots along the southern frontier to protect the people as much as possible from any future incursions.[51] Interestingly, the sepoys stationed in Cachar posed a new problem for the administration to reckon with, by creating disturbances in the *bazars* and a *bazar* day seldom passed without this evil. They insulted, ill used and abused the people, and would forcibly take commodities from the sellers even without paying. In case a merchant had refused and attempted to resist or some other buyer agreed to pay more than the price offered by a sepoy, the sepoys in the whole *bazar* would join together and start beating the people *en masse*. The matter reached at such a height that the people gradually withdrew themselves from the *bazars*. Verner asked *Subahdar* Puran Singh, the senior native officer, to put a stop to the scandal, but the latter failed to achieve anything positive. Ultimately, the Superintendent had to take the matter up with Col. Lister, and it took a long way to invoke discipline among the sepoys.[52]

Verner had proposed to organise a Levy consisting of the loyal Kukis and allied tribesmen to act as a local corps of defence against the invading Kuki clan and to restore confidence among the local people in South Cachar who were in a state of constant plight and removed themselves to the northern bank of the river Barak.[53] But the Kukis were a mobile Community, who subsisted on *Jhum* or shifting agriculture requiring to search a new field after every two or three years, the *teelahs* having lost their fertility with the first or second season as they were not supplied with sufficient manure other than being burnt in the winter. The implements of cultivation were spade and spikes, and the exhausted fields must remain fallow for some years to recover the productive capacity. Backed by the strange custom of hunting human heads for superstitious purposes, they were in a state of constant inter-clanish warfare and whenever a particular clan had become stronger the neighbours were obliged to resort to flight.

In the middle of the last century, especially, due to famine conditions in Lushai-Chin Hills, the Kukis became completely restless in search of new home which, on the other hand, added to their mutual rivalries. In the fifties, several Kuki chiefs sent their emissaries to the Superintendent of Cachar requesting help against the invading clans, but with no positive response.[54] In 1859, some Kuki clans made a desperate attack upon Manipur, and the Government gave ammunition worth Rs. 2,500 to the Raja of Manipur to protect his people from tribal inroads. By this time, the political situation in Manipur was extremely disquieting due to conspiracies and insurrections led by Debendra Singh, Kanhai Singh, Gokul Singh and other members of the royal family against Chandrakirtee Singh, Raja of Manipur, and many Kuki and Lushai raids in Cachar and Manipur were instigated by these rebel princes. In 1861, Vonpilal, Chief of the Mullah clan, sent an embassy to Captain Stewart, Superintendent of Cachar, asking aid against the western Kukis and the Pois of the south, but on this occasion too British assistance was denied. Again in January 1862, three outrages were committed in Sylhet in which three villages were plundered and a large number of villagers were killed or carried off. In April 1863, four of the captive women made their escape to Cachar and gave out the names of Muchoilo, Sukpilal, Rungbhoom and Lal Hoolien as the raiding chiefs. The district authorities of Sylhet wanted to send an expedition against the offending clans, but as Sukpilal had maintained friendly relations with the Cachar authorities for a long time by sending frequent deputations with presents, Sir Cecil Beadon, Lieutenant Governor of Bengal, directed the Superintendent of Cachar to induce

Sukpilal to release the captives and to undertake the protection of the frontier people from committing such raids and refusing to cooperate with other chiefs in any such attempt in future. The Chief was also offered an annual money payment in return for this service. This moderate step was proposed by the Government of Bengal only considering that a punitive exped- ition might antagonise the tribesmen to raid upon the fast spreading tea gardens in Cachar-Lushai borders. In 1864, the negotiations were initiated with Sukpilal and resulted in the surrender of four captive boys in 1866. The chief also inform- ed the Cachar authorities that the other captives were already married to the Lushais and expressed their unwillingness to return to the plains.[55]

Despite such measures, the frontier problem posed a real menace to the authorities in Cachar. The fugitive Manipuri princes in Cachar continued to exercise their best endeavour to dislodge Chandrakirtee from the throne of Manipur. In 1865, a large number of Manipuris assembled in the eastern frontier of Cachar to invade Manipur, while the Lushais were threeaten- ing the tea gardens in south Cachar and the authorities were engaged in suppressing the intruders. On 15 January 1869, the Lushais burnt the tea gardens of Loharband and made a most brutal attack upon Maniarkhal, both on the eastern fron- tier of Cachar, causing several casualties, and then marched to Manipur along with Kanhai Singh. The punitive expedition that was immediately despatched failed to achieve anything tangible due to difficult communication and inclemency of the weather.[56] However, economic blockade and beating off the intruders compelled some leading Lushai chiefs to meet the Deputy Commissioner of Cachar and pledge for improved mutual relationship. Accordingly, in December 1869, Edgar, Deputy Commissioner of Cachar, undertook a tour into the Lushai Hills with the object of placing the British relations with the Lushais on a more satisfactory footing. Upon his recommen- dations it was decided by the Government that the Deputy Com- missioner of Cachar or one of his subordinates should annually visit the Lushai country, interview as many of the chiefs, separa- tely, as possible, use his influence for the adjustments of quarrels and reward the well disposed chiefs.[57] The Government also approved of the grant of charters to the chiefs specifying the conditions on which they would be left in the undisturbed possession of their territory, the levy of tolls by the chiefs on the people going up to trade with the Lushais, the settlement of the villages along the frontier, the appointment of a Political Agent in Tripura, and opening of two paths—one from Mani-arkhal to Bonkong and the other from Dwarband to the Rengtu Range.[58]

But before long, the Lushais perpetrated extensive raids in Chittagong Frontier, the range of which was soon extended to Cachar, Sylhet, Tripura and Manipur. On 12 January 1871, the Lushais made the most marauding raid upon Ainerkhal, in the South of Hailakandi, in which 25 persons were butchered and 37 captivized. Next day, they plundered the Alexanderpur Tea Garden and with a few hours difference attacked Katli-chara. In the former they assassinated the manager and carried off his daughter, while in the latter killed five coolies and wounded several others. Three days later, they again attacked Maniarkhal, but a strong troop of armed police succeeded in driving back the marauders after a fierce battle of two days. Maniarkhal was hardly cleared of the enemies, when the Lushais raided simultaneously upon Dharmikhal and Nagdigram killing eleven persons and capturing three. A party of sepoys and police was overpowered near Nagdigram by the tribesmen and majority of the sepoys killed.[59] By the end of February 1871, the Lushais made an attack upon Jalnachara Tea Estate, killed four persons and wounded three.[60]

The Government took steps to meet the challenge of these unfriendly neighbours by increasing the strength of the police force in Cachar and revitalising the frontier guards, creating a large number of out-posts and detaching regular troops along the borders.[61] Similar measures were affected in the Chittagong frontier. But the local authorities wanted to deal with the tribes-men more effectively by beating them off in their own territory. Accordingly, a military expedition consisting of two columns was sent into the Lushai Hills. The right or the Chittagong Column was under General Brownlow and the left or Cachar Column commanded by General Boarchier. The Cachar Column consisted of half a battery of artillery, one Company of Sappers, 500 men each of the 22nd Punjab Native Infantry and 44th Assam Light Infantry, a coolie corps together with 178 elephants and 1,200 coolies for Commissariat purposes. The Chittagong Column was also of the almost same strength, but mainly composed of Gurkhas. As the previous expeditions had revealed the extreme difficulty of communication, the Cachar Column was accompanied by 2,764 coolies and the Chittagong Column by 2,791 to clear the path for the advancement of the contingent. Both the columns were accompanied by Survey parties which made the topographical survey of 6,500 square miles and filled up the gap that had separated Cachar from Chittagong in the survey map. The expedition, by the Columns, achieved spectacular success and most of the independent Lushai chiefs were compelled to submit to the British authority. They undertook to allow free access to the Government agents to their villages, surrendered the guns taken at Maniarkhal and Nagdigram, released the captives including the daughter of the manager of Maniarkhal Tea Estate, and paid a fine of two elephant tusks, one set of war-gongs, one necklace, ten goats, ten pigs, fifty fowls and twenty maunds of husked rice.[62] A line of strong out-posts was established along the whole southern frontier of Cachar and Sylhet, while the river Langai was taken as the boundary between Lushais and Tipperahs.[63]

Although occasional raids were reported from Manipur and Tripura, the Lushais created no serious problem for Cachar since the expedition of 1871. On the other hand, their relations with the British Government gradually improved and all contacts were made through Cachar. The Lushais were largely dependent upon the Cachar markets for their supplies, while the Dwarband-Aijal Road provided the only means of communication between Lushai Hills and the rest of India. No wonder, therefore, the tribesmen wanted to be in the good book of the officers in Cachar by presenting rare indigenous varieties. In December 1873, some chiefs visited the Deputy Commissioner of Cachar and offered him several presents. Next year, many Lushais came down to Cachar plains to purchase cattles and carried on the transactions without any bad blood. To faciliate Cachar-Lushai trades, three *bazars* were established in the border region, at Changsil, Sonai and Tipaimukh, and the native merchants of Cachar settled themselves down in the flourishing business. In January 1875, many Lushais came down in the south bank of Barak to cut rubber, but as they were forbidden by the forest officials all quietly disappeared. A few days later, Sukpilal, the prominent chief, informed the Deputy Commissioner of Cachar about serious food crisis in his territory when supplies were immediately rushed by the Government and native traders were induced to send more. During the cold season of 1875-76, the Government noticed a gradual northward advance of the Lushais as they were pressed in the south and east by other tribes. The Chief Commissioner of Assam forbade altogether the settlement of these tribes within the British territory, except in the sites specifically assigned to them and with permission. This was, however, not considered as a serious problem and Lushais exposed themselves more and more to the British authority.[64] The policy of sending one of the Cachar officers to visit the tribal chiefs in a friendly way from time to time was pursued with best regularity. The frontier posts were carefully maintained and armed police were eventually placed on a sound footing.[65]

Notwithstanding, the conflicts between the Lushais and Manipuris as well as eastern and western Lushais were bound to have repercussions in Cachar. In 1876, Tantam, a petty eastern Lushai chief, being unable to stand the feuds migrated to Cachar and settled near Tipaimukh, but the British Government objected to the encroachment and the chief retired with his followers. But soon after several families from Tantam's *punji* migrated to Cachar and sought British protection. These immigrants were settled on the west bank of Barak, opposite to the mouth of Jiri. The situation having drifted from bad to worse, Sukpilal and other western chiefs sent a deputation to the Deputy Commissioner of Cachar at Silchar, in July 1877, for support against their adversaries. But the Government declined to assist either of the parties and rather advised the chiefs to live peacefully with the neighbours. However, in January 1878, when both the eastern and the western Lushais expressed their desire for British mediation, the *mantris* and other representatives of the Chiefs were invited to a conference at Silchar. The Deputy Commissioner advised these emissaries to give up hostilities and live like good neighbours, with the warning that any threat to the breach of peace will not be tolerated by the British Government.[66] This incident brought the Lushais more under the control of the British authorities. In July 1879, the

Lushais of Senong *Punji* presented an elephant tusk to the Deputy Commissioner and represented that they were hard-hit by the scarcity of food. Thirty-five maunds of paddy were then purchased by the Government from the local market in Cachar and offered to the people in distress as gratuitous relief. In October 1879, a party of Lushais plundered the Changsil *Bazar*. Sukpilal had earlier pledged to protect the establishments in the *Bazar*, and the Government now demanded compensation from the Chief and closed down the *Bazar*. When the Chief agreed to pay Rs. 1,000 as fine on behalf of his people and to remit the *Bazar* dues to the same amount, the Government reopened the *Bazar* and the traders from Cachar resumed their normal business.[67] Again, in 1880, a party of Lushais who had come down to collect rubber fell in with some wood-cutters in a reserved forest within the Inner Line and demanded rent from them. Upon the report of the Forest Officers, the authorities in Cachar sent a note of protest to Sukpilal and the offenders were immediately apprehended and severely punished. The Chief, further, authorised the Deputy Commissioner of Cachar to punish any Lushai who might interfere with the British subjects within the British Indian territory. Shortly after, Sukpilal was indisposed and Rai Bahadur Haricharan Sarmah, Special Extra-Assistant Commissioner, Cachar, was officially deputed by the district authorities to enquire about the health of the Chief. About this time, owing to the oppressions of Khalkan, son of Sukpilal, and several families of Lushais sought refuge in Cachar and were settled at a distance from the frontier.[68]

But the troubles in Manipur became fierce in 1882. The matter reached its climax on 3 July when some Kuki subjects of the Raja of Manipur attacked a Lushai Village with fire-arms and set fire to the houses. In this raid twenty-five villagers were killed, seven wounded and fourteen captivised, while property worth Rs. 700 was looted and eleven huts were gutted. As the incident took place not far from the Tipaimukh *Bazar*, the neighbouring chiefs like Laho, Tantam, Banrum, Toiboi and Lengkam were asked by the Head constable in charge of Tipaimukh out-post to send adequate guard for the protection of the *bazar*. They were, however, cautioned to avoid any retaliatory measure, very common with these refractory tribes, against the raiders without permission from the Government. The chiefs detached a guard of ten persons for the *bazar* and agreed that if the Government would undertake to settle the matter they would accept their decision.[69]

In the wake of the severe famine of 1882, caused by the depredation of rats,[70] the prominent Lushai chiefs decided to cease their mutual hostilities and depute envoys to Cachar to obtain supplies. Several Lushai families migrated to Cachar and showed their anxiety to earn bread by manual labour or by begging. Many of them were employed by the Forest Officers for cutting bamboos and timbers, while others by the Tea Gardens for clearing the jungles. The traders were induced by the Government to supply foodgrains to the two important *bazars* of Tipaimukh in east and Changsil in the west. Some Government stores were opened at Tipaimukh and Guturmukh from which relief was issued to the distressed chiefs and persons whom their chief certified to be insolvent. Rai Bahadur Haricharan Sarmah and Mr. Place, Extra-Assistant Commissioner and Assistant Commissioner respectively of Hailakandi, toured in the famine striken areas. This gesture of the Government saved the Lushais from this havoc and made them more amenable to the British authority.[71] After the famine was over, the hillmen resumed the cultivation of their *Jhum* fields, but more than a thousand immigrants settled themselves in Cachar whose descendants are still to be found in various *punjis* of the district.

Nevertheless, the disturbances again raised their ugly head in 1888, in Chittagong Division originating from the massacre of the Survey Party by some Lushais on 3 February.[72] The situation soon drifted from bad to worse, and the local authorities made strong recommendations to the Government of India for effective military actions. Ultimately, the Governments of Bengal, Assam and Burma undertook a combined expedition from Chittagong, Cachar and Arakan Sectors in January 1890, which completely subjugated the Lushais. The stockades were built, at Aijal and Changsil; while in the south, Fort Tregear was established and Fort Lungleh augmented. The Political Officers were posted at Aijal and Changsil, line of communication was established between Bengal and Burma, military posts were raised at all strategic points and the offend-

ing tribes strongly dealt with.[73] But Captain Brown, the Political Officer at Aijal, was murdered by the rebellious western
Lushais in September 1890, and the hillmen attacked the stockades. R.B. MacCabe, next Political Officer, succeeded in bringing the situation under control and proper punishment was
meted out to the chiefs involved in the upsurge. The local
officers now hoped that the Lushais would gradually settle themselves down under the British rule, but in February 1892, they
suddenly attacked MacCabe. Although the insurrection was
turned down, in April 1892, the Lushais raided the Barunchara
Tea Estate; burnt five houses and killed 42 coolies. This created
the pretext for the complete annexation of the Lushai Hills in
1898.[74] The Southern Lushai Hills, which was administered by
the Government of Bengal, was amalgamated with the northern
tract and Rutton Poiya's area, in the Chittagong Hill Tract,
was also transferred to the same jurisdiction. This united Lushai
Hills and the District was put in charge of a single Superintendent under the Chief Commissioner of Assam.[75] Since then,
there was no notable Lushai raid in Cachar. The British rule
was gradually consolidated in the hitherto secluded 'country'
and all communication with the new district were made through
Cachar and by the Dwarband-Aijal Road. The famine was a
very frequent feature in Lushai Hills as the people clung to the
less productive *Jhum* system of cultivation and the authorities
had to organise supply from Cachar. On some occasions the
people would even complain to the Cachar authorities about
their various grievances.[76]

Similarly, the Naga disturbances from the north-east frontier of the district had also been gradually minimised. At the
time British Government had taken over the administration of
Cachar, the Naga problem was considered as an alarming
factor. The creation of the Naga Hills District in 1868, as has
already been mentioned, and stationing of a British Establishment at Samaguting proved effective against Naga hostilities
in North Cachar. The inclusion of the district in the Chief
Commissionership of Assam in 1874 further accelerated the
pace of innovation towards peaceful situation in the Naga
Hills· Although the traditional inter-clanish feuds as well as
occasional raids and plunder in Manipur endured with a lesser
intensity, Cachar was considerably relieved of the problem. In

1866, Captain Butler, Deputy Commissioner of Naga Hills, had advocated the complete subjugation of all the Naga tribes and Sir George Campbell, Lieutenant-Governor of Bengal, also came to the conclusion that the gradual establishment of political control would be the only satisfactory plan to normalise the Naga menace.[77] By this time, there was a huge gun-running in the frontier and the availability of sufficient fire-arms and ammunition was largely responsible for the ceaseless inter-tribal clashes. These were mostly procured secretly and illegally from Manipur and Cachar. The person who prepared cartridges for the Raja of Manipur used to keep a part of the total production for the use of the Raja and sold a significant part to the Nagas. The sepoys in Manipur, on the otherhand, sold caps and cartridges to the tribesmen, while they purchased guns and other arms and ammunition from the traders at the Barkhala *Bazar* in Cachar which was generally a secret mid-night fair. To avoid detection while taking to the hills, the Nagas detached the barrel from the stock and placed it in bamboo tubes and the stocks were wrapped up with cloth and plaintain leaves and then placed in the baskets. For the *Beparies*, as the traders were called in Cachar, it was a voluminous and profitable business.[78] Obviously, the possession of these arms added to the marauding practice of the Nagas and ultimately the Supreme Government, in 1874, approved the plan suggested by Sir George Campbell. The survey and exploratory missions were taken in all earnest, the policy of non-intervention was abandoned, villages after villages of the independent clans were brought under effective control, construction of roads as well as humanitarian works were taken up and in the beginning of the present century the supremacy of the British over whole Naga Hills became a *fait accompli*.[79]

In this process of the making of British 'empire', the Government had to reckon with the stiff resistance of the Naga clans and their occasional outbursts had serious incidental repercussions in Cachar. Thus in February 1877, the Mozemah Nagas attacked Gumaigaju, a Cachari Village in North Cachar, killed six people, injured two and carried off two guns, and the cause was an old feud which had started thirty years back. In the same year, the Angamis attacked a Kacha Naga Village in the same locality and the offending village was burnt under the instructions of the Government.[80] But in January 1880, an incident of most daring nature took place in the Baladhan Tea Estate. A party of Konemah Nagas killed the Political Officer of the Naga Hills and were beleaguered by the British troops. A section of these recalcitrants made their way to Baladhan and killed the Garden Manager and 16 of his coolies. During February and March, following year, the rebels encamped themselves in the Chakka Fort on the crest of the Barail Hills and maintained a typical guerilla warfare. The British troops besieged the fort and cut-off their supplies. Pressed hard by the blockade, the fort surrendered on 27 March, and the villages involved in these onslaughts were severely dealt with.[81] This was probably the last of the serious ravages caused by the Nagas in Cachar. In 1882, when the Naga Hills District boundaries were laid down, a triangular tract of territory, in- habited by the Kukis and Cacharis and bounded on the south by Langting and Langreng rivers, on the north-east by Lumd- ing and on the north-west by Dayang, which originally belong- ed to Cachar but was transferred to Naga Hills in 1866, was restored to North Cachar Sub-division.[82] Again, during the famous Kukis Rebellion of 1917-19, against forced recruitment of the Kukis by the Government for the Labour Corps, in Manipur, Cachar and adjoining areas, some Naga clans suffered badly at the hands of the Kukis and the Cachar frontier was reduced to a considerably disquieting state.[83] In 1927, a Kabui Naga, named Jadonang, professed a new faith on the Cachar-Manipur Road and proclaimed a *Kabui Naga Raj*. The people believed him to be a Prophet and the various Naga tribes, including the Kacha Nagas in Cachar, looked upon him as their *Messiah* and offered him tributes. His activities created a great stir in the region. However, the prophet was arrested during his mission in Cachar and sentenced to death in June 1931 on a murder charge.[84]

But by far the worst problem to be reckoned with by the Cachar administration was perhaps the repercussions of the feuds that centred around the throne of Manipur since the be- ginning of the 19th century. It may be recalled that the intri- gues of some of the claimants with Ava and the flight of their rivals to Cachar had led to invasion of Manipur and Cachar by the Burmese and also the Anglo-Burmese War. Gambhir Singh,

who was placed on the throne of Manipur by the British
support after the Treaty of Yandaboo, was all out to dethrone
Govindachandra and usurp Cachar. Whatever might be the official version of the tragedy, the part played by Gambhir Singh and
Manipuri collaborators in the assassination of the last Raja of
Cachar is well known.   Although Gambhir failed to establish
his claim to the throne of Khaspur, the British ceded a large
chunk of Cachar's territory to him in 1833 and a section of the
Manipuris who had taken shelter in Cachar during the Burmese
inroads in their state had permanently settled in Cachar. But
the problem seemed never-ending and for many years more the
palace trouble in Manipur had disturbed the law and order in
Cachar. To quote W.M. MacCulloch, Superintendent of Cachar,.
on 8 August 1842:[85]

> In this district the principal disturbances which have taken
> place have been occasioned by Munipoorie princes residing
> in the country assembling men for the invasion of Munipoor
> and these assemblies have been easily dispersed by parties
> of the detachment stationed here, which could not even if a
> military police were established to be dispensed with.

As a matter of fact, Gambhir Singh ruled over Manipur
with a strong hand and the unfortunate state was relieved of
the palace strife for some years, but his death in 1834 marked
the repetition of the old drama. Gambhir's infant son Chandrakirtee Singh ascended the throne and his *Senapati*, Nur Singh,
became the Regent, while other frustrated claimants fled to
Cachar and Burma.   From Cachar these princes made several
attempts to dethrone Chandrakirtee and instigated the refractory
Kuki and Lushai tribes to raids and atrocities in Manipur. In
1839, Setember Singh, a *Rajkumar*, who was fugitive in Cachar,
offered to collect Rs. 2,000 as capitation tax from certain Kuki
villages provided he would be furnished with some muskets.
But E. R. Lyons, Superintendent of Cachar, rejected his petition
on the ground that any of the Manipuri princes in Cachar
should not be entrusted with fire-arms as they were always
anxious to invade Manipur and occupy the throne.[86]   In 1840,
Tribhunbanjit, another *Rajkumar*, represented to the Superintendent that he was informed by his servant in Manipur that Nur
Singh and his brother Devendra Singh had sent a *Sardar* with
25 men to assassinate him.   Lyons reported the matter to the

Political Agent of Manipur and also alerted the Cachar Frontier Police to prevent the party from entering into Cachar.[87] Interesting enough, soon after, the Political Agent in Manipur wrote quite a few letters to the Superintendent of Cachar relating to the disquietitude caused by Rajkumar Tribhunbanjit in that valley. In this connection some comments of the Superintendent may be worth quoting:[88]

> .. but he is doing nothing openly calculated to lead me to suppose that he mediates an attempt on Manipore. However, Munneepoorees are great adepts in keeping the world ignorant of their plans and intentions, and I have no doubt but that the prince would be rash enough to follow the steps of Torrung. Komba and Juggendrojeet had the means of supporting a body of armed followers which I both believe and trust he has not. If however he does go it will be owing, in my opinion, to an invitation or promise of assistance by parties now at Manipore.

Tribhunbanjit was detained by the Superintendent; but as the prince did not commit any act sufficient to warrant the Magistrate's keeping him under restraint he was released on 6 April 1841. On 29 April, Lyons received an intimation that Tribhunban had made his way to Manipur by a circuitous route with a body of armed followers. The Superintendent despatched an express to the Political Agent of Manipur promising its bearers Rs. 20 in addition to Rs. 5 paid to them at the starting if they succeeded in relieving the letter to Captain Gordon, the Political Agent, before the prince could reach the valley. He also commissioned a contingent of the Sylhet Light Infantry to intercept the party, if possible. This was effectually done and several of the followers were apprehended together with a large number of muskets, ammunitions and flags.[89] On 20 May 1841, Lyons received a letter from Gordon informing him that Tribhunbanjit had been killed in Manipur after a hard fight for the *Gadi*.[90]

The troubles were not far to come from the official rulers of Manipur as well. Nur Singh, the Regent, proposed to levy duties on the timbers and other goods either to be exported from or imported in Manipur and for the purpose to establish a *ghat* at the mouth of the river Jiri. The treaty of 1833, by which Jiri frontier was ceded to Manipur, had clearly provided that the Raja of Manipur will in no way obstruct the trade carried on between the two countries by Bengali or Manipuri merchants, will not exact duties and will make monopoly of no article of merchandise. The treaty had further provided that the Raja will in no way prevent the Nagas of the locality from selling or batering ginger, cotton, pepper and every other produce of the country at the Banskandi and Udharband *Bazars* to which they were long accustomed. The treaty had authorised the Raja to establish a *Thana*, i.e., police station, on the eastern bank of the Jiri, and the Regent wanted to interpret it to be transit *ghat* for imposing duties. Naturally, the Cachar authorities sharply reacted to the proposal and requested the Political Agent to dissuade the Regent from introducing the change as it would be tantamount to a clear violation of the treaty and also injure the lessees of the Sealtekh *Ghat* in Cachar.[91]

Meanwhile, in January 1844, the *Maharani*, mother of Chandrakirti, made an unsuccessful attempt to assassinate Nur Singh and then fled to Cachar together with the young Raja. On 3 February, along with 40 guards they arrived at Silchar and solicited political asylum with the Superintendent.[92] Lyons then ordered the Commissariat to make room for them in any public building until the erection of two or three mat houses for their accommodation on the bank of the Barak, for which the *Maharani* was very much desirous, and also sent a *Havildar's* party for the security of the *Maharani* and her son Their departure from Manipur was so precipitate that they had left behind all their private property, so much so that they had scarcely a second change of clothes or cooking utensils. The Cachar authorities had, therefore, to supply every essential article.[93] In Manipur, on 28 September, Nur Singh was recognised by the British Government as the legal Raja. Naturally, it became the duty of the Government to protect the new Raja, but Gordon got an intelligence that the *Maharani* was intriguing with four other exiled *Rajkumars* to overthrow Nur Singh and, accordingly, requested the Superintendent of Cachar to restrict the activities of the *Maharani*. Lyons was also fully convinced that the *Maharani* was the chief instigator of a strong conspiracy against the Raja of Manipur. As a first step towards ensuring the peace of the Cachar frontier, he suggested that the *Maharani* and Chandrakirti should be removed from Cachar. Since there were already three other exiled princes at Dacca and Sylhet was too near the frontier, he recommended to the Government of India that they may be sent to Faridpur. To quote him:[94]

> Knowing as I do the extreme cunning of Munniporees I hold it next to impossible that the *Maharanee* should be ignorant of the project of the four princes, for it must be her chief care to learn what is going both here and at Munnipore amongst the chiefs and if she were opposed to the scheme she would immediately acquaint me. I entertain no doubt of the correctness of the Rajah's information which he obtains through the medium of his spies in Cachar but these Princes are poor and could do nothing without the promise of assistance from the disaffected at Munnipore which on similar occasions has invariably been afforded.
>
> I find that the *Maharanee* has been sending many hundred of rupees to Calcutta, for, as she asserts, *Durbar* expenses could be incurred. I doubt not her object is to buy musquets, as did the three princes (all killed) who made several attempts during the incumbency of my predecessor, and Prince Tribubunjeet in my time... .
>
> I deem it proper mainly to confine myself in this letter to recommending the removal of the *Maharanee* and her son to Fureedpur, where there are no Munnipoorees I believe and consequently less chance of plots being formed. They have 29 followers only now, any of whom who wish it might, I think, be allowed to accompany them, though probably not more than half would desire to do so, it would be advisable to send a guard from the Sylhet Light Infantry to escort them to Furreed Poor whence it would return.
>
> The Munnipooree princes in Cachar are as uncivilized as the Burmese, though excessively proud notwithstanding, gave a vast deal of trouble during the five or six years, antecedent to and in 1841.

But the proposal of the Superintendent about the removal of the *Maharani* and her son took an unnaturally long span of time to be considered by the Government of India. Meanwhile, in 1847, there were strong rumours that the Manipuri Princes in Cachar and Burma were making hectic preparations for invading Manipur. Accordingly, the princes in Cachar were warned not to disturb the peace in Cachar and that any one found guilty to do so would be removed to Dacca or Faridpur. In this situation, Nur Singh died and was succeeded by Debendra Singh. But Chandrakirti advanced his claim to the throne and was even reported to be prepared to support it by

force of arms.   The British Government immediately recognised the succession of Debendra Singh, and sanctioned the apprehension of Chandrakirti and removal of the ex-Raja and the
Maharani to Dacca.* This provoked the three *Rajkumars*
in Cachar, namely, Melai Koomba, Konenba and Cheba, to
try their luck in the troubled waters of Manipur. On 1 February,
1850, at 12 midnight, G. Verner, the Superintendent of Cachar,
received an intelligence through the Government spies that a
large number of followers they all had assembled in the house of
Melai Koomba and were prepared to start for Manipur the same
night.   The Superintendent immediately directed Puran Singh,
a *Subahdar* in the local corps, to proceed forthwith to prevent
the princes from launching their campaign. Although the *Subahdar* started with 30 men of his crops for Melai's house, he could
gather that the party had already left by the way of Khaspur
with about 100 followers all armed with muskets. He advanced upto the Cachar frontier but could not overtake the aggressors.[95]   However, on 1 March, Verner was informed by Captain
McCullock, Political Agent of Manipur, that the invaders were
dispersed by the Manipur Army and two of the princes had
been killed in the encounter.[96] On the other hand, Chandrakirti
was put under house arrest at Silchar and preparations were
being made for his removal to Dacca, as per the instructions
of the Government of India.   But, on 10 June, at 11 night, he
effected his escape notwithstanding a guard from Sylhet Light
Infantry Battalion of twenty men with five sentries watching
over him round the clock.   The *Dak* runners were immediately
sent to convey the message to McCullock and they were promised fabulous presents from the Cachar Treasury.[97] Hiding himself in the jungles for about a month Chandrakirti made preparations for a major offensive to recover his *Gadi*, and in the
second week of July appeared in the neighbourhood of Imphal
with a large number of armed followers. The resistance offered
by Debendra Singh was easily broken through, and people of

---

*In 1848, Maharani Indraprabha, widow of Raja Govindachandra of
Cachar and a cousin of Chandrakirti, requested the Superintendent of
Cachar to be permitted to visit Manipur. G. Verner, Superintendent of
Cachar, took up the matter with the Political Agent of Manipur, but in
view of the convulsed situation there Indraprabha's petition was rejected.
C.R. 147 of 1848.

Manipur generally sympathised with his cause and many openly sided with him. The following extract from McCullock's letter to Verner during the operations explains the situation:[98]

> The sepoys sent by the present Raja Debendra Singh against the Ex-Raja all fire in the air and then run away so that there appears to be little doubt but that Kirtee Chandra will gain the day, and most likely the next dak will bring in the news of his having regained the *guddea*. The sons of Nur Singh, the late Raja, have joined Kirtee Chandra and so it is said have many others. He was very popular here and I believe, without exception, every man in Cachar wishes he may be successful, and I suppose most do the same in Munipoor, for I often heard it said that there was not a Manipooree who would fire at the son of late Gumbeer Singh were he to return to Manipoor and it has turned out so far very nearly correct. If he does succeed it is to be hoped that peace will be restored and that there will be an end to these attacks.

True to the expectation of the Political Agent, Debendra Singh fled from Manipur in the evening of 17 July and Chandrakirti regained the *Gadi*.[99] History repeated one of its cruel ironies on 24 July when Debendra Singh with his wife, five sons and twenty followers arrived at Silchar and sought refuge in the Company's territory. He expressed his desire to stay in Cachar and offered his services to the British Government in whatever way the latter would like to utilise, and professed that he did not intend to return to Manipur at all. He was accommodated in the same *Manipuri Bari* where Chandrakirti had stayed with his mother only recently.[100] But the remark made by Lyons about the character of these Manipuri princes, quoted earlier, proved to be genuine in the evening of 17 October when Debendra Singh left with about 60 followers to endeavour to regain the lost throne. A detachment of the Sylhet Light Infantry Battalion was at once despatched by the Cachar authorities to overtake the party before crossing the Cachar frontier.[101] They actually came up with the gang a little beyond Lakhipur and asked the Raja to return with his men but he refused to comply. His men also fired a few rounds upon the sepoys and a short encounter ensued. There were casualties on both sides and the Raja's party then escaped into the jungles. The sepoys could not apprehend any of them but afterwards ascertained that five of the Raja's men were killed during the exchange. A wounded man surrendered, a couple of ponies were caught, and four muskets and few spears were recovered.[102]   In November, Debendra Singh entered Manipur with a large number of tribal followers recruited from the frontier hills and initiated a stiff fight with Chandrakirti's people. Unable to break through the wall of resistance, Debendra retired to the Kala Naga Hills and organised a section of these Nagas into raids and plunders. Pabitra Singh, another *Rajkumar*, who was detained at Dacca, also joined hands with Debendra Singh. From his camp in the Kala Naga Hills, Debendra wrote a letter, on 14 November, to Verner informing him that his first attack upon Manipur had failed, that he would renew his efforts, that he sought either *Gadi* or death, and begged to the Superintendent that till he could obtain either no armed people be sent from Cachar.[103] But all his attempts to recover the *Gadi* failed and the unfortunate prince was deserted by his own followers. As a result, without obtaining *Gadi* or death, he sent another letter to Verner, on 24 November, reporting his failure to unseat Chandrakirti and praying that he might be allowed to return to Cachar with only eight followers including his brother and four sons.[104] Naturally the Superintendent sought advice of the Government of India, but before anything could be decided, Debendra arrived at Silchar on 27 November. On the same day, he was sent to Sylhet along with his brother and sons and escorted by a section of the Sylhet Light Infantry Battalion.[105]

It would be crystal clear from the facts and circumstances that the Manipuri princes given shelter and hospitality in Cachar at a huge drain from the Cachar Treasury were constantly haunted by their tradition of blood feuds. They kept the frontier in alarm by the repeated attacks launched upon Manipur across the hilly tracts and with followers from the Manipur settlers in Cachar. The very character of these princes, the geographical advantages and the presence of a sizable immigrant Manipuri population in Cachar could be considered by the Government in favour of removing all the fugitive princes at a safe distance from the frontier. This Manipur episode had dearly taxed Cachar from the beginning of its contacts with the British and the extreme indulgence given to Gambhir had shaped the later history of the state. In the assassination of Raja Govindachandra the Manipuris in the palace guard collaborated with the contingent sent from Manipur and hence the authorities had every reason to be vigilant about the Manipuris in the local corps. Puran Singh, a Manipuri, who had acquired a large landed property in Cachar, and was a *Subahdar* and in charge of the section of the Sylhet Light Infantry posted in Cachar, was deputed by the Superintendent on 1 Febuary 1850, to chase the three princes who left Cachar that night for Manipur, but the *Subahdar* had reported that he could not overtake them within Cachar. Curiously, the suspicion of the authorities fell in course of time upon this officer and Puran was summoned to attend the Court of the Superintendent in December 1852 and was warned that "should it be proved that he affords aid and assistance either directly or indirectly to Munnypoorie Princes to enable them to attack the Rajah of Munnypoor, that he will thereby liable himself to punishment."[106] As early as 1844, Lyons had insisted that the Manipuri Princes should be removed from Cachar to ensure peace in the frontier. But the Government continued to give indirect indulgence to the rebels at the cost of the peace and tranquillity of Cachar and embarassment of the authorities. No wonder, therefore, in March 1851, another Prince, Bhagindra Singh, made extensive preparations for attacking Manipur and the situation could be saved only by the timely intervention of the Superintendent.[107] But this did not mean an end to his efforts. In April, two of his people, Chatra Singh and Eraibal, were detected in Sylhet smuggling away from there a quantity of ammunition. On this intelligence, the Superintendent of Cachar at once sent for Bhagindra Singh but the latter was missing from Cachar. It could, however, be gathered that with one or two brothers he had gone off towards Lakhipur to be joined there by many others on their way to Manipur. On the same day, it was ascertained that Ranjit Singh, another *Rajkumar* and a brother of late Tribhunbanjit, had also been absent from Cachar. Great many rumours spread in Cachar and on Manipur borders that the princes from Cachar would launch an attack on Manipur. The Cachar authorities immediately posted a police party at Lakhipur to prevent the armed persons, stores, ammunitions etc. from passing by that way and the Manipur Government was informed of all these developments so that the latter might put the Raja on guard.[108] Although their attempts were foiled by the Frontier police, the princes continued to harass the Government. In April 1852, there was a strong rumour in Manipur that seven princes from Cachar, named Nawal Singh, Kanai Singh, Bhuban Singh, Sangoe Taba, Khero, Maipha and Ujah, would attack Manipur and some people in that state including tribesmen were in league with them. Alarmed at the tension created by the rumour, Raja Chandrakirti requested Verner to apprehend all these princes and prevent their followers from proceeding to Manipur. But save Nawal and Kanai other princes were unknown to the authorities and the spies a!so failed to collect their antecedent. The police could arrest only Nawal as Kanai was missing from that morning. Nawal Singh, an infirm elderly man, was put under surveillance.[109] In May, Nawal represented to the Superintendent to be released on furnishing 'good security' on the ground of age and infirmity.[110] Verner having supported his case, the Government of India sanctioned his release but asked the Superintendent to watch his movements.[111] But in November, the princes again became active and restlessness relapsed on the frontier. The two names now mentioned were Pabitra Singh and Lulumber Singh. These two princes were detained for a time at Dacca but were allowed to return to Cachar in January 1853 and settled at Barkhola. On the other hand, Debendra Singh, his three sons (Heemabdoh, Lookanko and Chakockumbak) and Shekar Singh (son of Nur Singh) were removed to Dacca.[112] Pabitra and Lulumber had promised to maintain good conduct and settle down in Cachar like other Manipuris. But they could hardly keep their commitment and the reports received by the administration showed their involvement in the disturbances. On enquiry, it was found that Pabitra was at Barkhola but the whereabouts of Lulumber were not known. Nawal Singh was also wanted by the Superintendent but he was missing from Cachar.[113] He was a *Guru* of the Manipuris and lived on charity and constantly moved among the Manipuris settled in Cachar and Sylhet. The Manipuris were exceedingly close among themselves, and as a spiritual leader Nawal had the additional privilege of making private arrangements with the people without leaving any possibility for the Government officers to detect them.[114]

As the repeated warnings on the part of the Government

had failed to impress the Princes, Captain McCullock proposed in November 1851 that in the event of any attempt being made to attack Manipur by the Manipuri Princes in Cachar the Cachar authorities should send on troops after the party into the Manipur territory with a view to following it up to dispersing and with instructions for them to go on till they received orders from the Political Agent of Manipur.[115] But the Superintendent of Cachar observed that should any armed persons assemble in Cachar for illegal purposes he would be bound to apprehend and punish them, but the question of sending troops to a foreign territory to resist and punish the aggressors was beyond his jurisdiction. Verner, therefore, requested the Political Agent to ascertain from the Government of India whether he would be authorised to acts of this nature.[116] But, after all, the problem of these Princes was not only a threat to the Government of Manipur but also a real nuisance for Cachar. There were a large number of them in Cachar, most of whom subsisted on the charity of their countrymen settled in Cachar. They all nourished their utopian claim to the throne of Manipur and as soon as a few of their countrymen in Cachar promised to follow them they started off in the hope of being joined by a considerable section in Manipur where the attitude of the people was most uncertain and the Raja could put but little dependence on his own troops when engaged against some Manipuris. Verner felt that it would be impossible for the Cachar authorities to prevent these princes from leaving Cachar at their will as they did not form parties to go in bodies but would agree among themselves in the most secret and quiet manner and leave their homes at night and before morning and cross the frontier through jungles without affording any scope for suspecting their conduct. 'No person would be a security for a Munnypoorie prince, for their words and oaths are nothing to them, and indeed no dependence can be placed on any Munnypoorie.' The Raja of Manipur had many people and spies of his own in Cachar who must know everything that was going on, but they dared not tell him for the reason that were one of the princes successful in obtaining the *Gadi* they and their families in Manipur would be ruined. The Cachar authorities had made it known to all the princes and Manipuris in Cachar that every person who joined, aided or

assisted in any attack against the Raja of Manipur would be punished and they also posted a police force at Lakhipur to detect and
prevent the supplies of arms and ammunition or armed persons
from passing towards Manipur by land or water, but had no
means of preventing people passing through the jungles. Verner
also felt that these princes would never be deterred from
making similar attacks till a sufficient number of British troops
were posted in Manipur to assist and maintain the Raja in his
present position and only then the princes would realise the
futility and hopelessness of their attacks and would automatically desist from these adventurous endeavours. Accordingly
he suggested to the Government of India that some two or
three hundered men from the Sylhet Light Infantry Battalion
be posted in Manipur under the supervision of the Political
Agent.[117] As a matter of fact, he had made a similar suggestion
in November 1850 that two or three companies of the British
troops be kept in Manipur to protect the Raja[118] and was eventually even more convinced that in order to secure the peace of
Cachar and also that of Manipur the adoption of some measures of this kind was absolutely necessary.[119]

Before anything, on 24 November 1852, the *Rajkumars* made
the most concerted attack upon Manipur with a large band of
followers. In the encounter that followed Nawal Singh and his
son, Lulumber and his two sons, Kanai Singh and some others
were arrested by the sepoys in Manipur, while there were also
some casualties.[120] The invaders were pursued by the British
troops from Cachar and seven persons* were rounded up by
them and kept in Silchar Jail.[121] In pursuance of the instructions
of the Government of India, Verner wrote to the Political
Agent of Manipur, on 15 January 1853 that these prisoners
including those arrested in Manipur be made over to the Raja
of Manipur 'under a strict guarantee from him that their lives
shall be spared, and that they shall be treated as is consistent
with the usages of the civilised nations.' Captain McCullock
was requested to obtain from the Raja the requisite guarantee,
signed and sealed by him, and then make over the same to the
Superintendent of Cachar in original before delivering the

---

*They were Birjeet Singh, Mego Singh, Shubal Singh, Govind Singh,
Chaitan Singh, Chamo Singh and Khalendra Singh.

prisoners. He was also requested to suggest a place for the repatriation of the prisoners and to advice whether any of them were to have irons put on them before leaving Silchar. Verner at the same time desired the whole proceedings to be done in as public a manner as possible so that the Manipuris in Cachar might feel that the attacks of this kind were not to be made with impunity but that all who joined in them would be subjected to punishment and this might deter others from indulging in such offensives in future.[122] On the other hand, Ensign Stewart, Commander of the troops in Cachar, was requested by the Suprintendent to increase the strength of the jail guards till the delivery of these detenues to prevent the possibility of their escaping.[123] Anyway, the prisoners having been repatriated in due course, the problem of the Manipuri Princes in Cachar gradually subsided. The Manipur Government had posted one Purna Singh Dewan at Lakhipur, while at Silchar there was a *Vakeel*, Raj Kishor Samrah, under whom a number of spies were engaged in collecting information about conspiracies against the Manipur *Raj*.[124] Although McCullock reported to the Superintendent, on 27 January, of certain rumours in Manipur that one Bachun Singh from Cachar was preparing to attack Manipur, the authorities in Cachar had no knowledge of any one of the same name. However, enquiries were made through the Cachar Police in Manipur and Naga villages without being able to ascertain anything regarding the truth in the rumour. The Superintendent also had a dialogue with the *Dewan* and *Vakeel* of the Manipur Government in Cachar but they too failed to gather any information.[125]

In February 1861, the Civil Finance Commission had recommended that the Political Agency in Manipur be abolished and, accordingly, the Government of Bengal desired that the Superintendent of Cachar should act as the Political Agent of Manipur in addition to his normal duties. But it would be a huge affair for the Superintendent who was already overburdened with the multifarious duties in the Non-Regulated Province. On the other hand, Captain McCullock strongly advocated the importance of the Agency and the Raja of Manipur also requested the British Government for the continuation of the same. Ultimately, the Government of India decided to maintain the Agency on the ground of the Chiefs being cruel, oppressive and weak and the country being far from Cachar and difficult of access.[126] However, the death of Chandrakirti in 1886 ushered in another era of political restlessness in Manipur leading to plots and assassinations and with logical repercussions in Cachar. Surachandra, the eldest son of Chandrakirti, ascended the throne, and a rival claimant who tried to sieze the throne was defeated by the Military Police from Cachar and deported to Hazaribagh.[127] But, in 1890, Angou, Thangal, Jilliangamba and Tikendrajit led a forceful revolt against him. As a result, Surachandra abdicated in favour of his second brother Kulachandra and fled to Cachar wherefrom he submitted a memorial to the Governor General of India for his restoration to the throne. The memorial was rejected by the Government and it was ordered that Kulachandra be recognised as the Maharaja of Manipur and Tikendrajit be banished from the state. To execute this order, J.W. Quinton, Chief Commissioner of Assam proceeded to Manipur with an escort party. In the process, the British troops committed certain highhandedness and the Manipuris attacked the residency and rounded up Quinton, Colonel Skene and other officers, while Grimwood the Political Agent, was killed on the spot. The four British officers, including the Chief Commissioner, were tried by the Manipur Court according to local law, sentenced to death and executed by the Public executioner. The attack on the residency was dragged on, so the defenders retreated to Cachar. The British Government then declared war against Manipur and sent three columns from Cachar, Kohima and Burma respectively which occupied Manipur. The rebel chiefs were tried according to the Indian Penal Code. Tikendrajit, Thangal and some others were sentenced to death, while Kulachandra, Angou and others were transported for life. Subsequently, Manipur was regranted to Chura Chandra, a minor scion of a collateral line, and Major Maxwell was appointed as the Political Agent and Superintendent. The Superintendency came to an end in 1907 and Chura Chandra was formally installed on the throne. The Manipur *Darbar*, headed by a member of the Indian Civil Service as President, was the highest court in the state but the sentences exceeding rigorous imprisonment for five years required the confirmation of the Governor of Assam, while the President was responsible for the administration of the hill tribes living within the state and for all matters of revenue and finance. This arrangement with partial modifications from time to time continued till the end of the British Rule in India in 1947.[128] The chaotic conditions in Manipur were gradually obliterated and the more Manipur enjoyed peace the better it was for Cachar.

To guard the frontier from the inroads of the hill tribes certain active measures were undertaken by the authorities. The Cachar Levy, organised in 1830, was converted into the Cachar Frontier Police and held responsible for the defence of the whole north-east frontier. Its outposts ran along the foot of the Naga Hills up the Dhansiri Valley and through the North Cachar Hills into Cachar where they linked up again with the posts guarding the Lushai borders. This Force rendered invaluable services in repelling the repeated raids and plunders of the Lushais and the Nagas, and in suppressing the onslaughts of the Manipuri Princes. During the operations against the Lushais in 1871, Garoes in 1872 and the Nagas in 1879 the Cachar Frontier Policemen played a significant role. The Eastern Bengal Frontier Regulation of 1873 and the Inner Line Regulation of 1872 were extended to South Cachar in August 1875. The object of this measure was to restrict the dealings of the Europeans and other British subjects with the hill tribes in the frontier and no person was since then allowed to cross the inner line without permission. The line started from the Chatta-chura peak in Hailakandi and passing through Jalnachara, Barunchara, Newarband, Dwarband and Maniarkhal ended at the Moinadar outpost on the bank of Barak.[129] In 1881 the strength of the Frontier Police was increased to a great extent and was given the entire charge of the border posts. Two years later, for the improvement of their efficiency, the Cachar Frontier Police was broken up and reconstituted into battalions of Military Police whose commandants were borrowed from the regular army.[130] A complete battallion of this Military Police was stationed in Cachar and a large portion of the battalion was detailed on outpost duty. In 1888, there were three posts in North Cachar, two in the foot-hills and six along the eastern and southern frontiers of Cachar stretching from Jirighat to Jalnachara. The Cachar Military Police Battalion was highly appreciated by the frontier authorities for their discipline and efficiency, and had taken the most active part in the Lushai hills expedition of 1889-90, Manipur expedition of 1891 and Lushai Hills expedition of 1892.[131] Subsequently, the Military Police Battalions were rechristened as the Assam Rifles which was manned by all and sundry but officered from the Regular army.[132] In addition to the local corps, of the four Regular regiments stationed in Assam one had its headquarters at Silchar; two being at Shillong and one at Dibrigarh. In Cachar the regiment had its cantonments at Maniarkhal, Alinagar and Chargola.[133]

APPENDIX 4

Draft of a letter proposed to be written to Rajah Gumbheer Singh, 8 February 1830

You are sufficiently aware that the claim formerly preferred by you to the elaka of Chundipore was after enquiry disallowed for want of proof, and on the grounds, that supposing the alleged grant to have taken place the conduct of yourself and family to Rajah Govind Chunder had been such, as fully to justify the latter in the resumption of land.

2.   Notwithstanding this decision, however, considering it desirable that you should have a Magazine on this side of the hills for the reception of Military stores in transit to Munnipore, I prevailed with difficulty, upon Govind Chunder to cede to Government a tract of land containing 50 plough gates of Chundipore, which with the sanction of Govt. I assigned to you for the above purpose and no other.

3.   Now it would appear from the representation of Govind Chunder, the reports of our Vakil, and the accompanying copy of an order directed to your head-man at Chundipore that your people disregard the limit fixed by the Vakil, that they commit violence upon the natives of the country, and that by your order, a copy of which is annexed, they interrupt the navigation of the River and levy duties from boats, upon pretext of the commodities being produced in your country, a plea whether well or ill-founded cannot in the least degree justify such a demand.

4.   Now therefore I write to intimate you that such pro-

ceedings were never contemplated by the Government when it agreed to put you in possession of the land ceded by Rajah Govind Chunder, and that it is quite impossible that you should permit the continuance of conduct so injurious to the interests of that belief, under which circumstances, if it is your desire to retain a Magazine in Cachar, it can only be done on the following conditions.

1st. That your people should confine themselves implicity to the limits of the 50 plough gates of land pointed out by the Vakeel who will determine any dispute that may arise on this head.

2nd. That disputes arising amongst Munnipooree subjects within those limits, may be settled by the head person appointed by you, but that whenever one of the parties concerned may be a native of Cachar the case will be tried in Rajah Govind Chunder's court.

3rdly. That all offenders and defaulters retiring to Chunderpoure must be delivered upon the requisition of the Vakeel within two puhurs, and that they may otherwise be searched for and taken away by Rajah Govind Chunder.

4thly. That all interference with boats, navigating the river be discontinued, upon whatever pretext it may have been exercised, and that all persons so offending be liable to trial and punishment by the Rajah of Cachar.

5thly. That if the above conditions are not implicity observed, it will be necessary for the Munniporee settlers to withdraw altogether from Cachar, when an arrangement will be made in concert with Rajah Govind Chunder for transporting all military stores to the councy (sic) of his country where you can adopt measures for their reception.

(Sd.) D. SCOT
Agent to the Governor General
North East Frontier

CHAPTER VI

Consolidation

The creation of the Chief Commissionership of Assam, in 1874, ushered in a new era in the history of north-eastern India. By a proclamation issued by the Government of India, on 6 February 1874 the new province emerged with the districts of Cachar, Goalpara, Kamrup, Darrang, Nowgong, Sibsagar, Lakhimpur, Garo Hills, Khasi-Jaintia Hills and Naga Hills. On 12 September 1874 the district of Sylhet and on 1 April 1898 Lushai Hills were added to Assam. On 16 October 1905, following the Partition of Bengal, the Province of Eastern Bengal and Assam was created and placed under a Lieutenant Governor, with headquarters at Dacca. But the partition of Bengal was strongly resented by the Bengalees, leading to the historic *Swadeshi Movement*. The Government was ultimately compelled to withdraw the partition in 1911 and the two wings of Bengal were re-united. As a result, Assam, including Sylhet, Cachar and Goalpara, was again placed under a Chief Commissioner, at Shillong. In 1921, Assam was upgraded to the status of a Governor's Province.

Cachar thus became a part of Assam. In fact, Surma Valley being a natural continuation of Bengal plains and peopled by the Bengalees, it was logical that Cachar and Sylhet should continue as parts of Bengal. Similar was the case with Goalpara which was previously included in the Rangpur district but, in 1822, was converted into the Commissionership of North-East Rangpur to meet the Garo depredations.[1] The creation of the Chief Commissionership of Assam in 1874 had thus resulted in the first partition of Bengal. The separation of Assam, Cachar, hill areas and the adjacent districts from Bengal was suggested by Sir John Lawrence, the Governor-General of India (1864-69), in 1868, for administrative convenience.[2] As a matter of fact, the Chief Commissionership of Assam was created in 1874 for strategic reasons. But the transfer of Cachar and Sylhet was on economic considerations.[3] In 1873 the public opinion in Sylhet had strongly condemned the separation from Bengal and a memorial was submitted to the Governor-General opposing the transfer of the district to Assam.[4] However, the Government of India assured the people of full justice,[5] and the prospect of jobs in the Province, which the educationally advanced people of Sylhet could naturally expect. It was also declared that the form of administration in Sylhet will not be affected by the attachment of the district to Assam.[6]

Nevertheless, the normal rules and regulations of the Government were gradually introduced in Cachar [7] Formerly, like North-East Rangpur, Assam, Chotanagpur and Darjeeling, it was a Non-Regulated Province. As already mentioned, since its annexation in 1832, Cachar was placed under the Agent to the Governor-General, North-East Frontier, whose jurisdiction extended over Assam, Cachar, Manipur, Jayantia, Kuch Behar and other independent states in this frontier.[8] The Agent had, in the Non-Regulated Provinces, under him Principal Assistants, in charge of the districts, who, were assisted by Junior Assistants and Sub-Assistants.[9] In Cachar, the administration was headed by a Superintendent who, like Principal Assistant, in addition to the normal duties of a Collector of Bengal, had the functions of a Civil Judge, Magistrate, Police Officer, an Executive Engineer, Education Officer and also of the Post Master.[10] It was, of course, necessary to arm the Superintendent with such wide powers in view of the manifold problems of the Province, internal and external, and also its tradition. There were rival claimants to the Raj who engineered internal chaos and perpetrated crisis, while the frontier tribes, through plundering raids and incursions, made the lives of the inhabitants miserable. The province being educationally backward and used to the rule of medieval Chieftains, the Regulations of the Government were not found workable. The Superintendent had to be ready at all times either to proceed to the spot to initiate police enquiries or to conduct military expeditions against refractory tribes. He had, therefore, to be a military officer in civil employment and act in discretion.

When Cachar passed under the Commissioner of Dacca, in 1836, many of the departments had common heads for Cachar and Sylhet, viz., Superintendent of Police, *Abkaree* Superintendent, Sessions Judge etc. Also, the services of the Sylhet Light Infantry could be called at any time for actions against the predatory tribes. By Act V of 1835, Cachar was placed under the Control of the Board of Revenue for Lower Bengal in revenue matters. But although tagged with Sylhet in the same Division, in Cachar the Non-Regulated System was not abolished till 1921. As elsewhere in India, the high offices in the beginning were the monopoly of the Europeans. Although the Charter Act of 1833 had declared that 'no native of India was to be debarred from holding any office by reason of his religion, place of birth, descent and colour' until 1858, no Indian was appointed to the covenanted posts.[11] In Cachar, however, from the very beginning natives were offered some responsible uncovenanted posts. The 'country' had an unique tradition of *Khel-Raj* and the foreigners were unlikely to understand its ethic, customs and usages. Even the Rajas of Cachar, who ruled over the Valley for three hundred years prior to British Rule, did not dare to interfere with the local administration and they further tightened the hands of the *Mukhtars* with more administrative and judicial powers. The British Government also realised the situation and, as a result, confirmed the *Mukhtar System* and put Bengalee Officers to deal with the public. In addition to the *Tahsildar Munsiffs* and the Judges of the *Panchayat Courts*, one Goluk Chandra Bol was appointed in 1841, as the Deputy Collector.[12] In 1856, Dr. S.M. Sarkar, Assistant Surgeon of the Cachar Civil Hospital, was appointed as Assistant Superintendent in addition to his medical duties, at an extra allowance of Rs. 200 per month.[13] The Assistant Superintendent, in his civil capacity, exercised the powers of the Assistant Collector, under Regulation VIII of 1831, and of an Assistant Magistrate under Regulation III of 1821.[14] Gradually, however, with the attainment of local experience the European Officers were put in these responsible positions, but

Babu Goluk Chandra and Dr. Sarkar enjoyed the offices till their retirement. Thus in 1858, E.M. Reily was appointed as the Deputy Collector,[15] but on 24 March 1859, he was obliged to resign due to ill health,[16] and Dr. S.M. Sarkar was put in charge of the Treasury as Deputy Collector.[17] Following the retirement of Dr. Sarkar, on 15 February 1860, Dr. Clement Sconee was appointed as the Assistant Surgeon and also put in charge of the Treasury, while Lieutenant J.F. Sharer was posted as the Assistant Superintendent and held the charge of the Deputy Collector.[18] But on 4 December 1862, Sharer took over the charge of the Treasury as well.[19] In 1861, the Office of the Superintendent, like Principal Assistants in Assam was redesignated to be the Deputy Commissioner and the Assistant Superintendent came to be known as the Assistant Commission· er. In 1864, all Officers below the rank of the Judicial Commissioner then attached to the Non-Regulated Provinces of Bengal, viz. Assam, Chotanagpur, Darjeeling and Cachar, were formed into one amalgamated service by an executive order of the Government of Bengal. But two years after, in 1866, the Government of India revised the Uncovenanted Judicial Service and amalgamated it with that of Bengal.[20] In revenue matters, in 1864, the Deputy Commissioner was vested with the powers of a Collector and Assistant and Extra-Assistant Commissioners with those of a Deputy Collector, but only for the purpose of Rent Law.* In 1859, the Civil Procedure Code and in 1862, Criminal Procedure Code were introduced in Cachar. Since 1867, the District Judge of Sylhet used to stay in Silchar for a certain specified period to try the Sessions cases, and in 1872, the Deputy Commissioner of Cachar was vested with the powers of a District Judge and District Magistrate as provided in the Codes of Procedure.[21] Similarly, the Limitation Act (1859), Stamp Act (1860), Penal Code (1860) and Police Act (1861) came into force in Cachar. Gradually the judicial business of the district increased and the Assistant Commissioner was vested with the powers of a Munsiff. These arrangements continued, with minor changes, till the creation of the Chief Commissionership of Assam. In 1875, the Government of India, in supersession of all previous orders, vested the Judicial Commis-

---

*Act X of 1859.

sioner of Assam, *ex-officio*, with the powers of a District Judge and the Deputy Commissioners were vested with the powers of a subordinate Judge. In Cachar, however, the Deputy Commissioner was vested, *ex-officio*, with powers of the Judicial Commissioner. The Assistant Commissioner at the *Sadar* station had the powers of the Subordinate Judge, while the Sub-Divisional Officer of Hailakandi was a Munsiff.[22]

Needless to say, the British Government of India was an organised bureaucracy run by a hierarchy of officials. The 'Dominion of India' was divided into provinces, provinces into divisions, divisions into districts, and the districts into Sub-divisions and *thanas*. The Province of Assam, headed first by a Chief Commissioner and then Governor, had three divisions, each under a Commissioner, of which Surma Valley Division consisted of Cachar and Sylhet. The Commissioner of Surma Valley, with headquarters at Silchar, supervised the general affairs of the division and had both appellate and original jurisdictions, while the Deputy Commissioner of Cachar from Silchar was in general charge of the district. For the purpose of general administration, Cachar was divided into three Sub-divisions, viz. Silchar, Hailakandi and Haflong. Silchar was the *Sadar* Sub-Division and the seat of all district offices. On 1 June 1869, Hailakandi Sub-division was created and placed under an Assistant Magistrate. The North Cachar Hills were formed into a sub-division in 1880, under a Deputy Superintendent of Police, with headquarters at Gunjong but in 1898 was shifted to Haflong. Silchar was under the immediate charge of the Deputy Commissioner. In addition to the Sadar Sub-Divisional Officer, he was aided by three Subordinate Magistrates and a Sub-Deputy Collector. In Hailakandi the Sub-Divisional Officer was of the rank of an Assistant Magistrate and had a Sub-Deputy Collector under him. The Sub-Divisional Officer in Haflong had a distinct status, because some special rules and regulations for the administration of the tribal areas were in force. He also exercised some police and judicial powers more directly than the Officers in charge of other sub-divisions.[23]

In the matter of Judicial administration, the Deputy Commissioner was the District Magistrate and District Civil Judge. The Assistant Commissioner at Silchar was Subordinate Judge and the Sub-Divisional Officer of Hailakandi had the powers of a Munsiff. In criminal cases, appeals were made to the Deputy Commissioner from the orders passed by the Magistrates of the second and third class, and from the orders of the first class Magistrate to the Sessions Judge at Sylhet. The crime map of the Cachar plains was never alarming, but the people being conscious of their rights sought intervention of the state in the event of any offence. The majority of the offences were either against property or against person, both of which had been declared by the Penal Code as against the State. The worst offences were theft and house tresspass, reported from the rural areas. Some Stipendary and Honorary Magistrates were appointed to try minor cases with their local experience. In 1902, there were 9 Stipendary and 2 Honorary Magistrates in Silchar and Hailakandi Sub-divisions.[24] The Deputy Commissioner was vested with special powers by virtue of Sections 30 and 34 of the Indian Penal Code, and was authorised to impose sentences upto 7 years' rigorous imprisonment. In civil cases, the appeals from the Munsiffs' Courts were heard by the Subordinate judge at Silchar. The District Civil Judge heard a certain category of original cases as well as appeals. In all cases, the appeals from the Judges would go to the High Court of Judicature at Calcutta and in turn to the Privy Council at London.

Special rules were in force for the administration of justice in North Cachar Hills. Like other hill districts, the normal rules and regulations were not extended there in consideration of the geographical backwardness of the area and traditions, customs and usages of the people. The inhabitants were not found suited for the elaborate legal procedures laid down in the various Codes and several other enactments of the kind. They had to be governed in a simpler and more personal manner than those of the more advanced plains districts.[25] Therefore, the Scheduled Districts Act of 1874, prescribed a simpler system of civil and criminal justice, while the Frontier Tract Regulation (1880) provided that the operation of unsuitable rules might be barred in all the hill tracts including North Cachar Sub-division. Accordingly, the entire hill tract was excluded from the operation of the enactments relating to criminal procedure, stamp, court fees, registration and transfer of property, while the Civil Procedure Code was never extended to the hills. The jurisdiction of the High Court was barred except in criminal cases against European-British subjects. The Deputy Commissioner was empowered to pass sentences of death, transportation and imprisonment for 14 years. Sentences of death, transportation and imprisonment for 7 years and upwards, however, required the confirmation of the Chief Commissioner. No appeal would lie as a matter of right from any sentence of the Deputy Commissioner of less than three years imprisonment. The petty cases, both civil and criminal, were dealt with by village tribunals, presided over by the headmen chosen by the people themselves, whose procedure was free from all legal technicalities.[26] The Sub-Divisional Officer was the Chief Appellate authority in such civil and criminal cases. In 1930, the Governor of Assam, under Section 6 of the Scheduled Districts Act (1874), ordered that no Pleader should be allowed to appear in any case except in the courts of the Deputy Commissioner and Sub-Divisional Officer, and only with the Deputy Commissioner's permission. The pleader included *Mukhtar* or any professional agent recognised by the court.[27] Naturally, the agents were not allowed to practise in the village tribunals. On 25 March 1937, the Governor prescribed revised rules for the administration of Justice and Police in the North Cachar Hills Sub-division.[28] The administration of the Sub-division was vested in the Governor of Assam, Deputy Commissioner of Cachar, and Sub-Divisional Officer of Haflong, the Assistants to the Deputy Commissioner and the Village authorities. The Deputy Commissioner was empowered to nominate and appoint the village authorities, subject to the confirmation of the Governor of Assam, and to assign them their respective functions and define the local jurisdiction. The ordinary duties of police in respect to crime would be discharged by the village. They would arrest all criminals and maintain peace and order within their respective limits. Such authorities were deemed to be Police Officers for the purpose of Section 26 of the Indian Evidence Act and Section 162 of the Code of Criminal Procedure.

On the other hand, the civil police continued to be under the charge of an Assistant Superintendent of Police till the 1920s, when a Superintendent of Police for Cachar was appointed. Previously, the Superintendent of Police in Sylhet exercised his jurisdiction in respect of Cachar as well. Towards

the close of the last century, the strength of the police establishment in the district consisted of 1 Assistant Superintendent,
1 District Superintendent, 1 Inspector, 24 Sub-Inspectors and
210 Constables. But the police-work of the district having
gradually increased, the police forces were thoroughly augmented during the early decades of this century. To maintain law
and order and to protect the lives and properties of the people,
the police officials played a vital role towards the consolidation
of the British rule in Cachar. With red turban and colourful
costume, they could easily make the people feel the existence of
the Government and to submit to the Rule of Law. For the
purpose of Police administration, the district was divided into
a number of units, called *thana*. In Silchar, there were three
thanas, viz., Silchar, Lakhipur and Katigorah and two *Sub-thanas*
at Barkhola and Sonai. In Hailakandi, there was only one
thana at the headquarter and a *Sub-thana* at Katlichara. In
North Cachar, the chiefs were responsible for the police duties
within their respective jurisdiction, while a special class of
police, called Hill Police, were stationed in Haflong and at the
disposal of the Sub-Divisional Officer. In the plains, the *thana*
was in charge of a *Darogah*, of the rank of Sub-Inspector, who
was empowered to arrest suspected persons, to detain them and
even to hold preliminary trials before sending them to the headquarters. He was aided in his duties by a contingent of policemen, and had a regular establishment. But as in other districts
of Bengal,* the foundation of the police system in Cachar was
the village *Chaukidars* who reported all serious crimes and any
probability of the breach of peace in his area to the Police Station. Under this system, a *Chaukidar* had 64 houses under his
care and collected one rupee per month as his remuneration. Each house paid one pice a month and 3 annas a year. There
were 525 such *Chaukidars* in Cachar in 1858, and Rs. 3900 were
annually paid towards them by the villagers. The pay received by a *Chaukidar* was ridiculously low and precluded any idea
of the employees making it a serious profession. A *Chaukidar*
was hardly considered a public servant and did nothing more
than reporting heinous crimes. R. Stewart, the Superintendent

---

* There was no *Choukidari* System in Assam Valley districts where the
patgiris and the *mouzadars* were expected to assist the *Darogah* in the
detection and apprehension of the criminals.

of Cachar, therefore, considered that the pay of a *Chaukidar* should not be less than four rupees a month to enable him to maintain his livelihood and to secure his full time services.[29] The Superintendent offered a plan for placing the Cachar Rural Police upon a regular footing. He proposed that the pay of the *Chaukidar* be charged upon the land revenue at an enhanced rate of Rs. 6-4-0 per cent annually. A *Chaukidar* would have a particular beat assigned to him and receive his remuneration through the Superintendent. This would bind them to their duties and improve their own condition. For the town of Silchar and its suburb to the extent of 10 square miles, which required more careful watch, he recommended the levy of a tax upon the estimated value of the land, house and other property of an inhabitant to be annually fixed by the Superintendent. This area, he believed would require ten *Chaukidars* and Rs. 500 could be equitably levied. These recommendations of the Superintendent was favourably considered by the Government of Bengal and the *Chaukidari* System contributed considerably to the maintenance of law and order in the Cachar Valley.[30]

In addition to the regular police and rural police, a reserve of men was kept up at the district and sub-divisional headquarters, who were armed with smooth bore martinis and were employed on guard and escort duties. Up-countrymen, Nepalese and the local tribals were recruited to this contingent. The civil policemen were also armed with various weapons and the constables were required to undergo annual course of musketry. There was also a Volunteer Corps in Cachar. This was introduced in 1883 with a strength of 80 members, but was subsequently amalgamated with its counterpart in Sylhet to form the Surma Valley Light Horse. This corps rendered admirable services in the maintenance of law and order, in addition to their normal duties during famine, inundation and other calamities.[31] There was a Jail at Silchar and Magistrate's lockups at Hailakandi and Haflong. But the accommodation in the Jail was insufficient and the convicts who were sentenced to imprisonment for more than one year were transferred to the Central Jail at Sylhet. A Jailor was in charge of the Silchar Jail and guards were furnished by the Military Police.[32]

It was highly expedient for the British authorities to inspire

the people of Cachar with the confidence that the tribal raids
in the plains have come to an end and that there would be no
repetition of the Burmese menace. At the same time, to meet
any local insurrection and to explore its resources, no part of
the district could be left beyond the normal reach of the
administrators. All these needed a sound means of communication throughout the district. Strategic reasons, further
demanded the construction of strong out-posts along the
frontiers, which were to be linked up with the *Sadar* Station
and with one another. Although Cachar was found 'notorious
for communication' by Captain Verelst in 1763, who failed to
find a way from Khaspur to Manipur, the 'country' was
never cut off from the rest of the world. The pre-British
history of the tract, discussed in the first two chapters, reveals a
regular intercourse with the adjacent principalities. The
Assamese Chronicles refer to routes between Khaspur and
Assam through which repeated expeditions were despatched by
the Ahoms against Cachar.[33] As early in 1711, two Ahom
envoys proceeded by boat from Namdang to Dimarua and
then to Khaspur by land, wherefrom they went to Tripura.[34]
There was a major road in Cachar which originated from
Khaspur and connected the important places like Udharband,
Dalu, Katigorah, Badarpur, Jainanagar, Burhibail, Ganirgram
and Haritikar.[35] This was probably constructed during the
time of Raja Krishnachandra Narayana and is even now known
as *Rajar Sarak*. Lieutenant Pemberton, in his report prepared
in 1835, referred to several routes to and from Cachar.[35]
There were three such direct routes between Cachar and
Manipur; one from Banskandi in Cachar *via* Aquee to
Jainanagar in Manipur, another from Banskandi *via* Kala Naga
territory to Sanuyachil in Manipur, and the third from Jirighat
to Imphal. The total distance from Banskandi to Sanuyachilghat
was 203 miles, while a route from Sanuyachilghat by the
Ninghee and Irrawadi rivers to Ava had a distance of 300
miles.[36] Thus, Cachar had a line of communication with
Burma through Manipur and thence with China and other
South-East Asian countries. Pemberton also referred to a
route from Bikrampur pass in Cachar to Raha *chouki* in Assam.
The first part of the route extended from Katigorah to Dawsun
pass and then through the rocky bed of Jatinga descended on

the valley of Kapili and Jamuna rivers, and had a total distance of 150 miles.[37]   He also referred to a direct road between Sylhet and Cachar.[38]   Starting from Sylhet towards the east, *via* Karimganj and Badarpur, this road extended upto Silchar.   It served as the most vital line of communication for Cachar, for it connected the district with the rest of India through Sylhet.   It had also some important branches; one from Hatimganj to Dacadakshin, another from Kanaibazar to Jaiantiapur, a third from Karimganj to Latu and then to South Sylhet, and another from Karimganj to Durlavchara. There was a direct road from Sylhet to Jalalpur.   Jaintiapur had a traditional route with Raha, while the Sylhet-Gauhati Road, constructed in 1831, *via* Cherapunji, connected Surma Valley more intimately with Assam.   All these roads were either constructed or improved by the British Government in the nineteenth century.

Nevertheless, the road system in Cachar Valley was extremely backward and seriously handicapped material development and administrative efficiency. A sketch map prepared in 1862 shows twenty-five roads in Cachar.[39]   The first was a *Kutcha* road, of embankment earthwork, constructed in 1860, between Silchar and Banskandi, with *pucca* bridges or wooden platform over masonry pillars with the exception of Barak and Badri rivers which were covered by ferries.   The second was a continuation of the Banskandi road to Lakhipur and then to Manipur.   It was a *kutcha* road of embanked earthwork in the plains and scarped on the side of the hills, as it passed through the mountainous hill tracts, and was unbridged, but kept in good order by the Political Agency of Manipur.   The old circuitous road to Sylhet was partially bridged, while the old Banskandi Road could no longer be used.   A proposed short-cut to Sylhet was constructed upto Hathia where it temporarily joined and then ran parallel with the old Sylhet Road.   This part of the old road was also partially bridged, but was in bad repair.   Another proposed short-cut to Sylhet from Jainagar was surveyed, laid down and in use, but in no way constructed.   An old line towards Karimganj was under use, without any improvement. The section of the old circuitous road, which was proposed to be merged with the new Sylhet Road, was in wretched repair, unbridged and hardly traceable. The tenth was a road from the factory of M/s. Tyod & Co. at Silchar, which joined the Sylhet Road beyond Tarapur and was constructed at the expense of the Company. A bridled path from *Thana* compound at Hailakandi connecting the Assam Co.'s factories at Annugar and Robertabad and Chandi Company's factories at Sonai and Chupara joined the new Sylhet Road. Another road from Panchgoan to Luckinagar, all along the Valley of Hailakandi, was surveyed and laid down. There were seven *kutcha* roads from the tea factories of Dallidur, Chandipur, Ballikandi, Damanipur, Kanchanpur, Kachula and Banglanagar, joining the Panchgoan-Luckinagar Road. The Silchar-Barkhola Road, a high-way to North Cachar, was *kutcha* and unbridged. A road from the Valley of Madhura to Durgapur was in general use but not constructed. Similar was the Silchar-Sonaimukh Road. The Chatla Road, from Silchar to Dargakuna, constructed at the expense of the tea planters, was the only *pucca* and fully bridged road, while the more important Panchgoan-Badarpur road was in a deplorable condition. This shows how ridiculous was the road system in Cachar.

As a matter of fact, the management of the roads was entirely in the hands of the Magistrate who was preoccupied with the judicial and administrative problems of the district and could hardly spare time for the improvement of the lines of communication. Accordingly, in 1864, the Cachar District Road Committee was constituted with the Deputy Commissioner as the Chairman and the Civil Surgeon, Sub-Divisional Officer of Hailakandi and seven European civilians, mainly tea planters, as members.[40] In 1872, at the recommendation[41] of O.G.R. McWilliam, Deputy Commissioner of Cachar, Rai Bahadur Haricharan Roy and Babu Baikunta Chandra Gupta, 'two local Bengalee gentlemen of intelligence and position,' were included as members of the Committee.[42] This Committee was charged with the administration of the funds which might be available for expenditure on road and communication in the district and the general supervision of the works executed out of the funds.[43]

The Local Boards, constituted in 1881, were entrusted with the maintenance of the roads within their respective jurisdiction, while the Public Works Department was entrusted with the

maintenance of Provincial Roads and construction and main-
tenance of the large public buildings. The Public Works
Department was in charge of an Executive Engineer who was
assisted by one Assistant and five Subordinate Engineers.[44] A
Ferry Fund Committee, constituted in 1864, with the Deputy
Commissioner Executive Engineer, Civil Surgeon and five
European residents, was responsible for the management of the
ferries and roads connected by ferries and the bridges on them.
The executive establishment consisted of a Superintendent of
Roads, an English Writer and six Overseers, and the revenue
was raised by leasing out the ferries.[45]

All these organisations endeavoured to develop the means
of communication in Cachar. While in 1853, there was only
one major road in Cachar; in 1866 the Ferry Fund Committee
itself had six roads under its control.[46] At the initiative of the
P.W.D., the District Road Committee and other local organisations during the thirty years from 1870, a number of roads were
constructed in the district. The Trunk Road entered Cachar at
Badarpur, fifty miles from Sylhet, and crossed the Manipur
Frontier at Jirighat, forty miles from Badarpur. This road of
national importance was known as Cachar Trunk Road.
Another important road* from Silchar across *Chatla Haor, via*
Dwarband and Somaikuna, ran to Hailakandi. Worthy to be described as the heart-line of Cachar, this Silchar-Hailakandi Road
was divided a little to the north of Hailakandi, into two branches, one joining the Trunk Road near Badarpur and the other
extending to Salchapra Railway Station. The Dwarband-Aijal
Road, that joined the Silchar-Hailakandi Road at Dwarband,
provided the line of communication for the Mizo Hills. South
of Hailakandi, two minor lines merged into a bridle path and
joined the Aijal Road in the Cachar-Lushai boundary, while a
number of minor roads and bridle paths, branching east and
west, served the tea gardens in the area. East of Silchar, there
was the Maniarkhal Road and several bridle paths. North of
the Barak, there was the Natwanpur Bridle Path which ran
westward to the Jaintia Parganas. The Damchara, Nemotha,
Siberband and Baladhan Paths had numerous branches. Other
notable roads in the Cachar Plains were the Jatinga Valley

*Formerly referred to as Silchar–Dargakuna Road.

Road, Durganagar Road, Scotpur-Udharband Road and
Jalnachara Road. In North Cachar there was no road worthy
of the name. There was a bridle path from Haflong to
Garampani which extended to Shillong through Jowai. Another
bridle path ran from Ganjong to Doiangmukh and thence to
Garampani. A third bridle path from Maibong went to
Baladhan, while another path from Laishang ran to the border
of the Naga Hills.

The construction of border roads, connecting the out-posts
with each other and with district and sub-divisional headquarters, had received special attention. The important out-
posts along the southern frontier were at Nagdigram, Maniarkhal,
Moinadar, Dwarband, Jafferband, Jalnachara, Chattachura,
Kalashib, Bongkong, Rukni and Rupachara. The stockades
were built at these out-posts, while barracks were constructed at
Bhuban, Bonkong, Kalashib, Bairabi and Chattachura. In
1872, a scheme submitted by the Deputy Commissioner for the
improvement of the border roads was approved by the Government of Bengal. The scheme provided for the construction of
military roads from Nagdigram to Maniarkhal, Maniarkhal to
Moinadar, Dwarband to Noarband, Noarband to Maniarkhal,
Jafferband to Jalnachara, Jalnachara to Chattachura, Kalashib
to Jalnachara, and involved a project of Rs. 27,190.[47] The
District Road Committee was entrusted with the project and the
special fund was placed at the Committee's disposal by the
Government of Bengal.[48] Some of these roads were completed
during the next few years, but most of them were abandoned
due to paucity of funds.

In the thirties of the present century, P.C. Chatterjee,
Chairman, Silchar Local Board, took interest in the development of the roads. In February 1934, a plot of 4 *bighas*, 1
katta and 6 *chattaks* of land was acquired in Lakhipur
pargana for the construction of the Dixa-Jaypur Road.[49] In
the Happy Valley Road, which was constructed in the
twenties, a short diversion was effected in July 1935 in *mouza*
Goassainpur and 3 *kattas* and 3 *chattaks* land was acquired
for the purpose.[50] Same year, 9 *kattas* and 9 *chattaks* land
was acquired in Barakpur *pargana* at Rs. 70-2-0 for the
construction of the Uttar Krishnapur Road.[51]

The heavy rainfall combined with the tenacious character of
the clay had rendered the question of road development in

Cachar a serious problem. Like other East Bengal districts, it had innumerable streams, rivulets and *haors*. During rains the rivers would rise in high spate with extreme rapidity and render the construction of permanent bridges over large streams either impossible or highly expensive. Consequently, the ferries were largely used and there were more than a hundred ferries in the district. These were managed by a committee and auctioned off to the highest bidder. On the other hand, Surma Valley had an unique naval tradition. A number of *Kulangis* and *Panchalis* refer to the use of boats for commercial pursuits. There was a proffessional class, called *Manjhi*, and innumerable boat-songs have enriched Bengalee folk literature. The forests of Cachar were rich with *Jarul* timbers, necessary for boat-building, which were supplied to the other districts of Bengal.[52] Obviously, the country-boats played an important role in the transport business of the district. The all-weather navigable rivers were Amjuri, Badri, Barak, Bohali, Chiri, Dalu, Dhaleswai, Katakhal, Gagra, Jatinga, Jiri, Madhura, Rukni, Salganga and Sonai. The Barak, which passes through the heart of the district and con-fluences with Dhaleswai, Meghna and Padma, facilitated stea-mer service with Calcutta, *via* Narayanganj. The steamers owned by the General Steam and Navigation Company were in use in the route. During the rainy season even big steamers could easily ply upto Silchar, but in winter the water surface would go down and require five days to reach Calcutta. The ports of call for the large steamers in Cachar were Badarpur, Sealtekh, Jatingamukh and Machimpur. In summer the larger steamers could also be used for inland traffic; up the Barak, Madhura, Gagra and Katakhal from Silchar to Lakhipur, Chandighat, Hattichara and Kukichara respectively.

The actual line of communication with the outside was, however, opened with the extension of the Rail-link. The Assam-Bengal Railway covered Silchar in 1899. The rail line entered into Cachar near Badarpur Junction, across Sylhet. A branch line from Badarpur, through the south bank of Barak pushed upto Silchar, past Katakhal, Salchapra and Gagra. The main line crossed the Barak, by a magnificient bridge, 454 yards in length, immediately after Badarpur and then made its way up the Jatinga Valley, through North Cachar Hills, into

Assam.† This 113 miles Badarpur-Lumding Hill Section, with 36 tunnels and 81 bridges was constructed by the Indian Railway Company at a huge expenditure and through difficult tracts.[53]

The extension of road, rail and steamer link not only minimised the problem of communication within Cachar but also brought Calcutta nearer to the people. A steamer from Silchar would require 5 days in winter and 3 days in summer to reach Calcutta. For the passengers, the quickest link was the railway, and by Surma Mail one could reach Calcutta, *via* Chandpur and Narayanganj, within 24 hours. Cachar was also provided with Air-link in the twenties of the present century when the Aerodrome at Kumbirgram was commissioned.

In addition to the roads, the Public Works Department and the Local Boards were entrusted with the construction of buildings both of administrative and public utility. The P.W.D. was responsible for the jail, government offices, schools, hospitals at the district and sub-divisional headquarters and circuit house, Dak Bungalow and Inspection Bungalow on the provincial roads, while the inspection bungalows on the district roads were maintained by the Local Boards. On the Cachar Trunk Road the dak bungalows were at Badarpur, Salchapra and Silchar, and inspection bungalows at Salchapra, Lakhipur, Jirighat and Banskandi. The inspection bungalows were also at Bikrampur and Gumra on the Natwanpur road, at Bakhola on the Jatinga Valley road, Tikalpur on the Durganagar road, Udharband on the Scotpur-Udharband road, Narainpur on the Banimukh road, Lala, Katlichara, Jainanagar and Merogang on the Jalna-chara road, Borojalinga on the Hailakandi road and at Lohar-band and Kangli on the Aijal road. In North Cachar, rest-houses were at Haflong, Gunjong, Derabara, Baga, Karungwa and Garampani on the Haflong-Garampani road and at Gui-long, Laishung and Hangrum on the Baladhan road.

A letter from the Superintendent of Cachar, to the Post Master General, on 8 June 1836,[54] shows that there was no Post Office in Cachar and that the jurisdiction of the Post Office at Sylhet theoretically extended to Cachar. The official packets and letters were carried between Silchar and Sylhet and

†The important stations in the route were Hilara, Bihara, Harangajao, Jatinga, Haflong, Mahur, Maibong, Lanting, Hatikhali, etc.

Silchar and other sub-divisional headquarters and *thanas* in Cachar by some messengers attached to the Superintendent's establishment. However, in 1852, a Post Master for Cachar was appointed,[55] and post offices were established at Hailakandi, Katigorah and Haflong in addition to the Head Post Office at Silchar. In 1861, regular post and telegraph service was introduced in Cachar and 30 post offices were inducted in the district, of which 19 had tele-connection.[56] Between Silchar and Calcutta the mail was served through the Assam-Bengal Railway, while between the head-office and the branches in Cachar there were regular runners. The postal service was made more efficiently available to the people in the present century with the opening of more branches and the expansion of bus-routes in Cachar.

Attempts were also made to extend medical facilities to the people by eradicating malaria, *kalazar*, cholera and diarrhoea which were endemic in Cachar and led to a great loss of human lives every year. Inoculation was introduced soon after British occupation and the people were induced to take to modern medicine in lieu of the traditional herbal drugs. The hospitals and dispensaries were instituted by the Government at Silchar,* Hailakandi, Katigorah, Haflong, Laksmipur, Barkhola and Fenchara. The tea gardens had their medical centres, mostly under Pharmacists. The district was in the medical charge of the Civil Surgeon posted at Silchar, while the hospitals at Hailakandi and Haflong were under the Sub-Divisional Medical Officers who were of the rank of Assistant Surgeons. The jail at Silchar had an attached dispensary under an Assistant Surgeon. The Civil Surgeon supervised all the hospitals and dispensaries in the district. He was in charge of the Vaccination Department and was required to visit the medical centres in the tea estates and report on the death rate. In August 1929, G.D. Walker, Deputy Commissioner of Cachar, had ordered that the dead-bodies in all unnatural cases must be brought to the Police Station before disposal. On the request of the Secretary, Surma Valley Branch of the Indian Tea Association, to exempt the tea gardens from the purview of the

---

* The medical centre at Silchar, opened in 1835, was improved to be a hospital in 1864.

notification, the Deputy Commissioner ordered that such dead bodies need not be sent to the *thana* as the tea gardens had qualified medical officers to certify.[57]

By far, the most significant were the revenue measures of the government which touched the common people in their very means of subsistence and resulted in the steady increase of revenue, thus contrary to the doubts of a section of the British officers regarding the fiscal viability of Cachar. As a matter of fact, the consolidation of the administration of an alien government, with commercial origin, was no wonder primarily concerned with the land and its vitality. Special attention was therefore, given towards the revenue matters which gave a confidence about the benefits that would ultimately accrue. The Deputy Commissioner himself was the Collector, while there were Sub-Deputy Collectors at Silchar, Hailakandi and Katigorah. The Deputy Commissioner was also the Registrar of the district and there was a Special Registrar at Silchar and Rural Sub-Registrars at Hailakandi and Katigorah. For the collection of revenue, the traditional *Mukhtars* were ultimately replaced by *Peadahs*. The radical reforms in land revenue were initiated with the assessment of land, scraping the traditional *Khel* system and grouping all lands into *Parganas** and *mouzas* in the line of Bengal. The Stamp Law was introduced in Cachar in the sixties of the last century, and registration and stamps added to the revenue. Thus in 1903-4 the receipt under stamps amounted to Rs. 66,738 and Cachar occupied second position in the list of districts in Assam, being only next to Sylhet.[58]

The 15 years' settlement made in 1843-44, discussed in an earlier chapter, expired in 1858 following which a twenty years' settlement was made by Captain Stewart in 1859. All cultivated lands were now divided into two classes. The first consisted of the lands easily irrigable and the second of undulating lands. Each of these two classes was again divided according to advantages of situation and other similar circumstances, and assessed at rates varying from Rs. 2 to 3½ per *hal* for first class lands and

* There were 22 *parganas* in Cachar Plains (Silchar and Hailakandi), viz., Udharband, Katigorah, Kalain, Gumra, Chatla, Jainanagar, Jalalpur, Davidsonanbad, Fulbari, Banraj, Barkhola, Barnarpur, Barakpur, Banshikunda, Jatrapur, Rajnagar, Rupaibali, Lakhipur, Leverputa, Saraspur and Sonapur.

from Rs. 1 to 3 for the second class. The area thus assessed was 132,077 acres and the revenue Rs. 92,712. In 1862, there were 7447 estates in Cachar, consisting of 219,673 acres, divided into *mahals*; each containing an average area of 29 acres, 1 rod and 24 poles, and was settled upon 9,473 persons, allotting to each rent payer roughly 3 acres and 33 poles. Beyond these estates were the waste lands.[59]

This settlement was based on the professional survey under Lieutenant Theuiller in 1842 which was brought up-to-date by the local *Amins*. On its expiry in 1879, a fresh survey was undertaken and a settlement affected by Major Body in 1883, for 15 years, upto 31 March 1898. The *tahsils* of Silchar, Hailakandi and Katigorah were each divided into four circles and rates were determined in accordance with the assessment capacity of each circle. The constitution of the circle was on the consideration of the productiveness of the soil, facility of communication, liability to inundation, exposure to the ravages of wild animals and the proximity to dense forests. The rates for the first class were the same for each *tahsil*, but in respect of other circles there was a considerable difference between the *tahsil* rates. The land was divided into four classes, viz. (i) homestead and garden, (ii) paddy land, (iii) tea and (iv) waste land. The rates varied from Rs. 4-12-0 to 8-4-0 per *hal* for homestead, Rs. 3-12-0 to 7-2-0 for cultivation other than tea, Rs. 6 to 7-2-0 for tea and a uniform rate of Re. 1 per *hal* for waste land. The total area settled was 253,728 acres, of which 149,449 acres were cultivated and 104,279 acres were waste. The unsettled area, then reported, was 6,791 acres. A notable feature of this settlement was the introduction of Bengal *bigha* for official use in Cachar. Formerly, the units of measurement current in Cachar were the *hal* (4.817 acres) and *Keyar* (one-twelvth of a *hal*). Now an acre was equivalent to 3.025 *bighas*.

The next settlement was carried out by Rai Bahadur Sarat Chandra Banerjee in 1900 and was preceeded by a professional survey of the whole district by the survey of India.[60] This complete re-survey was necessitated by the fact that the previous survey excluded tea grants and waste lands. The villages were now broken up and grouped into blocks of convenient size and all boundaries were permanently demarcated with stones. The lands were primarily divided into homesteads, riceland, other crop land and waste land. The rice land was divided into four classes and the class of the majority land determined the class of the village. The homesteads were assessed at 13, 11, 8 and 6 annas, rice land at 11, 9, 7 and 5 annas, other crop land at 8, 7, 5 and 4 annas, and waste land at 2, 2, 1 and 1 annas per *bigha* for 1st, 2nd, 3rd and 4th classes respectively. All tea land was assessed at 11 annas a *bigha*, while there was a special rice land rate of 4 annas a *bigha* in certain flood affected villages. The *khels* which were held in large blocks since the time of the Rajas of Cachar, were broken up and the number of estates increased from 11,292 to 61,284. The number of *Mirasdars*, who were land-holders in their own right and paid revenue direct to the government, also increased. The total area resettled was 375,464 acres and the revenue was increased from Rs. 3,05,624 to Rs. 4,51,568. The settlement was for 15 years, to expire on 1 April 1915.

A large proportion of Cachar's territory was evergreen forests of useful timber and bamboo scrub. The low swampy valleys were covered with canes and reeds. The most valuable timbers of the district were *nageswar, gamari, sundi, cham, rata, korta, haris, simul, odal, kathal, haritaki, satri, jarul, agar, chandan*, etc., all of which had great demand in Bengal. Pemberton recorded their regular supply before the British rule. *Jharul* of Cachar, for example, was required in the eastern districts of Bengal for boat-building.[61] The forest industry was highly prospective in Cachar and, therefore, special attention was given from the beginning by the government to the forests which were grouped into government-reserved and unclassed state forests. But due to genuine demand for land in Cachar a part of the reserved forests was thrown open to cultivation. In 1896, the Dhaleswari Reserved Forest, which covered an area of 22,164 acres in Barnarpur Pargana, was deforested, but only 7,000 acres were available for settlement as the rest was unfit for cultivation. In 1902, about 4,000 acres were allotted at the rate of 12 annas an acre for flat and 3 annas an acre for hilly land, with a revenue-free period of three years. In 1903, an area of 3,600 acres of the Barak Reserve, which covered 75 square miles, were made available for settlement, but only 1,300 acres, found fit for cultivation, were allotted at 15 annas an acre after the expiry of revenue-free period of three years.

The same year, 6,728 acres of the Sonai Reserve were deforested and 1,800 acres were immediately settled. About 10,500 acres of the huge Inner Line Reserve, which covered an area of 509 square miles in the south-west corner of the district, were also offered for settlement and 7,000 acres were immediately allotted to cultivators. These two reserves were settled at the rate of Barak Reserve. As a result of these operations about 18,600 acres were available for settlement, of which nearly 13,600 acres were disposed of by 1 April 1902.[62] In 1904, the total area of the reserved forests in Cachar was 807 square miles and of the unclassed forests 711 square miles.[63] The most important reserve forests were Jiri, Katakhal, Barak, Loharband, Lungting-Mupa and Barail. The reserve forests were under the general control of a Forest Officer at Silchar. In unclassed state forests the settlement-holders were allowed to graze their cattle and to remove any forest produce other than timber free of charge, provided it was for consumption and not for sale. The professional herdsmen paid a fee of 8 annas for each buffalo and 4 annas per horned cattle. Evidently, these forests contributed a good share to the government treasury. The trade in imber in Cachar was brisk and the out-turn from the unclassed state forests was generally larger than that from the government reserves. The bamboos and canes were notable among the minor forest products.

A reference may now be made to the waste lands which were settled gradually upon the newcomers and under different rates. As a matter of fact, the practice of offering waste lands at progressive rates with a revenue-free term had been in vogue in Cachar ever since the British Government had obtained the possession of the district. In 1855, Major Verner made some jungle settlements for 15 years at rates varying from 4 annas to 3 rupees per *hal*, being rent-free for 3 years, Re. 1 per *hal* for the next four years, Rs. 2 for the subsequent four years and Rs. 3 for the last four years. In this way, 972 *mahals* were settled, containing 14,577 *hals* with a *Jumma* of Rs. 37,123. These were done under the Assam Grant Rules and to facilitate tea grants. During Stewart's settlement, in 1859, waste lands producing thatching-grass and reeds were settled at the full rates charged for cultivated land in the neighbourhood, but jungle lands that required clearance were leased at liberal rates commencing with a revenue-free term of three years and then assessable at full rates. Upto 1864, altogether 660 *jungle-mahals* were settled with an annual revenue of Rs. 16,926. In 1861, Assam Rules were substituted by Fee Simple Rules and several European Planters applied for grants. Same year, 179 grants were issued, covering 484,760 acres. In 1864, however, the Government of Bengal issued fresh orders laying the principles on which such leases were to be given in tenure. In accordance with these orders, which were generally known as the *jangalbari* or Wasteland Reclamation Rules leases were sanctioned. These leases were available for special as well as ordinary cultivation. The leases were for thirty years ; the first three years revenue-free, next five years at 3 annas per acre, another five years at 8 annas, still five years at 12 annas, and the last twelve years at 1-8-0 per acre. But, in 1875, the Government of India ordered for the reclamation of all these waste land leases and terms for new leases were reduced to 20 years ; first 2 years revenue-free, next 4 years at 3 annas per acre, another 4 years at 6 annas and last 10 years at 12 annas per acre. In 1876, new 30 years' waste land leases were issued only for special cultivation in Cachar. Only 15 leases, covering 4,904 acres, were granted while 142,751 acres of land were held in Fee Simple. Anyway, the *jangalbari* leases began to fall in before the settlement of 1900 and the lands were resettled with the rest of the district. The only distinction now made was, that, waste land in these *mahals* continued to pay at previous rates, but this too had disappeared since 1912.

The next settlement of the district was made by W.L. Scott during 1913-18, for another 20 years.[64] The lands were classified into six classes, viz. (i) *barhi* or good homestead, (ii) *bhit* or poor homestead, (iii) *sailura* or land growing transplanted winter rice, (iv) *asraura* or land growing broadcast winter rice, (v) *Chara* or land growing miscellaneous crops other than rice, and (vi) *patit* or waste land. The area reassessed was 854 *bighas* held for ordinary cultivation and 366,185 *bighas* held for special cultivation. The revenue from land held for ordinary cultivation increased from Rs. 4,37,238 to Rs. 5,84,488. The tea garden lands were assessed on a dual system ; a fixed rate of 15 annas per *bigha* was taken on land actually growing tea and three annas per *bigha* for waste land in tea gardens. The result of assessment of tea lands was an increase in revenue from

Rs. 1,19,612 to Rs. 1,51,149. Taking ordinary cultivation and
tea gardens together the enhancement of revenue was from
Rs. 5,33,171 to Rs. 6,99,964. The term of this assessment
expired on 31 March 1938, but due to the situation created by
the war its term was extended upto 31 March 1948.

The revenue-free estates in Cachar were generally known as
baksha. These were originally granted by the Rajas to their
priests and officials for maintenance. Their validity was enquired
into in 1859, but it was difficult to ascertain whether these were
intended to be rent-free in perpetuity. It was, therefore, decided
to recognise them as revenue-free so long as they would remain
in possession of the family of the original holders but would
become liable to assessment in case of transfer other than by
inheritance. As a result of the working of this rule, the number
and size of the estates gradually decreased. For example, in
1896 there were 142 estates covering an area of 2,381 acres,
while in 1916 the number reduced to 98 estates covering 1,039
acres ; in 1929 only 77 estates covering 711 acres and on the
eve of independence 50 estates with 200 acres. The fallen estates
were assessed from time to time, resulting in the enhancement
of the land revenue due to the government.[65]

The land system, discussed so far, related only to the plains
sub-divisions of Cachar, namely, Silchar and Hailakandi. The
North Cachar Sub-division, like other hill areas of North-
Eastern India, was exempted from normal land taxes. The
tribesmen used to pay a house-tax at the rate of Re. 1 per
house, while a *dao-tax* at the rate of Rs. 5 per head was levied
on the foreigners living in Haflong and a grazing duty was paid
by the Nepali graziers. Only the flat valley of Jatinga, which
contained a considerable area of ordinary cultivation and held
mainly by the non-tribals, was assessed at ordinary land revenue
at par with Cachar Valley. The total revenue demand of the
Sub-division in 1929 was Rs. 35,225 ; Rs. 22,729 house-tax,
Rs. 2,978 grazing duty, Rs. 4,610 as land revenue from Jatinga
Valley and the rest *dao*. In 1931, one Monbir Thapa was
appointed as the *Gurkhali Mouzadar* for the collection of *Dao*
and grazing duty from the Nepalis in North Cachar on the
basis of 10% commission on the total collection. In 1934-35, the
Mouzadar credited to the Treasury an amount of Rs. 1647,
less the commission. Even the tribal villages in the plains

sub-divisions were required to pay only the house-tax, and in 1853 there were 113 such villages which paid a tax of Rs. 2324.[66]

Cachar was thus beneficial to the British rulers for land revenue, and the small district occupied a unique position in the revenue map of the country. As early as 1872, the demand on account of land revenue amounted to Rs. 1,53,345, which increased to rupees seven lakhs on the eve of the departure of the British from India, while another two lakhs came as miscellaneous land revenue. The most important head of receipt as miscellaneous land revenue was the rent of fisheries which were of two classes. The first class fisheries in the principal rivers were sold by auction from year to year, while the second class fisheries in the villages were let out at an annual rent for a fixed period. However, before the issue of the Board's order in 1859 for farming the fisheries in navigable rivers, the fisheries in Cachar consisted of *jheels* and *nullahs* which were scattered all about the district. These were leased for one year or for terms of years as might be considered most convenient. These classes of land were not of great value, but as cultivation extended and new fisheries were discovered in the jungles and also with a steady growth of population, the *jheels* and *nullahs* were gradually brought under cultivation. In 1853, there were 42 such *mahals* yielding a revenue of Rs. 619-8-0, while in 1873, the number increased to 93 *mahals* and the revenue to Rs. 7,396.[67] The farming of the river fisheries multiplied the revenue, and in 1944-5 the government earned Rs. 40,001 as rent from the fisheries.[68]

Indian rubber was discovered in Cachar in 1862 and in that year about 3,000 maunds were sold in the local market. In 1863, the Board offered the monopoly to the highest bidder for Rs. 18,000 on the condition that the farmer would plant 400 trees during the year and that the collection would be limited to the months between November and April. In 1867, the value of the rubber in Silchar market was Rs. 10 to 15 per maund. The traders from Bengal collected them in the important transit stations of the district. An import duty of Rs. 10 per maund was imposed on the rubber from Manipur and Lushai Hills. To make rubber trade more profitable, Mc-William, Deputy Commissioner of Cachar, in 1872 divided the rubber areas into *mahals* and since then letting them off to the highest bidder for one year became the usual practice. There was a very stiff competition for the commodity and Cachar rubber fetched a high price in the following year.[69] Although the figures are not available, Allen reported, in 1905, that in 1900-01 "there was a considerable revenue derived from rubber, but the trees seem to have been killed out by overtrapping, and since that year very little caotchone has passed through Cachar."[70] Unfortunately, smuggling was a serious handicap to the growth of this trade. In 1871, the Collectorate *Nazir* siezed smuggled rubber worth Rs. 1,000. The smugglers were convicted of receiving stolen property under Section 411 of the Penal Code and the High Court on appeal, upheld the sentence. But this could hardly bring the innumerable smugglers to book, who carried on a good deal of illegal traffic every season. The government, on the other hand, was keen on the collection of this valuable article of trade. In 1874, the Commissioner of Dacca accepted the offer of Rs. 7,000 per annum for the monopoly of rubber trade in Cachar by Babu Braja Govinda Dey of Beliaghata, Calcutta.[71] Although the Deputy Commissioner of Cachar considered the offer as 'ridiculously small' as the price of Cachar rubber in Silchar market by that time was Rs. 60 per maund,[72] the Commissioner had probably agreed to the offer as a measure to stop smuggling. Meanwhile, McWilliam's proposal for an extensive establishment to deal with rubber smuggling was approved by the Government of Bengal, and Harish Chandra Sarmah, *Tahsildar* at Hailakandi, who had rendered appreciable services during the Lushai expedition, was promoted, in recognition, as Special Extra Assistant Commissioner to look after the frontier tribes and to supervise the Rubber *mahals* at a pay of Rs. 150 per month and was also conferred upon the honour of *Rai Bahadur* 'giving him a social status that would make him more useful in his new appointment.'[73] It is not very clear from the records how far this arrangement was effective in preventing the rubber smuggling. However, the revenue under this head considerably increased in the subsequent years.

There was a large number of salt wells in Cachar and the notable among them were in Saraspur and Bhuban Hills. Cachar was formerly supplied with salt entirely from its own wells and the greater part of the native manufacture was bartered with the hill tribes for cotton, bee-wax and ivory.[74] The salt wells were leased out to the highest bidders in public auction for three years. The salt was prepared by a simple process of the evaporation of the water by boiling and the quality was rather coarse and dirty. Under scientific management, more and finer salt could be produced from these indigenous raw materials, but instead foreign salt was pushed into Cachar which in no time developed a distaste for the local salt. As a result, there was a gradual decline in the revenue. For instance, while in 1852 nine such *mahals* were leased for Rs. 1030, in 1872 only one salt *mahal* was leased for Rs. 95.[75]

Like the Garo *hats*, and Naga *khats*, the *ghats* played an important role in the revenue and commercial history of Cachar. In these *ghats*, where the hillmen bartered their hill products with the merchants of Bengal, certain duties were levied by the Rajas. In the early British records we have references to a number of such *ghats* in Katigorah, Lakhipur, Sonai, Banraj, Banskandi, Loharband and other places on the borders with tribals areas, besides custom *choukies* on the Assam-Cachar border at Jamunamukh, Dharampur and Roha. The rivers being the principal routes of communication with Bengal, duties were collected from the river *ghats* at Jirighat, Sonabarighat, Madhuraghat and Sealtekhghat. In the early years of British rule, these transit stations were leased to the merchants from Bengal who received certain commission, but when their exactions became manifest, the *ghats* were brought under the direct control of the government in 1833. But the exactions and occasional oppressions of the local officers discouraged the merchants and impeded trade. As a result, all the *ghats* in Cachar, except Sealtekh, were abolished, which now developed into local *bazars*. The Sealtekh *ghat* had since then throve well as all the articles of export and import had to pass through it. The *ghat* was farmed out by public auction for a term of three years. The lessees levied toll on specific indigenous and hill products like timber, bamboo, cane, thatching-grass, cotton, wax and ivory. In 1832, the Sealtekh *ghat* yielded a revenue of Rs. 3,200 which increased to Rs. 10,244 in 1872.[76]

The tusked elephants in the jungles were an additional source of revenue in Cachar. The question of *Kheddah* was raised in 1851 when Major Verner's enquiry revealed that the right to catch elephants exclusively belonged to the former Rajas. Accordingly, on 16 July 1852, the Board of Revenue formally declared that that right had been logically inherited by the British Government and that the licences would be issued at the discretion of the Commissariat. The forests were then farmed out and the farmer was bound to give one-fifth of what the caught to government and authorised to sell others, but if he caught none he had nothing to pay. Evidently, no one would loose by failure and the *kheddahs* were carelessly conducted and failed. In 1861, the Government of Benga decided to abolish the Dacca Elephant Commissariat and called upon the Superintendent of Cachar to report on the prospect of the establishment of a commissariat in Cachar. The latter observed that with a proper system of leasing the forests and reserving the right of pre-emption to the government of all elephants over seven feet at Rs. 300, from 50 to 150 elephants might be caught annually. He anticipated a revenue of Rs. 5,000 from the leases. The plan found favour with the government, and in February 1862, the Superintendent was directed to lease the forests on the condition proposed by him. However, it was decided that, for that year the government would be entitled to 20 per cent of the captives. Of these, the elephants above 7 feet would be retained and others sold by auction. But after a long correspondence with the Commissariat Department regarding an establishment for the preservation of elephants, it was decided to dispose of all elephants whether above or below 7 feet. Captain Stewart, the Superintendent of Cachar, asked for the proceeds of the *Kheddahs* for the improvement of the district roads, but his request was turned down. Anyway, the license system continued for some years. In 1862-63 the revenue realised as license fees amounted to Rs. 3,711, while next year it was only Rs. 200 and in 1864-65 Rs. 700. In 1865-66 the plan of leasing out the elephant *mahals* was actually enforced and leased for Rs. 4,250 in public auction. The revenue under this head had since then steadily increased.[77]

Much to the dissatisfaction of the people, *Abkari* opium was introduced in Cachar. The drug was derived from the juice of a plant commonly known as poppy and extensively cultivated, and swallowed in the form of pills or mixed with water and drunk. *Madok* was prepared by mixing boiled opium with

pieces of dried betel-leaf and stirring it over a fire. The compound
was then rottened up in pills and smoked. This drug hardly
found favour with the inhabitants of Cachar Valley and only
the hillmen of North Cachar, particularly the Mikirs, were
addicted to it. In 1903, the revenue realised from opium in
Cachar amounted to Rs. 35,000, while Lakhimpur which had a
smaller population yielded Rs. 5,12,000. The country spirit
manufactured by native method was profitable in Cachar. The
raw materials required were either flowers of the *mahua* plant or
rice and molasses, while the apparatus consisted of large brass
or copper boxes to be placed over the fire on the top of which
an earthen jar was fitted. The industry naturally attracted the
attention of the government, which was then regularised and
dealership licence introduced. In 1861, the question of opening
a government distillery was considered. By this time there was
only one distillery in Cachar at Silchar, run by a Bengalee
under government licence. The Superintendent's report shows
that except the military and a small number of Bengalees, there
was no spirit consumer in Cachar.[78] R. Stewart, the Superintendent, therefore, did not support the idea of opening any
more distillery. However, due to the pressure of a section of
the officials, in May 1861, one more distillery and two sales-
rooms were sanctioned.[79] In 1859-60 country spirit yielded a
revenue of Rs. 205-8-0; in 1860-61 Rs. 365 and in 1861-62
Rs. 948-8-0. The growth of population, particularly of tea labourers, demanded more supply of the liquid and more liquor shops
were consequently set up. In 1874, revenue realised from 141
shops amounted to Rs. 42,596 and in 1900, Rs. 1,29,948.[80] In
1935, there were more than two hundred country spirit shops
in the rural areas alone, particularly in tea gardens.[81] Although
the high caste Bengalees were never used to drug of any kind,
ganja was fairly popular among a section of the cultivators. The
drug yielded Rs. 2273-1-0 in 1859-60, Rs. 2737-8-0 in 1860-
61, and Rs. 3947-8-0 in 1861-62 to the government as duty.[82]

In the beginning, the *Abkari* administration of Cachar was
entrusted to the *Abkari* Superintendent of Sylhet and Babu
Dwarakanath Banerjee held the office from 1852 to 1853 with
his headquarters at Sylhet.[83] In February 1851, Babu Krishna
Prasad Sarma was placed in charge of the *Abkari mahals* of
Cachar as a subordinate to the *Abkari* Superintendent. How-

ever, in 1853 the office of the *Abkari* Superintendent was done away with and the *Abkari* department was incorporated in the revenue department of the district.[84]

The discussions in the foregoing pages must have reflected the multiplication of the state revenue from year to year, while the expansion of agriculture, trade and commerce will be discussed in the next chapter. The government also earned a substantial sum as income-tax, half of which was contributed by the salaried tea garden managers and their subordinates. The receipt amounted to Rs. 25,800 in 1888 and Rs. 38,500 in 1899. The Act XI of 1903 raised the minimum taxable income from Rs. 500 to Rs. 1000 per annum and this resulted in decrease in revenue to Rs. 28,879 in 1904. The Professional taxes were paid by the money-lenders, contractors, dealers and pleaders whose contribution amounted to Rs. 10,730 in 1904.[85]

The consolidation of administration, on the other hand, brought into prominence new townships. Hamilton's report shows that in 1828 Khaspur the capital, was the only town in Cachar.[86] Immediately after British annexation the headquarters was shifted to Silchar which had since then fast developed into a modern town. The history of Silchar began with Janiganj Bazar which was settled by Raja Krishnachandra upon the *Mirasdar* of Ambicapur Estate towards the close of the eighteenth century but was resumed by Govindachandra before his assassination, in 1830, probably with the idea of converting it into the capital.[87] Anyway, the Sadar Station was now fixed at Silchar and a portion of the resumed land was occupied for *Katchari,* Jail, court and other office buildings, while the remaining area was settled by the *Amlahs* and traders. Upon this, the *Mirasdar* of Ambicapur appealed for compensation and Captain Fisher referred the claim to the Government of Bengal, which directed him to pay compensation for only such lands as were actually required for official purposes. Accordingly, Fisher paid the compensation for two *hals* of land and directed the *Amlahs* and traders to pay for their holdings at the rate of Rs. 18 per *hal.* The area of the Janiganj Bazar was then twenty-three *hals.* But the government soon interfered on behalf of the new settlers and directed the *Mirasdar* to refer the matter to the Civil Court. The *Mirasdar* did nothing for about ten years and Janiganj was shown as unsettled wasteland in the records of the Collectorate.

During these ten years, Cachar was twice resettled, in 1838 and 1843, and in the papers of both the settlements Janiganj was shown as government *khasland*. In 1844, the representatives of the *Mirasdar* filed a suit to recover the land from the occupants. But the *Mirasdars* were persuaded by the *Amlahs* to resign their claims and they executed a deed of sale transferring their rights to the occupants, receiving Rs. 18 per *hal*. The government, however, did not recognise this deed of sale and in the Collectorate records the *Bazar* continued to be shown as *khasland*. In 1859-60, Major Stewart granted the occupants a rent-free *Pattah* for twenty years, subject to cancellation by the introduction of Chaukidari Act or Municipal Act. On 29 November 1865, Act III of 1864 was extended to Silchar and the *pattahs* were liable to be cancelled. The Government of Bengal, on 5 October 1860, directed the profits of the *bazar* to be made over to the Municipal Commissioner.[88] The existing *Pattahs* were considered void and the Commissioner proceeded to assess the land in possession of the occupants preparatory to granting fresh *pattahs*. The rates proposed by the Commissioner were very high and the occupants appealed to the government for reduction. In his report, McWilliam, the Superintendent of Cachar, proposed that the land should be settled upon the occupants at the highest rate paid for rice land in the district. This proposal was supported by the Commissioner of Dacca and the Board of Revenue, and the Government of Bengal ultimately approved the rate.[89] Accordingly, a settlement was made in December 1868, but before the confirmation of the Commissioner of Dacca could be obtained the earthquake*

---

* On 10 January 1869, a terrible earthquake had occurred in Eastern India and its shock was felt from Upper Burma to Patna over a total area of 250,000 square miles. The shock probably originated in a fissure about 20 miles long, situated at a considerable depth below the surface on the northern border of Jaintia Hills, and Silchar was worst affected. The jail wall, the church tower, the cemetery gates and the military hospital were all thrown in ruins to the ground. The Deputy Commissioner's bungalow, including several official buildings, were wrecked. The Barak rose in high waves and washed out the bamboo and mat houses in the town taking a heavy toll of human lives. Situated in a seismic zone, Cachar was bound to bear the brunt of tremors and another earthquake in 1897 also taxed the district heavily. Although felt in a lesser degree than in 1869, the sub-divisional buildings and Inspection bungalows in Hailakandi and Haflong were damaged, The bridges sustained heavy injuries, hundreds of private houses were demolished and the *tahsil* office at Katigorah subsided into the Barak. See B.C. Allen, *n. 23*, pp. 15-7.

of 10 January 1869, completely destroyed the boundary marks and necessitated a fresh settlement. But it was decided to observe the further encroachment that the river might make and the extent of injuries done to the land by the earthquake. Meanwhile, two rainy seasons passed, and a fresh settlement was made with the actual occupants of the land in 1871 for 30 years. The land occupied by government buildings, streets and used for other public purposes was excluded from the settlement. Despite, 23 acres, 2 rods and 21 perches of land was assessed and settled at the rate of Rs. 1-8-0 per acre and the estimated annual *jumma* was Rs. 35-7-1.[90] But the Commissioner of Dacca considered the rate of assessment to be mere nominal in view of the prospect of Silchar becoming a good town in near future.[91] Upon his recommendations, the Lieutenant-Governor of Bengal ordered that the land annexed to buildings as compounds or pleasure ground be assessed at Rs. 10 per acre.[92]

The daily and weekly *bazars* were held in the site of the old jail, popularly known as Fatak Bazar, and the traders paid some nominal duty. The settlement of 1871 embodied the conditions that the lessees would put permanent marks around their respective holdings, assist the Collector in carrying out such measures as he might from time to time think fit for protecting the town from fire, ravages of the river, for conservancy and sanitary improvement and should pay such dues as the Collector might demand, and that the Collector alone would regulate the *hats* and *bazars*, change its site or establish new *hats*.[93] The next settlement for another 30 years was made in 1902. The trade sites were assessed at Rs. 75 per acre and residential sites at Rs. 36, while in special trade sites the rate varied from Rs. 3-8-0 to 8 annas per cubit.[94]

The evolution of the district administration gave Silchar a very urban look and the growth of population and sanitary problems demanded the formation of a municipal organisation. Accordingly, in 1865, under the Bengal District Town Improvement Act (1864), Silchar was constituted into a Municipality.[95] The Magistrate, Executive Engineer and the Superintendent of Police were the members of the Municipal Body, while the District Magistrate was the ex-officio Chairman. It could levy tax on houses and landed property and apply the proceeds for the maintenance of a police force and improvement of sanitation. But the experiment did not prove satisfactory and the municipality was withdrawn in 1868. However, in 1882, under Bengal Municipal Act (1876), which divided the urban areas into first and second class municipalities, stations and unions, based on population, Silchar was constituted into a Station.[96] Meanwhile, in 1881, the Government of India had provided that the local bodies should not consist of government servants and the strength of the non-officials in the board should be at least half of the total membership. The Station Committee had no authority to impose tax on latrines, carriage, animals and for the supply of water. Naturally, its resources were limited and with the fast growth of population the sanitary condition of the town was very unsatisfactory. In 1872, the population of Silchar Town was 4,925 and it increased to 6,567 in 1881. In 1891, the population was 7,523, the density per square mile being more than 4,000 souls, while more than three-fourth of the people were engaged in pursuits other than agriculture. Persuaded by Babu Kamini Kumar Chanda, a nationalist leader and a lawyer, who headed the Station Committee, the Deputy Commissioner of Cachar, in 1891, recommended to the Government of Assam that the Silchar Station be converted into a second class municipality.[97] Accordingly, on 1 April 1893, the station was upgraded to the status of a second class municipality[98] and this was retained during the remaining years of British Rule. In 1906, Hailakandi was constituted into a Union and in 1921, the Haflong Bazar Fund was introduced. However, in 1926, Hailakandi and in 1946, Haflong were constituted into Town Committees. In 1930, membership of the Silchar Municipality was raised from 20 to 25.[99]

The history of Local Boards in Cachar, like other districts in Bengal, began with the Committees, viz. District Road Committee and Ferry Fund Committee, for the construction of roads and bridges. In 1874, some new Funds were constituted, namely, District Revenue Fund, District Primary School Fund and the Miscellaneous Improvement Fund.* The local authorities and funds were created for local purposes and the Assam Local Rates Regulation (1879) levied certain taxes to meet their expen-

---

*These funds were the break-up of Government Estate Improvement Fund.

diture. Ultimately, there was a District Committee at Silchar and a Branch Committee at Hailakandi headed by the Deputy Commissioner and Sub-Divisional Officer respectively. The Committees consisted of officials and non-officials appointed by the Chief Commissioner at the recommendation of the Deputy Commissioner. The Cachar District Improvement Committee consisted of fourteen members; the Deputy Commissioner was the Chairman and the District Superintendent of Police a member.[100] The Cachar District Road Committee consisted of seventeen members, headed by the Deputy Commissioner as Chairman and Civil Surgeon as Vice-Chairman.[101] The Cachar District Committee consisted of nine members, of whom five were ex-officio. The Deputy Commissioner and Senior Extra Assistant Commissioner were Chairman and Vice-Chairman respectively. The Branch Committee at Hailakandi was headed by the Sub-Divisional Officer and had two other members.[102] The functions of the District and the Branch Committees were the preparation of the budget, allotment of funds for the improvement of the roads and bridges and the management of the schools.*

The existence of a number of Committees created confusion. Most of the committees were dominated by the tea planters. This was a common problem for all the districts, and the Commissioner of Assam wanted that there should be only one Committee in each district performing all the local functions.[103] Meanwhile, in 1881, Lord Ripon suggested an increase in the strength of the non-official members from one-half to two-third and the transfer of certain services and revenues to the District Committees. The Government of Assam opposed the proposal on the ground of the backwardness of the province and wanted the District Committees to be only consultative. But the Government of India decided that the District Committees be endowed with real powers and functions. Consequently, certain services and revenues were de-provincialised. In 1882, in addition to primary education, Aided Middle and Lower Middle Schools were transferred to the District Committees. The permanent grants to the dis-

*Besides these Committees, there was a Dispensary Committee in each sub-division and a District School Committee for the management of the funds raised by subscription and fees from the students.

pensaries were made through the District Committees and the hospital employees were put under their control. The provincial roads and buildings were retained by the Public Works Department, but all other works, including sizable section of the Public Works employees were transferred to the District Committee.[104] The Ripon Resolution of 1882 also provided that the local authorities be charged with specific duties and trusted with definite funds, their jurisdiction be limited to ensure local knowledge and interest on the part of the members, the chairman be a non-official and preferably elected, the non-official members to be majority and elected by rate-payers and the Chief Executive Officer of the district should watch the proceedings. The local officers in Assam did not favour the resolution. The Deputy Commissioner of Cachar, like his counterparts in Darrang and Goalpara, did not feel it exepedient to make any change in the existing arrangement, although the Deputy Commissioner of Sylhet welcomed the proposal. Ultimately, however, due to the insistence of the Government of India, the Government of Assam decided that the administrative area of the Local Board would be a sub-division, number of members between 8 and 24, and that in Cachar, like Sibsagar and Lakhimpur, the strength of the tea planters should not be less than half of the non-official members. The Deputy Commissioner, Civil Surgeon, District Superintendent of Police and an Extra Assistant Commissioner would be ex-officio members, while either an official or non-official could be elected as chairman. The Boards would be concerned with the execution of public works, management of postal services, primary education, medical charity, fairs, circuit houses, inspection bunglows and the distribution of grants-in-aid to lower middle schools. The entire proceeds from local rates, in addition to grants from provincial revenue, were placed at the disposal of the Local Boards. Accordingly, in 1882, the District Committees were abolished and the Sub-divisional Boards were introduced. The Assam Local Self Government Act, 1915 authorised the Local Boards to appoint District Engineers and Health and Sanitary Officers, and to levy tolls on new bridges and a special tax for the construction of railways and to manage primary and secondary education. The Act also provided for an elective majority of members and for

the election of non-official Chairman and Vice-Chairman.

Incidentally, the Committees and the Boards were an Official and European monopoly. In 1872, all the seven members of the Cachar District Road Committee were Europeans; namely, Dr. J.G. Coulter, R.B. Davidson, S.C. Davidson, Dr. J. Nelson, J.P. Stuart, J. Stewart and H.H. Wekor.[105] Same year, however, Babu Haricharan Roy and Babu Baikunta Chandra Gupta, two local Bengalees, were included in the Committee.[106] In 1878, the Cachar District Improvement Committee consisted of the Deputy Commissioner, District Superintendent of Police and sixteen others. Of these sixteen, majority were Europeans and official.[107] In 1880 the Cachar District Committee had nine members, five of whom were ex-officio.[108] In 1882, the Silchar Municipality consisted of 15 members. Of them ten were elected, but of the ten elected seven were government officers.[109] In 1883, the Silchar Local Board consisted of 2 official and 24 non-official members. Of the non-official 12 were elected and 12 nominated. Similarly, the Hailakandi Local Board consisted of 2 official and 8 non-official (4 elected and 4 nominated) members. A sizable majority of the nominated members, in both cases, were European tea planters.[110] In 1918, however, the Silchar Board consisted of 5 nominated and 13 elected members. Of the elected members, 7 were planters, 1 mercantile, 1 from headquarters and 4 from rural areas. But of the total 14 members in Hailakandi Board 6 were nominated and 8 elected. The elected members were 4 planters, 1 mercantile, 1 from headquarters and 2 from rural areas. The ex-officio members were Deputy Commissioner in Silchar and Sub-divisional Officer in Hailakandi and the Civil Surgeon, Executive Engineer and Deputy Inspector of Schools in both the Boards. In 1920, the strength of the ex-officio members was reduced to two and the Civil Surgeon and the Deputy Inspector of Schools continued to be 111 members.[111]

Although the Assam Local Self-Government Act of 1915 had provided that the Chairman of the Board might be elected by the members of the Board, this idea was never translated into action. The Chief Commissioner of Assam had suggested this noble experiment be made in Silchar and Gauahti Boards.[112] W.J. Reid, Commissioner of Surma Valley, had accepted the

proposal.[113]   But due to the opposition of the Commissioner of Assam Valley and Deputy Commissioner of Cachar, the proposal was ultimately dropped. The Assam Local Self-Government Act, 1926, provided all the members of the Board to be elected, the government might nominate officials to supply expert advice and the Chairman to be an elected non-official. The elective constituencies were divided into General, Non-Muslim and Muslim. To facilitate better communication, water supply and other public needs, the Local Boards were authorised to levy tax on carts, carriages and other vehicles using their roads. The Silchar Local Board had 4 nominated and 19 elected members. Of the elected members, 7 were planters, 7 Non-Muslims and 5 Muslims. The Hailakandi Board consisted of 4 nominated and 18 elected (5 planters, 5 Non-Muslim and 6 Muslim) members. The Chairmen were elected non-officials.[114]

Notwithstanding, the genesis of the local self-government in Cachar has to be traced from the *Panchayat* system which had a unique tradition in Bengal. In Cachar there were the *khels* or voluntary organisations for carrying on a specific undertaking. The members were obliged to discharge their share, for the guilds possessed powers to enforce their authority. With the British ascendency *Panchayat* and Village *Chaukidari* system made their way into Cachar. In North Cachar, every village had a *Panchayat* headed by the headman. The Regulation XIII of 1813 had laid down the principle of local taxation for local purposes. The Magistrate was authorised to constitute *Panchayats* consisting of members elected by the inhabitants of the locality. The *Panchayats* had the power to appoint and control the *Chaukidars* and to levy and collect taxes for the payment of their salaries. The Act XX of 1856 authorised the government to extend the *Chaukidari* system to any town, suburb or *bazar* in which there was a Police station. The Bengal Village Chaukidari Act of 1870 laid down that the District Magistrate might constitute a *Panchayat* in any village consisting of more than sixty houses. In case of lesser number of houses, two or more villages might be grouped into a *Panchayat*.[115] Cachar, like Sylhet and Goalapara, was a Bengal district and all these Bengal Regulations were in force in the district. The Local Rates Regulation, 1879, made further

provisions for local taxation and their utilisation for local purposes.[116] The Assam Local Self Government Act, 1915, provided for the constitution of village authorities in certain areas and for the delegation by the Local Boards to Village Authorities of powers and functions in connection with village sanitation; petty village development works and primary education under the control of the Board. The village authorities were also to perform duties relating to village police and civil and criminal justice under the supervision of the District Officer. In Cachar a Village Bench and Village Court was constituted at Lakhipur under the Bengal Village Self-Govt. Act, 1919, as modified in its application to Assam by Notification No. 1507J, dated 16 February 1920. The authority also maintained a pound of their own. In 1923, the Government of Assam directed that the surplus accuring under Section 18 of the Assam Cattle Tresspass Act of 1871 in respect of the pound situated at Lakhipur within the jurisdiction of the Lakhipur Village Authority, under Silchar Local Board, be placed to the credit of the Village Fund constituted for the said Village Authority. The Government also transferred powers of the Magistrate to try and find in respect of the Cattle Trespass to the Village Authority.[117] The Commissioner of Surma Valley took immediate action.[118] The working of the system was appreciated. The Rural Self Government Act of 1926 provided for a village authority in each village, to be constituted of 9 members on the basis of adult franchise. The Act aimed at a machinery for all the villages to undertake the management of their own affairs.[119] In 1929, the Registrar of the Village Authorities, Assam, requested the Deputy Commissioner of Cachar to submit proposals for the establishment of Village Benches and Courts.[120] The Deputy Commissioner immediately directed the Extra Assistant Commissioner to prepare the proposal and the Commissioner of Surma Valley notified that the Village Bench and Court at Lakhipur would continue to function until they were reconstituted under the Assam Local Self Government Act, 1928.[121] However, the spirit of these legislations developed their fuller personality only after the independence of India through the Assam Rural Panchayat Act of 1948 and the Assam Panchayat Act of 1959. Nevertheless, the Panchayat System had carried the British banner deep into the

rural areas and minimised the work-load of the government officers.

APPENDIX 5

Revenue Tables

TABLE I
ESTIMATE OF RECEIPTS AND DISBURSEMENTS IN CACHAR FOR THE BENGAL YEAR 1237

RECEIPTS	Rs.	As.	P.
Land Tax as levied in 1236	20,101	7	0
Estates settled on the Rannees	610	9	0
for the supply of rice to the Raja and family	767	14	0
for the supply of the Raja's cookroom	27	8	0
for various services	1,221	8	0
Debottara	571	9	0
Brahmonttara	993	12	0
Total	24,294	3	0
Sayer duties as now leased	3,135	0	0
Opium Tax as levied in 1236	1,200	0	0
Salt Tax as levied in 1236	800	0	0
Fees on Registry of Sunnunds levied in 1236	500	0	0
Fees on succession	250	0	0
Fines in Foujdari (average of 3 preceding years)	2,000	0	0
Fines on Collectors (average for 3 preceding years)	500	0	0
TOTAL (Sicca Rupees)	32,679	3	0

DISBURSEMENTS			
Allowance to the Rannees and dependents of the late Raja			
Estates as settled	610	9	0
Estates for cookroom	27	8	0
Estates for supply of grain	767	14	0
	1,405	15	0
Cash	480	0	0
Allowance for Debottara	571	9	0
Allowance for Brahmonttara	993	12	0
Allowance for various services	1,221	8	0
	2,786	13	0

$\frac{1}{4}$ Fines claimed by the Burra Bundari and others who

serve for land	625	0	0
Establishment and Miscellaneous charges	5,820	0	0
Tribute to the Honourable Company	10,000	0	0
TOTAL (Sicca Rupees)	21,117	12	0

(Sd.) THOS FISHER
In-charge of Cachar Affairs

TABLE II
LAND SETTLEMENTS IN 1830-31, 1838-39, 1843-44 and 1858-59

Settlement	Area of land (in acres)	Full Jumma (in rupees)
Lands as settled in 1830-31 under the Government of Rajah	35,735	21,433
Lands as settled in 1838-39 for 5 years	56,855	24,975
Lands as settled in 1843-44 for 15 years	1,07,275	58,518
Lands as settled in 1858-59 for 20 years and under other settlements	3,71,260	1,49,312

(Sd.) R. STEWART
Superintendent

TABLE III
REVENUE RECEIPTS IN 1855-56, 1860-1861 AND 1861-62

	1855-56			1860-61			1861-62		
	Rs.	As.	P.	Rs.	As.	P.	Rs.	As.	P.
Land Revenue	69,268	12	4	99,506	12	5	1,63,483	7	0
Sealtekh Ghat	7,675	0	0	12,300	0	0	15,000	0	0
Hill house tax	2,740	0	0	3,249	0	0	3,594	0	0
Fisheries	834	8	0	1,661	8	0	3,416	0	0
Salt Well	995	0	0	480	0	0	480	0	0
Opium (Sale Tax)	13,212	0	0	17,918	0	0	25,920	0	0
Ganjah	1,380	6	0	2,990	0	0	3,947	8	0
Madok	91	8	0	136	10	0	182	8	0
Country spirit	129	10	0	377	0	0	948	8	0
Post Office and Stamp	864	0	0	9,149	3	6	15,000	0	0

Income Tax		—		12,872	0	0	14,000	0	0
Misc. Revenue		576	2	0	1,365	4	8	1,425	0	0
Misc. Dewani		65	5	0	289	10	6	300	0	0
Misc. Foujdari		762	7	4	2,182	2	6	4,000	0	0
TOTAL	98,594	11	7	1,64,477	7	7	1,91,696	15	0

(Sd.) R. STEWART
Superintendent

TABLE IV
NET REVENUE IN 1834-35, 1845-46 AND 1859-60

	1834-35			*1845-46*			*1859-60*		
	Rs.	As.	P.	Rs.	As.	P.	Rs.	As.	P.
Land Revenue	31,113	8	9	49,170	4	5	95,039	4	0
Revenue from other sources	9,594	7	6	10,530	2	10	40,759	2	6
Gross Income	**40,708**	**0**	**3**	**59,700**	**7**	**3**	**135,798**	**6**	**8**
Gross Expenditure	30,281	3	8	29,334	10	7	38,555	9	1
NET REVENUE	10,426	12	7	30,365	12	8	97,242	13	2

(Sd.) R. STEWART
Superintendent

TABLE V
LAND REVENUE IN 1874-75 AND 1944-45

Land Revenue	1874-75	1944-45
Ordinary	1,49,529	7,96,919
Miscellaneous	88,390	1,76,990
TOTAL	2,37,919	9,73,909

Source : The Assam Land Revenue Manual, pp. xxviii-ix.

Material Progress

For some time after the reinstatement of Govindachandra as the Raja of Cachar the British authorities had serious doubts about the resources of Cachar and the capacity of the Raja to pay the annual tribute of Rs. 10,000.[1] But more they came in closer confact with the 'state' more optimistic they became about its prosperity. On 30 May 1829, George Swinton, Chief Secretary to the Government of Bengal, on the basis of the various reports received from the local officers, advocating the resumption of the 'country' by the Company, observed that "Cachar under a better rule would become the granary of the surrounding regions, and while it would thus afford adequate supplies to the Manipur Country . . . would thereby conduce to the security and tranquility of our North Eastern Frontier."[2] Captain Fisher, who was posted in charge of Cachar affairs following the assassination of Raja Govindachandra in 1830, thoroughly examined the resources of Cachar and had foreseen its prospects in various developing fields. In his report on Cachar, in May 1832, Fisher observed :[3]

> The soil of Cachar containing often a large admixture of land and silicean particles than that of the country to the westward, is capable of yielding a greater variety of products. Besides several kinds of rice; wheat, pulse and potatoes have been reared successfully, and though political circumstances, and want of capital have prevented the inhabitants from making any considerable experiments, yet enough has been done to shew the feasibility of cultivating with advantage many of the more valuable products. The climate is unfavourable to Indigo, but it appears that much success was obtained some years ago in an endeavour to improve the sugarcane for which the land appears eminently well qualified. Ginger and Safflawer also grow well.

Lieutenant Pemberton, who visited Cachar in 1835 in connection with the survey of the North East Frontier, remarked :[4]

The fertility of the soil of Cachar is so great, as to have attracted the particular attention of all the natives of the more western provinces, who visited it during the war, and it possesses a variety of site, arising from the intermixture of hill and plain, which gives a degree of beauty to its appearance, and a facility for the culture of varied produce, never found in the tracts of Bengal.

Lieutenant Burns, the Superintendent of Cachar, also had great hopes about the fertility of the soil of Cachar. In his own words :[5]

...I know no country which affords a finer field for such speculations than Cachhar where there is ample room and scope for industry and its remuneration.

MacWilliam, the Deputy Commissioner of Cachar, in his 'Report on the Annual Revenue Administration of the District of Cachar for 1871-72' observed :[6]

There can be no doubt of the great prosperity of the inhabitants of Cachar. The country is extremely fertile, and yields heavy crops with hardly any cultivation.

As a matter of fact, the soil in Cachar was highly fertile for agriculture. The land contained huge mineral deposits and the jungles were rich in timber, cane, bamboo and tusked elephants. The *Raj* in good old days was held in guild by the agriculturists and the commonwealth provided them with green summer and golden winter. With a scanty population, Cachar always yielded surplus products in foodgrain. Certain areas were depopulated during the Burmese and Manipuri invasions and misrule. Therefore, large scale immigration had to be encouraged by Thomas Fisher and the newcomers were settled in several colonies. Despite the growth of population and natural calamities like flood and inundations and ravages of the wild animals, the production of rice continued to be surplus to the local demand. As a result, a good quantity was exported to Sylhet and the adjacent districts of Bengal. The traders from Sylhet used to purchase rice from Cachar and carry them by boats to Lower Bengal. In 1846 the price of rice in Cachar was only eight annas per maund[7] and that year the value of the

paddy collected by the Sylhet traders was estimated by the Superintendent of Cachar at one lakh and ten thousand rupees. A larger quantity was consumed by the Manipuris, Nagas, Lushais and other tribesmen in the neighbourhood.[8] In 1847, the rice crop in Sylhet and westward districts was luxurious and, as a result, the demand was less than usual. Very few *mahajans* came to Cachar and the farmers' granaries were overstocked.[9]

On the other hand, Cachar had always a scanty population. Further, certain areas, as has already been mentioned, were thoroughly depopulated during the Manipuri devastations and the Burmese war. The local officers were alive to the fact that unless the depopulated lands were resettled and fallow tracts brought under tillage, the material development of Cachar could never be effected. A systematic policy was, therefore, followed by the government to increase the population. Captain Fisher settled a number of Manipuri villages in the Cachar-Manipur borders, of course, in the long run resulting in the merger of a tract of Cachar with Manipur. Invitations were extended to the Bengalee cultivators of the Lower Province to accept land in Cachar at liberal terms. The Valley of Cachar was only a geographical continuation of Bengal and the people were mostly Bengalees. The hundreds of agriculturists immigrated from Sylhet, Mymensing, Comilla and even from Burdwan and Birbhum. They were followed by the traders and fortune seekers.

The newcomers were settled in the sparsely populated divisions of Cachar, especially in the frontiers exposed to tribal incursions. The waste lands were leased off at progressive rates, with a revenue-free term to be followed by assessable years. For example, under the thirty-years' waste land settlement of 1864, for the first three years the lease was revenue-free, for the next five years the revenue was 3 annas per acre, next five years 6 annas, then another five years 12 annas and the last 12 years Rs. 1-8-0 per acre per annum. During the settlement of 1876 the term of the lease was reduced to 20 years, divisible into 4 terms of 2 years, 4 years, 4 years and 10 years. The first term was revenue-free and the revenue for other terms were 3 annas, 6 annas and 12 annas respectively. The lessees undertook to clear and develop the land at stated phases, failing which the grants were liable to be resumed. The tea grants, which

will be discussed in appropriate pages, offered under Rules for Special Cultivation, were also liable to resumption in case the grantees would fail to maintain the stipulated speed of clearance and plantation. These resulted in the rapid disappearance of the fallow lands and, consequently, withdrawal of the offer of leases on specially favourable terms. Pending the expiry of the existing leases, the lands were assessed at normal rates towards the close of the last century.[10] In 1900, the traditional *khels* were broken up in accordance with the actual possession and assessed under normal rules. The number of revenue paying estates then increased from 11,292 to 61,284 and the revenue from Rs. 3,05,624 to Rs. 4,51,568. That the land revenue in the district increased to Rs. 9,73,909 in 1944-45 against Rs. 2,37,910 in 1874-75 gives an impression of the extent of material progress achieved by Cachar during British Rule.[11]

Cachar was essentially an agricultural 'country' even under the native government when the socio-economic units were based on agricultural guilds, called *khel*. As expected by the early British officers, Cachar supplied foodgrains to the neighbouring districts for a long time. But the unnatural growth of population caused by the immigration of the coolies in tea gardens and workers engaged in various construction projects increased the internal comsumption of rice resulting in the rapid fall in the quantum of export. While the waste lands were generally leased off for special cultivation, the rice lands in some cases were converted into non-agricultural use. The growth of new towns and *Bazars* and cantonments, and the construction of roads and buildings deprived the agriculturists of a vast chunk of land. Moreover, the mode of cultivation was too traditional and the fertility of soil was gradually used up. The production under such circumstances was bound to fall. Anyway, in 1904, rice covered 66% of the total crop area ; tea 19%, oil seeds 5%, sugarcane 2% and the rest other grains.[12] Rice was grown in three season-varieties, viz. *aus* or summer rice, *sail* or winter paddy and *aman* or spring paddy, yielding 22%, 70% and 8% of the total crop product. The mustard seeds were raised in three different systems known as (i) *dhupi*, grown in highlands, (ii) *hainna*, in *chur* lands and (iii) *haoria*, in *haors*. Wheat, barley, maize were grown in small patches. Rhea and Jute fields yielded satisfactorily.

Nevertheless, agriculture did not mark much improvement. The mode of cultivation continued to be traditional. The floods and innundations were annual features. The pigs, monkeys and birds did much injury to the crops. Sometimes grave damages were done by the insects called *lehari* and *kharts*. The government did very little towards agricultural improvement. The tribals in North Cachar resorted to their age-old unproductive method of *jhum*. As a result, a good quantity of paddy from the Cachar Valley was required to subsidise their demand. Ivory, bees, wax and cotton of good quality were brought down to the border *hats* by tribesmen, all of which found their way to Bengal.[13] Encouraged by the quality of indigenous cotton and its demand in Bengal, the government, in 1862, distributed cotton seeds in North Cachar, but the attempt completely failed.[14] Interestingly enough, the agricultural prospects of Cachar drew the attention of some European capitalists. In 1837, two French gentlemen desired to establish themselves as farmers and introduce the cultivation of sugar, coffee, etc. Burns, the Superintendent, strongly recommended the case to the Government of Bengal on the ground of "great advantage that would accrue to the country from the introduction of European skill and energy."[15] But it is not clear from the records whether these gentlemen actually obtained any farm in Cachar or dropped the idea in process.

The cultivation of poppy was very popular in Cachar and it was never prohibited. The land-holders grew it in any part of their *taluk* at pleasure and without any permission from the Superintendent, but paying a revenue of Rs. 48 per *Kulbah* in addition to the common rate of land tax. No one cultivated as much as a *Kulbah* of poppy, seldom more than half and in many instances even less. Despite this, in the Bengali year 1245 the Government derived Rs. 1,300 as revenue from poppy. There was large scale consumption of this drug in Cachar and a bulk of it was smuggled out to Sylhet. The plantation marked rapid expansion, but the government desired to put a stop in view of the objection raised in Sylhet. In 1839, commenting on the suggestion, Lyons, the Superintendent of Cachar, observed that the measure would apprehend no difficulty but would be uneconomic and injure a section of the inhabitants of Cachar who favour the drug.[16] The plantation, however, seems to have died

a natural death and the poppy fields were converted into other agricultural farms.

By far the most commendable innovation of the British rulers towards the material development of Cachar was the introduction of the Tea Industry which, although primarily intended to serve the commercial aspirations of the Company's government, had completely changed the very look of the district through rapid socio-economic transformation. The indigenous tea plants grew wild in almost all parts of Cachar Valley. In February 1831, David Scott, Agent to the Governor-General, North East Frontier, had collected some specimens of tea plants in Cachar and forwarded them to the Government of Bengal and observed that the government should attach importance to this discovery in view of its growing unfavourable relations with China.[17] The Chinese, who then enjoyed a monopoly of tea trade, had adopted a rigid closed door policy against the British merchants. As a result, the East India Company had to search for an alternative source. In 1834, the Government of India appointed the Tea Committee for preparing a plan for the cultivation of tea plant in the sub-continent, ushering in a new era in the economic history of India. The Committee undertook rapid survey in the Himalayan region, Nilgiris and the valley and hill-slopes of north-eastern India.[18] In February 1834, immediately after the appointment of the Committee, G.T. Gordon, Secretary of the Tea Committee, requested Captain Fisher, Superintendent of Cachar, to learn from the Chinese merchants coming to Cachar from the province of Yunan in China the conditions regarding soil, rainfall, climate etc. required for the cultivation of tea and to report if Cachar satisfied them.[19] Upon Fisher's report and other informations, the Tea Committee, in August 1839, observed that "Assam and the lower range of the Naga and Cachar countries will be found equally well adapted for the culture of tea."[20] Meanwhile, indigenous tea plant was discovered, in 1835, in Sadiya (Assam) and some Companies had undertaken plantation there. In February 1855, R. Stewart, Superintendent of Cachar, forwarded specimens of Cachar plants to Dr. Thomas, Superintendent of the Government Botanical Garden at Calcutta, who recognised them as genuine tea plants.[21] Further explorations in the jungles of Cachar established that the plants were available

in abundance in the south and south-east of Silchar.[22] The Tea Committee immediately resolved to begin Plantations in Cachar, while the Board of Revenue, on 12 January 1856, decided that the land would be granted under Assam Rules of 1854 and, as such, should be compact, not less than five hundred acres, and that the whole plot of land comprised within the limits, whether adapted for tea or rice should be included therein subject to some conditions like clearance in stipulated phases and bearing cost of survey.[23]

The Superintendent of Cachar then invited the planters to undertake tea cultivation in Cachar. On 12 February 1856, G. Williamson, Superintendent of Assam Tea Company, and Major J. Graham, a retired officer of Bengal Army, applied for grants of 1,500 and 8,000 acres in Hailakandi and Chatla *Parganas* respectively.[24] Till 26 June, thirty applications were received by the Superintendent.[25] Meanwhile, on 1 May 1856, Williamson was offered the first grant of 742 acres in Burrahangun for 99 years at 16 years rent-free, 10 years at Rs. 104-5-10 and 73 years at Rs. 208-11-8,[26] while I. Davidson, of Cachar Tea Company received five grants aggregating 12,057 acres.[27] Next day, Boakara grant was alloted to A. Tyod of Wise & Co. and Chandipur to M. Herring. Charles Mackey, a businessman in Sylhet, received a grant of 500 acres in Barakpur.[28] On 5 May 1856, the Superintendent reported that the Planters have commenced their work and appeared to be well satisfied with the prospects and expected to make large profits by the cultivation and manufacture of tea in Cachar.[29] On 12 May 1857, the Superintendent again reported that tea plants in Cachar had been attracting large number of European capitalists and that about 30 gardens had already emerged in the hitherto fallow lands. The speculations promised in every respect to be successful. There were about one million acres of land calculated for the cultivation and each acre was expected to yield 200 lbs of tea.[30] The progress made by the pioneer-planters attracted more capitalists and large number of applications poured in for leases. The Cachar Tea Company, Silchar Tea Company, Sylhet and Cachar Tea Company, Cachar Tea Association, Badarpur Tea Company and Jirighat Tea Company were among the competitors. These were all foreign concerns and the tea industry was a monopoly of the European 'gentlemen' till the

beginning of the present century. However, one Babu Parbati Charan Banerjee, a banker of Sylhet, was among the earliest applicants for tea-grants in Cachar, but it is not clear whether he himself withdrew from the field or his case was not considered by the authorities. Anyway, in 1851 the government issued 54 tea-grants roughly covering 80,000 acres under the Assam Rules.[31] The Bengal Tea Co., Moran & Co., Burradaile Tea Co,* Silchar Tea Co. and the Equitable Tea Co.† were important among the new entrants. Some companies secured lands outside their gardens to settle the labourers.[32] The Silchar Tea Company, for example, had taken up a large chunk of riceland at the normal rates of the district.[33] Some companies were engaged in other trades simultaneously. The Burradaile Tea Co., for example, were dealers in motor-parts and assessories and supplied ivory, wax and medicinal plants from Cachar. The Co. was financialy sound and the working capital was taken into consideration for registration and grants.[34] R. Stewart, Superintendent of Cachar, in his report on the Company expressed satisfaction. The Cachar Company had received a grant of 12,508 acres on 1 May 1856 and the survey of the grants was completed in the next year. In 1858, the Company obatined further grants of 16,508 acres and invested the capital of Rs. 1,25,000 and the estimated *jumma* was Rs. 16,508.[35] This company supported several public utility measures and I. Davidson, the proprietor of the company was associated with many public bodies.[36] In 1858, the government also considered a proposal for government plantation in Cachar, but the Superintendent having considered it unnecessary on the ground that many companies had entered into the enterprise with earnest spirit and were prosecuting their business extensively and vigorously the idea was utimately abandoned by the Government of Bengal. As a matter of fact, by 1860 the plantation had vastly increased and the prominent planters were W.H. MacArthur of Sereespur, James Abertnutty of Monachara, W. McArthur of Lakhipur, H C. Gibson of Mohonpur and Sanderman of Rosekandi.[37] In 1861 Cachar yielded 3400 maunds of finished tea and Rs. 2,50,000 was

*The Burradaile Tea Company had the following gardens : Dalbeer, Chandipur, Banskandi, Kanchanpur and Kalachara,

†The Equitable Tea Co. was a good competitor and had an annual *Jumma* of Rs 1,139-6-0.

invested as capital during the year.[38]

The survey of the provisional grants were undertaken from the year 1859 and the final adjustments were carried on simultaneously. The grantees who could fulfil the necessary conditions were confirmed, while others were redeemed, readjusted or relinquished. In 1861 five grants were confirmed, namely, one each to Sanderman of the Equitable Tea Company (538 acres), J. Davidson (634 acres), F. Tyod (1,804 acres) and two grants to J.M.L. Comertic of Peterson & Co. (706 acres and 672 acres).[39] In 1862, *pattas* were issued to D.G. Moorgan of Sereespur Tea Estate, Thomas Mamekin of Doodpatil Tea Estate and G. Brownlow of Kanchanpur Tea Estate.[40] Dr. J.B. Barry of Eastern Bengal Tea Co. who had obtained a number of grants from the government and purchased some established gardens from the Cachar Tea Company, was an important planter. In 1862 he applied for the redemption of Lalamukh, Khoza, Monachara, Lalkandi, Morraghat, Goongoor and Bharakhai gardens. Like three other grantees, the redemption was allowed by the government.[41] Same year, the Assam Waste Land Rules were revised and regularised by Act XXII of 1863 which relaxed the rule that the grant should not be less than 500 acres and fixed the price at Rs. 2-8-0 per acre. But there were 278 pending applications registered under the old rules ; and out of these, 179 grants were made in 1870, covering a total area of 484,760 acres,[42] In 1870, final adjustment was made in respect of 24 tea gardens. Tarapur and Labac were redeemed. Jaipur grant was reduced to 2,088 acres against the original area of 3,038 acres and Alipur to 1,907 acres from 14,249 acres, the grantees having failed to meet the clearing condition. For the same reason, Dwarband was reduced to 1,077 acres from 2,664 acres, Diksha to 404 against 2,806 acres, Jafferband 1,760 against 2,043, Barjalenga 2,220 against 12,926. Kalainpur 219 against 1,041, Nowarband 279 against 1,723, Salgonga 737 against 1,713, Jirighat 1,853 against 3,997, Khaspur 758 against 2,227, Mynadur 870 against 1,340 and Bengalnagar 5,860 against 10,184 acres. In Dilkush, Rupachara, Log, Dudpatil, Cleverhouse, Leburband, Muderpur and Chandipur minor adjustments were made. Narainpur and Cossipur were commuted to Fee-Simple Estates which did not involve clearing conditions. Indraghar and Telka were confir-

med without any modification.[43] But by the end of the year, it was found that the clearing condition could not be fulfilled by many grantees and cultivation has not been attempted. Some grants were then abandoned. The government had, therefore, to interfere with the deserving grants. Seventy-one* grants were resumed, four** relinquished and forty-two† commuted to Fee-Simple Rules. Consequently, in 1871, only 64 grants remained under the Old Assam Rules and altogether covered an area of 146,356 acres. Eight became liable to rent in 1971, the 15-year rent-free term having expired, and the demand amounted to Rs. 3,324. Similarly, 5 grants were in the rent paying list; rent would be due from 5 grants in 1872, 1 in 1875, 11 in 1876, 8 in 1877 and 31 in 1878.[44]

Of the 42 grants†† commuted to Fee-Simple Estates in 1871, nine were redeemed before the issue of *Pattah*. Alipur was proposed to be sold for arrear of interest but was ultimately resumed as there was no bid in the auction. Badarpur grant was relinquished by the grantee with the sanction of the Board of Revenue. Four other grants were revised. Consequently, there remained 36 grants redeemed in Fee-Simple, covering 66,023 acres and the purchase money amounted to Rs. 1,81,770. The Fee-Simple tenure did not find favour with the planters. Till 1871, only 26 grants, aggregating 21,666 acres, were issued for Rs. 54,179. Same year, five grants were relinquished and sold for arrear of interest and converted to *Khas*.[45] On 23 August 1872, Sir George Campbell, Lieutenant Governor of Bengal, issued some interim rules which required that the land should be fallow, not occupied or utilised by anybody, and was priced at Rs. 5 per acre.[46] Of the applications, submitted before the issue of the rules, 16 grants were issued under the former tenure.[47] But the condition of clearance was rather strictly persued by the Government and, in 1872, seventy tea gardens were resumed for the failure of the grantees. The Rupabally Tea Estate belonging to M/s Gregson & Coy of London was an important resumption. Tilka Tea Estate of the same Company was converted to Fee-Simple Estate.[48] Ultima-

---

* Total area 204,120 acres.
** 5,123 acres.
† Introduced in 1862.
†† The total area covered by the 42 grants amounted to 69,023 acres and the purchase money to Rs. 1,89,270.

tely, in 1872, there were 80 Tea Estates in Cachar, covering 91,000 acres, and the revenue demand in 1871-72 amounted to Rs. 1,53,346.[49]

The gardens were laid out on the top of the low spurs projected from the Barail hills towards the Barak and south of the river in undulating land and the low round topped hills. In 1875 an experimental plantation was done on the thoroughly drained marsh land and this rich soil yielded exceptional large return. The small drains were placed at intervals and considerable allowance was made for shrinkage of the soil. This type of gardens quickly grew up and high yields attracted the planters. The quality was not at par with the product of the foot-hill gardens, but the difference in market price was insignificant and there were ready buyers. Four disinct varieties of plants throve well in Cachar, viz. Cachar or Lushai indigenous, Assam plant, Manipur or Burma plant and Naga plant. The experimental cultivation of China variety and different kinds of hybrids also responded favourably. The Burma plant came into bearing very quickly and yielded good return. Kalain, Jatinga, Kasipur, Alyma and Goabari, amongst others, were noted for the cultivation of this variety.[50] In the beginning only black tea was manufactured in Cachar, but subsequently many companies cultured green tea as well to meet the demand in American markets.

It would be interesting to note that when the plantation started in Cachar it was considered as a mere speculation than a solid industry by many concerns. To quote Edgar, the Deputy Commissioner of Cachar, in 1873. :[51]

> Scarcely one interested looked forward to obtaining his return from the produce of his tea cultivation ; every one looked forward to becoming suddenly and immensely rich by getting a piece of land, planting it out with tea, and then selling it for a vastly greater sum than he had expended on it.

Edgar was very justified in his observation, because it is in record that many gardens were sold for seven or eight times more than their actual cost and in some cases the plantation existed in paper only.[52] Dr. J.B. Barry, for example, purchased a number of established gardens in the sixties of the last century from the leading concern like the Cachar Company.[53] This unhealthy state of affairs proved to be a real devil to the industry. Again, a crash came in 1866 and the period of depression continued till 1869.[54]

As a matter of fact, the planters in Cachar had to overcome a number of problems. They were required to import mechineries, seeds and skilled personnel. Even the manual labourers were not available locally. The indigenous people of Cachar were traditional agriculturists and possessed sufficient land and the surplus yield could be bartered or sold for other necessaries of life. The paid labour was unknown and no one would, therefore, volunteer to be wage-workers. The question of labour thus posed to be a serious problem. The government could not take up the normal development works, even the construction of essential roads, due to the dearth of workmen. The carrying of military stores to Manipur also created an additional charge upon Cachar. J.G. Burns, Superintendent of Cachar, in 1838, regretted 'the extremely unpleasant predicament that he was placed by the requisition of men, by the military department'.[55] Again in 1848, when the Commissariat Gomastah of Manipur applied to the Superintendent of Cachar for 80 coolies to carry military stores to Manipur, the *Darogah* was ordered to recruit the coolies. But the *Zamindars* went to Court of the Superintendent and prayed that he 'should not insist on their *ryots* being taken from them and forced to go, for that they are one and all busy in the land and that by taking them away they would be very considerable losers'.[56] The Superintendent, therefore, observed that except by imprisonment, which was strictly prohibited by the government, the Cachar authorities could afford no assistance.[57]

This being the normal state of labour in Cachar it would be anybody's guess that the plantation industry, requiring large number of coolies, was bound to be handicapped by the dearth of workmen. Curiously, R. Stewart, during whose Superintendency the industry began in Cachar, cherished false hope about the prospect of tea labour. He did not "anticipate there will be any great difficulty in obtaining the quantity which may be required, if not in Cachar, in the neighbouring district of Sylhet, the inhabitants of which district and of Jynteah come very willingly to Cachar and settle down in it".[58] This was too much for the Superintendent, being well aware of the fact that the administration was facing a serious problem to meet very common demand of coolies for the works of the district. Even in Assam the growth of the industry was seriously handicapped by the dearth of labour. Several inducements on the part of the government and the planters having failed to attract the local men, the Tea Committee represented to the Government of Bengal to allow the immigration of the coolies from the South-West Provinces. The authorities in Calcutta having agreed, the immigration commenced in late fifties.[59] No wonder, therefore, the planters in Cachar from the very beginning were blessed with this problem. The over optimism of Stewart about the local labour soon belied, but was hopeful about Sylhet and the western districts for sometimes more. In his report on 12 May 1857, the Superintendent observed[60]:

> There are a million acres calculated for this (tea) cultivation in the district, each acre in full bearing is supposed to yield 200 lbs. of tea, but each acre require the constant labour of one man, and the great problem at present is how to secure such immense quantity of labour as that which will be necessary from so small a population, from a population too already so thoroughly employed in its own agriculture. Labour will have to be obtained from the neighbouring and densely populated district of Sylhet and there further westward, and from such prolific sources, is but small doubt that the neccessary quantity will be forthcoming and in that in time Cachar will export its millions of lbs. of tea.

Unfortunately, the expectations of the Superintendent about the neighbouring districts as well never came true. The Bengalee working classes at the time were essentially agriculturists and en masse showed a marked disinclination to be enrolled as tea labourers. On 13 May 1858, Sanderman, Manager of Goongoor Tea Estate, suggested the importation of coolies into Cachar from north India to end the problem of labour. Stewart also opined that "it would be a measure attended with much benefit to the country, and to the tea planting interest".[61] He also thought it very probable that the imported coolies would settle in Cachar for good and form a permanent population. He desired that every facility should be given to the coolies to prosecute cultivations of their own as well as labouring in the tea gardens. Once settled on a piece of land which they would clear themselves and know to be their own, it was very probable that the coolies would hardly ever think of quitting

and would thus become a lasting source of supply of labour. During those years the coolies from north India were obliged to ship themselves off to Mauritius and West Indies for subsistence. They would naturally prefer Cachar to a distant foreign land.[62] The Superintendent, however, desired that before leaving Calcutta for Cachar the coolies must enter into an agreement to serve for a certain minimum number of years and a breach of this agreement would subject the delinquent to one month's imprisonment and to another month if he still refused to fulfil the contract and the advantages which might have been made to him would be recoverable through the civil courts.[63] The proposal piloted by the Superintendent readily received the approval of the Government of Bengal and the immigration started in early sixties.[64] This also provided opportunity to a handful of persons to make money as professional labour agents, supplying coolies to the gardens according to requirements.[65]

During the period from May 1863 to January 1868, a total of 52,155 coolies were imported to Cachar. Of them, 2,456 died during the voyage. The journey having occupied less than a month, the rate of mortality was characterised to be alarming. In the beginning the mortality among the imported coolies was very high and the relations between the planters and the coolies was often far from being satisfactory. The Waste Lands suitable for the growth of rice were not allowed to be within the grants or in their neighbourhood. Consequently, when a coolie left the garden, had to settle in the remoter part of the district and his service was lost to the industry. Stewart had rightly anticipated that the companies would not like to invest large sums as importation cost without some guarantee that they would be able to retain the coolies for a minimum period. The Government of Bengal too gradually realised the position and the Act XIII of 1859 empowered the Magistrate to compel a coolie to fulfil his contract and to punish the delinquent with imprisonment.[66] A coolie was, however, at liberty to give up his work after the term of his contract was over and look for other means of subsistence in the developing district with plenty of fertile but fallow land and growing townships to be emancipated from the bargain of the planters at poor wages.[67]

This state of affairs in the gardens posed a new threat to the development of the industry. On 18 May 1881, the Indian Tea Association was formed for united action among the proprietors to deal with the matters of common interest like following up the work of the Tea Syndicate in its endeavour to promote the sale of Indian tea, eradication of the diseases affecting the plants, improvement of communication with 'Tea District',* tennure of land, inland migration, etc. The Associations also established the Calcutta Tea Traders' Association for organising and regulating sale of tea in the Calcutta Auction Centre. To assist export promotion, the Association had suggested in 1890 a levy of cess on tea and the proceed to be utilised to stimulate consumption in foreign markets. The government, accordingly, had set up a Tea Cess Committee which was the forerunner of the Tea Board. For the eradication of malaria, *kalazar* and such other scourages, the Association initiated the establishment of the Ross Institute of Tropical Hygiene. A Scientific Department was set up by the Association, in 1900, for conducting research in tea and its benefits were made available to the entire industry in North Eastern India.[68] The endeavours of the National Trade Union Congress and other local organisations, both planters' and workers', and the introduction of the various statutes by the government, relaxation of waste land rules, computation of grants in the early decades of the present century, had gradually ameliorated the condition of the coolies and improved the employer-employee relation. In the last decade of the 19th century, Babu Bipin Chandra Pal, the well-known nationalist leader, raised a storm of protest against the exploitation of the labourers by the planters. Aided by his friend Dwarakanath Ganguli, Bipin Chandra championed the cause of the down-trodden tea-workers and publicised the deplorable condition of these people and demanded better wages and lesser working hours through his book, *The New Economic Menace of India* and the Bengali journal, *Samhati*. The Indian National Congress took up the matter in the annual session in 1896, and

---

*Assam, Cachar and Sylhet were included in the same tea district even before the creation of the Chief Commissionership of Assam in 1874 In 1873, the Government of Bengal considered a proposal to divide the tea districts into two whereby Cachar and Sylhet would form a separate tea district, and to permit the planters in Cachar the free recruitment of tea labourers. But the planters in Assam and their sympathisers took an exception. *Hindu Patriot*, 18 August 1873.

the Government of Assam introduced certain measures to remove the greivances of the tea garden labourers.[69] During the historic Coolie Oxodus of 1919 Arun Kumar Chanda and Chittaranjan Das appeared as the emancipators of the coolies, to which reference would be made in the last chapter.

Notwithstanding, the immigration of the coolies was rather in a massive scale in the last century. During the decade ending in 1890, a total of 51,894 coolies were imported, while in the nineties it was 75,412. In 1901, a total of 129,063 coolies immigrated into Cachar; of them, 50,287 were from Assam, 49,309 from Bengal, 13,725 from the United Province and 11,921 from Central Province.[70] Obviously, the coolies stated to be immigrated from to Assam were not the local men of the state but those who had come to Assam from U.P. or C.P. and for some reasons or other did not stay in Assam and preferred to migrate to Cachar. Any way, by this time the coolie population in Cachar had numbered about four lakhs. This rapid growth of the working population naturally reflects the steady progress of the plantation and quantum of the finished products. The depression in the sixties taught the planters to mind their profession seriously. The seed was also available at cheaper rates, ranging from Rs. 20 to 40 per maund. The Bubble Companies worked steadily and made substantial progress. The other concerns too learned to follow and gradually settled themselves to the profession. In 1869, Cachar had 24,151 acres under tea and yielded 4,255,000 lbs. Till 1876, however, the production in the Brahmaputra Valley advanced more rapidly than in the Surma Valley but since then the balance dramatically reversed.[71] In 1882, the area under cultivation in Cachar had risen to 48,873 acres and the yield to 12,721,000 lbs 'which was considered in excess of that returned from any other district in the province'.[72] In 1885, of the total production of 53,617,020 lbs of the province, Surma Valley, with only two districts of Cachar and Sylhet, yielded 20,998,978 lbs, while Brahmaputra Valley which had seven districts could return 32,618,042 lbs. Of the tea producing districts, Cachar topped the list and was followed by Sibsagar, Lakhimpur and Sylhet.[73] But in 1895, Sylhet took the first position, followed closely by Cachar, Sibsagar and Lakhimpur. That year Brahmaputra Valley yielded 56,640,815 lbs and Surma Valley 52,879,759 lbs (Sylhet 22,710,626 lbs and Cachar 20,169,133 lbs). With the Hill Division producing 4,000 lbs, the total yield of Assam in the year was 99,524,574 lbs.[74] Cachar continued to be one of the largest tea manufacturing districts and till the close of the last century it had the highest number of tea gardens. In 1895, for example, Cachar had 199 gardens, while Sibsagar had 174, Lakhimpur 141 and Sylhet 133.[75] In 1898, the area under cultivation in the district was 62,179 acres and the out-turn 20,898,000 lbs. This was followed by a succeeding favourable season and, as a result, in spite of the decrease in the cultivated area, the yield in 1901 was 31,088,000 lbs.[76] The yield per acre was higher in Cachar than most of the districts in Assam and was on an average about 500 lbs of finished tea. A good *beel* garden sometimes even yielded 14,000 lbs per acre.[77]

Tea was, therefore, an exceptionally paying industry for the British in India. The Indian tea was exported to international markets in Europe, Australia and America. India emerged as the largest tea exporting country in the world. Assam became the highest tea manufacturer in India and Cachar contributed its due share. In 1865, at an exhibition in Paris, where Indian indigenous goods including tea were displayed, the sample of Cachar tea was highly admired and the Manager of the Lalamukh Tea Estate was rewarded for quality manufacture.[78] The price varied from time to time, but the industry never suffered from unnatural decline in demand or value. In 1868, it was presumed that tea must be sold at 2s a pound in London to cover the cost of manufacture and transportation and profit, and in 1882 the Deputy Commissioner of Cachar complained that the average price had fallen to 1s 2d a pound. This was a matter of concern as the companies would hardly produce tea for less than a shilling. The cost of production was reduced to meet the situation. This economy as well as the gradual increase in the market value and quality culture returned satisfactorily. The Cachar gardens had so far manufactured only black tea, but in America green tea had greater demand. Accordingly, in 1902, the Indian Tea Association offered a bounty of $1\frac{1}{2}$ annas a pound for green tea. In the following year one million pounds of green tea was exported from Cachar to North America and Midland.[79]

Nevertheless, since the beginning of the present century the tea record of Cachar had marked a gradual decline. Many tea fields were exhausted and the European concerns began to wind up their investment. The local capitalists endeavoured to take up the position. The Cachar Native Joint Stock Company had since then emerged as a leading concern. Some nationalists, inspired with the spirit of economic nationalism, had started tea estates. But all these could hardly fill up the vacuum and the number of estates began to decrease. Thus in 1915, Cachar had 159 gardens, covering 2,77,033 acres, of which only 60,549 acres were under tea and the total yield amounted to 30,084,829 lbs. Although in 1928 the number of gardens had risen to 176 covering 2,83,601 acres, the area under tea had declined to 57,314 acres and the manufacture to 26,731,490 lbs.[80] Many tea fields were deserted by the planters and were requisitioned for the rehabilitation of the refugees from East Pakistan (Bangladesh).

The tea industry was an innovation during British rule and was sponsored by the Europeans. The people of Cachar had certain indigenous and cottage industries. These included weaving, pottery, bell-metal utensils, blacksmithy, carpentry, grinding and fishing. The craftsmen in all these industries formed themselves in professional castes, but all of them were tillers of the soil. In Cachar, unlike in other parts of Bengal, the natives were primarily agriculturists. The immigrants from Bengal, before and during British rule, received grants of land they required and held them in guilds and took up peasant's life. During 'off seasons' only, they could indulge in other professions. But the products were sufficient only for local consumption. The bell-metal utensils were prepared mostly by the Manipuris. The knives, axes, hoes and such equipment were manufactured in a small quantity by the local blacksmiths. These were generally supplied by the blacksmiths of Sylhet. The potters of Cachar used glutinous clay and the articles manufactured were cooking pots, water-jars, plates, cups and lamps. The pottery was, however, inferior in quality than that imported from Bengal. During the early years of British rule many *Kumars** families migrated from Cachar and settled in Jainanagar, Chatla, Banraj and Kalain *parganas* in Silchar and

*Traditional potters of Bengal.

Rangauti, Matijuri, Bishnupur and Sibarttar in Hailakandi Sub-division. But they gradually abandoned their traditional occupation and took to agriculture and manufactured only few articles in their leisure. The mustard oil was grinded by the ordinary bullock-pulled mills and *telis*† attached to the craft were confined to Silchar town. The *Jugis*†† were strongly represented in the weaving industry and they are the original weavers of Cachar, but in the 19th century they gave up their profession. The Bengalees of Cachar became used to the cheap fabrics of Manchester. As a result, this important handicraft was gradually extinguished. Only the Manipuris, Kukis, Dimachas, Mikirs and Nagas utilised their leisure hours in weaving and mostly used their cottage products. The women were especially suited to this craft and manufactured the garments they required. The Manipuri *Khesh* and Kuki *Pal* and the curtains knnited by the Kuki and Naga women were highly popular among all sections of the people. The silk worms were reared by the Dimachas both in the hills and plains of Cachar, but the clothes manufactured were generally intended for personal use and very little of them came to the markets. Lac was produced only in North Cachar and reared by the tribesmen. The ants and caterpillars did much damage to the insect and heavy storms sometimes crushed them totally. The Marwari merchants collected the products and exported them in crude form.[81]

The fishing industry needs special mention. The fisheries in Cachar were divided into two classes. The first class consisting of the larger and more important ones were auctioned off to the highest bidders annually, while the smaller fisheries were settled for a term of three years with the persons having stronger claim on equitable grounds. The revenue varied from Rs. 1 to Rs. 200, but in most cases from Rs. 5 to 15. Allen found 40 fisheries of the first and 304 of the second class in Cachar in 1904. But the industry was not of a great importance to the locals of Cachar and was a monopoly of *Mahimal* and *Patins* castes of Sylhet.[82] The saw mills would be highly profitable in Cachar in view of the abundant timber and numerous tea com-

†The professional Bengalee oil-grinding caste.
††The weaving caste of Bengal.

panies. But the Lakhipur Saw Mill and the Barak Mill at Sonaimukh were the only two noteworthy factories, owned by the Europeans The principal products were tea-boxes, for which there was a large local demand. Such boxes were also manufactured by the native carpenters at Silchar.[83] The furniture and other timber goods were also supplied to the people of the district by these carpenters. Cachar has an all time repuation in cane industry.

Cachar had a long trading history with Bengal and through Bengal with the rest of India. She exported her natural products and imported basic necessaries of life. The neighbours in the hills depended on her for their supplies and there were a number of *hats* on the borders with the Nagas and the Lushais. The historic kingdom of Manipur too maintained her relations with Bengal through Cachar and there was regular trade across the Jiri frontier. As a matter of fact, the early European visitors to Cachar have noted the trade and commerce in and across Cachar. Felix Carey, who visited in June 1817, mentioned the profit earned by the traders by supplying the indigenous products of Cachar to Bengal like timber, ivory, lac, wax elephants, cotton, *augur*, bamboo, cane and other minerals. He also reported that since Burma had become a formidable country, the trade in ivory, wax, lac, silk, cotton, copper, tin, lead, zinc, silver, gold, sapphire and rubies had completely "been drained by that country and exported through that channel to Bengal and other parts of India."[84] Thomas Fisher, the first Superintendent of Cachar, has left behind detailed descriptions of the timber, bamboo, cane and other trades of Cachar with Bengal. According to him, *Jarul, sundi, gandru, gamer, siliatha, sepai, gandi, jam, chika* and many other costly timbers were transported from Cachar. The river Barak, divided into Surma and Kushiara, was the channel through which Cachar timbers, bamboo and cane were conveyed to Sylhet, Habiganj and Nabiganj and thence transported to other parts of Bengal. The price of the timber, volume of trade and the cost of transportation given by Fisher show that the trade was huge and highly profitable. The *Jarul* timber of Cachar was in great demand in Bengal for boat-building and with Surma Valley having its unique tradition of boating and water trade a significant part of these timbers were worked up in Sylhet alone, at

Ajmeregarh, Chatak and Sunamganj. They were also carried beyond the district in logs and sometimes exported in planks for the same enterprise.[85]   Fisher's information have all been confirmed by Lieutenant Pemberton in his report in 1835.[86] Before the annexation of Cachar, the Rajas of Cachar had a good deal of trade with the British merchants in tusks, wax, ivory, timber, cane and bamboo ever since the East India Company had ascended to the Dewani of Bengal. The traditions suggest that Cachar had maintained, in early times, regular commercial contacts with Burma and other countries of South East Asia, and some historians have accepted these views.[87] Felix and Fisher have mentioned these routes in their reports. Pemberton also endorsed them and quoting from the journals of the Anglo-Burmese War he opined that starting from Calcutta it would be possible to reach Ava through Assam in 170 days and by Cachar route in 107 days.[88]   The fact that in 1834 the Tea Committee had asked Captain Fisher to collect certain information from the Chinese merchants coming from Yunan definitely establishes Cachar's trade relations with China even during the British rule.[89]   The official records also reflect the *hats* in the frontiers where the tribesmen from the neighbouring hills traded with the Bengalees.[90]   The chief production of internal consumption was paddy which had a supply much beyond the demand and the surplus was drained to profitable markets. In 1829, three maunds of rice was sold for a rupee in the villages and $2\frac{1}{2}$ maunds in the internal markets. There was a brisk trade between Sylhet and Manipur through Cachar in wax, ivory, silk and cotton and duties were levied by the Raja on the merchandise at the *ghats*.[91]   In the northern frontier there was extensive trade with Assam and the Nagas. In addition to a number of *choukies* in the frontier, Mahung-Dijua was a flourishing area on the Cachar-Assam border. There was considerable cultivation of rice, cotton, poppy and mustard and extensive plantations of Endi and Muga silk worm. The capability of the place for agriculture, traffic and commerce was highly commended by the early official visitors. Its position appeared to be singularly happy as it had routes leading to Upper Assam, Cachar plains, Manipur, Naga hills and Gauhati. There was a very brisk trade in the *bazar* at Mahung between the people of Cachar, Assam and the Naga hills.[92]

During British rule the import trade was chiefly controlled by the European merchants who had opened various firms immediately after the annexation of Cachar. Flour, salt, sugar, cloth, kerosene, oil, medicine, coal and iron and steel were the principal articles that required importation from Bengal. During the closing years of the last century even rice had to be procured from outside the district. There was a large population employed in the plantation industry and the same industry was responsible for cutting the arable land to size. Tea, timber, bamboo, cane, elephant tusks and some other forest products were exported from Cachar. Manipur exported to Cachar timber, cattle and Indian piece goods and received European piece goods, dried fish and betel-nuts. The major part of the trade was carried through the water routes. Roads and rail links took a long time to establish their claim as lines of communication and could never come at par with the water routes largely due to the boating tradition of Bengal and to its viability. The Barak, with her tributaries and branches, having links with the major rivers of Bengal confluencing with the Bay of Bengal was bound to be the heart line of communication. Katigorah, Badarpur, Sealtekh, Silchar, Sonai, Jirighat and many other *ghats* could develop into flourishing *hats* because of their portships. Jirighat was important for Cachar-Manipur trade, while Sealtekh was known as the transit station of Cachar. The merchandise transported through rivers would move to Barak and invariably touch Sealtekh near Badarpur, both ways. The government earned considerable revenue by levying transit duties on the articles passing through Sealtekh ghat. The timber, bamboo and cane were floated down the river, while other goods and cargoes were shipped by boats and steamers. The tea boxes were directly shipped from the factories to the auction market at Calcutta. The internal trade was carried on at the weekly markets. Silchar, Hailakandi and Haflong had daily markets and there were several permanent shops. There were also permanent *bazars* in some mofusil areas. The important weekly markets were Udharband, Lakhipur, Matijuri, Sonaimukh, Dwarband, Bhanga, Lala, Bhaga, Katigorah and others. The markets were held on certain weekdays and had permanent shops and grocers.

As has already been mentioned, important trades were

carried mostly by the Europeans resident. In October 1831, when the question of disposal of Cachar was still under consideration and the British Government had taken temporary charge of the 'country', one H.L. Chistiana, a European gentleman, applied to Lieutenant Fisher for permission to reside in Cachar and trade with the inhabitants.[93] Forwarding the application, Fisher recommended that Chistiana and the Europeans in general should be required to reside at or near the *Sadar* Station, should be altogether prohibited from visiting the hills, should submit to the local laws and customs of Cachar and should agree to abstain from all interference in the political disputes among the chiefs and people of Cachar and its neighbourhood. Under these restrictions, Fisher felt, trade might be carried on to the advantage of all parties.[94] W. Cracfort, the Agent to the Governor General, fully coincided in the opinion expressed by Fisher and suggested that some specific terms of agreement might be drawn up.[95] But pending the unsettled state of the question regarding the disposal of Cachar, the Government of Bengal did not deem it expedient to grant any license to foreigners to reside and trade in Cachar. The government, however, desired that the Political Agent and the Officer-in-charge of Cachar would exercise their own discretion in granting or refusing permission to persons to visit Cachar for the purpose of trade subject to such terms and conditions as might appear necessary.[96] Meanwhile, Cachar was formally annexed to the British Dominion in 1832 and the European traders were encouraged to invest their capital in Cachar. The restrictions on the foreign traders were gradually relaxed and bulk of the trade was in their hands. Besides tea planters, there were a number of European concerns in Cachar. M/s John Small & Co., Cachar Club & Co., Standard Oil & Co., Wise & Co., Webster & Co. had established themselves as leading traders since the last century.[97] M/s John Small & Co. of Silchar were the suppliers of gun, cartidges and other amunitions in the region, including Chittagong.[98] The profitable oil trade was in the hands of the Europeans. B.O.C.'s field agent at Badarpurghat was allowed to store 80,000,00 gallons. The Standard Oil Company had their units at Silchar, Tarapur, Badarpur, Hailakandi and Lalabazar.[99] M/s Harish Chandra Bhuiya of Janiganj and M/s Ramani Mohan Das of

Tarapur were notable among the natives who maintained close competitions with their European counterparts.[100] The manager of the Cachar Club was granted license to transport patrol.[101] Similar license was granted to Miss M.S. Michel, daughter of the manager of Kubhir Tea Estate.[102] The Burradaile & Co., which was primarily a tea concern, had other trades.[103]

The majority of the shop-keepers were emigrant Bengalee and some from United province. The local people have shown little interest in commercial enterprise and to share the profit that accrued from retail trade. The number of Marwari merchants was also small, although since the twenties of the present century some of them had established firms in towns and some even entered in the plantation industry. The petty shop-keepers in the villages dealt in grain, pulse, ghee, mustard oil, sugar, molasses, salt, tabacco, spices, umbrellas and piece goods that were basic for subsistence. The villagers brought in the weekly markets rice, fruits and vegetables they grew in their farms and also cows, goats and poultry. They could procure their requirements for the whole week and carry them to the distant villages. For rare and costly goods, cloth for example, they would go to the town, but such cases were exceptional and rather ceremonious. To fight a case, to stand a trial, pay the revenue or persue any official matter the villagers would go to towns. Even recently, the people in the villages had the impression that the towns were meant for the *Babus*. Besides the periodical markets, we have reference to an annual large fair held at Katigorah since the last century during the bathing festival, attended by several thousand people from Sylhet and Cachar and merchants from Bengal where a considerable volume of trade and business was carried on.

It may not be out of place to refer to the problem of currency faced by the traders, people and the government immediately after the British annexation. Till then former native coins called *Tulik* or *Sonat* were in circulation. *Sicca Tanka* which was the unit of circulation in medieval Bengal, was obviously the common media. Finally, the introduction of British rule brought in Company's rupee. The circulation of all these currency at the same time naturally created confusion. None could refuse, and even the government had to pay its employees both in Company's rupees as well as in *Sicca*. For example, in 1836, the Superintendent, Native Surveyor and *Mohurir* were paid in Company's rupee and the *Bara Bhandari*, Native Doctor and the *Naksha Navish* were paid in *Sicca* rupees.[104] Captain Fisher had fixed the remuneration of a certain employee at *Sicca* Rs. 49-5-17-0 or Company's Rs. 52-10-3.[105] This shows the difference in value between the two, while the value of *Tulik* was still higher. The traders at Sealtekh and Banskandi *ghats* refused to pay their duties in *Tulik* on the ground that the *Ghatyals* paid to the government in Company's rupees and they too should be charged in the same rate.[106] In 1838, Burns, the Superintendent, complained to the Collector of Sylhet that a large quantity of old coins of Cachar having been imported to Cachar had depreciated their value. In Sylhet these old coins could be procured at the rate of 40 *gandas* (two annas) for rupee.[107] Ultimately, however, all other units were gradually replaced by the Company's rupee which became the only standard of circulation as elsewhere in India.

APPENDIX 6
Progress of tea industry in Cachar

Year	No. of gardens	Total area (acres)	Area under plant (acres)	Yield (lbs.)
1861	54	80,000	16,000	34,000
1869	71	86,000	24,151	4,55,000
1872	80	91,000	23,000	5,000,000
1882	150	n.a.	48,873	12,721,000
1895	199	2,80,172	58,216	20,169,133
1898	199	2,80,172	62,179	20,898,000
1901	180	n.a.	56,000	31,088,000
1915	159	2,77,033	60,549	30,084,829
1928	176	2,83,601	57,314	26,731,490

Impact of British Rule

The introduction of the British ⌈rule and gradual opening of Cachar in various fields had immediately resulted in a substantial increase in population with marked changes in political, economic, social and cultural life of the district. Although the actual figures are not available, Cachar had undoubtedly a sparse population during the passing years of the Heramba rule. The Manipuri occupation and the Burmese invasion had resulted in a large scale depopulation of many prosperous villages. To quote Pemberton :

> . . . the country of Kachar was the arena, on which the several Muneepooree brothers, Choojeet, Marjeet, and Gumbheer Sing, contended for supremacy; and as might have been anticipated, the inevitable result of their disputes was the most serious injury to the country, from the cessation of agricultural pursuits, and the flight of a very considerable portion of the inhabitants to the adjacent districts of Sylhet, Jynteeah, and Tripurah.[1]
> The total area of Southern Cachar...may be estimated at 2,866 square miles, of which 1,850 lie on the southern, and the remaining 1,008 on the northern bank of the Barak river. Of the former tract, Captain Fisher estimates that there are 1,711 square miles of the finest plain, almost wholly unoccupied, through which the rivers Dullaseeree and Soonaee flow from south to north, and pour their waters into the Soormah, near Panchgaon and Sonarpoor. The sites of numerous villages are still discernible along the banks of these streams, which were densely inhabited during the reign of the Rajah Kishunchundruh, the irruptions of the Poitoo and other Kookee tribes

became so frequent, as to spread dismay among the peaceable cultivator of the soil, and led to the desertion of these favourite localities: the invasion of the Burmahs completed the havoc which had been partially effected by the cruelty of the Kookees, and the rapacious imbecility of Govindchundruh ; the flight became general, and this most fertile portion of the province relapsed into a state of nature, ..[2]

On his assumption of the charge of Cachar, Fisher had estimated the population of South Cachar to be 50,000 and there was about 1,800,000 *bighas* of waste land to which there was no claimant.[3] Many of the Manipuri refugees, who had escaped from their 'country' during the Burmese occupation of Manipur, had permanently settled in Cachar. According to an official report in 1832, "a large proportion of the new settlers consist of Munipoories, who averse to the system of Government in their own country, have determined not to return to it, and have in consequence obtained grants of land in Kachar—one of the largest and most flourishing of the villages thus founded has been established on the banks of Madura Nulla...and its inhabitants consists principally of Muneepooree Sepoys from the Sylhet Light Infantry who have resigned that service and invested their little capital in the soil."[4] A large number of Manipuri villages were established by Fisher in the eastern part of Cachar. Many of the fugitives, who had retired to Sylhet during Burmese invasion, were also induced by him to return to their villages and resume cultivation. Pemberton, during his survey duty in Cachar, reported that during the first eighteen months of Fisher's administration 12,000 people had returned to Cachar from Sylhet and "relying on the continued exercise of British authority they have produced the most marked amelioration in the condition of the country and established flourishing villages in spots which... in 1826 were covered with dense jungle—nearly the whole line from Buddurpoor to Banskandee now presents an animated picture of successful industry enhanced by the substitution of an equitable or an iniquitous administration of Government and the hope that they will be allowed to retain those lands under the form of rule they most approve."[5] As a matter of fact, Fisher genuinely believed that the vast fertile but fallow land in Cachar could never be developed, and the revenue improved, without the increase of population. With the approval of the Government of India, he had extended invitation to the cultivators in the adjacent districts of Bengal and even in the distant districts of Burdwan and Birbhum.[6] In the next few years many people from Bengal emigrated into Cachar and the new-comers received land in liberal terms and had become the permanent population of Cachar. Several Naga and Kuki clans had also settled in Cachar during the early years of the British rule.[7] For example, in May 1831 a Naga clan of 100 families *en masse* migrated to Cachar from Kachha Naga territory and settled in the neighbourhood of Lakhipur. The Government extended gratuitous financial support for their rehabilitation.[8] Similarly, in March 1831, a body of Kukis consisting of 250 families came down to Cachar and were settled by Fisher in the hill areas within Cachar and extended financial support for rehabilitation.[9] The Agent to the Governor-General, North East Frontier, had authorised the Superintendent of Cachar to make necessary advance in terms of money and implements for husbandry.[10] In the following years there was a general exodus of Kukis and across the Cachar Valley they settled themselves in several colonies in the North Cachar Hills.[11]

Evidently, the population in Cachar marked a gradual in-crease, since the British occupation of the Valley. But the offi-cial estimates were highly superfluous. As stated above, in 1831 Fisher had estimated the population of the Cachar Valley at 50,000 and Pemberton reported that 12,000 people had immigra-ted from Sylhet during the first eighteen months of Fisher's administration. This was followed by many more from Bengal, and the Nagas and Kukis. Despite, Burns, the next Superin-tendent, estimated the population of the Valley to be 50,000.[12] However, Lyons in 1842 reported that the population of the plains had increased to 80,000.[13] A census taken in 1844 re-turned the same figures.[14] Another census taken in 1851 returned the figure at 85,522. Of them 30,573 were Bengalee Hindus, 29,708 Bengalee Muslims, 10,723 Manipuris, 276 Assa-mese, 62 Europeans, 6,320 Kukis, 5,645 Nagas and 2,215 Dimachas. Verner, then Superintendent, however, believed that the actual number would be 100,000 and that because of some inaccuracies in enumeration the number had been less.[15] In 1857 the population of the Valley was estimated at 137,000 and of North Cachar Hills, 30,000; the total being 167,000. This census reflected an increase in the number of Manipuri and Naga settlers in Cachar plains, and Naga and Kuki settlers in the North Cachar Hills.[16] It may be mentioned, the population of the North Cachar Hills was ascertained by a census during the reign of Raja Krishna Chandra to be 14,000.[17] But the disturbed political situation in the tract during the tenure of Tularam Senapati had compelled some people to migrate to the adjoining areas. As a result, Burns in 1837 estimated the population of the hills to be 6,000.[18] However, in 1851 the population increased to 20,000[19] and, as stated above, in 1857 to 30,000. Meanwhile, tea plantation had begun in the Cachar Valley and the immigration of the labourers from North India commenced in 1861.

The first regular census of India was taken in 1872 and the second in 1881, and since then it has become a decennial affair. In 1872 the population of the Cachar Valley returned at 2,05,027 and in 1881 at 2,93,738. In North Cachar Hills it was 30,000 in 1871, but 20,121 in 1881. In 1885, the Cachar Valley and North Cachar Hills were amalgamated after more than half a century, of course in a truncated form. Consequently, in 1891 the total population of Cachar stood at 3,86,483, of which 3,67,542 were in the plains and 18,941 in the hills.[20] The Subdivision level population returned at 2,67,673 in Silchar, 99,869 in Hailakandi and 18,941 in Haflong. In the plains the total increase was 73,804 or 25%, of which 19·9% was due to natural increase, 2% immigration from other districts and 5% from other provinces.[21] Of the immigrants from the neighbouring districts, 218 were found in North Cachar and 25,380 in the plains, and of the latter 21,626 came from Sylhet, 1,714 from Manipur and 787 from the Khasi-Jaintia Hills.[22] According to this census, the largest population per village in any plains district in Assam was in Cachar and the smallest in Darrang. In North Cachar, the exteremely small hamlets of the Mikirs brought down the average.[23] In 1901, the population of Cachar was 4,55,593; of them, 4,14,781 in plains and 40,812 in the hills. The Silchar Sub-division returned 3,01,884, Hailakandi 1,12,897 and Haflong 20,490. The density of population was 321 in the plains and 12 in the hills per square mile, the density of the district as a whole being 121.[24]

To quote Allen, in the beginning of the present century;

"A century ago the eastern end of the Surma Valley was very sparsely populated, but the population has grown with remarkable rapidity, and outside the reserved forests there is little land remaining in the plains available for settlement."[25] Nevertheless, the unnatural growth of population was in the last century only and that too with declining ratio. For example, while the total growth from 1832 to 1872 was more than 400 per cent, the percentage of increase was 43·3 from 1872 to 1881, 25·1 from 1881 to 1891 and 12·1 from 1891 to 1901. On the other hand, in North Cachar Hills the population was extremely sparse and did not mark any significant increase throughout the British rule. In the last century, the population in the hills had shown a downward variation. The census of 1872 returned the figure at 30,000, but in 1881 it came down to 20,121 and in 1891 to 18,941, while from 1857 to 1872 the population remained static at 30,000. In 1901 the population increased to 40,812, but it included 20,324 outsiders engaged in the railway constructions. The actual population of North Cachar in 1901 would, therefore, be 20,488, with an increase of 1,547 since 1891. The downward variation from 1872 to 1891 might have partially resulted from the stationing of sepoys to check Naga disturbances in the fifties and sixties and their withdrawal in seventies and eighties and the gradual reduction of the territory. The possibility of inaccuracies in enumeration in the hills can not also be altogether ruled out. According to Gait, the editor of the 1891 census report, however, the fall of 1,179 souls was 'due to the absence of the working coolies..., migration of the Nagas to Naga Hills and Jaintias to Jaintia Hills.'[26]

In the present century, therefore, the growth of population in the rural areas was bound to be optimum. The expansion of the townships, administrative and commercial centres, attracted job-seekers and businessmen from the rural areas as well as distant parts of the country. The population in the district increased to 499,475 in 1911, while 529,301 in 1921 and 570,531 in 1931.[27] The upward variations were 43,053 in 1901-11, 29,826 in 1911-21 and 41,230 in 1921-31.[28] The urban population in Silchar was 9,256 in 1901, 8,785 in 1911, 10,204 in 1921 and 13,069 in 1931, while in Hailakandi the figure returned at 1,462 in 1911, 2,228 in 1921 and 2,002 in 1931.[29]

The density of population in 1921 was 369 in the plains and 16 in North Cachar Hills per square mile.[30]

A natural extension of Bengal Plains, the Cachar Valley was peopled by the Bengalees. For sometimes, in the medieval period the valley was under the Tipperahs and their capital was at Khalangsha on the bank of the Barak, but the Tipperahs gradually migrated to the Tipperah Hills. The North Cachar Hills were then under the Dimachas and in the seventeenth century they shifted their capital to Khaspur in the Cachar Valley. The Dimachas generally remained in the hills and there were only few villages in the plains. The British records and the records of the Heramba Government testify the existence of large Bengalee *Khels* in the valley.[31] The official language of the Heramba Government was Bengali and the inscriptions and coins were inscribed in Sanskrit in Bengali script. The high officials and ambassadors were Bengalees. That the Cachar Valley was predominantly Bengali speaking can be ascertained from the fact that the members of the royal family and the Barmans in the plains were gradually Bengalised. The *Raj Darbar* was adorned by a galaxy of Bengali scholars and some of the Rajas are well known for their contribution to Bengali literature. Krishnachandra and Govindachandra made correspondence with the East India Company's Government in Bengali.[32] Govindachandra issued several statutes, popularly known as *Govindachandra Ain*,[33] in Bengali with parallel Sanskrit in Bengali script. Maniram Barman, a member of the *Darbar*, was a poet and his Bengali poems have been highly acclaimed. A number of Bengali scholastic works were composed in the *Haramba Darbar* and notable of them are *Naradiya Purana*, *Vivad Darpan*, *Kalmi Puthi*, *Rindan Vidhi*, and *Ranachandi*.

The Bengali population in the Cachar had increased in the nineteenth century, after the British annexation. Many Manipuris migrated to Cachar, Sylhet and Tripura during the Burmese occupation of Manipur. The North Indians came mostly as the workers in the tea gardens. The Europeans came as the officers of the British Government or as traders and planters. The traders from Rajputana and Ajmer-Marwar came in commercial pursuits.[34] The Manipuris, Hindustanis and Bengalees, who emigrated during British rule, have since made Cachar their permanent home, and the bulk of them use

Bengali as the spoken language. In North Cachar, Dimacha
was the widely spoken language, besides Rangkhol and Naga
dialects.[35]

The official census taken from time to time, since the
British occupation, show that the Bengalees had a good
majority in the Cachar Valley. Burns, in 1837, had found that
'a large proportion' of the population was Bengalee.[36] Of the
total population of 85,522 in 1851, there were 60,281
Bengalees.[37] The immigration of the Hindi-speaking tea
labourer since 1860's, however, brought down the percentage
of the Bengalees. In 1901 the Bengalees were 61% of the total
population, Hindi-speaking 21%, Manipuris 11% and the rest
7%. However, according to Allen, 'Bengali' was "the common
language."[38] Of the total population of 529,301[39] in the whole
of Cachar in 1921, Bengali was the mother tongue of 5,951
persons per ten thousand.[40] Thus about 60% of the total
population of the district were Bengalees. In 1931 the Bangalees
in the district were 6,280 in every ten thousand.[41] Even in the
North Cachar Hills 333 in every ten thousand were Bengali-
speaking.[42] The percentage of the Bengalees in 1931 in Cachar
as a whole was about 61% while, in the valley the percentage
would obviously be higher.

The two major religious communities in Cachar were the
Hindus and Muslims. In 1881, there were 92,393 Muslims and
767 Christians in the plains and 3 Muslims in the hills. The remaining 200,578 in the plains and 20,118 in the North Cachar
Hills were Hindus and 'Animists'. In 1891, the plains returned
1,12,846 Muslims, 809 Christians, 2 Buddhists and 47 Jainas,
while North Cachar Hills had 15 Muslims and 1 Christian.[43]
In 1901, the 67% of the people were Hindus, 31% Muslims
and 2% 'Animists'. Of the Hindus, 49% were *Saktas*, 42%
Vaisnavas and 9% *Saivas*. The *Kishori Bhajan Sect*, introduced
by one Kalachand Vidyalankar of Bikrampur in Dacca for
obtaining salvation by immitating anourous actions of Krishna
at Brindaban, had some 'young widow' associates of 'low
caste' in Cachar.[44] The Hindu festivals like *Saraswati Puja,
Suryabrata, Sivaratri, Dol Yatra, Barani Puja, Rathayatra,
Bishori Puja, Durga Puja, Laksmi Puja, Kali Puja, Kartik
Sankranti, Rash Yatra, Uttarayan Sankranti* were popularly
observed. The *Nauka Puja* and *Dasha-Avatar Puja* were

occasionally celebrated in the rural areas in the winter and *melas* held in these connections were added attractions. As in these days, the *Sidheswar Mela* during *Baruni Yatra* and *Bhuban Mela* in *Siva-ratri* were colourful celebrations. A *Kalibari* was founded at Silchar in 1833 and another in Tarapur in 1871. The *Kalibari* at Hailakandi was established towards the close of the last century.[45] The *Baram Than* in Silicoorie and *Shyamananda Ashram*, *Radhamadhaber Akhra*, *Mahapravur Akhra* and *Shyamsundarer Akhra* in Silchar were established in the present century. The *Kachakanti Bari* in Udharband and *Ranachandi Mandir* in Khaspur were founded during the Heramba rule and have been kept in high esteem by the devout Hindus. A *Siva* temple in Subhang has references since 7th Century A.D. and the images of *Hara-Parvati* in the Bhuban Hills were probably installed by the Tipperahs,[46] while the *Siva temple* in Badar-purghat is said to have been established by Kapil Muni, the celebrated author of *Sankhya* philosophy. These are held to be sacred shrines and have continued to be places of pilgrimages.[47]

The Muslims in Cachar were mostly of the *Sunni* Sect. Although Allen had written, in 1905, that there were 'no mosques of special sanctity' and the prayers were 'usually said in a thatched hut,'[48] several permanent mosques have been constructed during the early decades of the present century. The *Imam Medhi Mukam* and *Langer Shar Mukam* at Phulertal, *Kari Pirer Mukam* near Badarpur[49] are very old Muslim shrines and are held in high esteem both by the Hindus and the Muslims. The Muslims also subscribed to the funds raised by the Brahmanas 'during the smallpox epidemic to promote the worship of the Goddess *Sitala*.'[50]

The members belonging to other religious communities were practically none in Cachar. As has already been discussed, in 1881, there were only 767 Christians in the plains and none in North Cachar. In 1891, the plains returned 809 Christians, 2 Buddhists and 47 Jains, while in the hills there was only 1 Christian. In 1901, there were 49 Brahmas, 22 Jains, 23 Buddhists and 165 Sikhs, but they were employed in the Assam Bengal Railway Company.[51] The number of the Jains was reduced to 22 against 47 in 1891, but the number of the Christians increased to 1,040.[52] As a matter of fact, a branch of the Welsh Prebyterian Mission was established in Silchar on 4 August, 1861.[53] A plot of land was secured from a private individual in the heart of the town and the Lord Bishop of Calcutta laid the foundation of the Church and named it 'St. Andrews Church in Cachar.' A sum of Rs. 4,691* was collected as donation on the occasion and five thousand rupees was promised. The Lord Bishop himself had promised Rs. 1,500 from a fund of which the Governor-General of India was the trustee. Col. Reid prepared the plan and estimated the cost at Rs. 8,000. R. Stewart, Superintendent of Cachar, took the leading part in the matter and called upon the Government of Bengal to share two-third of the expenditure. During his visit to England, soon after, the Superintendent requested the 'Church of England Society' to send a Missionary as Clergyman to Cachar. With the cooperation of the Government of India, Church of England and the European residents in Cachar, the 'St. Andrews Church in Cachar' engaged itself in proselyterian activities. The Superintendent issued a circular† to the European residents to contribute to the fund. But from the beginning, 'Cachar appeared to be a barren field for missionary enterprise.'[54] No wonder, therefore, in 1881, after twenty years had elapsed since the establishment of the Church, there were only 767 Christians in the Cachar plains, of whom 476 were natives and 291 Europeans. In 1891 the plains returned 809 Christians, 488 of them being natives.[55] In North

---

* The donors were : Capt. R. Stewart (Rs. 1000), Lt. J.F. Sharer (Rs. 600), G. Sonee (Rs. 400), J. Davidson (Rs 350), A. Forbes (Rs. 200), G.S Lackie (Rs. 200), A P. Sanderman (Rs. 350), J.B. Barry (Rs. 200), M. Thomson (Rs. 100), J. Obbard (Rs. 50), J. Wateon (Rs. 100), Capt. E.A Rowlatt (Rs. 50). I. Sandaman (Rs. 350), M. Smith (Rs. 45). Capt. Scott (Rs. 50). R.A. Word (Rs. 30). The Bishop of Calcutta (Rs 50), A. Daneon Fruth (Rs. 16), J P. Wise (Rs. 300), A. Webster (Rs. 100) and B P. Shelan (Rs. 150).

The monthly subscriptions promised by these donors varied from Rs. 10 to 2/8 as. C.R., No. 42 of 1861.

†The Circular read as follows :

"The time has arrived that something should be done by the European Residents of Cachar towards the erection and support of a suitable building for Divine Worship. The Christian Community being now a considerably large and a potent one, it is sincerely hoped that we will come forward to further this good work, and that such a sum will be subscribed as to enable a handsome edifice to be erected and supported in which God will be praised and his worship manifested to the heathen." C.R., No. 42 of 1861.

Cachar Christianity could not make any influence in the last century.[56]   In 1881 there was no Christian there, and in 1891 the figure was 1 and that too an 'European', in all probability the Officer-in-Charge of the Sub-division.[57]   Although 4 missionaries, three of them ladies, had since engaged themselves in the noble profession, in 1901 Cachar returned 1,040 Christians including 683 natives.[58]   The establishment of two hospitals, at Alipur and Labak, had hardly enabled the 'Gospel' to infiltrate into the ecclesiastical tradition of the people.   Of the total population of 570,531 in 1931, the Hindus were 359,238, Muslims 196,196, Animists 10,319, Jains 26, Buddhists 58 and Christians 4,602.[59]

Allen had found that the original Bengalees of Cachar were 'low caste Hindus' who occupied a 'humble position in the Hindu social scale,' and they were all agriculturists.*[60]   *Patni*, a boating and fishing class in Sylhet, had taken to agriculture. *Namasudra*, another boating and fishing caste, had also taken up the same profession.   The *Jugis* had given up their traditional weaving profession. The *Brahmanas* held rent-free *Brahmattara* lands and were attached to the traditional priestly profession. The *Kayasthas* were appointed by the former Rajas as state officials.   During the British rule, the Bengalees of all castes had immigrated in Cachar and had settled themselves in various professions—Government or industrial employees, traders, shop-keepers and agriculturists. The Manipuris claimed themselves as *Kshatriyas* but in Cachar they were all agriculturists and weavers in leisure.   The North Indians most represented were *Bauri, Bhuiya, Chamar, Munda, Musahar* and *Santal* castes.   *Shah*, a trading caste, and *Das,* a noted agriculturists' class, of Bengal were also of good number.   The merchants from Rajputana and Ajmer-Marwar were known as *Kaiyas*. There were some Kabuli money-lenders and a few Nepalese. The working class from North India was engaged in the tea gardens as plantation labourers.   The Dimachas in North Cachar were mostly Hindus but the Kukis and Nagas were 'Animists' who believed in their traditional tribal religion.   The Dimachas generally lived in the valleys intersecting the hills.   In every village the houses were built in two lines facing each other and,

*Nakpate in Garo Hills and Morung in Naga Hills.

in the centre there was the youngmens' club or *Nodrang*, being
a common feature in the tribal villages of north-eastern India.
In the plains the Dimachas were known as Barman who had
assumed the system of wearing sacred thread like the *Brahmanas*
and the *Kshatriyas*. The *Shemsharas* were the cross between
the Dimachas and the Nagas, they spoke in chaste Dimacha
but had Naga countenance. The Kukis were divided into four
tribes, viz. Rangkhol, Bete, Jansen and Thadoi. Formerly
they lived in the Lushai Hills, but the perpetual unrest in the
hills engendered by inter-clanish feuds had compelled them to
migrate, across Cachar Valley, to North Cachar Hills in the
18th century. The Kuki immigration continued even after the
British annexation of North Cachar in 1854 and the Kuki colonies were established by the Government to act as a buffer
against the Nagas. The Rangkhols and the Betes were a demo-
cratic community and their village affairs were managed by a
group of officers, viz. the *Galun* or headman, *Qubir* or Chief's
Assistant/and two subordinates, the *Chapia* and the *Chapia Qubir*.
The offices were not heriditary and an incumbant had to begin
his career from the bottom of the ladder as *Chapia Qubir*. The
Jansen and Thadoi villages were administered by Rajas who were
supported by the contribution levied from each house and were
aided by *Mantris*. The Kukis planned their village on the hill-
tops on either side of a common road. The houses were built
on bamboo platforms with a *veranda* in the front and partitioned off into rooms. An interesting custom among the
Rangkhols was to render service to the father-in-law for three
years before the marriage and two years after. They were
exempted from the bride's price which the Jansens had to pay.
The Nagas lived in village-clans and their houses were built of
planks and thatched walls disappearing in the roofs which was
brought down almost to the ground. The Dimachas, Nagas,
Kukis all had patriarchal system.[61]

True to the Indian heritage, Cachar was essentially a rural
area and the people in general were agriculturists. In 1901,
almost 89% of the people in the plains were agriculturists, while
the tribesmen in the North Cachar subsisted on the *Jhum* cultivation. Tea was the principal industry of the district, but the
plantation labourers were no better than agricultural workers.
The fishermen, weavers and potters were primarily agriculturists.

The traders and employees in the Government and private concerns returned an insignificant section of the population. As a
matter of fact, the fertile and fallow land in Cachar had attracted the agricultural communities from Bengal during Heramba
rule and, as has already been mentioned, all of them possessed
several *Koolbahs* and every one could claim himself to be a
Mirasdar. Even in the early days of the British rule, traders
from Sylhet, Mymensing and other distircts of Bengal used to
procure the surplus product of the cultivators and drain them
out.[62] The Cachar Valley also supplied food crops to Lushai,
Naga and other adjoining hills including its own northern wing.
But the growth of urbanhood and increase of population during the British rule proved to be a heavy charge upon the local
granary. On the other hand, the introduction of tea estates,
growth of administrative and commercial centres and, above
all the mushroom growth of homesteads had cut down the size
of the cultivable land. Not only export was adandoned, at
times rice was even required to be imported from Sylhet. The
increase of the agricultural population had also resulted in the
rise of the tenant class. The waste land rules introduced by the
Government encouraged the former inhabitants to extend their
holdings and the *Khel* system gradually became extinct. The
Khas lands were all used up and sub-letting became a considerable feature. The land revenue was liberal and in no case was the
demand made in advance. In case of the failure or des-
truction of the crops, remissions were allowed by the Government. In spite of the 'age old method' of cultivation and the
large scale destructions caused by frequent inundations and wild
animals and insects, the yield was very high. Naturally, no one
would be willing to relinquish the land, while in and around
Silchar there was very little land for the *Mirasdars* to spare.
The value of the rice land systematically went up, varying from
Rs. 40 to 60 per acre in the beginning of the present century.
The infiltration of capital resulted in inflation and transfer of
ownership. The Cachar Re-Settlement Report of 1898 shows
that 13% of the cultivated land in Silchar, 18% in Hailakandi
and 20% in Katigorah *tahsils* were held by the tenants. Only
16% of the total area was under the sub-tenants. The tenants
were proportionately numerous in Banraj, Lakhipur, Barnarpur,
Kalain, Jalalpur, Gumra and Chatla *Parganas*. In 1901, there

were 1,58,080 cultivating land-holders, 2,109 non-cultivating land-holders and 80,256 cultivating tenants. Evidently, the number of agricultural workers largely surpassed the owners. To quote Allen, in 1905 : "The large number of cultivating land holders shows that Cachar is still a country of peasant proprietors, and that the landlord class is still numerically a small one."[63]

Besides the agriculturists, there were industrialists, traders, workers and artisans. There was no major industry other than tea. In the beginning, the planters were all Europeans and subsequently few Indians entered in the industry, but until the independence of the country most of the concerns were in the hands of the foreigners. The major trades were also the monopoly of the European companies. The Government and the various companies employed a good number of educated as well as illiterate personnel. The bulk of the paid labourers were engaged in the tea garden and some of them in the construction of roads and buildings. The artisans were mainly carpenters and blacksmiths.[64] A report from R. Stewart, Superintendent of Cachar, in 1862 gives a list of arts, trades and dealings in which the natives in Cachar were engaged.[65]

Agur sellers, Apathecaries, Artists, Bakers, Bamboo sellers, Barbers, Basket makers, Bread sellers, Bird fanciers, Blacksmiths, Beat merchants, Book sellers, Bone turners, Boxwallahs, Braziers, Brass and copper Vessel sellers, Brick makers, Brokers, Bannias, Butchers, Cane sellers, Carpenters, Cattle dealers, Charcoal makers, Cloth merchants, Confectioners, Coppersmiths, Conster mongers, Cotton dealers, Cutters, Dairymen, Daftaries, Dyers, European stone sellers, Ferrymen, Fishermen, Fishery tillers, Fish mongers, Flour merchants, Fruiterers, Ganja sellers, Goldsmiths, Goat farmers, Grass sellers, Gwallahs, Hide dealers, Hooke smoke makers, Horse dealers, Hunters, Idol makers, Innoculaters, Ivory sellers, Khansama, Kaviraj, Mahoots, masons, mat-makers, Miscellaneous dealers, Money changers, Money lenders, Massala men, Musicians, Native doctor, Oil men, Opium sellers, Ornament seller, Overseer, Paddy dealers, Painters, Pan sellers, Parched rice sellers, Pattern drawer, Pawn brokers, Pedlars, Potters, Poulterers, Rice dealers, Rope makers, Salt makers, Salt merchants, Salt water sellers, Sawyers, Sheep farmers, Shoe makers, Silk marchants, Silver smiths, Soap sellers, Soopari sellers, Spirit sellers, Stone cutters, Sugar makers, Sugar sellers, Tailors, Tea makers, Teklahs,

Hatchers, Timber merchants, Tin smiths, Tobacconists, Toy makers, Turban makers, Turners, Vaccinators, Washermen, Wax dealers, Weavers, Weighmen, Wicker workers, Wood cutters, Wood merchants, Writers.

The economic condition of the people of Cachar was fairly satisfactory.[66] The fertility of the soil was notably great, and the rainfall was regular. Although floods and inundations were almost annual features, the bulk of the rice land lay above the risk of flood. The peasants had either *Khas* land or land held in sub-tenancy. There was hardly any unemployed agricultural labourer in the rural areas. They could grow abundant paddy, wheat or sugar. There were ready markets scattered all over the district. With their limited 'want' the agrarian population had no reason to be poverty-striken. During the re-settlement of Cachar in 1898 an attempt was made to divide the agrarian population into the following classes : (i) *Mirasdars* who derived their chief income from rent, (ii) *Mirasdars* who sublet part of their land but were cultivators themselves, (iii) *Mirasdars* who cultivated their entire land, (iv) *Mirasdars* who had to hire land in addition to their own holdings and (v) *Ryots* who owned no land.[67] But the relations between the *Mirasdar* and the *ryots* were good and the protection afforded by the former was considerable in order to prevent the latter from quitting their lands, which would otherwise be the case owing to great demand for labourers in Cachar. The following extracts from a letter of E.R. Lyons, the Superintendent of Cachar, will explain the situation : [68]

8. The Ryots are well clothed and have an abundance of food, but from long habit and custom the quality...is not in proportion to their means, this is they are very frugal and content with simple food, and use less condiment with it than there is any absolute necessity for. There are salt wells in Cachar and the poorer classes usually boil their fish or vegetables in the brine obtainable from the wells, and add a good quantity of chillies and a little termeric but I doubt if the Ryots of many other districts get so good. Use could be found for many more bullocks than are in the district but the people may be considered well supplied in this respect and the supply is increased by animal importations from Munnipore and Assam. There are good many buffaloes in the province and these animals are highly prized, a fine female being worth Rs. 35/- or 40/-....

10. Mendacity is most uncommon; there is scarcely a 'Fuqueer' in the district for I give them but little encouragement, and there is no class in a state of destitution, the extraordinarily small amount of burglary and larceny affords the strongest evidence of this fact.

11. Slavery is common, but slaves can obtain their freedom in accordance with Regulations in force but petitions for emancipations are rarely presented owing to slaves being unusually well treated here...their condition for the most part is that of servants.

That the ecomomic condition of the local people was really sound is best supported by the fact that no villager would agree to act as labourer, and the Government was faced with the unusually difficult problem of labour.[69] Otherwise, the 'bulk of the inhabitants of Cachar' belonged 'to castes which in other parts of India' were 'employed as labourers.'[70] But the facilities to obtain land had been so great that they succeeded in rising to the position of peasent proprietors, or at least cultivators. The land itself was considered the property of the party in whose name it was settled and he had the right to dispose it off in the manner he might consider favourable. Almost every man in Cachar was a *Mirasdar*, being a landholder in his own right and paying the revenue direct to the Government. Most of the states belonged to a number of shareholders and in some parts of the district the want of *ryots* was much felt.[71] No wonder, the labour was both scarce and dear. The Census Report of 1891 shows that the total number of persons supported by general labour in the Cachar plains was only 3,751. In 1901, the number increased to 4,626 or barely 1 per cent of the total population. As a result, the wages were very high, and in 1852 a man could earn 10 *pie* a day from oil pressing, 9 *pie* from rice-husking, 5 *pie* from bamboo works and 2 to 3 *pie* from mat-making in their off seasons.[72] In 1876, an ordinary labourer could earn Rs 7 per mensem in addition to his food and the rate varied from 7 to 10 rupees in the beginning of the present century when the daily wage was 4 to 8 annas.[73] These rates were considered high, but it was the common complaint that the labourers were scarce and difficult to obtain. In Hailakandi, especially, the people flatly refused to work on hire, either because they were 'Meerasdars themselves or relatives of Meerasdars.'[74] The peasantry had a unique sense

of dignity and cultivated their lands themselves, but considered it to be a disgrace to work for others and particularly
as paid labourers. The agricultural enterprise was sanctioned by
ancient usages and the villagers believed it to be a special
blessing of *Laksmi* to work in their own fields. Earlier, the
wealthy *Mirasdars* used to bribe their poorer neighbours to
work by offering a bonus of Re. 1 to $1\frac{1}{2}$ a day, in addition to the
daily wages of 6 annas. Subsequently, the day labourers were
imported from Sylhet under the control of the *daffadars* who
appropriated a portion for the bonus paid for the coolies. This
system of workmen trade was discontinued in 1904, but the
price paid for unskilled labour continued to be enormous, tend-
ing to suggest that the level of prosperity in Cachar must
have been very high.[75]

The planters and the large traders, mostly European, constituted the capitalist class in Cachar and maintained a distinct gap
with the working classes. The petty traders in the towns
and *bazars* could earn to their need. But the employees in
the Government and other European concerns were subjected to
indiscrimination, if not poverty. The Indians were rarely appointed to the high posts, at least during the first century of
the British rule in India. Their scope for promotion was limited
and even in the same capacity the pay, allowances and privileges of an European employee was not extended to his Indian
counterpart.[76] The Indians could be found mostly in the cleri-
cal jobs and these *Babus* or *Badraluks* were hard pressed. More
difficult was the condition of the daily or weekly wage earning
tea labourers. They had to live in the strange distant 'country.'
Ultimately, certain workmen' organisations raised their voice
focusing the deplorable condition of the labourers and trade
union activities started in the tea estates. The nationalist leaders
took up the cause of the coolies and successfully prevailed upon
the Government to institute commissions of inquiry and afford
redresses that could be expected under the system.

The economic condition of the Dimachas, Nagas and Kukis
in the North Cachar Hills was more or less satisfactory. They
grew rice in their *jhum* fields and had patches of sugarcane and
vegetables round their houses. The Naga villages had gardens
of grapes, mangoes and peaches. But the small community
of the Mikirs was 'improvident' and mostly in debt to the *Kaiya*

creditors who gave them advances and brought their cotton at much cheaper rate than in markets. The Rangkhol Kukis, like Mikirs, too could not grow sufficient rice to feed them throughout the year and the quantity of opium they consumed was a very serious drain upon their resources.[77] The standard of living being very simple, the labour was comparatively cheaper in this Subdivision and was paid 2 to 4 annas a day in the beginning of the present century. The Dimachas were the principal employers and engaged Rangkhol, Mikir, Kuki, and Nagas. They seldom worked on hire and never employed from their own people.[78]

The essential commodities were very cheap in Cachar in the last century, but had marked a steady rise in prices. During the reign of Raja Krishnachandra 25 maunds of paddy could be grown in one *Keyar* of land.[79] There was a tradition that Cachar had never acknowledged a famine in its history, and that paddy, rice and milk were never sold or exchanged and that such an act would be looked down by others. There is also tradition that during the Burmese occupation, the Burmese soldiers bought these commodities from the local people, and it is only since then that people in Cachar had learnt to trade in such commodities.[80] In 1829, eighteen maunds of paddy were sold for one rupee.[81] In December 1835, the price of rice was 9 annas, paddy 4 annas, mustared seed Rs. 3-4, cotton Rs. 4, betelnut Rs. 1 and salt Rs. 5 per maund.[82] In 1839-40, Cachar exported goods worth Rs. 19,850 and imported goods worth Rs. 36,800.[83] In 1853, the export goods included paddy, rice, *Chhan*, bamboo, cow and elephant, while the imported commodities were *ghee*, oil, salt, *ganja*, opium and steel. The price of paddy per maund was 2 annas and 2 paise.[84] Even in 1872, twenty-one seers of rice could be purchased for a rupee, but in the seventies the value of the rupee went down to 19 seers and in the eighties to 15 seers. In the beginning of the twentieth century, 12 seers of rice were sold for a rupee in Silchar. In Hailakandi this commodity was cheaper and in 1905 twenty-two seers were sold for a rupee.[85] Hailakandi was a vast paddy growing valley, but sparsely populated. As a result, the price of essential commodities was commendably low. The mustared oil, salt and pulse were also cheap.[86]

The people had a general tendency to keep themselves free

from debt. They cleared the revenue with appreciable regularity and this exhibited their fiscal position. The actitivies of the various banks, including the local Industrial Bank, Bharat Bank and Cachar Central Co-operative Bank, covered the urban areas. In rural areas the agriculturists received petty loans from the *Kabuliwallas, Kaiyas* and *Mirasdars.* An assessment made by Rai Bahadur Sarat Chandra Banerjee, the Settlement Officer, in 1903, shows that only 10% of the house holders were in debt.[87] Banerjee's report also shows that the rate of interest varied according to the amount borrowed. A debt was generally incurred to pay for a wife, land or cattle, lawyer's fee and only sometimes to pay land revenue. The revenue was generally paid by selling surplus paddy, vegetables, poultry, goats or cattle. The Deputy Commissioner in his report for 1902 observed that there had been a marked advance in the economic condition of the people. The readymade garments had come into common use. The coats, cigarettes and other foreign luxuries had gained a large demand. In the years that followed the price level became radically higher as part of the country-wide phenomenon. The colonial economy and imperial exploitation had exhausted the natural wealth of the country and Cachar could hardly be an exception. The fertility of the soil was reduced, production in the tea estates declined, salt wells were exhausted, tusked elephants found their way to the *Kheddahs* and massive exploitation without reinforcement had converted the green forest into barren hillocks. To make matters worse, the two world wars imposed a heavy drain upon the Indian economy. The major role of the British Power in these international crises had taken the otherwise indifferent Indians to fuel the cause of the imperialists in man and material. The Second World War particularly has left behind the harrowing tales of human sufferings. Cachar and the adjacent frontier region received irregular and short supply of essential commodities. Even what they produced of their own, the people had to keep their stores open to feed the defence personnel encamped in several cantonments all throughout the district. The advance of the I.N.A. had at once lifted this frontier into prominence. The British Government was seriously concerned with the safety of its empire and had hardly any time or reason to think for the people. The scarcity of essential commodities and their spiralling prices added with the feeling of insecurity caused by the war propaganda of the Government had taken the people to an unaccountable degree of miseries. An idea about the price index during the last 60 years of British Rule in Cachar and its war-time variations are available from messing dues charged from the borders in Silchar Government High School Hostel. The changes in the messing dues in a Government educational institution, particularly noted for its role in India's Freedom Struggle, make the general price index anybody's guess. The messing charges of each border is given below:[88]

Year	Charge for each border		
	Rs.	As.	P.
1888-89	3	4	8
1892-93	3	14	0
1904-05	7	0	0
1919-20	8	1	6
1922-23	11	4	0
1924-25	7	5	10
1925-26	10	2	2
1930-31	11	10	0
1935-36	8	9	0
1936-37	6	8	0
1937-38	8	1	0
1938-39	6	4	0
1939-40	7	0	0
1941-42	6	6	0
1942-43	9	4	0
1943-44	16	1	0
1944-45	16	11	2
1946-47	19	5	0
1947-48	27	8	0

The progress of education during the British rule was indeed commendable. It was a cooperative achievement of the Government and the people. During the Heramba rule, the Rajas encouraged and patronised education. The *Raj Darbar* was adorned by a galaxy of scholars who had composed a number of scholastic works in Bengali. Rani Chandra Prova, queen of Tamradhwajnarayan, was an admirer of Bengali literature. The celebrated poetical work *Naradiya Rashamrita* was translated into Bengali by Pandit Bhubaneswar Bhattacharya Bachaspati during the reign of her son, Suradarpa Narayan. Suradarpa himself composed some *Malashi* songs. *Brahma Purana* was also translated during this time. The royal priest regularly recited the *Bhagwat Purana* and explained the *slokas* in Bengali to the Raja and his courtiers. The tradition was followed by the succeeding Rajas. *Vivad Darpan*, *Rin Dan Vidhi*, *Heramba Rajyer Danda Vidhi*, *Rana Chandi* were composed in the eighteenth century. Some *puranas* and chapters from the epics were also translated into Bengali. Notable among them were *Vishnu Purana*, *Gaya Purana*, *Prahlad Carit*, and *Ajodya Kanda*, *Kiskinda Kanda*, *Sundar Kanda*, *Lanka Kanda*, *Viravahu Yudha*, *Laksmaner Sakti Shel* and *Uttar Kanda* from *Ramayana* and *Drona Parvan* and *Virat Parvan* of *Mahabharata*. The names of the translaters are not known as we could not go through the manuscripts. Babu Mukunda Datta, a noted poet of Cachar, composed the book *Raghunather Aswamedha*. The last two Rajas of Cachar, Krishnachandra and Govindachandra were well-versed in Bengali and Sanskrit. They have left behind a large number of *Rasha* and *Malashi* songs. The *Pala Git* of Krishnachandra are still popular. Govindachandra's collection of self-composed songs *Maharashatsov Gitamrita* is a treasure of Bengali literateur. His translation of *Rasha Panchadhyay* is highly scholastic.[89] One Sambhunath Sarma Deshamukhya prepared a long map indicating the physical features from Udharband to Kashidham (Benaras) to facilitate the visit of Raja Krishnachandra.[90] Chandra Mohon Barman, a Dimacha, was a noted literateur. His *Hairamba Bhasa Prabesh* and score of poems have enriched the nineteenth century Bengali literature.[91]

These facts lead to easy conclusion that the pursuit of learning was held in high esteem by the former rulers of Cachar. As a matter of fact, they granted scholarship to the Brahmins and *Kayasthas* alike for studies in Bengal. They also entertained few *Pandits* who 'gave instructions in Bengali and Sanskrit'. The education was, however, 'confined to the Brahmins' while the Muslims were, 'in a state of as complete ignorance as the bulk of the same persuation in Sylhet.'[92] The Rajas of Cachar had granted *Brahmattara* land to the Brahmins and the traditions suggest that the Brahmins ran *tols* in their houses. The existence of regular *tols* and *Pathshalas* in the noted temples of *Ranachandi* and *Kachakanti*, where learned Brahmins were appointed by the Rajas as herditary *Sebayats* can not be ruled out, considering that *adhyapana* or teaching was an additional duty of the temple priests in India in the former times. It is, however, not unlikely that in an agricultural 'country' like Cachar the bulk of the common people had little interest in learning and the education was confined to the Brahmins and people of high castes. The officials might have received their education in Sylhet which had produced eminent scholars from a remote period of history.

No wonder, therefore, urging upon the Government to extend educational facilities to the people of Cachar without delay, Fisher, the first Superintendent of Cachar, in his report in June 1834 observed :[93]

> ...the business of public instructions appears now generally to be considered the duty of the state, the absence of it has long been among the better informed natives the approach of our rule in India.... Christian education alone could not be proposed without incurring the most alarming risques [risks]. The scholars should be allowed to receive instruction in their own faith. At the same time 1 think it would be desirable to furnish a portion of the pupils with the means of prosecuting their studies under more advantageous circumstances either at Calcutta or Serampore, where they might enlarge their minds, and prove on their return perhaps the means of effecting great improvements among their countrymen.
> ...The entire instruction in this district is to be conveyed in the Bengali language.

Fisher also proposed that a competent *Pandit* from Sylhet be appointed as a teacher in the first ever school to be started in Cachar by the British Government. But his pious desire took a long time to be materialised. On 22 September 1837, J.G. Burns, then Superintendent, while considering that "the means of instructions would indeed be a boon and gratefully received as such by the inhabitants of Cachar" feared that "the resources of the country would not admit but a very limited scale of its introduction."[94] But on 25 April 1838, Burns wrote:[95]

> The places most suitable for schools in Cachar are the 3 Thanas viz. Silchar (the Sudder), Hyliakandi and Kattee-

gora and the large pargunnah of Sonapoor. The spots are
the central and accessible to scholars from the neighbouring
Pargunnahs except during a portion of the rainy season.
With regards to teachers there are none in Cachar no native
of the Zillah capable of this task, but competent men can be
had from Sylhet where there is a Pundit whom Capt. Fisher
proposed employing should schools ever be established here.
There is also a competent man in the Colectorate Sershta
here. I imagine Rs. 20/- monthly would be sufficient salary.
The expense of stationary can be ascertained and settled
hereafter and either be charged as expended of a consolidated sum allowed.

As school rooms must be built there would be a difficulty for
want of grass in doing so till after the rains, and as I have
some doubts of the people of Cachar availing themselves of
the opportunity I would recommend beginning with one at
the suddar station as an experiment. As there will be many
candidates for admission on the part of the families of the
Amla and hangers on here as also from Sylhet I wish to be
informed if the school is intended only for the natives of
Cachar or whether all applying indiscriminately to be
admitted.

Accordingly, a school was established at Silchar and maintained by the voluntary subscription of the *Amlahs* and the
Superintendent. But the subscription gradually fell off and, as
a result, the school was abolished.[96] In 1851, a petition was
made to the Commissioner of Surma Valley, on behalf of the
guardians, to provide educational facilities to the local lads.
Consequently, the Superintendent was called upon to ascertain
how many persons would pay at the rate of one anna per
month, if a public school was established. It may be interesting
to note that no one came forward to subscribe the amount for
the education of his children. On the other hand, a section of
the people requested the Superintendent 'to endeavour to have
a Government School established, where all children would
receive schooling gratis.'[97] The request moved G. Verner, the
Superintendent, who felt that if some Government schools were
established in Cachar they would benefit the district and 'the
children of the more respectable portion of the community
would gradually get into the habit of attending regularly and
learn to read and write which but few of them can do now.'[98]

Unfortunately, the recommendations of the Superintendent
did not find favour with the Government of Bengal. However,

in 1857, three schools were started at Silchar, Hailakandi and Katigorah on private subscriptions. The enrolment in the Silchar School was 128, while the schools at Hailkandi and Katigorah averaged 30 each.[99]   But the schools did not receive any financial assistance from the Government. The enrolment in the Silchar School came down to 13 in 1861 and the school was closed down in 1862. During the five years that the school lasted many local boys received instructions in Bengali and English. Some of them were provided as Writers in public offices, while others were employed by the tea planters. None but the ruling Government has to be blamed for the extinction of the school. To quote R. Stewart, the Supreintendent of Cachar:[100]

> The denial of Government assistance made it languish and not only did the attendance gradualy lessen but the subscription began to fall until latterly they ceased altogether, and the last few months of its existence it lived entirely upon its capital until that too was exhausted and then it closed.

Anyway, the Katigorah and Hailakandi Schools continued to exist on private subscription, Naturally, it makes an interesting note that the inbabitants at the outstations at Hailakandi and Katigorah could maintain private schools when the only school at the Saddar Station had to be abandoned for the lack of patronage. Stewart, therefore, opined that the opening of school at Silchar should be the duty of the Government as it would be impossible to set up a school again on private subscription, the public having been disgusted with the apathy of the Government to extend financial assistance. Believing that the 'money spent in establishing a Government school here would be by no means thrown away and would be but a measure of justice' to the people whose revenue was 'so rapidly increasing and whose resources' were 'so important', the Superintendent felt that the Government should first built a school house and then appoint a good English teacher and a Bengali one. The monthly expenditure, he estimated, would be Rs. 100 to 150. On 17 July 1862, he requested R.L. Martin, Inspector of Schools, South East Circle, Bengal, to 'obtain Government sanction for the same and set this useful institution once more again.'[101] In continuation, on 16 September, he proposed that Rs. 1800 be allowed for the construction of a large 'kutcha pucca' house as school building. He also proposed to the Inspector that the 'Government should be solicited to grant to the Cachar School the same allowance that were accorded to the lowest class of Zilla schools in the Regulation Provinces' and that 'at first the whole staff of school masters' be not required at the Sudder Station and the junior teachers 'be deputed to outstations of Katigora and Hailakandi.' At the outstations, 'the school houses would be erected by the parents of the pupils themselves, and contingencies and repairs of the Sudder School house could be paid out of the amount of fees collected from the scholars.[102]

Meanwhile, the Wood's Despatch of 1854 had already recommended the system of giving grant-in-aid to the private sponsored schools so that the financial commitment of the Government did not become heavy. But 'in districts remote from the great centre of civilisation and activity,' the Government was prepared to take upon itself greater responsibility. On 10 August 1863, the Lieutenant Governor of Bengal assigned strong reasons for the establishment of Government schools in Cachar, Deoghar and Dibrugarh.[103] Evidently, a favourable atmosphere was created for starting a Government School at Silchar. But at the moment Reverend William Pyrse of the Sylhet Presbyterian Church appeared in the field.[104]

Popularly known as the pioneer of English education in the Surma Valley, Rev. Pyrse had started a school at Sylhet and in the Entrance Examination of the Calcutta University in 1859 Babu Nabakishore Sen, a student in the Pyrse's School, came out successful.[105] Elated by his success in Sylhet, Pyrse wanted to extend his field of operation to Cachar and, accordingly, wrote to the Superintendent of Cachar for necessary permission. R. Stewart, the Superintendent, welcomed the proposal and allowed Pyrse to start his school in the former school house at Silchar.[106] In November 1863, Pyrse came to Silchar and on 1 December started the Cachar High Grammar School with 80 students. Babu Nabakishore Sen was appointed as the first Headmaster and the Superintendent of Cachar sanctioned a monthly grant of Rs. 80 on behalf of the Government.[107] The school continued under the grant-in-aid system till August 1868 when it was converted into a Government Zilla School. Some years later, in October 1872, the school came directly under the management and control of the District Committee. But on 2 May 1879, the secondary education was transferred to the control of the Inspector of Schools, while the Deputy Commissioner and the members of the District Committee were regarded as the visitors of the school.[108] Despite the donations, private subscriptions were realised for the maintenance of the school. During all these changes, Babu Abhay Charan Bhattacharjee was the Head master of the school, while Babu Nabakishore Sen, the first Headmaster, was the Deputy Inspector of Schools, Surma Valley.

The establishment of a High Grammar School in 1863 under Rev. Pyrse should be taken as the beginning of English education in Cachar. But a very pertinent question should not escape attention. Could there be a High or Secondary School without feeder schools ? The officials from time to time reported that there was no school in Cachar.[109] Maybe, this indicated the absence of an English or Government school. This apprehension finds support in the General Administration Report of Cachar for 1861-62 wherein R. Stewart, Superintendent of Cachar, recorded that "Report of Education in Cachar for the year 1861/62 is blank, there being no Government institution in the District."[110] Again, in the report for 1863-64 he repeated "Report on education in Cachar for the year 1862/63 is blank, there being no Government in- stitution in this District."[111] But we definitely know, as dis- cussed above, there was a school run on private contributions for five years, from 1857 to 1862, and that in 1863 Rev. Pyrse started a High Grammar School. R. Stewart, Superintendent, in his Annual Report for 1863-64, stated about this school as follows :[112]

The Welok Presbyterian Mission have established a school in Cachar, which is supported by public subscriptions and a Grant-in aid made by the Government. This institution, commenced on 1st December last, is thriving and deserves every support. About 80 boys attended.

There might have been also some *pathshalas* maintained purely on private basis and some *tols* run by individual priests or *Pandits* of which the officials either failed to take note of or was beyond the perview of their correspondence.   Rev. Pyrse's school appeared in the Superintendent's report because it received grant-in-aid from the Government.

The *pathshalas* were not brought within the scheme of the grant-in-aid until 1872 and, as a result, there is no mention of such institutions in the official records. The Report of the Director of Public Instructions for 1870-71 shows that there were 5 Government and Aided schools in Cachar which were attended by 248 pupils; the classification being Government English School 1, Government Vernacular Schools 3, Aided Vernacular School 1. The Report for 1871-72 shows that there were 1 Government Higher English School, 3 Government Primary Schools, 1 Aided Primary School and 1 Unaided school, which were attended by 211 pupils. Sir George Campbell's reform, in 1872, extended the benefit of the grant-in-aid system to the *pathshalas* and also provided that even unaided schools would be subject to annual inspections. As a result, the Report for 1872-73 shows that there were 1 Government Higher English School, 3 Government Lower Vernacular Schools, 1 old *pathshala* and 19 new *pathshalas* and 104 Unaided schools. The number of schools under inspection had thus increased to 128 and the number of pupils to 2,259. In 1874-75 the district returned 131 schools, attended by 2,508 pupils. There were 108 primary schools, with 1,987 boys and 132 girls in the roll. The Middle Vernacular Schools numbered 6 and were attended by 238 pupils. The number of higher schools had increased to 7, attended by 373 students. The Cachar Zilla school or the Silchar Government High School was attended by 135 students. Same year, a Normal School was started at Silchar to cater to the need of both Cachar and Sylhet, and there were 16 teacher-trainees in the roll. In addition, there were two secondary schools under the missionaries.[113]

In 1876 two Middle English Schools were started in Silchar, of which one was aided and the other a private institution. Meanwhile, an Aided High School had started in Hailakandi and Middle English and Middle Vernacular Schools were opened in the rural areas of Barkhola, Katigorah and Narsingpur. A good number of primary schools were established in the sub-divisional and *thana* headquarters as well as important *bazars.* The big tea estates also established primary schools for the education of the children of their employees. Sir Edward Gait, the editor of 1891 Census report, had observed that "the proportion of literate males is highest in Cachar plains" and turning to the females "the largest proportion of learners is in Cachar."[114] The Welsh Presbyterian Mission started a Girls' High School at Silchar in 1895, which was subsequently taken over by the Government. The Narshing M. E. School at Silchar was upgraded to be an Aided High School and another Government High School was started at Hailakandi.

The medium of instruction in general was Bengali. The High Schools were affiliated to the Calcutta University. There was no Entrance Examination centre at Silchar till 1906 and the candidates had to appear from the Sylhet Centre. In 1906, Kamini Kumar Chanda and Rai Bahadur Haricharan Das took the initiative for having University Examination Centre at Silchar and the Silchar Bar Association actively backed the demand. Ultimately, the University opened an examination centre at Silchar.[115] In Silchar Government High School a law class was introduced in the nineties for preparing the candidates for the pleadership examination. It was an independent institution and Rai Bahadur Haricharan Das, who was the first student of the Silchar Government High School to pass the Entrance Examination (1868) and also the first B. L. in the legal profession in Cachar, was the first Lecturer in Law. During his illness, resulting in retirement, Babu Kamini Kumar Chanda M.A., B.L. was appointed as a Lecturer.[116]

Some references may also be made to the inspecting staff. In the beginning, Cachar was included in the jurisdiction of the Inspector of Schools, South Eastern Circle, Bengal, while Cachar, Sylhet, Commilla and Mymensing were under one Deputy Inspector. In 1865, Sylhet and Cachar, known as the Surma Valley, were made a seperate circle under a Deputy Inspector and Babu Nabakishore Sen, the first Headmaster of Silchar High School was appointed as the first Deputy Inspector of the Circle.[117] Since the creation of the Chief Commissionership of Assam, in 1874, the Surma Valley had one Inspector of Schools with headquarters at Silchar. Cachar had two Deputy

Inspectors, one at Silchar and the other at Hailakandi, and the Deputy Inspector at Silchar was aided by a Sub-Inspector.

The progress of education in Cachar in the last century can be realised from the following table:[118]

Year	No. of secondary schools	Pupils	No. of primary schools	Pupils	Total No. of pupils
1874-75	7	373	108	2,119	2,492
1880-81	7	446	99	2,565	3,001
1890-91	3	413	190	4,708	5,121
1900-01	4	654	248	7,188	7,842

In the present cetnury, education made a marked progress in Cachar. The Silchar Government High School grew both in size and performance of the students. In 1910 the school had 430 students, and in the Matriculation Examination of the Calcutta University that year 16 candidates appeared from the school. Of them, 15 came out in first division and one in second division, while seven secured scholarship. One Brojendra Kumar Biswas headed the list of successful candidates in Assam and secured 6 medals.[119] By the time the Hailakandi Government High School had received solid foundation and very few students would come to Silchar from that Subdivision. During the Non-Cooperation Movement many nationalist students left their schools at the clarion call of Gandhiji. A National School was then started for the rebel boys, although it proved to be short-lived. But the Dinanath-Nabakishore Balika Vidyalaya, better known as Swadeshi School, established during the period by the nationalist leaders still provides an ideal centre of women education in Cachar. Similarly, during the Civil Disobedience Movement many students left the Government High School as a protest against the Cunningham Circular and to accomodate them the Cachar High School was established at Malugram. With the establishment of the Ambikapur* High School the number of such schools rose to six. In the rural areas there were five high schools, while Hailakandi had two. Haflong had no high school during the British rule. As a matter of fact, the actual emphasis during the colonial period was on the primary

*Adharchand High School.

education. In addition to the primary schools run by the Local Boards and the Government, the tea estates also sponsored L. P. Schools for the instruction of the children of their employees. No wonder, therefore, in 1931, Cachar returned 51,692 literates; 46,271 of them being males and 5,421 females,[120] while the percentage of literacy was eleven.

The establishment of Gurucharan College at Silchar, on the other hand, marked the beginning of higher education in Cachar. The bulk of the matriculates from Cachar could not pursue their collegiate education at Sylhet or Calcutta for obvious reasons. At the initiative of Arun Kumar Chanda and purse donated by Mrs. Kiranshashi Naug, the Gurucharan College was started in 1935 in a dilipidated bungalow at Rangpur. Arun Kumar Chanda himself served the college as the Honorary Principal, while Mahesh Chandra Dey, Digindranath Bhattacharjee, Dhirendra Kumar Bhattacharjee, Nikhil Sen, Khushi Mohan Das, Upendra Shankar Datta, Pramesh Chandra Bhattacharjee, Rabindranath Datta, Kamini Kumar Adhikari and Rev. T. W. Rees were among the members of the teaching faculty during the formative years of the college. The college began with 60 students in First Year Arts. Ramendra Deshamukhya, Sudhir Sen, Kapil Bhattacharjee Arzan Ali were among these poineers. The college was affiliated to the Calcutta University and an examination centre was opened at Silchar from the very beginning. In 1946 the college was temporarily shifted to the normal school building and the classes were held in the morning. Shortly afterwards, the college was shifted to its present site at Tikarbasti. The Gurucharan College had opened a new horizon for higher education in Cachar. It has gradually been developed as one of the premier institutions of collegiate education in North East India.

The progress of education is closely linked with the facilities for booksellers, libraries and printing presses. In Cachar these problems could be solved not without much initial difficulties. The earliest book stall in Silchar was started by Babu Mahananda De at Dewanjibazar and the next was Students' Library at Janiganj. The Calcutta Book Society, which used to supply all the text books of the university, had no agent at Silchar. The Headmaster of the Government High School had, therefore, to procure the required text books for his pupils from the Society's Calcutta Office. The books for the school library and for awarding prizes to students were also obtained from Calcutta. The leading suppliers were M/s. S. K. Lahiri & Co. and M/s. Thaker Spink & Co. However, the opening of a book stall by Mahananda De and the Students' Library came as a great relief to the teachers and the taught. But these book-sellers could not supply text books. The establishment of the Saraswati Library by Babu Baidyanath De to some extent solved the problem. But it indulged in the circulation of note-books among the students.[121] This was considered as a serious problem by the guardians of education. The Director of Public Instruction, Eastern Bengal and Assam, in 1910, suggested the running of a book-stall by the teachers of the Silchar Government High School as a remedy. But the teacher did not take the risk of competing with the existing book-sellers.[122]

The Government High School had a school library almost from the very beginning. The other schools also maintained their own libraries according to the resources at their command. The normal school Library was known for its rare collections. Similarly, the Gurucharan College authorities had taken interest in developing the library and reading habits of the students. In 1935, Dr. H. K. Mukherjee, Vice-Chancellor of Calcutta University, was happy over the display of newspapers and journals in the students' common room. As early as in 1876, a public library, known as Keatinge Library, was established at Silchar during the visit of Sir H. Keatinge, Chief Commissioner of Assam (1874-76). Renamed as Arun Chanda Granthagar since independence, it has recently been merged with the District library.

The educational institutions and public organisations also endeavoured to promote extra-curricular activities among the students and youths. Silchar has a great sporting tradition and is proud of the unique distinction of having staged the world's first official polo match played in 1853. The army officers, tea planters and British civilians posted in Cachar had developed keen interest in this game. Captain R. Stewart, Superintendent of Cachar, was an ardent polo enthusiast and due to his personal initiative the first official match could be played at Silchar.

The game gradually attracted business men and army personnel from many parts of India and official matches became an annual feature in winters. The enthusiasm temporarily subsided during the Sepoy Mutiny but was revived by Captain Stewart in 1861. Lieutenant J. Sharer, Assistant Superitendent of Cachar, was another polo enthusiast and joined Stewart in organising the game. As a result, the Silchar Polo Club was established in 1861 as the first official polo club in the world. The game did not remain confined to Cachar for long. In 1862 it was introduced in Dacca by Captain E. Hill of the Lahore Light Horse who was introduced to the game during a sojourn in Cachar. As a matter of fact, the game had gradually become a craze in the town and the greatest attraction for the vistors. The European merchants of Calcutta on their various missions to Silchar evinced keen interest in the game which was eventually introduced in Calcutta.[123] The football and *kabadi*, on the other hand, were the most popular games among the local youths. Besides, local games and inter-institutional competitions, the sporting teams from the educatianal institutions participated in various tournaments in Bengal and the school teams from other parts of Bengal also reciprocated. The football, cricket and hockey clubs in Silchar participated in all-India competitions, while the football clubs of national fame took part in the tournaments held in Silchar. The India club, Town Club and Silchar Sports Association were popular sports organisations in Cachar, while Nolini Mohon Gupta, Ashu Datta and Narendra Gupta were among the local talents of Cachar who achieved distinction in the sporting history of India. The Silchar School Cricket and Debating Club provided a unique forum for the culture of sporting and oratorical zeal of the students. The Gurucharan College Students' Majlis, introduced since the tenure of A. K. Chanda, helped the students to cultivate their aptitude through games and sports, debate and symposia, theatrical and literary competitions, besides leadership training. Bani Parishad, a study circle in Silchar Normal School, organised weekly literary discussions.

Cachar had its first printing press in 1885. The Silchar Press, which even now exists on Central Road, was the first printing press founded by Babu Hara Kishore Gupta.[124] Soon after, Sadhya Press was established by Babu Radhakanta

Sadhya. In the beginning of the present century, Aryan Press was established by the Aryan Insurance Company, Silchar. This was closely followed by the Cachar Press of Babu Satyadas Roy and Jayanti Press of Babu Gajendra Chandra Datta. In the forties, few more printing presses came into existence.

The growth of printing presses facilitated the progress of journalism. The earliest known newspaper of Cachar was a Bengali weekly *Silchar*. This was printed in the Silchar Press and edited by Babu Bidhu Bhusan Sen, a teacher in the Narshing M.E. School.* Popularly known as *Bidhu Pandit*, the editor "had a very powerful pen, and he used it unsparingly against both officials and non-officials. His writing was full of satire and wit. So fearless was he that though serving a school aided by the Government, he did not hesitate to attack the Inspector of Schools and the D.P.I."[125] Enraged by his satires, Wilson, the D.P.I., on one occasion, threatened to withdraw the grant from Narshing School if the *Pandit* continued to be the editor of *Silchar*. As a result, the paper was discontinued for some years, but revived in 1897 when Wilson was no longer in the office. The editor soon resumed his fiery columns and carried on attacks on the District authorities and the Head Master of the Government High School.[126] The Head Master sought the permission of the D.P.I. to prosecute the editor for defamation, while the Deputy Commissioner refused to recommend the exchange of the Assam Gazettee with this paper.[127] Bidhu Babu was a conservative caste Hindu, and this conservatism brought him into tussle with the Head Master. The cook in the Hindu Hostel of the Government High School was a non-Brahmin and *Silchar* raised the demand for a Brahmin cook. In its issue of 29 July 1903, the paper said : "Great inconvenience is felt by the students in the Silchar Boarding for want of a Brahmin cook. The Head Master does not like to take any step in this connection, because he is neither a Brahmin nor a Kayastha. We request the Director to see his way to remove the inconvenience."[128] This episode reflects the contemporary social scene in Cachar. Untouchability was definitely practised. Even Bidhu Bhusan, who not a Brahmin himself, was serious for a Brahmin cook in the students' hostel.

*Later upgraded to High School.

Incidentally, the Head Master was Babu Abhaya Charan Das, and the charge of the editor that he did not take any step was unwarranted. As a matter of fact, the Head Master for a long time had been pressing the authorities for a Brahmin cook.[129] Although Bidhu Bhusan was censored for 'scurrilous writings,'[130] it may be said that the Government High School was the actual target of his attack, and not the Head Master. This school, inspite of its brilliant performances, had incurred the displeasure of many as a Government institution. During Swadeshi movements several guardians had refused to send their children to this school and some public institutions had sprang up in the town to provide the alternative. Moreover, the caste rules had not changed much towards the close of the 19th century. Untouchability was a universal social problem in India and continued to be so till very recently. What could be expected from Cachar which had emerged from Feudal Hindu Rule only in 1830 ? A society has to be studied in the context of age, background and situation. Bidhu Bhusan was the product of his own age, and what appeared in the columns of his paper might not necessarily be his own views. As a journalist, he might have represented the contemporary public opinion. Nevertheless, Bidhu Bhusan Sen was the pioneer of journalism in Cachar. *Silchar* was the only newspaper in the district in the last century, and it played a commendable role in guiding public opinion and focusing attention on social and political problems.

In 1911, *Surma*, another Bengali weekly, began its publication from the Aryan Press. The first editor was Pandit Chandraday Vidyavinode, and was succeeded by Pandit Bhuban Mohon Vidyarnava. The Aryan Trading Company at Silchar was the owner and publisher. In 1914, the paper was converted into a daily and it kept the people informed about the developments of World War I. Being discontinued for some years in the twenties, the *Surma* resumed its publication in the thirties under the editorship of Babu Nagendra Chandra Shyam, the noted lawyer-literateur of Cachar. In the forties the paper was edited by Shri Hurmat Ali Barlaskar, now editor of another Bengali weekly *Azad*. Daring in spirit and constructive in criticism, the *Surma* played a great role in guiding the public opinion in Cachar and on occasions forced the Government to note its comments.[131] It also acted as a fillip to the literary pursuits in Cachar by opening columns for the young talents. Nagendra Chandra Shyam, Ashoke Bijoy Raha, Ramendra Deshamukhya and Sudhir Sen were among the regular contributors.

Like Bidhu Bhusan Sen, Pandit Bhuban Mohon Vidyarnava is a great name in the history of journalism in Cachar. Besides his association with the *Surma*, he edited *Deshabrata* and *Janasakti* from Sylhet. Earlier he was associated with *Hitavadi* and *Sadhana*, published from Calcutta and Dacca respectively. Bhuban Mohon was an ardent nationalist without belonging to any political party and wielded his pen forcefully for the national cause. As a journalist, he preached the Swadeshi spirit and enthused the young men with the high ideals of the culture of ancient India. He became the editor of the *Surma* in 1912 and continued to edit the paper when it was converted into a daily in 1914. Bhuban Mohon had thus the unique distinction of editing the first daily newspaper published from Cachar.[132] He was also the editor of *Brahmans Parishat Patrika*, a Bengali feature journal. This was the organ of the *Silchar Brahman Parishat* and was first published on 25 April 1929. Printed by Babu Radhakanta Sadhya at the Sadhya Press, the *Patrika* was published by Pandit Kalijay Nyayapanchanan of Silchar.[133] The object of the journal, as stated in the declaration before the court, was the 'Social Reform of Brahmin Society.' It is interesting to note that the spirit of reform had reached the Brahmin society in Silchar and an organisation was formed to reform the society. The *Patrika* was a media for the self-criticism of the guardians of the Hindu society in Cachar, and Bhuban Mohon and his colleagues had responded to the needs of the time. Similarly, the *Vaidic Brahmins* of Cachar were associated with the *Shreehatta Vaidic Samiti*. The proceedings of the *Samiti* were printed at the Sadhya Press and edited and published by Babu Ram Chandra Bhattacharjee of Silchar in 1929.[134]

Bhabishyat, a Bengali monthly, also came into publication in 1929. It was edited by Babu Aswini Kumar Chakravarty of Shillongpatty. *Silchar*, was printed at the Calcutta Printing Works, Calcutta, and published from Ukilpatty, Silchar.[135] The Gurucharan College Majlis brought out its handwritten magazine, *Kundakali*, in 1935 and poet Rabindranath Tagor sent his blessings. The College Magazine, *Purbasree,* came into publication since 1940. Earlier, *Vijoyini,* was published in 1930 as the organ of the *Silchar Mahila Samiti.* Edited by Professor Khushi Mohon Das and printed at the Jayanti Press, *Saptak,* a literary magazine, was published in 1937. In these publications initiative was taken by Principal A.K. Chanda and Tagore blessed them all.

Besides these newspapers and magazines, a large number of literary works were published from Cachar. But this is beyond our perview to discuss their details in this volume leaving this theme to be dealt with in an appropriate study in future. A few among the innumerable books which were written during the devastating flood of 1929 (Bengali year 1336) may be named here. Babu Suresh Chandra Bhattacharjee, a teacher in the Silchar Government High School, published his book *Cachare Mahaplaban.* Moulavi Monawar Ali Mazumdar's *Jaler Kabita,* and Amiruddin Barbhuiya's *Jal Plabaner Ganer Puthi* and *Bam Cachare Banyar Kabita* were printed in the Sadhya Press and published in September 1929.[136] Same month, *Sambandha Chintamani* by Surya Kumar Tarka Saraswati, *Jailkhanar Puthi O kaler Baibaran* by Kala Mia and *Matri Adesh* by Baikunta Charan Das were registered.[137] These books were also printed in Sadhya Press and published from Silchar. Some copies of Kala Mia's book were transferred to the India Office Library, London, by an order of the Director of Public Instruction.[138] The registration of seven books in the same month and their publication from the same printing press would project an idea of the literary pursuits in Cachar. That the Bengalees are poetic by nature may be supported by the information that one Shri Barenya Bejoy Choudhury, a student in the Silchar Government High School in the thirties; after a teacher had narrated in the class how his affectionate grandmother would preserve sweets for him two months before the vacations when the teacher himself was a student, immediately wrote a poem *Amar Thakurma* and presented it to the teacher.[139] A similar incident was reported in 1911. On the Coronation Day of King George V, a procession of the school boys paraded through the streets of the town. A student of class IX in the Government High School had composed a poem synchronising the occasion and it was sung by the boys when they marched in procession. The poem was full of noble sentiments and possessed excellent literary merit. The composer was awarded a special medal by the Director of Public Instruction and printed copies of the poem were distributed among the students in schools and colleges.[140] Cachar had thus a great literary heritage. In 1933, the Third Surma Valley Literary Conference was held at Silchar, and many local poets and writers presented their compositions.

Evidently, the impact of British rule on Cachar was commendable. It had put an end to the feudal legacy. The hitherto fallow lands were brought under cultivation and the products were exported abroad. The tremendous increase of population, opening of the country, progress of education, growth of towns and the facilities for trade and commerce and employment ushered in radical socio-economic transformation. A landless agriculturist was unknown in Cachar in the pre-colonial period, but the increasing pressure of population now reduced the size and fertility of the arable land. The fallow lands were mostly leased for tea plantation. The frequent transfers of the agricultural lands, on the other hand, converted a section of the cultivators into landless peasantry and forced them to be wage earners. Many agriculturists also sold their land to provide for the education of the children. Once educated, the youths preferred to live only in the towns and, as a result, there was mobilisation of the population from rural to the urban areas. The people, whose traditional occupation was agriculture, had now to live with the plantation workers in the tea estates and the traders and *babus* in the towns. The agrarian community found new sources of earnings and their younger generation secured employment in the government and private sectors. The hitherto purely agricultural tract thus achieved a mixed economy, resulting in the emergence of an economically dominant middle class. The progress of education added to the consciousness of the people and the role of the intellectual middle class in social, economic and political behaviour of the people exposed its inherent characteristics. The Regulations of the Government were gradually introduced and the people became concerned with their rights and greivances, while the improvement of the means of communication established more closer contacts between the different parts of the district as well as with the rest of the country. The spirit of Bengal renaissance imme-diately swept over this eastern sentinel of the greater valley. The caste rules gradually lost their rigidity and there was a rapid upward mobility. The cross-section of the people deve-loped a new society, while the fast acculturation of the North Indians, Manipuris and other outsiders provides interesting areas of sociological study.

APPENDIX 7

Population Tables

TABLE I

Year	South Cachar	North Cachar
1831	50,000	14,000
1837	—	6,000
1842	80,000	—
1851	85,522	20,000
1857	137,000	30 000

TABLE II

Year	Cachar Plains	North Cachar Hills	Total
1872	2,05,027	30,000	2,35,027
1881	2,93,738	20,121	3,13,859
1891	3,67,542	18,941	3,86,483
1901	4,14,781	40,812	4,55,593
1911	4,69,984	29,491	4,99,475
1921	5,00,388	28,913	5,29,301
1931	5,37,687	32,844	5,70,531

TABLE III
POPULATION IN 1931

Subdivisional		Linguistic	
Silchar	386,695	Bengali	3,38,772
Hailkandi	150,992	Hindi	1,03,789
North Cachar Hills	32,844	Manipuri	55,550
TOTAL	570,531	Dimacha	13,547
		Oriya	9,611
		Bodo (Plains Kachari)	9,068
		Kuki (all tribes)	8,885
		Naga (all tribes)	6,871
		Mundari	4,128
		Santhali	3,327
		Mikir	3,132
		Assamese	2,215
		Telegu	2,097
		Khasi	1,737
		Nepali	1,671
		Oraon	1,604
		Tipperah	852
		Gondi	773
		Turi	676
		Lushai	412
		English	331
		Kandhi	298
		Karku	229
		Pashto	175
		Punjabi	168
		Bhumji	155
		Tamil	147
		Gujrati	133
		Marathi	123
		Rajasthani	20
		Khamti	16
		Miri	9
		Chinese	9
		Koch	7
		Magari	5
		Limbu	4
		Chutiya	2
		Garo	1
		Bhotia	1
		Others	51
		TOTAL	5,70,531

CHAPTER IX

Epilogue

The discussions in the foregoing chapters are expected to provide a graph of the machination of British Raj in Cachar. As a matter of fact, the British Rule had provided a great relief to the local people hit hard by the misrule of Raja Govindachandra, atrocities perpetrated by Tularam, turmoils created by the Manipuri princes, Kuki incursions and Naga raids. The last two, accompanied by natural calamities, continued to pose problems even after the annexation of the kingdom. The security measures and works of public utility undertaken by the ruling Government might have attached the people of Cachar by a sense of gratitude.[1] But hardly had the British Government consolidated its position in Cachar, the national struggle for freedom began to gain ground in the country. The nearness to Sylhet, which had produced the freedom fighter of national stature and shared the storm and stress of the national movement, immediately drew Cachar to join the challenge. The sense of loyalty was immediately shaken and the spirit of nationalism raised its gallant head. The Surma Valley had a joint response to the call for national agitation and the two districts, Sylhet and Cachar, were partners in the political programmes.

In the Sepoy Mutiny of 1857, which is regarded by a section of the historians as the first war of India's independence, Cachar had no part to play. But three companies of the 34th Native Infantry, which had mutinied at Chittagong, entered Cachar with the intention to push on into Manipur. They were encountered by the British troops at several places. At Latu, the mutineers succeeded in killing Major Byong of the Sylhet Light Infantry. But they were exposed to great hardship and only a few could escape death or arrest. The detenues were tried summarily and sentenced to be shot. The Manipur princes, then detained in Cachar and having designs on the throne of Manipur, endeavoured to befriend the mutineers, but failed to organise and thereby exposed themselves to British wrath.[2] The tea-planters of Cachar had raised a volunteer force which fought with the mutineers and compelled them to retire in the jungle to the east. A notable encounter took place at Dwarband wherefrom the volunteers under one Mr. Hogg chased the mutineers in the Lushai hills and discovered a treasure. Mr. Hogg and several others from Cachar received the Indian Mutiny Medal.[3]

Reference may be made to some sporadic risings that had taken place in Cachar against the British. In 1882, Sambhudhan, a Dimacha, claiming himself to be a directly inspired agent of God and an expert in miraculous cure, had collected a small body of followers. Pitching up his *ashram* at Maibong, the *Deo*, as Sambhudhan was known to his followers, forced the neighbours to contribute and led a reign of terror in the adjacent villages. Major Byod, Deputy Commissioner of Cachar, rushed to Maibong with a force of armed police, but Sambhudhan proceeded to Gunjong, burnt the station and killed two officials and a policeman. Considering the liberation of North Cachar Hills complete, Sambhudhan returned to Maibong with his followers. Major Byod and his party encamped there for the night and early next morning commenced operations against Sambhudhan's *ashram*. In the encounter many people lost their life, but Byod received a severe injury from a hatchet to which, resulting in tetenus, he succumbed within a couple of days. For sometime Sambhudhan evaded arrest but was ultimately cordoned by the police in his hiding hut. In his attempt to escape, Sambhudhan contracted an injury due to which he bled to death. Man Singh, the chief priest of Sambhudhan, was arrested, tried and sentenced to transportation for life.[4] Sambhudhan is still a legendary name in Cachar and many considered his movement as a mission to revive the local institutions and a reaction to the British rule.

The next incident took place in 1893 when one midnight some persons entered into the bungalow of a manager of the Baladhan Tea Estate; the manager and the *chaukidar* were assassinated, a woman was mortally wounded and the contents of the safe were removed. The incident, popularly known as the Baladhan Murder Case, is well known in India's legal history. Six Manipuris and one Gurkha were apprehended and sent to stand the trial before the Sessions Judge at Sylhet. The Judge, relying upon the purported confessions obtained under heavy torture, sentenced four of the accused persons to death and the rest to transportation for life. Their case was taken up by Babu Kamini Kumar Chanda and the High Court at Calcutta, on appeal, acquitted all the accused. The case had created a great stir all over Bengal. Maharshi Devendranath Tagore and other nationalist leaders of Calcutta helped Babu Kamini Kumar in collecting funds for the case. The success in defending the accused gave Chanda wide fame as a lawyer. W. S. Caine raised questions in the British Parliament about some irregularities in police investigations, magisterial enquiry and trial in the Sessions Court and thus Baladhan Murder Case was publicised in England.[5]

Another alarm was created in 1898 when Mr. Wilde, the Railway Executive Engineer was murdered by two pathan contractors and an aide. The engineer was riding along a narrow part of the road and called upon the Pathans, mounted on the ponies, to move aside and let him pass. The contractors refused and there were violent altercations, some jostlings and a Pathan was hustled off his pony. The enraged persons then dragged Wilde into the jungle and hacked him to death. The perpetrators were subsequently arrested. One of them committed suicide in the jail and the others were ultimately hanged.[6]

Political activities in Cachar had begun during the Swadeshi Movement. In Cachar the apostle of the new era was Babu Kamini Kumar Chanda. Born at Chhatiain in Sylhet, on 4 September 1862, Kamini Babu passed the Entrance Examination of the University of Calcutta in 1789 from Silchar Government High School. He then joined the Presidency College at Calcutta and passed the F.A. in 1882,

B.A. in 1884, M.A. in 1886 and B.L. in 1888 from Calcutta University with credit and then joined Silchar Bar. The fame won from the Baladhan Case early in his career gave him a flourishing practice in criminal cases all over in Bengal. In 1904 he was enrolled as a *Vakeel* in the Calcutta High Court and in 1925 he became an Advocate.[7] Kamini Kumar showed his rare administrative skill as the first non-official Vice Chairman of the Silchar Municipality and then as its first Chairman for twelve years. A Director of the Hindustan Insurance Society, he was interested in the industrialisation of the Surma Valley and extended financial support to many local enterprises. A strong supporter of female education, he offered active help to the Welsh Presbyterian Mission when they started a Girls' High School in Silchar in 1895 by convincing many orthodox guardians to send their daughters to the school and himself set the example by sending his daughter. He was also one of the founders of the Dinanath Balika Vidyalaya during the Non-Cooperation Movement. A generous personality, he provided free board and lodging to many students who came from the mofusil areas to study in Silchar. A distinguished public speaker and writer, he has left behind many of his fiery speeches in the legislative proceedings and memory of his younger contemporaries and contributions to journals including Tagore's *Bhandar*.

A born leader of men, Kamini Babu displayed his qualities from studenthood. As a student in Calcutta, he was an active member of the Students' Association, led by Surendranath Banerjee, and *Shrihatta Sanmelani*, sponsored by a student from Sylhet in Calcutta. Prominent among his friends from Sylhet in Calcutta were Babu Bipin Chandra Pal, Sitananth Datta, Mahesh Chandra Datta, Tarakishore Choudhry,* and Dr. Sundari Mohon Das. He had close association with *Brahmo* leaders of Calcutta like Sibnath Sastri and Devendranath Tagore. Although not within *Brahmo* fold, he was one of the founders of the *Brahmo Mandir* at Silchar in 1897. He was a leading member of the party of youngmen sent by Surendranath on a touring mission in North India for propagating social and political ideas.

Kamini Kumar Chanda became associated with the Indian

Santadas Babaji Maharaj.

National Congress† from its second session held in Calcutta
in 1886 when he was a post-graduate student. This was the
beginning of his long association with the Congress and he
soon made his mark as an all-India leader. For several terms he
was a member of the Congress Working Committee. Since
his joining in the Silchar Bar, he started political activities in
Cachar, but continued to take part in the national programmes
and attended the annual sessions of the party held at different
places.[8] Cachar, Sylhet and Goalpara districts of Assam
were included in the Bengal Provincial Congress, must be for
ethnic reason, and Kamini Babu was althrough an influential
member of the Bengal Congress. The leaders of the National
Congress were divided into extremists and moderates. The
extremists like Bipin Chandra Pal, Bal Gangadhar Tilak and
Lala Lajpat Rai wanted active resistance but the moderates led
by Surendranath Banerjee believed in passive resistance. But
Kamini Kumar being an old co-worker of Surendranath
Banerjee in the Students' Association and a personal friend of
Bipin Chandra was an active link between the two and at
times was successful in bringing the two giants of Indian
politics together. No wonder, a man of high stature in
all-India politics, Kamini Kumar Chanda was the real spirit
behind the nationalist activities in Cachar.

In 1899 Bipin Chandra Pal came to Cachar as a *Brahmo*
Missionary and was a guest of Kamini Kumar. He delivered
learned speeches on *Brahmo* philosophy in several public
meetings. Notable among them was on Indian Religion
delivered in the Narshing M. E. School* and attended, among
others, by a large number of the European residents. Born on
at 7 November 1858, at Poil in Sylhet, Bipin Chandra belonged
to the era of tremendous social upheaval that had originated
in Bengal and owed its philosophy to Raja Ram Mohan Roy
and Bankim Chandra Chattapadhyay. The movement for
political freedom was a sequel to the reformist urge initiated by
Brahmo Samaj. Bipin Babu was an active organiser of the
Samaj and an impressive propagator of its philosophy. A

---

†Founded at Bombay in 1885 under the Presidentship of W. C. Banerjee,
a Bengalee Barrister.
*Now High School.

prolific writer and an impassioned orator, he had created a
social and political firmament which stirred the whole nation.
Together with Lala Lajpat Rai and Bal Gangadhar Tilak,
this trio of the early nationalist movement in India had
made popular distinction as 'Lal-Bal-Pal.' Naturally, his
visit and addresses had created the horizon for socio-political
thought and action in Cachar.[9]

Meanwhile, the political consciousness in Bengal had taken
a deep root and the British Government hatched in secret a
sinister plan to partition the province, on the plea of administrative convenience, to wreck the solidarity of the Bengalee race
and intelligentsia and thereby to weaken the political agitation
in Bengal. There were loud protests all over Bengal against
the scheme and the Indian National Congress passed resolutions condemning the plan in 1903 and 1904. On 11
January 1905, about 300 delegates from all the districts of
former Bengal met in a conference in Calcutta with Sir Henry
Cotton in the chair. Sir Cotton, an ex-Chief Commissioner
of Assam, in his address not only opposed a fresh partition
of Bengal but also demanded that the Bengali-speaking districts of Cachar, Sylhet and Goalpara 'be added to Bengal
from Assam much to the satisfaction of the Bengalees.'[10] It
may be recalled that when Assam was constituted into a
separate province in 1874, three districts of Cachar, Sylhet
and Goalpara were transferred from Bengal to the new province. As stated already, there were agitations in the Surma
Valley against the separation. But it is not clear if this
agitation had any repercussion in Calcutta or Dacca.
Naturally, Bengal having been already partitioned in 1874, the
scheme of 1905 must be termed as the 'Second Partition of
Bengal.' Anyway, 1874 and 1905 meant already a generation gap and the conference now demanded that the views
of the Bengalees should be considered before taking a final
decision.[11]

Inspite of this popular demand, on 20 July 1905, Lord
Curzon, the Viceroy of India, declared that the Dacca, Chittagong and Rajshahi Divisions of Bengal including Assam*
would be constituted into a separate province with effect

---

*Including Sylhet, Cachar and Goalpara.

from 16 October 1905. No wonder, therefore, the declaration was greeted with outbursts of indignation all over Bengal and a tremendous national upheaval at once swept over the province. Anti-partition meetings and demonstrations were organised under the leadership of Surendranath Banerjee, Bipin Chandra Pal, Aurobindo Ghose, Abdul Rasul, Aswini Kumar Datta and others. The newspapers strongly criticised the scheme and focused public reaction. On 7 August 1905, the delegates from all the districts of Bengal met in a conference in the Calcutta Town Hall. The students of all the educational institutions of the city and its suburbs paraded the streets of Calcutta with black flags inscribed 'United Bengal,' 'Unity is strength', 'Bande Mataram', 'No Partition', etc. in Bengali and then proceeded to the Town Hall, while factories and shops observed general *hartal*. The conference, presided over by Maharaja Maninidra Chandra Nandi of Cassimbazar, emphatically condemned the partition of Bengal, declaring it to be unnecessary, arbitrary, unjust and calculated to seriously interfere with the socal, intellectual, moral and industrial advancement of the Bengalees and stressed that the entire scheme was a deliberate disregard of the public opinion. It then resolved to continue the agitation till the partition was reversed and to pressurise the government by boycotting British goods and using *Swadeshi* or indigenous goods. The call to use the indigenous goods fostered a spirit of patriotism and self-help and the agitation came to be known as *Swadeshi* and became the fashion of subsequent political struggle for freedom from the British yoke.

Rabindranath Tagore called upon the Bengalees to observe on 16 October (30 *Asvin*, 1312 *Bangabda*) *Rakhi Bandhan* to indicate the indelible unity of the Bengalee race and *Arandhan* i.e. to live on milk and fruit, all indigenous. On 22 September, in a public meeting in the Calcutta Town Hall, the representatives of Bengal decided to organise a Federation 'to maintain the unity and the solidarity of the Bengali race and to tighten the bonds between the two Bengals after the partition takes place.'[12] Thus 30 *Asvin*, 1312 B.S. is a memorable day in the history of Bengalee solidarity. There were *prabhat feri*, *Sankirtan*, *Rakhi Bandhan*, *Arandhan*, patriotic songs and meetings all over Bengal. In Calcutta, the youngmen from dawn paraded the streets singing *Bande Mataram* and large crowds from all walks of life marched towards *Ganga* to take bath in the holy water and then tied *Rakhi* on each other's arm. In the afternoon the foundation of the Bengalee Federation Hall was laid in Upper Circular Road and Ananda Mohon Bose, a veteran leader, presided over the meeting attended by 50,000 people. The public leaders, journalists, educationists and literateurs took active part in the day's programme. Notwithstanding, the ruling Government carried out their colonial scheme. The Province of Eastern Bengal and Assam, including Cachar, Sylhet and Goalpara, was constituted with Dacca as the headquarters and Joseph Bamfylde Fuller, the Chief Commissioner of Assam, as the first Lieutenant Governor.

But this was the signal for stronger political agitation. The failure to achieve any conspicuous success by the National Congress had already strengthened the radicals led by Bipin Chandra Pal and they now assumed a more militant attitude and demanded bolder action against alien domination. Curzon's action added fuel to the fire and totally convulsed the highly inflammable political situation in Bengal. Not only the extremists took exception, even moderate leaders like Surendranath Banerjee stood at the forefront of the anti-partition movement. Openly defying the government, the students picketed the shops and factories and made bonfires of foreign goods, while the cities and towns rang with the fervour of Bankim Chatterjee's *Bande Mataram*. Krishna Kumar Mitra's *Sanjibani*, Surendranath's. *The Bengalee*, Bhupendranath's *Jugantar*, Aurobindo's *Bande Mataram*, and many other newspapers injected the Bengalees with the spirit of nationalism and inspired them to resist foreign rule. In Surma Valley, *Sylhet Chronicle*, *Silchar*, *Paridarsak*, *Shribhumi* played a commendable role in focusing the public opinion.

To defeat the cause of the *Swadeshi*, the Government attempted to alienate the various sections of the people by encouraging Hindu-Muslim feuds and demanding strict discipline from the Government servants. The European Companies threatened to dismiss their employees having any link with the movement. On 10 October 1905, R. W. Carlyle, Chief Secretary to the Government of Bengal, issued a circular to the

District Magistrates asking them to censor the students of the schools and colleges who would participate in political activities and threatened to withdraw their scholarships, to disaffiliate their institutions and discontinue grants-in-aid.[13] In a public meeting held in Calcutta on 24 October 1905, under the Chairmanship of Abdul Rasul, Bipin Chandra Pal not only condemned the Carlyle Circular but also suggested National Education.[14] The Anti-Circular Society, formed shortly after the meeting, spearheaded a strong movement and ultimately a National Council of Education was set up and National Schools and Colleges were established in various parts of Bengal. With the programme of boycott and *Swadeshi* was now added National Education. The real motive behind the partition was to wreck the solidarity of the politically conscious Bengalee intelligentsia and to encourage Hindu-Muslim rift. But to the disappointment of the British authorities, it gave the people a feeling of oneness. Although the Muslim League, founded by Nawab Salim Ullah of Dacca, in 1906, supported the partition and opposed the boycott and *Swadeshi*, the bulk of the Bengalee Muslims stood solidly behind the national leaders in condemning the British move to destroy the bond which had united the Bengalees in all phases of history.

The people in Cachar took active part in *Swadeshi* Movement under the leadership of Kamini Kumar Chanda. In 1905 the *Cachar Swadeshi Sabha* was established, with Kamini Kumar Chanda as the President and Abantinath Datta as the Secretary. Mahendra Chandra Datta, Kali Mohon Dev, Radharaman Datta, Durga Shankar Datta, Dr. Nagendra Chandra Datta, Dinanath Datta, Ramtarak Bhattacharjee, Nur Muhammad Laskar, Kushiram Namasudra, among others, were the members of the Executive Committee. The *Sabha* successfully spearheaded the agitation in Cachar and preached the *Swadesi* ideals. Almost everyday protest meetings were organised and the students made large-scale bonfires of British goods.[15] In Sylhet the movement was highly successful and the repressive measures of the government could not in any way suppress the agitation. The Surma Valley had a common response to the political programmes under the leadership of Bipin Chandra Pal, Kamini Kumar Chanda, Dr. Sundari Mohon Das, Shrish Chandra Datta, Satish Chandra Deb,

Dulal Chandra Dev, Shyama Charan Deb and a host of other illustrious sons of Shribhumi. Under their leadership, Surma Valley responded equally with any other part of Bengal to the partition issue, although Sylhet and Cachar had already been separated from Bengal and attached to Assam. The people of these two districts because of their historical, linguistic and cultural oneness never felt the existence of the different political systems. They maintained all ties with Bengal and psychologically never recognised the separation since 1874. No wonder, therefore, Sylhet and Cachar were joint partners to the Surma Valley Political Conference. In July 1906, the first session of the Surma Valley Political Conference was held at Telihowr under the presidentship of Kamini Kumar Chanda.[16] Besides the leaders of Cachar and Sylhet, Bipin Chandra Pal, Shrish Chandra Datta and some other Calcutta based Surma leaders participated in the conference. The well attended meeting condemned the partition of Bengal and urged upon the people to boycott foreign goods and use indigenous goods. A National school was then established at Sylhet with Babu Abhinash Chandra Datta as the first headmaster. Shrish Chandra Datta of Karimganj, Suresh Chandra Deb of Habiganj and Bhuban Mohon Vidyarnava of Silchar were the teachers. Shrish Chandra Datta, who served the school from 1906 to 1912, had succeeded Abhinash Babu as the headmaster. About the same time, another National School was established in Habiganj with Mahendra Chandra Dey of Moulavi Bazar as the headmaster.[17]

Same year, in course of his extensive tour over East Bengal and Assam to popularise the *Swadeshi* philosophy, Bipin Chandra Pal came to Silchar. Bipin Chandra's fiery speeches had already created a tremendous upheaval in East Bengal and how anxious the people of Cachar would be to see him and listen to his speeches was not unknown to the local leaders. A public pandal was constructed in an open field near the house of Dinanath Datta of Malugram and a Volunteer Corps was organised under the leadership of Radhakishor Pande, Kedarnath Sen and Kamini Kumar Kar to maintain discipline.[18] This first ever mass gathering on a political issue had created a great stir in Cachar. Babu Brajendranath Ganguli of Mymensing, who had specialised in Bipin Pal's self composed lyrics,

presented some *Swadeshi* songs. There were also some chorus
from Tagore, besides Bankim's *Bande Mataram.* Ignoring the
prohibitory orders of the authorities, the students of Silchar
Government High School attended the meeting, while
Sourindra Mohon Endow, a student of the school, read a
welcome address to Bipin Chandra Pal on behalf of the
students community of Cachar. The people of Cachar pledged
to boycott British goods. Many people for quite a long time
had really boycotted foreign salt, cloth, medicine and other
goods and used only indigenous goods. The washermen of
the town had organised an address of Bipin Chandra at
Sadarghat and in the meeting they decided not to wash foreign
clothes. Bipin Chandra's tour also infused moderation in the
social outlook of the people. The Bengalee society in Cachar
was still conservative about the women. In Bengal the literateurs
had rightly exposed the lamentable condition of the women in
the society and the leaders of the 19th century Bengal renaissance agitated for their emancipation. The beginning that was
made by the abolition of *Sati* system and Widow Remarriage
Act was carried further and in the urban areas the women
were already allowed in public institutions. In Cachar, however,
things took a long time to change. Although Kamini Kumar
Chanda was a strong advocate of women education and a
girl school was established in 1895, the women in Cachar
could not think of attending a public meeting in 1906. In the
meeting at Malugram no woman gave audience. But
Bipin Chandra as an orator had assumed a legendary name and
a section of the women expressed their desire to listen to him.
Ultimately, an arrangement was made in the house of Mahesh
Chandra Datta where the women from the upstair families of
the town listened to his address, but from behind a screen.
Some ladies made a chorus of Bipin Chandra's song, *nā jāgile
sab Bhārat lalanā, ai Bhārat ar jāge nā* ; but that too behind
the screen. This was the first meeting attended by the women
in Silchar and undoubtedly made a good beginning. In the
Non-cooperation Movement Chandraprabha Chanda, wife of
Kamini Kumar Chanda, took part. Saudamini Devi, wife of
Shyama Charan Deb, was a teacher in Silchar Mission's Girls'
High School since 1917 and joined Swadeshi High School
from its very inception in 1921. In the twenties of the century,

the women workers of the Congress formed *Silchar Mahila Samiti* and in the thirties their monthly organ *Vijoyini* was published. In the Quit India Movement, Jyotsna Chanda, among others, took part.

Evidently, the tour of India's top nationalist leader of the time, in 1906, popularised the *Swadeshi* cult in Cachar. The people took pride in using national costume and consuming local products. *Arandhan* and *Rakhi Bandhan* were observed on 30 *Asvin* every year throughout the continuance of the *Swadeshi* or *Banga-Vanga Āndolon*. Tagore's '*Bānglār māti Bānglār Jal*,' '*Uthre Uthre torā Hindu Musalman*,' '*Māyer deoā motā kāpār mātay tole ne re Bhāi;*' and Bipin Chandra's '*Ār bājoyo nā Mohon bānshi*' were popular public chorus of the old, young, women and children of all castes and creeds during these occasions.[19] The new spirit engendered in the young minds a sense of hatred against the British. The students of Silchar Government High School, the premier institution of Cachar, started taking part in the agitation. Babu Abhaya Charan, the headmaster, although a government servant, inspired the boys with patriotic ideals and encouraged them to use *Swadeshi* goods. A Negro servant of an English military officer was assaulted by a student of the school for his attempt to manhandle some boys of tender age. The military officer lodged a complaint in the court and the incident created a great sensation in the town. But the headmaster defended the student so strongly that the case had to be ultimately withdrawn. On another occasion, a student of the school alone came to blows with four *Firingis* for their misbehaviour with a Bengalee peon of the telegraph office. Three other boys noticed the scene but took to their heels, Abhaya Charan appreciated the boy who came to blows with the *Firingis* and rebuked the escapists for their cowardice. Thus the boys became gradually conscious of the ignominy of foreign yoke and learned to protest against anything that injured their national prestige. The new spirit played so high that when the students were asked to contribute for decoration on the occasion of the visit of Fuller, the Lieutenant Governor, the boys refused to pay.[20] Disregarding the Carlyle and Risby Circulars, the students continued to attend public meetings and take part in the demonstrations. A Volunteer Party was raised with the students of the school and the second anniversary of the *Banga-*

Vanga Āndolon was colourfully observed. Consequently, the
Director of Public Instruction, Eastern Bengal and Assam,
suspended 39 students of the Silchar Government High School.[21]
Of them, 38 rejoined the school after offering an apology, but
Apurba Kumar Chanda, son of Kamini Kumar Chanda, did
not submit to the humiliation. Kamini Babu did not allow his
son to offer an apology and, instead, sent him to Tagore's
Santiniketan at Bolpur.

Meanwhile, the *Swadeshi* Movement had already achieved
an all India character. The annual session of the Congress, held
in Calcutta in 1906, not only endorsed the *Swadeshi* plan but,
for the first time in its history, laid down *Swaraj* as its goal.[22]
The session was a victory of the radicals, and Bipin Chandra
took a lecture tour in the country publicising *Swaraj* or self-
rule. In his speeches and writings in *New India*, *Bande Mataram*
this oracle of Indian nationalism singularly laid down that
Swaraj can not come by resolution and must be achieved. By
Swaraj he meant an absolute autonomy free from British
control, that it will be *Swaraj* of Indian people and not of any
section of it. His inflammatory speeches stirred the whole nation
and the spirit of nationalism now acquired a dynamic character that was needed to offer a positive challenge to the British
rule. *Swadeshi* was an all India phenomenon and wherever he
addressed a meeting the people upheld the extremist method.
Evidently, Bipin Chandra's activities posed a serious threat to
the British Raj and the Government soon sent him behind the
prison bar. In October 1907, he was sentenced to six months
imprisonment and sent to Boxur Jail.[23] His absence created a
great political crisis. The moderate leaders could not keep pace
with the Radical Resolution of the Calcutta Session and were
all out for a change in the Congress policy. As a result, in
the Surat Session, in 1907, held under the presidentship of Dr.
Rash Behari Ghose there was an open split in the Congress.
The extremists now kept themselves out of the Congress for
sometime and pursued the *Swadeshi* plan more vigorously.

On 9 March, 1908, Bipin Chandra Pal was released from
jail. He was accorded a public reception at Calcutta and
there was general illumination in his honour.[24] Even the moderate leader Surendranath Banerjee's *The Bengalee* wrote :[25]
"On the technical question as to the propriety or significance

of Babu Bipin Chandra's conduct, there may perhaps be a difference of opinion. But who can doubt that his patient and unremitted suffering has raised Babu Bipin Chandra immensely in the estimation of the country ? If all suffering has a tendency to enlist public sympathy on behalf of the sufferer, most of all have the sufferings of those who make the cause of the country of their own." *The Eastern Chronicle*, published from Karimganj, welcomed his release and referring to the recent crisis in the Congress wrote :[26] "...the citadel of Moderation is yet averse to reconciliation and a constitution for the Congress is being hatched in secret. The expectant eye of our people is now upon the coming hero who is to guide us to our destination." As expected, Bipin Chandra immediately resumed his activities and undertook an extensive tour, first in Surma Valley.

The leaders in Surma Valley generally belonged to the radical section of the nationalists, and in the twenties of the century the Swarajya Party had become a dominant force in the valley to be reckoned with by the opponents. A reason might be the active link maintained by Bipin Chandra Pal with his home region. *The Eastern Chronicle, Paridarsak, Silchar* and other local papers subscribed to the radical thought and highlighted the views of Bipin Chandra through their columns. The political thinking of the local leaders is well understood from the proceedings of the Second Surma Valley Political Conference held at Karimganj on 18 April 1908, under the presidentship of Babu Radha Benode Das, a leading criminal practitioner. Bipin Chandra was an active organiser of the conference and Shri Aurobindo graced the occasion as the Chief Guest. In his presidential address, Babu Radha Benode "deplored the Congress split and appealed to the leaders to forgive and forget and stand shoulder to shoulder under the Congress banner...condemned the repressive policy of Government with fearless independence, encouraged the victims of the bureaucratic despotism to remain unshaken in their unflinching devotion to the country's cause fortified by the conviction that Swadeshi was a divine dispensation destined to work our country's salvation." Adverting to Hindu-Muslim problem, he "exposed the despicable dodge resorted to by the Government to alienate the sympathy of the Mohomedans from the Swadeshi movement by gilded baits of state patronage, but he added that truth would ultimately triumph and our Mohomedan brethren will soon shake off this hypnotic spell and see through the will-of-the-wisp policy of the Govt. He exposed the present policy of the Govt. with apt quotations from standard works. He exhorted his countrymen to become alive to the present industrial bondage of our country and seek her emancipation by the promotion of limited companies and by other means of increasing national wealth."[27] The illuminating speeches of Shri Aurobindo, Bipin Chandra Pal, Kamini Kumar Chanda, Ramani Mohon Das added to the determination of the people to actively resist the British rule and to attain *Swaraj*. In the proceedings of the Third Surma Valley Political Conference, held in Jalsuka in 1910, also the spirit of radical nationalism ran high and another National School was established where Babu Shyama Charan Deb acted as the Headmaster till 1917.[28]

Meanwhile, the *Swadeshi* cult had become a redoubtable force to be reckoned with by the British Government and the latter let loose a campaign of repression. The peaceful pickets were beaten and sent to jail, political meetings were broken by police with merciless *lathi* charges and popular movements were suppressed with all severity. Many nationalist leaders were tried and imprisoned under Regulation III of 1818, while some were deported without trial.[29] Bal Gangadhar Tilak was sentenced to six years transportation and a fine of Rs 1,000. Lala Lajpat Rai was deported from the country and Bipin Chandra Pal had an enforced exile in England from 1908 to 1911.[30] But these measures could hardly check the nationalist programmes. Many prominent leaders went underground, clubbed into secret and revolutionary societies and sought to terrorise the Government by killing the British officials and their Indian collaborators. Bombs were secretly prepared and the reports of political murders almost daily poured in from various parts of Bengal. The Anarchist or Terrorist movement now became a part of Indian politics.[31] The *Jugantar* and *Anushilan* parties had attracted many revolutionaries from Cachar and Sylhet and the underground activities, including political murders, had shaken the Government machinery in a positive manner. The prominent revolutionaries of the valley like Shrish Chandra Datta, Basanta Das Purkayastha, Debendranath Choudhury, Jnanendra Chandra

Dhar, Ramani Mohon Roy, Upendra Roy, Monoranjan Singha, Mohini Barma had formed the *Suhrid Samiti*. Upendra Dhar Tara Kishore Bardhan, Kaliraman Bhattacharjee ran the *Tarun Sanga*. *Sree Sangha*, led by Lila Nag, the well-known revolutionary lady of Sylhet, attained almost legendary character. In 1900, Thakur Dayanand and Tarakishore Roy Choudhury had founded the *Arunachal Ashram* near Silchar and, sometime after, Mahendra Nath Dey started the *Jagatshi Ashram* near Moulavi Bazar. Many revolutionaries harboured around these *Ashrams* and the suspicion of the officials had fallen on them. On 3 June 1912, Thakur Dayanand publicly issued a statement asking the people for Non-Coperation with the British Government. Soon after a big party of the armed police led by top European officials made a planned midnight swoop upon the *Ashrams*. The *Ashrams* were cordoned and members, both men and women, were brutally tortured and several rounds of shots were fired. Mahendra Nath Dey was seriously injured and ultimately passed away in Sylhet Jail. Thakur Dayanand and several others were arrested and imprisoned. The incident created a great stir in the valley. Many eminent persons became vocal and the revolutionaries let loose a terroristic campaign against the officials.[32]

The repressive policy having failed to foil the movement, the Government sought to rally the moderates by granting the Morley-Minto Reforms, embodied in the Act of 1909. This Act amongst others, provided for the appointment of an Indian member in the Viceroy's Executive Council, the appointment of Indian members in the Provincial Executive Councils, creation of such councils in the states where they did not exist and the enlargement of Legislative Councils, both in the centre and the provinces, by nominated and elected members. But this did not satisfy the people. Ultimately, on 12 December 1911, the Government declared the modification of the partition. Bihar, Chotanagpur and Orissa were constituted into a province under a Lieutenant Governor. Assam including Surma Valley and Goalpara, was reverted to Chief Commissionership and the rest of Bengal was constituted into a province under a Governor. In 1912, the capital of India was shifted from Calcutta to Delhi and the new arrangements were immediately carried into effect.

Evidently, the annulment of the partition was only partial. Cachar, Sylhet and Goalpara, were again transferred to Assam The public leaders in Surma Valley, therefore, continued to press their demand for the transfer of Cachar and Sylhet to Bengal. The Sylhet-Bengal Re-Union League, formed with the prominent leaders like Brojendranarayan Choudhury, Rai Bahadur Girish Chandra Nag, Rai Bahadur Ramini Mohon Das and others, spearheaded this movement. In 1926, the question of the transfer came up in the Assam Council and although the resolution was passed by the Council in favour of the restoration, the scheme did not materialise.[33] The injustice done to the people of Cachar and Sylhet did not escape even the eyes of Rabindranath Tagore who in one of his celebrated poems regretted the absence of *Shribhumi* in Bengal.* In Goalpara as well the people were unhappy over the separation. The Goalpara Zamindars Association and various local organisations continued to demand the transfer of Goalpara to Bengal.[34] Despite the popular demands, these three districts were retained in Assam and have contributed to the development of the province. In the first ever Council of Assam since 1913, Kamini Kumar Chanda of Silchar was a member. He continued as such till 1917 when he became a member in the Indian Legislative Council and continued till 1926.[35]

Meanwhile, remarkable changes had occured in the Indian political scene. The introduction of the separate electorate for the Muslims under the regulations of the Act of 1909 alienated the moderates from the Government. The death of Pheroz Shah Mehta and G. K. Gohkale had on the other hand, weakened the Indian National Congress. With the outbreak of the First World War in 1914 the Indian soldiers were sent abroad to fight for the Allied Powers. During the War

---

*mamatābihin kāloshrote
    bānglār rāshtrashimā hate
nirbashitā tumi
    sundari Shribhumi
bhārati āpoh punyahāte
    bāngālir hridayer sāte
bānimālya diyā
    bānde taba hiyā
se bāndane chiradin taba kāche
    bāngālir āshirbād gānthā haye āchhe

1,161,789 soldiers were recruited in the army, of whom 1,215,338 were sent overseas and 101,739 became casualties.[36] The war also proved to be a heavy drain upon the Indian economy. Naturally, the Indian leaders were unhappy over the war policy of the British Government and the release of Tilak in 1914 brought the nationalists in the forefront of Indian politics. The moderates too realised the necessity of a rapprochement with the radicals in national interest and the constitution of the Congress was amended in the Bombay session, held in 1915, to accomodate the extremists. The next session of the Congress, held at Lucknow, resulted in the reunion of the moderates and the radicals. On the other hand, the British attack upon Turkey created a strong anti-British feeling among the Indian Muslims and paved the way for cooperation between the Congress and the Muslim League. The Lucknow Session, in 1916, held jointly by the Congress and the League, concluded the 'Lucknow Pact' by which the Congress consented to the separate electorate and both the parties raised the demand for Dominion Status.[37] Earlier, on 28 April, same year, the Indian Home Rule League was formed during the Belgaum session of the Nationalists, with Joseph Baptist as President, Kamini Kumar Chanda as Vice-President and N. C. Kelkar as Secretary. After the Lucknow Session, the Congress and the League carried on an intensive propaganda in favour of the scheme. On the other hand, in pursuance of the avowed object of the war to secure self-determination for the subject people and to make the world safe for democracy, added with the pressure of the Home Rule Movement in India and the lesson of the Bolshevik Revolution in Russia, Edwin Montagu, Secretary of State for India, made the famous announcement, on 20 August 1917, in the House of Commons, that the policy of the Government was to increase the "association of Indians in every branch of the administration and the gradual development of self-governing institutions with a view to the progressive realisation of responsible government in India as an integral part of the British Empire."[38] Montagu came to India in November 1917 and made an extensive tour in the country to ascertain public opinion. His report on the Indian Constitutional Reforms was published in 1918 and formed the basis for the Government of India Act, 1919. Like various organisations in the country, the Peoples' Association of Sylhet, the Surma Valley Muhamedan Zamindars' Association, Sunamganj Mahisya Samiti, the Surma Valley Branch of Indian Tea Association submitted memorandums to the Reforms Committee.[39]

The question of the acceptance of the reforms of 1918 led to another split in the Congress. The moderates accepted the reforms but the radicals dismissed them as inadequate, disappointing and unsatisfactory. The Bengal Provincial Conference, in a special session held under the presidentship of Kamini Kumar Chanda, on 14 July 1918, expressed the opinion that the scheme of reforms was disappointing and did not present the real steps towards responsible Government. The Indian National Congress also, at Bombay in August 1918, declared that nothing less than self-government within the empire would satisfy the legitimate aspirations of the Indian people.[40] Most of the moderates then left Congress, formed the Indian Liberal Federation and decided to support the working of the Act. On the other hand, a series of coercive measures, known as the Rowlatt Acts, passed by the Government in 1919, sought to perpetuate the extraordinary powers conferred on the Government during the war. M. K. Gandhi organised a passive resistance movement, and a wave of demonstrations, strikes and riots spread over India. The Government tried to put down the agitation with a strong hand and in the process became guilty of the Jallianwala Bagh Massacre when the troops under General Dyer fired 1600 rounds into the unarmed crowd, killing and wounding several hundred people. In a special session held at Calcutta in September 1920, the Indian National Congress adopted the famous resolution on Non-Cooperation recommending the renunciation of Government titles, boycotting of legislatures, law courts and Government educational institutions. In the meantime, Maulana Abdul Kalam Azad, Mohammad Ali and Shaukat Ali had started the Khilafat Movement focusing the Muslim sentiment over the defeat and dismemberment of Turkey in the World War. The Congress now strongly espoused the Khilafat cause.

The Non-Cooperation and Khilafat Movement evoked a hearty response throughout the country and there was an unprecedented fraternisation between the Hindus and the Muslims. In Surma Valley, the movement was acclaimed with enthusiasm. The Khilafat Movement had already stirred the Muslims in the valley. Maulana Abdul Mushabbir, Maulana Abdul Haque, Maulana Safiqul Haque and Maulana Abdul Rashid of Sylhet undertook extensive tours in Cachar to popularise the programme. The Cachar Khilafat Committee was formed in 1909 with Maulana Pir Mahammed Ali of Madhurband as the President and a permanent office was established at Silchar. Maulana Pir Mahammed Yakub, Khan Saheb Rashid Ali Laskar, Maulana Mahashin Ali, Maulana Umar Ali, Maulana Tabaqar Ali Barlaskar, Maulana Umed Ali, Maulana Ibrahim Ali, Maulana Uchman Ali were among the prominent Khilafat leaders in Cachar. The movement is also memorable for the unique Hindu-Muslim fraternity in Cachar. Babu Mahim Chandra Biswas, Dr. Nagendra Nath Datta, Dinanath Datta, Gangadayal Dixit, Sanat Kumar Das, Sanat Kumar Datta Choudhury, Ashoka Kumar Chanda,* Satindra Mohon Dev, Jatindra Mohon Deb Laskar deserve special mention among the Hindu leaders who stood by their Muslim brethren and suffered all the vengeance of the British Government. A ninety thousand strong Volunteer Force was raised in the district. Satindra Mohon Dev and Md. Gulezar Ali Mazumdar were the Captain and Secretary respectively, while Maulana Alimuddin, Md. Hamidur Reza, Maulavi Khushed Ali, and Munshi Manshad Ali were the organisers of the Volunteer Force.[41]

The Fourth Surma Valley Political Conference, held in Karimganj in July 1920, under the presidentship of Bipin Chandra gave the signal for a stronger movement and Shrish Chandra Datta, the principal organiser of the Conference, took a leading role in the new movement. During the Non-Cooperation Movement the Hindu and Muslim leaders worked hand in hand. The bulk of the voters abstained from taking part in the election to the Council held in November 1920. Many members of the Silchar and Sylhet Bars, like Satish

---

*Ashoka Kumar Chanda, third son of Kamini Kumar Chanda, had a chequered career and retired from service as the Auditor and Controller General of India.

Chandra Deb, Khirode Chandra Deb, gave up legal practice.
Satish Chandra Deb and some other nationalist leaders renun-
ciated the Government titles, while Kamini Kumar Chanda
had already refused to accept the title offered by the Government. The students from various educational institutions in
Cachar boycotted the Government institutions. The nationalist leaders of Cachar branded the Silchar Government High
School as 'Golam Khana' and called upon the students to
boycott the school. Many guardians refused to send their
children to Government institutions, while students' boycott of
such schools was almost spontaneous. A National School
was established in Silchar and Arun Kumar Chanda,* who

*Born at Silchar on 17 February 1899, Arun Kumar Chanda, the
second son of Kamini Kumar Chanda, received his early education in
Silchar Government High School, Murari Chand College at Sylhet, St.
Columbia's at Hazaribagh and Bangabasi College in Calcutta. He passed
the B.A. Examination with first class Honours in English, winning Abinash
Chandra Gold Medal. Obtaining his L.L.B. degree from Calcutta University in 1927, he proceeded to London and was called to the Bar from the
Lincoln's Inn. As Barrister, he practised law in Singapore but came back
to Silchar due to his father's illness. He built up a lucrative practice in
Cachar and Sylhet, but took more interest in educational, political and
social life of the Surma Valley. During the Non-Cooperation Movement
he made his mark as a leader of national stature. He worked as a teacher
in the National School at Silchar and National College in Calcutta, when
in close contact with Chittaranjan Das. As a student in London, he was
associated with the British Labour Party and took active part in Party's
electioneering. A socialist and trade unionist, he was an excellent speaker
in Bengali and English and exhibited his progressive social thinking by
associating the various communities in *Sarbajanin Durga Puja* at Silchar
in 1931. He was also the founder Principal (honorary) of the Gurucharan
College, Silchar, established in 1935. He was the President of the Cachar
Postal and Railway Mail Service Union for 12 years and presided over the
all-India conference of the Union in 1945. He was elected the first president of the Assam Provincial Trade Union Congress and was intimately
connected with the movements of the labourers in various tea gardens
and Assam Oil Company at Digboi. He popularised the Indian National
Congress in Cachar and drew the rural masses to the struggle for freedom.

From 1937 till death, he was the President of the Cachar District Congress Committee. In 1937, he was returned to the Assam Legislative
Assembly and was elected the Deputy Leader of the Congress Legislature
Party and played a vital role in the installation of the Congress coalition
ministry in 1938. He offered *Satyagraha* against the war policy of the
British Government in 1941 and was sentenced to one year's imprisonment, but in 1942 he was again arrested, along with top ranked leaders of
the Congress, at Calcutta under the Defence of India Act and, even after
release, was not allowed to enter Assam till 1945. In 1945, he was elected
to the Indian Legislative Assembly, but died at Calcutta on 26 April 1947.
A rare genius, Arun Kumar's interest touched all aspects of social life.
Under his guidance and writing, *Saptak*, published from Silchar in 1937,
had become a strong organ of public opinion in Surma Valley. His wife,
Shrimati Jyotsna Chanda, daugher of Babu Mahesh Chandra Datta, also

later made his mark as an all India leader, was a teacher. Kamini Kumar Chanda and many others started the Dinanath-Nabakishore Balika Vidyalaya, better known as the Swadeshi High School for girls. Shyama Charan Deb,* the Secretary of the Cachar District Congress Committee, who was earlier a teacher in the National School in Sylhet, joined as the first Headmaster of the School. Saudamini Devi, wife of Shyama Charan Deb and a teacher in the Mission Girls' High School, also joined the school. Certain native companies too came up during the movement. Finding that the tea industry in Surma Valley was dominated by the European planters, Shrish Chandra Datta, a prominent leader, along with some nationalist youngmen, set up a tea garden in Karimganj. Besides an economic venture, this garden gave shelter to many underground revolutionaries.[42] The Cachar Cooperative Apex Bank was also established in 1921.

The prominent leaders of the Non-Cooperation Movement in Cachar were Kamini Kumar Chanda, Shyama Charan Deb, Sanat Kumar Das, Sibendra Kumar Biswas, Prakash Chandra Bhattacharjee, Gangadayal Dixit and others; in Karimganj, Satish Chandra Deb, Shrish Chandra Datta, Radha Benode Das, Khirode Chandra Deb and in Sylhet, Basanta Kumar Das, Brojendra Narayan Choudhury. The students, in response to the call given by the All India Students Conference held at Nagpur in December 1920, launched a strong movement. Not only they boycotted their institutions, but picketed the liquor and opium shops and foreign goods' sellers. Enlisting them-

took part in Congress politics and carried the tradition of the Chanda family in Cachar even after independence. She was a member of the Assam Legislative Assembly from 1957 to 1961 and had resigned from the Assembly, in 1961, in demand for the recognition of Bengali as an official language in Assam. She was a member of the *Lok Sabha* since 1962 and died at Delhi in 1973. See S. P. Sen, ed., *Dictionary of National Biography*, 4 vols., Calcutta, 1972-1974. 258-9.

*Born in Habiganj on 21 November 1870, Shyama Charan Deb was a gifted teacher and dedicated freedom fighter. His chequered teaching career began from the Habiganj High School in 1893 and then joined the Ratanmani High School at Karimganj. In 1909, he started a National School at Jalsuka and served as the Headmaster till 1917. In 1917, he joined the Silchar Mission Girls High School and since 1923 was the Headmaster of the Dinanath Nabakishore Valika Vidyalaya. During the Non-Cooperation Movement he was the Joint Secretary of the Cachar District Congress Committee and later succeeded Kamini Kumar Chanda as its President. This *Silchar Gandhi* took leading part in the freedom struggle and was twice imprisoned. See S. P. Sen, *op. cit.* 416.

selves in large volunteer batches, the students carried on propaganda in favour of *Swadeshi* and *Swaraj*. There were open bonfires of foreign clothes, and the cheap *Khadi* became a badge of honour. The women also came forward to join the movement. Sibsundari Devi, wife of Kamini Kumar Chanda, and Saudamini Devi, wife of Shyama Charan Deb, carried the banner of women awakening in Cachar. The women workers of the Congress formed the *Silchar Mahila Samiti* and published their organ *Vijoyini*. The *Panchayat,* *Ryot* and *Kishan Sabhas* emerged in the rural areas. The crowded public meetings were addressed by the leaders almost everyday and the sky rang with the lyrics of Mukunda Das.[43]

A notable aspect of the Non-Cooperation Movement in Cachar was the labour strike in the tea gardens. Gangadayal Dixit, a cloth merchant of Lakhipur, along with Deosharan Triparti and Ramprasad Choubey, Trade Union leaders, worked among the labourers and persuaded them to refuse to work in the gardens owned by the European planters. The condition of these ill-paid labourers was highly deplorable and due to slump in the tea trade there was large scale retrenchments in many companies. As a protest against the incredibly low wages at which the labourers were forced to work, there was a general exodus of thousands of workers from Sylhet and Cachar in May 1921. About 12,000 men and women left the gardens and proceeded to their distant homes in North India. The planters took a vindictive attitude and laid the whole blame on the Congress volunteers who worked in the gardens propagating the cult of *Swaraj*. The Government had natural sympathy for the management and resorted to cruel action. When the coolies reached Chandpur, they were prevented from crossing the river by the Sub-Divisional Officer of Chandpur under the instructions of the Government of Bengal. Macpherson, a representative of the European Tea Association, arrived at Chandpur and through the S.D.O. tried to pressurize the coolies to return to the gardens. To escape the retreat and possible torture, large number of coolies rushed to the waiting steamer in the *ghat* but many fell in the river when the gangway was removed at the S.D.O.'s order. The coolies were then led to the Railway station in course of which, according to Government version, the S.D.O. was manhandled by some coolies. The Divisional Commissioner wired for a contingent of Gurkhas from Narayanganj. At about midnight next, when sleeping at the railway shed, the coolies were asked to vacate immediately. Some of them having refused, the Gurkhas fell upon the unarmed coolies and by kicks and beating with sticks and butt ends of their guns forced the men, women and children to leave the station and take refuge in an open ground although it was raining heavily. Thousands of coolies were stranded at Goalando, Rajbari and other stations, C. F. Andrews, who visited Chandpur next day, has left behind a touching account of the oppression and persecution of the stranded coolies. On 26 May, in a public meeting at Mirzapur Park, Calcutta, organised by the Bengal Central Labour Federation, he made a statement of the coolie situation. A large number of students and volunteers in Calcutta made collections for the relief of the coolies by singing songs describing the miserable condition of the stranded coolies and carried a canvas of a coolie woman being tortured by a European planter.[44] Meanwhile, Shrish Chandra Datta and Khirode Chandra Deb, the Congress leaders of Surma Valley, had rushed to the spot and arranged relief for the victims. A complete *hartal* was observed in the Chandpur town for the next few days. Chittaranjan Das and Jatindra Mohon Sen Gupta organised Railway and Steamer Strike since 20 May and for more than three months land and water traffic to Chittagong was in complete deadlock. Sir Henry Wheeler, a member of the Executive Council, inquired into the incident and in his report justified the official actions. But the non-official Inquiry Committee, appointed by the Tippera Congress with J.M. Sen Gupta as Chairman, endorsed the brutal assault by the Gurkha soldiers. Even K. C. De, the Commissioner of Division, who was on the spot of the incident, subsequently admitted that the assault had begun immediately with the arrival of the Gurkhas.[45]

The Chandpur incident had tremendous repercussions in Surma Valley. The young volunteers carried on demonstrations and picketings all over Cachar and Gangadayal Dixit urged upon the labourers not to work. The continuous strike in the gardens proved a heavy drain for the European planters. When the movement was in full swing, Mahatma Gandhi came to Silchar, in August 1921, accompanied by the Ali Brothers, Mohammed Ali and Shaukat Ali and stayed in the Chanda Bhavan as the guest of Kamini Kumar Chanda. A mammoth procession was organised by the Khilafat volunteers with Gandhiji and Mohammed Ali over all the important roads of the town. Gandhiji and Ali then addressed a public meeting attended by about 10,000 people at Fatak Bazar, the people taking their seats on the branches of the trees and roofs of the houses in the neighbourhood. They emphasised the need of *Swadeshi* and *Swaraj* and Hindu-Muslim unity. Kamini Kumar Chanda and Shrish Chandra Datta, amongst others, also addressed the meeting. How conscious the people of Silchar were even in these can be understood from the fact that Gandiji was questioned from the audience in course of his speech whether there would be any state religion in India under *Swaraj*. Of course, Gandhiji replied in the negative. A decent collection of funds was made on the spot to be sent to Angora. Gandhi, Mohammed Ali and Begum Saheba then addressed a womens' meeting at the Theatre Hall.[46] Gandhi's visit gave a fillip to the Congress movement which had already gathered momentum. Under the leadership of Kamini Kumar Chanda, the Congress President, the contemporaries and younger generation made a determined bid to achieve India's *Swaraj*. Gangadayal was soon sent behind bars and sentenced to imprisonment. The other leaders of Cachar, who were sentenced to imprisonment during the Khilafat and Non-Cooperation Movement, included Shyama Charan Deb, Dhirendra Kumar Gupta, Pekuram Kanu, Satindra Mohon Dev, Jatindra Mohon Dev Laskar, Imran Mia Barbhuiya, Suryamani Roy, Jafar Ali Barbuiya, Mabarak Ali Barlaskar, Rezam Ali, Munshi Gulam Robbani, Sanat Kumar Das, Md. Tabarak Ali Barlaskar, Md. Alimuddin, Md. Nur Ali, Hazi Suruj Ali, Munshi Abbas Ali, Md. Usman Ali, Md. Ibrahim Ali, Hazi Khushed Ali, Munshi Shikandar Ali, Gulzar Ali Mazumdar, Basarat Ali Mazumdar, Munshi Mansur Ali, Hazi Hashan Mia, Sabid Raja Mazumdar Mashad Ali, Maulavi Umar Ali, Md. Mahsin Ali, Md. Mauzraf Ali Laskar and Masraf Ali Choudhury. Even the villagers were not spared from the repression. Collective fines were imposed on the villages of Kalain, Barkhala, Bhuribail, Udhar-

band, Banskandi, Bhaga and in the adjacent village of Hailakandi. On 12 March 1922, an amount of rupees six thousand was
collected from the single village of Bhuribail as collective fine
within four hours.[47]

Meanwhile, the Non-Coperation Movement was so successful
all over the country that the Government machinery was paralysed in many quarters. As a result, the Indian National Congress, in the Ahmedabad session in 1921, not only expressed its
determination to continue the movement with greater vigour
but took steps to organise Civil Disobedience and appointed
Mahatma Gandhi as the sole leader to lead the movement.
But the Chouri-Choura riots in Uttar Pradesh, in which a
police station was burnt and twenty-four policemen killed,
brought a change in Gandhi's programme. Realising that the
movement was taking a violent character, he called off the
agitation for a couple of years. This produced a feeling of frustration among the political workers and adversely affected the
Hindu-Muslim relations. The Muslim League revived its old
ideas and gained more influence. A series of communal riots
broke out in various parts of the country in 1923 and introduced the cult of communal violence in Indian politics.

Assam was upgraded to the status of a Governor's province
in 1921. The new province, as provided in the Government of
India Act, 1919, had a Legislative Council consisting of the
members of the Executive Council, members nominated by the
Governor and the members elected by the people. Seventy per
cent of the members of the Council, which had a normal life
of 3 years, were elective and the rest official and nominated.
The total strength of the Assam Legislative Council was 53, of
whom 38 were elected, 6 nominated non-official and 9 *ex-efficio*.
The Congress had decided to non-cooperate with the Govern-
ment by boycotting the election under the Act of 1919 and
hardly one-third of the voters exercised their franchise. The
Councils were, therefore, manned by the European civilians
and the moderates, mostly title holders. Rai Bahadur Romoni
Mohon Das, Rai Bahadur Bipin Chandra Deblaskar and Khan
Saheb Rashid Ali Laskar from Cachar and Rai Bahadur Pro-
mode Chandra Datta, Khan Bahadur Abdul Mazid, Khan
Bahadur Abdul Hamid and Maulana Munahawar Ali from
Sylhet, amongst others, were returned to the Assam Council in

1921. Abdul Mazid became the Education Minister and next year Promode Chandra Datta was appointed as the Minister for Local Self-Government. But all of them had taken active part in the political movement in the Valley and some even underwent imprisonment during the Non-Cooperation and Khilafat Movements.

In the election of 1923 also the Congress was insistent upon the boycott, but C. R. Das was bent upon the Council-entry to wreck the constitution from within. Pandit Motilal Nehru was of the same opinion and they were joined by Hakim Ajmal Khan, V. J. Patel, N. C. Kelkar, Satyamurti and Jayakar. But the majority of the leading members of the Congress were opposed to the idea. C. R. Das, who was also the Congress President, threatened to resign from the Congress and ultimately the party endorsed the election-plan. The Swarajya Party was then formed within the Congress with C. R. Das as the President and Pandit Motilal Nehru as the Secretary. The leaders carried on the election propaganda vigorously all over the country—Nehru in Upper India, Patel in Bombay and C. R. Das in Bengal, Assam, Central Province and South India. During electioneering, C. R. Das came to Surma Valley where Khirode Chandra Deb, amongst others, was an active organiser of the Party. Tarun Ram Phukan of the Assam Valley was a close associate of C.R. Das, while Hem Chandra Baruah moved from district to district to select suitable candidates for the party. Despite the short preparation, the Swarajists routed the Moderates in the general election and even the doyen of the Moderates, Surendranath Banerjee, was defeated. Of the 105 elective seats in the Central Legislative Assembly, the Swarajya Party occupied 48 and joined by 24 Independent members under M. A. Jinnah, they came to be known as the Nationalist Group and Pandit Motilal Nehru was elected as the leader of the Nationalist Group. In the Legislative Council of Central Province the Swarajya Party secured the absolute majority. In Bengal it appreared as the largest single party and a good number of the Independents joined them. C. R. Das, the leader of the Party, was invited by the Governor to form the ministry, but in pursuance of his party's policy of non-cooperation, he declined. In Bombay, Uttar Pradesh and Assam the Party was fairly strong. Tarun Ram Phukan was returned to the Central Legis-

lature from the Assam Valley, while in the Assam Legislative
Council the party captured 8 seats and was joined by another
8 Independents. In this Council amongst others, Bipin Chandra
Deb Laskar, Romoni Mohon Das and Rashid Ali Laskar from
Cachar and Khirode Chandra Deb, Brojendra Narayan Choudhury, Abdul Hamid, Promode Chandra Datta and Munawar
Ali from Sylhet were returned. Abdul Hamid was elected President of the Council and Rai Bahadur Promode Chandra Datta
was again appointed as the Minister for Local Self-Government.
Maulavi Faiznur Ali of Dibrigarh was the leader of the Swarajya Party and Brojendra Narayan Choudhury, who was originally returned as an Independent but joined the Swarajya
Party, was elected the Deputy leader. The Swarajists functioned
with considerable effectiveness in criticising the Government
actions, voting out the unpopular measures and carrying
through the resolutions of public importance, and thus carried
out the party's method of obstruction from within. Although
the Swarajya-Independent Group had 16 members, they were
often joined by others. Bipin Chandra Deb Laskar of Cachar,
a ministerialist, for example, would generally sit with
the Swarajists. As a result, Gopendra Lal Das, a Swarajya
member, could be elected the Deputy President of the
Council.[48]

Unfortunately, the sudden death of C. R. Das. on 16 June
1925, weakened the party. Motilal Nehru, Madan Mohan Malaviya and Ragavendra Rao tried to activise the party, but the
opposition of Gandhi and withdrawal of some important party
leaders stood in the way. In addition to the non-changers,
there was a section of the Congressmen who favoured respon-
sive cooperation. A section of the Muslims undertook propaganda against the Non-Cooperation and some Hindus felt that
the cooperation of the Muslims with the British would put the
Hindus at a great disadvantage. As a result, in the election
of 1926 the Swarajya Party suffered losses. In the Central
Legislative Council they gained notable success only in Bengal
and Madras. Bombay returned only two Swarajya candidates,
while C. P. and U. P. one each. The results to the Provincial
Legislatures were equally disastrous. In U. P. their number
went down from 31 to 19, and in C. P. from 44 to 15. The
Punjab Council had only two Swarajists and Bombay returned

eleven. Only in Bengal and Madras their position was happy. In Assam the party maintained almost its previous position. But in the Surma Valley the position of the Swarajists was even improved. To the Central Legislative Assembly, Tarun Ram Phukan and Shrish Chandra Datta were returned from Assam Valley and Surma Valley respectively. Incidentally, the Surma Valley constituency included the Shillong town and was known as Surma Valley-cum-Shillong Non-Mohamedan Constituency. Shrish Chandra Datta, the Congress candidate, was elected with 1,444 votes, while his rivals Satish Chandra Datta and Khirode Chandra Datta polled 1,245 and 740 votes respectively. About 54 per cent of the voters exercised their franchise and 141 votes were rejected.[49] Jatindra Mohon Dev Laskar, was returned to the Assam Council from Cachar General Constituency.† Even the Cachar Mohamedan Constituency was captured by the Swarajists. Moulavi Arzan Ali Mazumdar was elected with 2,723 votes, defeating Moulavi Rashid Ali Laskar a ministerialist and sitting member for past six years, who polled 2,227 votes. In this constituency, about 80 per cent votes were polled and 45 declared invalid.[50] There were thirteen seats from Sylhet to the Council. The Swarajists won five non-muslim consituencies. None of their Muslim candidates was successful. All the Mohamedan Constituencies returned Independent candidates.[51] Two important inclusions in the Swarajya Party were Nabin Chandra Bardaloi from Assam Valley and Basanta Kumar Das from Sylhet. On the other hand, Kamini Kumar Chanda, a nominated member to the Indian Legislative Assembly, retired from active politics on health ground in 1926 and Promode Chandra Datta, a Minister of Assam, was nominated to the Central Assembly in 1927. Datta, however, soon returned to the state politics and was appointed as the Law and Finance Secretary in which capacity he continued upto 1936. In 1928, Maulavi Abdul Hamid of Sylhet was appointed as the Education Minister and continued till 1936.

On the other hand, the reforms of 1919 having not satisfied the aspirations of the Indian people, the demand for political advancement had gradually increased. The Indian National Congress, in the Madras session in 1927, declared the indepen-

†Sanat Kumar Das was elected from this constituency in 1929.

dence of India as its only goal. The British Government then
appointed a Statutory Commission, headed by Sir John Simon, to report on the working of the reforms. But when the
eleven-member commission landed at Bombay, it was boycotted
by the Congress, Muslim League and the Liberal Federation
as it did not include any Indian member. This incident provided an opportunity for the restoration of amity among the
different communities and political parties. The Congress, Muslim and the Liberals then met in an All-India Convention towards the end of 1928 to frame a constitution and agreed to
accept dominion status if granted by 31 December 1929, failing which the Congress would pursue its goal of complete independence and organise non-violent non-cooperation. The preparations were in the process for a country-wide movement by
the end of 1929. Unfortunately, in June that year, Surma Valley
was struck by a disastrous flood and Cachar was worst affected. About three-fourth of the people were rendered homeless
and had to take shelter in the hill-tops. The Silchar town had
been completely submerged, in some places there was five to
ten feet water.[52] The public leaders had, therefore, to engage
themselves to the service of the people. The Cachar-Sylhet
Flood Relief Committee, formed with Brojendra Narayan Choudhury as the Secretary, organised commendable relief work.
Both officials and non-officials came forward. The students and
teachers of the Silchar Government High School and their
Boy Scouts worked round the clock, taking the people to camps
and attending them. The Judge, Sub-Judge and Magistrates in
Cachar were all engaged in relief work.[53] The Cachar Relief Committee was formed under the joint Presidentship of the Divisional Commissioner and Kamini Kumar Chanda.[54] Attempts were
made to raise funds. The Government sanctioned gratuitous
relief and agricultural loans.[54] The local unit of the Ramakrishna
Mission opened a Relief Fund and appealed for contributions.[55]
Bipin Chandra Pal went upto Bombay to collect funds. The
charity shows[56] and matches[57] were organised in various parts
of Bengal and the proceeds were handed over to the Relief
Committee.

The people of Cachar had thus suffered an acute distress
for a couple of months and the recession of the flood water was
immediately followed by a tremendous political upheaval. In

response to the demand of the Congress for Dominion Status, the Government declared that a Round Table Conference of all the political parties would be held in London to discuss the recommendations of the Simon Commission. But the Congress, in the Lahore Session, held in December 1929, reaffirmed its demand for complete independence and decided to boycott the Legislatures and the Round Table Conference and took steps to launch a programme of Civil Disobedience. The Independence Day was observed all over the country on 26 January 1930. With the rest of the country, the National Flag was hoisted at Silchar and Sylhet and the Surma Valley witnessed popular excitement.[58] As directed by the Congress High Command, the members to the Legislatures from Cachar and Sylhet resigned their seats. Twelve Congress members of the the Assam Council, including four from Surma Valley, submitted resignation. Shrish Chandra Datta, the lone member to the Indian Legislative Assembly from the Valley, also resigned his membership. These seats were immediately filled up by the moderates and title-holders. The Sylhet District Congress Committee, however, had put the diarchy to ridicule by getting two unlettered cobblers, Chirtan Muchi and Kalicharan Muchi, returned to the Assam Council, in 1930, from the South Sylhet and Sunamganj constituencies, to sit with the *Rai Bahadurs* and *Khan Sahebs*.[59]

Shyama Charan Deb, President of the Cachar District Congress Committee, and Brojendra Narayan Choudhury, President of the Sylhet District Congress Committee, were at the vanguard of the Civil Disobedience Movement in the Surma Valley. Shyama Charan Deb had succeeded K. K. Chanda as the President of the Cachar District Congress Committee in 1926, while Direndra Mohon Deb was the Vice-President and Manindra Lal Mallik the Secretary. Subsequently Sunil Mohon Endow, Birendra Kumar Purkayastha, Achinta Kumar Bhattacharjee, Monomohon Bhattacharjee and Nikunja Behari Goswami had held the position of the Secretary, in turn. Any way, in the Civil Disobedience Movement Dhirendra Kumar Gupta, Satindra Mohon Dev, Gangadayal Dikshit, Prithish Naug, Sabid Raja Mazumdar, Kurshed Ali had taken active part. The Silchar Mahila Samiti played a significant role in popularising the campaign.

The agitation involved defiance of repressive laws and ordinances, boycott of British goods and use of indigenous goods including preparation of salt in the native method. The students took part as volunteers. But in May 1930, Mr. Cunningham, D.P.I., Assam, issued a circular requiring students of the Secondary schools and their guardians to give a written undertaking that the students would refrain from participation in any kind of political activity. The students and the guardians refused to be humiliated by signing the undertaking and the circular was condemned in public meetings. As a protest against the Circular, sixty students of the Silchar Government High School immediately left the school. The students from the Government-aided schools in Cachar also followed suit. Many guardians refused to send their children to the schools run by the alien Government. Dhirendra Kumar Gupta, Satindra Mohon Deb and others then started the Cachar High School. B. C. Gupta, a generous Bengalee tea planter of Silchar, donated a significant amount for the establishment of the school. Many other local businessmen and members of public contributed to the school fund. Dhirendra Kumar Gupta served the school as the Secretary and honorary teacher. Girija Mohon Datta, Promode Kumar Bhattacharjee, Kamini Kumar Chakravarty, Golam Chhabir Khan and many others also served the school as honorary teachers.[60] The Cunningham Circular thus led to the establishment of a school in Silchar and the present generation should remember its historic past. On the other hand, the agitation against the Circular had gained momentum all over Assam and ultimately the Government had to relax the Circular to facilitate the re-entry of the students in the Government and Government-aided schools. But the students continued to participate in meetings, demonstrations and picketings.

The political leaders tried to enhance their influence in the rural areas. Harendra Chandra Choudhury, a prominent leader of Sylhet, carried on massive propaganda for the abolition of capitalism and *Zamindari*. The Sylhet Ryots' and Peasants' Conference conveyed the message of non-cooperation and civil disobedience, including the non-payment of taxes, to the farthest villages of Surma Valley. Brojendra Narayan

Choudhury advocated the boycott of Government servants. He had little respect for the officers of Indian Civil Service and Police Service and wanted the true Indians in such services to follow the example set by Subhas Chandra Bose by resigning from the I.C.S.[61]

Gandhi's famous Dandi march, on 6 April 1930, to make salt on the sea shore in defiance of the salt law, was the signal for a fresh movement involving mass demonstrations, boycott of British goods, grave cases of terrorism like the armoury raid in Chittagong and the setting up of parallel governments in many places. The Government, on the other hand, adopted stern measures of repression involving police firing resulting in death and injury, imprisonment and indiscriminate beating of men and women. The scenes were similar in Surma Valley as elsewhere. The prominent leaders were soon sent behind the bars and the police resorted to rough tactics of dispersing meetings and picketeers. Gangadayal Dikshit was arrested immediately after the movement had begun. Dhirendra Kumar Gupta* was sentenced to six months simple imprisonment and sent to Tezpur Jail.[62] Many other Congress leaders, including Shyama Charan Deb, underwent imprisonment.

Meanwhile, the Round Table Conference was held in London, in November 1930, without any Congress representative and on 4 March 1931, the Gandhi-Irwin Pact was signed agreeing, on behalf of the Congress, to suspend the Civil Disobedience and join the Round Table Conference and the Government withdrew the repressive ordinances and released the political prisoners except those guilty of violence. The suspension of the movement offended a section of the Congress leaders including Subhas Chandra Bose who played a key role in the movement and was detained in Arracan Jail. Subhas now launched an anti-pact movement, but was banished from India to Europe to return not before 1937. A popular excitement was caused by the execution of Bhagat Singh, Sukh Dev and Rajguru for their terroristic activities in Punjab. The protest meetings were held all over the country deploring the execution, while the Subhas group directly blamed Gandhi

*Ex-chairman of Silchar Municipality and ex-Vice-President of the Cachar District Congress Committee.

for not including the release of these three patriots in the terms of the Gandhi-Irwin Pact. A public meeting at the Sylhet Town Hall, in March 1931, under the presidentship of Dwarikanath Goswami expressed the feeling that as a result of these executions there was the chance of a split in the Congress.[63] The Surma Valley Youth Conference, held at Moulavi Bazar in July, called upon the youth of the valley to be inspired by the fearless sacrifices of the martyrs like Bhagat Singh, Sukh Dev Raj Guru, Dinesh Gupta and Harikishen.[64] The terrorist movement that had started in Bengal during the Swadeshi movement was althrough in full swing through various secret societies and revolutionary organisations like *Yugantar* and *Anushilan Samitis*. The revolutionaries, dangerous according to the British, under hidden identity let loose a reign of violence in Bengal by killing the European officials and their Indian collaborators by surprise, ambush and sabotage. The attempts of the Government to supress through inhuman torture made them bolder and sanguine to expel the alien element from the Indian soil. Some of the prominent revolutionaries even escaped from the country and through foreign assistance and organisations abroad endeavoured to fuel the fight inside. The abrupt suspension of the movement by Gandhi caused frustration to many nationalists and drew them closer to the anarchists. In Surma Valley several secret societies carried on underground activities with often outbursts. On 27 March 1913 an attempt was made on the life of Mr. Gurdon, the District Magistrate, at Moulavi Bazar, but the bomb had burst before time and killed one of the revolutionaries. Again in May a *Chaprassi* was killed by a bomb aimed at Gurdon.[65] During the Civil Disobedience Movement, a young man named Rashamay Acharya wrote some letters to G. D. Walker, Deputy Commissioner of Cachar, in which he claimed himself to be the organiser of a revolutionary party and threatened that unless the Deputy Commissioner had adopted conciliatory measures in dealing with the Congress workers he would burn all the Government offices and bungalows in Silchar. The espionage being very intensive in those days, Rashamay was ultimately arrested under Section 109 of Cr. P.C. and some of his collaborators were also subsequently arrested.[66] This happened immediately after the veteran Congressman Gangadayal Dikshit was arrested and sentenced to imprisonment. It is heartening to note that when Gangadayal was produced before Walker, the District Magistrate, and the latter asked his name, Gangadayal replied that his name was '*Shveta-mlechha uccheda Dikshita Gangadayal.*'[67] This shows that the revolutionary parties were not always hostile to the Congress and when the Congress showed determination the revolutionaries supported the Congress scheme, while some Congressmen themselves had revolutionary spirit. Unfortunately, Gandhi could not sometimes rely upon his own schemes. To quote C. R. Das[68] : "The Mahatma opens a campaign in a brilliant fashion ; he works it up with unerring skill; he moves from success to success till he realises the zenith of his campaign—but after that he loses his nerve and begins to falter." Although he had called off the Civil Disobedience movement in January 1931 and himself attended the second session of the Round Table Conference in December 1931, Gandhi had to renew the movement immediately after his return to India because of Prime Minister's declaration of Communal Award. The Government started fresh repression and some top leaders, including Pandit Jawaharlal Nehru and Khan Abdul Gaffur Khan, were arrested and Gandhiji's request for an interview with the Viceroy was refused. On 1 January 1932, the Congress Working Committee decided to renew the Civil Disobedience and on 4 January Gandhi was arrested. Anyway, the people again responded to the call and a fresh spell of movement at once swept over the country. The revolutionary activities proceeded side by side and the Government launched an unprecedented campaign of coercion. The physical outrages, shooting and beating, punitive expeditions, collective fines on villages and seizure of land and property are recorded in the India League Delegation Report issued in 1933 and according to Congress estimate more than 1,20,000 people were arrested by the end of March 1933.

In this second phase of Civil Disobedience Movement also the Surma Valley contributed her ungrudging share. Brojendra Narayan Choudhury still lives in the memory of the older generation almost as a legendary figure for his role in organising civil disobedience in Surma Valley. A strong advocate of radicalism and a close associate of Subhas Chandra Bose, he toured North and East Bengal, while Subhas toured West Bengal in 1931, to enlist popular reaction to the Hijli incident, notorious for inhuman torture of the political prisoners, and the Chittagong Armoury Raid. Basanta Kumar Das and Shrish Chandra Datta were also active organisers of the movement and were sentenced to two years' imprisonment. A very daring role was taken by Khirode Chandra Deb in organising *Kisan Satyagraha* in Bhanubil and did it with equal success as Sardar Patel in Bardoli. He led thousands of peasants in defiance of the repressive measures of the Government and the *Zamindars*. The Bhanubil Satyagraha created a great stir in India and the British parliamentary circle. Khirode Chandra was arrested and sentenced to rigorous imprisonment for one and a half year.[69] Shyama Charan Deb, Satish Chandra Deb, Harendra Chandra Choudhury, Prakash Chandra Bhattacharjee, Sitanath De, Gangadayal Dikshit,. Hem Chandra Datta,Hem Chandra Chakravarty, Sanat Kumar Das also never lacked behind and were exposed to all repressions. of the imperialist Government. Sunil Mohon Endow, Mahitosh Purkayastha, Satyadas Roy, Achinta Kumar Bhatacharjee had practically converted the Congress into an active force in Silchar. Parmananda Debnath, Sazid Raja Mazumdar,. Rajendra Ghandra Purkayastha, Kazi Rahman Baksh, Rajchandra Deshamukhya, Umakanta Deb, Hurmat Ali Barlaskar, Gulam Chhabir Khan and many other Congress workers. carried the movement through the rural areas of the Sub-Division.[70] In Hailakandi, Moulana Abdul Matlib Mazumdar, Bidyapati Singha, Harendra Kumar Chakravarty were among the active workers. Under the leadership of these dedicated nationalists men, women and young children of Cachar and Sylhet responded to the campaign and their fearless sufferings would live as symbol of nationalism and. sacrifice for all times.

The oneness of purpose, ceaseless sufferings and determination to liberate the country had lifted Indian patriotism to the Himalayan height. Even the public opinion in Britain had gained momentum against the coercive actions of the Government. The publication of the India League Delegation Report created a great stir in Britain and the Government faced heavy storms in the Parliament. In 1933, the Government published the

White Paper, embodying the proposals for the reform of the Indian Constitution on the basis of the Round Table Conference and, with certain modifications, was converted into the Government of India Act, 1935. On 8 May 1933, Gandhi again suspended the movement. This came as a stunning blow to the political leaders in India. Vithalbhai Patel and Subhas Chandra Bose issued a statement condemning the suspension from distant Vienna. K.F. Narriman, the famed Congress leader of Bombay, immediately after his release from the jail made a bitter attack on Gandhi's ideology and conduct. In the election to the Legislative Assembly, in 1934, the Gandhi-Congress participated over the blood, sweat and tears of hundreds of partiots—the victims of the movement. A strong section of the Congressmen, led by Malaviya, sought to revive the Swarajya Party and fought the election under the name of Congress Nationalist party. The new party secured all the seats in Bengal. The Congress returned only one member from Punjab, but was successful in some provinces. Basanta Kumar Das was elected from the Surma Valley Constituency.

The Government of India Act, 1935, had provided for a bicameral legislature, with a Council of States and a Federal Assembly, in the Centre, while in the provincial legislatures, in Governor's provinces, there were two chambers—Legislative Council and Legislative Assembly. The Assam Legislative Council had 22 seats and the Assembly, 108. The seats were distributed on the basis of the communal electorate. Gandhi accepted the reform, but many Congressmen left the party. Shyama Charan Deb retired from politics.[71] Brojendra Narayan Choudhury had also decided in favour of defection but was persuaded by Dr. Bidhan Chandra Roy, Sarat Chandra Bose and Bhulabhai Desai to fill up the seat in the Central Legislature made vacant by the return of Basanta Kumar Das to Assam politics.[72]

It was a coincidence that the Act was passed in 1935, due for the Congress to celebrate the Golden Jubilee of its foundation. Cachar had celebrated the Jubilee in a befitting way. Kamini Kumar Chanda, the veteran Congress leader, was carried from his sick bed to address a mammoth public meeting at Silchar, on 25 December 1935. The Jubilee Celebration Committee was formed with Kamini Kumar Chanda as President, Dhirendra Kumar Gupta as Vice-President, Manindralal Mallik as Secretary, while Satindra Mohon Dev, Satyadas Roy, Haran Chandra Boxi and others were members.[73] The celebrations created a new spirit in the general public. But, shortly after, on 1 February 1936, Kamini Kumar Chanda passed away after long years of public service. In him Cachar, with the rest of India, lost a parliamentarian, an organiser, a leader of men and a true friend of the people. One of the beginners of active Congress politics in India, this 'Uncrowned King of Assam' has left behind a unique social and political career and will always find a place in the annals of modern India in his own deeds. The bunch[74] of letterrs written to him by contemporary national leaders and officials including Surendranath Banerjee, Bipin Chandra Pal, Mohammad Ali, Syed Samsul Huda, Ashutosh Mukherjee, M. A. Jinnah, Sir Bamfylde Fuller and preserved at his Silchar house would amply testify his personality and his role in Indian struggle for freedom. Fortunately for the country, the vacuum caused by his death was immediately filled up by his worthy son, Arun Kumar Chanda. Elected as the President of the Cachar District Congress Committee, Arun Kumar took the message of the Congress throughout the length and breadth of Cachar and converted the Congress politics into a mass struggle in the district. As the President of the Assam Branch of the Indian National Trade Union Congress, he took interest for the improvement of the condition of the workers and tea labourers and won the sympathy of the working classes in favour of the Congress politics. In the first general election held under the new Act, in 1937. Arun Kumar worked hard for the success of the Congress. The Congress won 33 seats in the Assam Legislative Assembly and emerged as the largest single party. The Muslim League captured some predominantly Muslim seats. The Assam Independent Muslim Party, founded by Moulana Abdul Rashid Choudhury in 1936, fought with the Muslim League and won 8 seats. The Moulana himself was elected to the Indian Legislative Assembly. Arun Kumar Chanda was elected to the Assam Assembly from Cachar General Constituency defeating his rival Jatindra Mohon Deb Laskar by a margin of 8,000 votes.[75] Other important returns to Assam Legislature from Surma Valley were Hem Chandra Datta and Harendra Chandra

Chakravarty in Cachar, and Basanta Kumar Das, Moulana Munawar Ali, Khirode Chandra Deb, Promode Chandra Datta* in Sylhet. Brojendra Narayan Choudhury was elected to the Central Legislature without contest.

Syed Md. Saadulla, leader of the Muslim group in Assam, formed the ministry with the support of the European, Tribal and other members and himself became the Prime Minister of Assam. But Basanta Kumar Das, a Congress nominee, was elected as the Speaker. Gopinath Bardoloi was the leader of the Congress Legislature Party and Khirode Chandra Deb of Karimganj, the deputy leader. Unfortunately, in July 1937, Khirode Chandra passed away and with him the country lost a valiant freedom fighter and the Congress, a zealous worker. Arun Kumar Chanda was then elected as the deputy leader. The Congress members, under Bardoloi and Chanda, carried on sophisticated attack upon the Government and the Ministry suffered eleven defeats through cut motions and resolutions in the very first budget session. They exposed many misgivings of the ministry and there was a storm of protests throughout the province. Ultimately, to avoid the no-confidence motion, Saadulla tendered the resignation of his ministry on 13 September 1938. On 19 September, Gopinath Bardoloi formed the Congress Coalition Ministry. Subhas Chandra Bose, the Congress President, and Moulana Abul Kalam Azad, a member of the Indian Parliamentary Sub-Committee, came to Shillong to put the coalition ministry in office. Arun Kumar Chanda and Satindra Mohon Dev had played a significant role in dismissing the Saadulla Ministry and bringing the Congress to office.

In the following years dramatic developments had taken place in Indian politics. Subhas Chandra Bose had resigned from the Congress, due to his differences with Gandhi, and formed the Forward Bloc. With the outbreak of the Second World War in 1939 the British Government drew India closer to the War. In protest, the Congress Ministries resigned. The Muslim League formed ministries, extended support to the war effort of the British and in 1940 put their demand for the

* Promode Chandra Datta resigned from the Assembly in 1938 and was appointed as the Advocate-General of Assam.

creation of Pakistan. Subhas Chandra miraculously escaped from India to organise fight from without and with the Indian National Army tried to liberate the country. The Congress Working Committee, on 14 July 1942, decided to organise a mass movement to achieve complete independence. The Quit India Movement in August 1942 was an open war against the British for India's independence and the whole country was electrified and the Government machinery successfully paralysed. The prominent Congress leaders were all arrested. Arun Kumar Chanda was arrested at Calcutta on 9 August 1942. His arrest, particularly, created stir in Cachar and there were protest meetings and demonstrations.[76] Following the German attack upon Soviet Russia, the Communists in India decided to support the war efforts of the British and declaring it to be Peoples' War the Communists organised rallies.

Situated on the eastern frontier, Cachar was supposed to be an immediate casuality of the Japanese invasion. The Government was constantly haunted by the Japanese phobia and since 1942 there was an unprecedented agglomeration of the troops in Cachar. Hundreds of military camps were opened in the small district and the educational institutions were made over to the military authority. The supply of essential commodities was far from being regular and a bulk of it was consumed by the armymen in the barracks. As a result, there was volcanic inflation in the market. The labourers and wage earners lost their means of subsistence, while the British propaganda made the people panicky. The local communist leaders also carried on the war slogans. The fall of Rangoon in March 1942 was followed by an influx of the refugees from Burma in Cachar and the political leaders and students had to work in the relief camps. To make matters worse, the bombing of the Darbey Tea Estate by the Japanese and the frequent appearances of the aircraft led the district authorities to ask for a total evacuation of the town. But nothing could suppress the patriotism and hunger for independence. Netaji's call to 'strike when the iron is hot' and Gandhi's call to 'do or die' had completely electrified the people.

Meanwhile, Netaji had appreared on the Indian frontier. On 4 July 1943, he took over the leadership of Indian indepen-

-dence movement in East Asia and formed the Indian National Army with the Indian prisoners of war and himself became the Supreme Commander. On 21 October, he proclaimed the Provisional Government of the *Azad Hind* or Free India, of which he was the Prime Minister. In November, Andaman and Nicobar Islands were liberated by the I.N.A. and in January 1944 the I.N.A. headquarters were shifted to Rangoon. Netaji then began his famous 'March to Delhi' and across the Burmese border reached Indian soil on 18 August when his columns moved upto Kohima and Imphal. But the British Government and a section of the Indians did their best to misguide the people by branding the I.N.A. advance as Japanese invasion. Cachar was practically converted into a battle field by the presence of innumerable army personnel and the war preparations. The local people were not given to understand that Netaji himself was only at a little distance from them. Subhas had come to Silchar and Sylhet in 1939 and his legendary activities had made a great impression in the people of the Valley. It is not at all unlikely that the people of Cachar and Sylhet would have defied the Government in extending whatever support they could to Netaji. But the British Government and their Indian allies exploited the situation to keep them away from their most beloved leader. Unfortunately, the tables were completely turned with the U.S. bombing of Hiroshima and Nagasaki which compelled the Japanese to surrender and Netaji to retreat. Hoisting the Indian national flag on Indian soil, the leader of the leaders marched off to an unknown destination in August 1945, leaving behind the history of his heroic role in India's struggle for freedom.

Gandhi was released from the jail in May 1944 and the Congress had called off the movement. In March 1945, Lord Wavell, the Viceroy of India, on behalf of the British Government declared that the members of the Council, except the Viceroy and the Commander-in-Chief, would be Indians and selected from the political parties. On 25 June 1945, he summoned a conference at Simla, but as the Congress and League could not come to an agreement the discussions broke down. Soon after, the Labour Party came to power in Britain and made an earnest effort to end the political deadlock in India. The new Government decided to hold elections to the central and provincial legislatures, to reconstitute the Viceroy's council after the election and to summon a constitution making body at the earliest. The general election held in the beginning of 1946, gave a sweeping victory to the Congress in the general constituencies and Muslim League won the Muslim seats.

In Assam the Congress Coalition Ministry that came to power in September 1938 resigned on 17 September 1939, following the party's directives and Saadulla Ministry again came to power. On 24 December 1941, this ministry was forced to resign as it had failed to control the law and order situation and lost the confidence of its coalition partners. Governor's rule was then introduced in the province. Again on 25 August 1942, during the mass movement, the Saadulla Ministry was installed. In the general election, held in January 1946, the Congress secured 50 seats, against 33 in 1937, in the House of 108 and with the support of the few unattached members the party formed an absolute majority. On 10 January, the Congress Ministry came to power with Gopinath Bardoloi as the Prime Minister and Basanta Kumar Das, the Home Minister. In Cachar, the Congress Party had gained an unprecedented success. Satindra Mohon Dev and Nibaran Chandra Laskar were elected from Silchar and Moulavi Abdul Matlib Mazumdar and Bidyapati Singha from Hailakandi to the Assam Legislative Assembly. Arun Kumar Chanda was returned to the Central Legislature without contest.[77] However, his untimely death, on 26 April 1947, had cast a shadow of gloom all over the country.

The Cabinet Mission, sent by the Labour Government, came to India in March 1946 and after a series of discussions with the Congress and League leaders declared their plan on 16 May. The plan envisaged a federal type of Government for India including the princely states. The Federal Government would deal with foreign affairs, defence and communication, while other subjects would be administered by the provinces and the states. India was to be divided into three groups of provinces; one comprising the Punjab, North West Frontier Province, Sind and Baluchistan, the second comprising Bengal and Assam, and the third would include the rest. On

6 June, Muslim League accepted the Plan. The Congress was also in favour of the acceptance. Gandhi, Nehru and Moulana Azad, the Congress President, appreciated the British gesture. But some leaders from the Assam Valley raised objection to the grouping of Assam with Bengal. Gopinath Bardoloi, Prime Minister of Assam, was persistent in his opposition and submitted a memorandum to the Congress Working Committee. On 16 July 1946, the Assam Legislative Assembly adopted a resolution moved by Bardoloi himself expressing disapproval of the plan and directing the Assam members in the Constituent Assembly not to sit in any group with the representatives of any other province.[78] Ultimately, Gandhi also changed his mind and gave support to Bardoloi.[79] In the meantime, the Muslim League had also revised their stand and rejected the Cabinet Mission Plan. The Viceroy's Executive Council was reconstituted without any representative of the Muslim League, and a Constituent Assembly was formed with the members elected by the provincial legislatures. This provoked a violent reaction of the separatist Muslims, and the Muslim League declared 16 August 1946, to be a day of 'Direct Action.' This was one of the blackest days in the history of Hindu-Muslim relationship in India, leading to the worst type of communal violence. In the Muslim-dominated areas of Cachar, Sylhet, Nowgong, Goalpara, Barpeta and Mongoldoi the Muslim League supporters raised the slogans in favour of Pakistan. Abdul Hamid of Sylhet was a strong advocate of Pakistan and was key to League's activities in Cachar and Sylhet. But many Muslim leaders in Surma Valley opposed the Pakistan demand of the League. Maulana Pir Md. Yakub of Badarpur, for example, had condemned the activities of the League and creation of Pakistan in strong terms.[80]

On 2 September 1946, the Interim Government was formed with Jawaharlal Nehru and the Constituent Assembly met on 9 December under the Presidentship of Dr. Rajendra Prasad. Ultimately, the Muslim League also joined the Assembly, but the representatives of the League continued to press their demand for Pakistan and the Congress members opposed to it. Lord Mountbatten, who came as the Viceroy of India on 24 March 1947, held a series of discussions with the Congress and League leaders. On 3 June, he issued the White Paper declar-

ing the basis for transfer of power from the British Government
to the Indian people. His plan had envisaged the demand for
Pakistan and provided that Bengal and Punjab would be partitioned if the leaders of the Hindu majority districts in the legislatures of these provinces had so desired. A referendum would
be taken in the N.W.F. Province to ascertain whether it should
join Pakistan. The Muslim majority areas of Sylhet would also
be tranferred to Pakistan after ascertaining the views of the
people by a referendum. The relevant part of the declaration
may be worth quoting:[81]

13. Though Assam is predominantly a non-Muslim province, the district of Sylhet which is contiguous to Bengal is
predominantly Muslim. There has been a demand that, in
the event of the partition of Bengal, Sylhet should be amalgamated with the Muslim part of Bengal. Accordingly if it
is decided that Bengal should be partitioned, a referendum
will be held in Sylhet District under the aegis of the
Governor-General and in consultation with the Assam Provincial Government to decide whether the district of Sylhet
should continue to form part of Assam Province or should
be amalgamated with the new province of Eastern Bengal, a
boundary commission with terms of reference similar to
those for the Punjab and Bengal will be set up to demarcate
the Muslim majority areas of Sylhet District and contiguous
Muslim majority areas of adjoining districts, which will then
be transferred to East Bengal. The rest of Assam Province
will in any case continue to participate in the proceedings of
the existing Constituent Assembly.

The Muslim League, whose original demand included whole
of Bengal, Assam and Punjab, was not happy with the plan, but
soon declared their acceptance. The Congress also could not
maintain its earlier stand for 'United India' and Gandhi,
Jawaharlal and other leaders gradually agreed to the plan.
Surharwady, Sarat Chandra Bose and some prominent leaders
of Bengal raised a demand for 'Sovereign Bengal', but in vain.
The majority of the political leaders in Cachar and Sylhet were
against the partition of the country and had raised their demand
for the independence of 'United India.' In February 1947, a
Students' Convention was held at Silchar. Major-General A.C.
Chatterjee, a former I.N.A. man, Niharendu Datta Mazumdar,
a youth leader, and Dr. Amiya Chakravarty came from
Calcutta to take part in the convention. The two-day conven-

tion unanimously resolved in favour of the complete independence of the undivided India. On 20 February, Assam Nationalist Muslims' Convention was held at Silchar under the initiative of Moulana Makaddak Ali, Moulana Mashman Ali, Moulana Hurmat Ali Barlaskar, Md. A.K. Nurul Haque, Kazi Rahman Baksh, Md. Sazid Raja Mazumdar, Md. Ibrahim Ali Choudhury and others. Moulana Ibrahim Ali of Jaintia presided over the conference, while Md. Abdul Matlib Mazumdar inaugurated. Moulana Mohammad Mashahid and Moulana Abdul Jalil strongly criticised the demand for Pakistan by a section of the Muslims. The conference adopted a resolution condemning the partition proposal and demanding the independence of undivided India. About fifteen thousand Muslims paraded the streets of Silchar with nationalist slogans.[82] The declaration of the Mountbatten Plan and proposed partition of Sylhet created a great stir in the Surma Valley. The people of Sylhet and Cachar were bound by a common language, culture and way of life and since the separation from Bengal in 1874, the Surma Valley was but a 'little Bengal' in Assam. No wonder, the people in the Valley received the most cruel shock by the declaration of the Government. Satindra Mohon Dev, M.L.A. and Chairman of the Silchar Municipality, immediately convened an emergency meeting of the political leaders of Surma Valley at Silchar. Held on 8 June 1947, the meeting was presided over by Basanta Kumar Das, the Home Minister of Assam. Brojendra Narayan Choudhury, Rabindranath Aditya, Baidyanath Muhkerjee, Abdul Matlib Mazumdar, Lalit Mohon Kar, Kamini Kumar Sen, Harendra Narayan Choudhury, Mazzummal Ali, Labanya Kumar Choudhury, Girindra Nandan Choudhury, Gopesh Chandra Pal in their fiery speeches demanded the retention of Sylhet in India.[83] The leaders then organised public meetings in various parts of Sylhet and urged upon the electorate to vote against the partition. But all went in vain, the cruel irony of history being predestined. The partition of Bengal and Punjab was effected by two commisions appointed by the Government under the chairmanship of Justice Radcliffe. Sylhet, with the exception of four *thanas* of Karimganj, Rathabari, Patharkandi and Badarpur, was put to referendum. Altogether 2,39,619 votes were polled in favour of the partition and 1,84,041 against. Thus the partition became a *fait accompli*.[84]   The Karimganj Subdivision, consisting of the Karimganj, Rathabari, Patharkandi and Badarpur, was transferred to Cachar which has continued to be a part of Assam.   After independence, Cachar had four sub-divisions, namely, Silchar, Hailakandi, Haflong and Karimganj.   The Haflong Subdivision was subsequently seperated from Cachar and eventually constituted into the present district of North Cachar Hills.

Abbreviations Used in Notes

A.R.	Asiatic Researches.
A.R.C.P.	Agricultural, Revenue and Commerce Department Proceedings.
A.S.R.	Assam Secretariat Records.
B.J.C.	Bengal Judicial Consulations.
B.P.C.	Bengal Political Consultations.
B.R.C.	Bengal Revenue Consultations.
C.R.	Cachar Records.
F.G.P.	Foreign Department General Proceedings.
F.J.P.	Foreign Department Judicial Proceedings.
F.P.C.	Foreign Department Political Consultations.
F.P.P.	Foreign Department Political Proceedings.
F.R.C.	Foreign Department Revenue Consultations.
F.S.C.	Foreign Department Secret Consultations.
H.J.P.	Home Department Judicial Proceedings.
H.P.P.	Home Department Political Proceedings.
H.R.C.	Home Department Revenue Consultations.
H.Pol.C.	Home Department Political Consultations.
H.Pub.P.	Home Department Public Proceedings.
J.A.S.B.	*Journal of the Asiatic Society of Bengal.*
P.A.S.B.	Proceedings of the Asiatic Society of Bengal.

Notes

Chapter One : Introduction

1 Census of India, 1961, *Cachar District Hand Book*, 1.

2 F. Hamilton, *An Account of Assam*, 83.

3 S K. Chaube, *Hill Politics in North East India*, Calcutta, 1974, 1.

4 R. B. Pemberton, *Report on the Eastern Frontier of British India*, Calcutta, 1835, 199.

5 *Ibid.*, also B.C. Allen, *Assam District Gazeteers*, vol. II (Cachar), Allahabad, 1005, 1.

6 Allen, n. 5, 6.

7 A.C. Choudhury, *Shrihatter Itibritta*, Sylhet, 1317 B.S., 96; P.N. Bhattacharjee, *A Critical Study of Mr. Gait's History of Assam*, 14

8 R.C. Majumdar, *History of Ancient Bengal*, Calcutta, 1971, 1.

9 U.C. Guha, *Cacharer Itibritta*, Gauhati, 1971, 20.

10 *Ibid.*, 5-6.

11 *Ibid* , 8.

12 *Ibid.*, 7; J.B. Bhattacharjee, "Some Important Sources of the History of Medieval and Modern Cachar," *Shodhak*, Vol. 4, pt. A, No. 10, Jaipur, 1975, 457-70.

13 *Ibid.*, 1.

14 Majumdar, n. 8, 79-81 and 510-1; R.N. Nath, *The Background of Assamese Culture*, Shillong, 1949, 75.

15 *Ibid.*, 3.

16 S. Endle, *The Kacharis*, London, 1911, 14. The Bodos are believed to have come to this part of India from Tibet. Several tribes of North East India like the Garos, Koches, Meches, Dhimals, Dimachas, etc. belong to the Bodo group of people.

17 Choudhury, n. 7, 48.

18 Guha, n. 9, 15.

19 Choudhury, n. 7, 204.

20 *Ibid* , 205.

21 E. Gait, *A History of Assam*, Calcutta, 1925, 248.

22 S.K. Bhuyan, (ed.), *Kachari Buranji*, Gauhati, 1936, xv.

23 *Ibid.*

24 Gait, n. 21; L. Devi, *Ahom-Tribal Relations*, Gauhati, 1968, 78.

25 S.K. Bhuyan (ed.), *Deodhai Asom Buranji*, 78.

26 Devi, n. 24.

27 K. Phukan, *Assam Buranji*, 18,

28 Bhuyan, n. 25, 19-20.

29 Bhuyan, n. 22, 13.

30 R.M. Nath, *The Background of Assamese Culture*, Shillong, 1949, 73.

31 *Ibid.*, 73-4.

32 J.B. Bhattacharjee, *Jayantia-Heramba Relations*, Proceedings, Indian History Congress, Muzzafarpur, 1972, 251-4.

33 Gait, n. 21, 53-4.

34 Guha, n. 9, 30-1.

35 Nath, n. 30, 73-4; Devi, n. 24, 84.

36 Guha, n. 9, 32-3.

37 Nath, n. 30.

38 Gait, n. 21, 303.

39 S.K. Datta, (ed.), *Jayantia Buranji*, 11-3.

40 Gait, n. 21, 304.

41 Bhattacharjee, n. 32.

42 Gait, n. 21, 305.

43 Bhuyan, n. 22, xxii.

44 Datta, n. 39, xii.

45 Gait, n 21, 304.

46 *Ibid.*, 303.

47 *Ibid.*, 305. This invasion is believed to be the subject-matter of a Bengali novel, *Kanachandi*. Satrudaman, the hero of the novel, has been identfied with Jasanarayan, the Raja of Heramba.

48 Datta, n. 39.

49 M I. Borah (tr.), *Baharistan-i-Gaibi*, vol. II, Gauhati, 1936, 156-75.

50 Bhattacharjee, n. 32; Nath, n. 30.

51 Bhuyan, n. 22; Gait, n. 21, 176-7.

52 Gait, n. 21, 178. Gait writes : "As the Ahoms advanced, the inhabitants of the villages along the line of march deserted their homes and fled towards Maibong. Demera was occupied without opposition. A garrison of 3,000 men was left there, and the army then entered the hills and continued its arduous march to Nadereng, 23 miles distant, which was reached in thirteen days. Here the letter was received from the Par Barua saying that he had already occupied Maibong. The Pani Phukan pressed on to join him, and covered the remaining distance of seventeen miles in two days. During his march he had taken in all 322 prisoners and a small quantity of loot."

53 *Ibid.*, 179; Bhuyan, n. 22.

54 Bhuyan, n. 22, xxiv.

55 Gait, n. 21, 180-2.

56 Bhuyan, n. 22.

57 Gait, n. 21, 293.

58 P.N. Bhattacharjee, *A Critical Study of Mr. Gait's History of Assam*, 14, quoted in Choudhury, n. 7, 96.

59 Bhuyan, n. 22, xvi.

60 F.P.P., 5 March 1832, No. 70.

61 Nath, n. 30, 74.

62 Guha, n. 9, 49.

63 Nath, n. 30, 74-5.

64 Guha, n. 9, 96.

65 *Ibid.*, 95-7.

66 A.S R., File No. 636 of 1872; Report on the Annual Revenue Administration in Cachar.

67 Choudhury, n. 7, 102. The appointment letter of the *Uzir*, in Bengali, has been appended in p. 102-5.

68 Nath, n. 30, 75.

69 Choudhury, n. 7, 105.

Chapter Two : Early Contacts

1 S.K. Bhuyan, (ed.), *Tungkhungia Buranji*, Gauhati, 1933 51-2; A C. Choudhury, *Shrihatter Itibritta*, Sylhet, 1317 B.S., 103-5.

2 *Ibid.*, 53-4; also R.B. Pemberton, *Report on the Eastern Frontier of British India*, Calcutta, 1835, 39-40.

3 Pemberton, n. 2, 195-6; R.M. Nath, *The Background of Assamese Culture*, Shillong, 1949, 92-3.

4 Nath, n. 3.

5 Pemberton, n. 2.

6 *Ibid.*

7 E. Gait, *A History of Assam*, Calcutta, 1925, 308; also C.U. Aitchinson, *A Collection of Treaties, Engagements and Sanands*, vol. II, Calcutta, 1872, 146.

8 R.M. Lahiri, *Annexation of Assam*, 45-7.

9 Gait, n. 7, 309; W.W. Hunter, *Statistical Account of Assam*, vol. II, London, 1879, 403. Although of tribal origin, the Dimachas were Hindus, and their rulers, as evident from the coins and inscriptions, were worshippers of *Sakti*, *Vishnu* and *Siva*. But the matrimonial relation with the ruling family of Manipur, where the people had *en masse* been influenced by the ideas of *Shri Chaitanya Mahaprabhu*, the *Vaisnava* reformer of Bengal, led to their formal adherence to *Vaisnavism*, in 1790, when Krisnachandra and his brother, Govindachandra, entered the body of the copper effigy of a cow and when emerged were taken to have a new birth, proclaimed by the Brahmins as *Vaisnavas* and belonging to the *Kshatriya* caste.
This incident has been described by some scholars as 'conversion' of the Dimachas into Hinduism; but acceptance of Hinduism is a matter of acculturation and not conversion. Although originally worshippers of their traditional deities *Kashaikhati* at Sadiya and *Umananda* near Gauhati, the Bodos by virtue of their long settlement in north-eastern India were gradually accultured into Hinduism. The Dimacha ruler,

Dershong-pha was the first to assume the Sanskrit-Hindu name of Nirbhoynarayana and since then the process of Hinduisation was rapid. The coins and inscriptions were issued by the Rajas to testify their faith in Hindu religion. Jasanarayana, for instance, issued a silver coin claiming himself as the "worshipper of *Hara-Gari, Siva* and *Durga.*" Biradarpanarayana issued a conch shell with ten *Avataras,* or incarnation of *Krishna.* A gold coin of Biradarpanarayana carries the text, on the reverse. "*Sri Sri Siva charana kamala madhu karasya.*" Same text is found in another gold coin issued by Harishchandra Narayana. The *Kali* temple at Khaspur, known as *Ranachandi,* and at Udharband, as. *Kacha-kanti* or *Kiratesvari,* are identical with *Jayantesvari* in Jayantia and *Tripuresvari* in Tripura. Like *Kamakhya*(Ka Meikha)who was originally a deity of the Khasis, in course of the time, *Umananda* came to be compared with *Siva* and *Kashaikhati* with *Kali* and have become highly popular among all sections of the Hindus. The Heramba Rajas were also patrons of scholars who composed literary works bearing aspects of Hindu religion. For details see Nath, n. 3, 71-5; Gait, n. 7, 306-9; V. Choudhury and P. Roy, *A Unique Gold Coin type of the Kachari Kings, J.A.S.B.*, Vol. XII, 153-4.

10 Gait, n. 7, 309; also E. Hamilton, *An Account of Assam,* 83.

11 S.N, Sen, (ed.), *Prachin Bangala Patra Sankalan,* letter Nos. 100, 106-8.

12 *Ibid.,* No. 65.

13 W.K. Firminger (ed.), *Sylhet District Records.* Vol. I, Nos. 32 and 43.

14 Sen, n. 11, No. 77.

15 F.P.P., 14 November 1823, No. 19.

16 Sen, n. 11, No. 77.

17 *Ibid.,* No. 80

18 S.K. Bhuyan, *Tungkhungia Buranji,* Gauhati, 1933, 122-6.

19 Sen, n. 11, No. 112.

20 *Ibid.,* No. 118.

21 D. Datta, (ed.), *Cachar District Records,* Silchar, 1969, 3.

22 Sen, n. 11, Nos. 112-5.

23 *Ibid.,* Nos. 106 and 124.

24 *Ibid.,* Nos. 112-4.

25 Firminger, n. 13, vol. III, No. 166.

26 *Ibid.*

27 *Ibid.,* vol. IV, No. 100.

28 A.C. Banerjee, *The Eastern Frontier of British India,* 212-4; Lahiri, n. 8, 44-5.

29 Sen, n 11, Nos. 141, 162-3.

30 F.P.P., 30 May 1829, No. 2.

31 Sen, n. 11.

32 *Ibid.,* No. 148.

33 *Ibid.,* No. 141.

34 *Ibid.*

35 F.P.P., 14 November 1823, No. 19.

36 *Ibid.*; also Sen, n. 11, Nos. 153, 156 and 162-6.

37 Sen, n. 11, No. 163.

38 *Ibid.*
39 *Ibid.*, No. 167.
40 *Ibid.*
41 F.P.P., 14 November 1823, No. 19.
42 Sen, n. 11, No. 166.
43 *Ibid.*, Nos. 162-3, 166.
44 F.P.P., 14 November 1823, No. 19; also Pemberton, n. 2, 46.
45 Pemberton, n. 2, 198-9.
46 F.P.P., 19 December 1823, No. 21.
47 *Ibid.*
48 Datta, n. 21, 11.
49 Pemberton, n. 2, 198.
50 F.P.P., 17 January 1823, No. 6.
51 *Ibid.*
52 Secret Letters to the Court of Directors, 9 January 1824, para 16.
53 *Ibid.*, para 17.
54 *Ibid.*, para 18.
55 *Ibid.*, para 19.
56 F.P.P., 28 November 1823, No. 6.
57 Secret Letters to the Court of Directors, 9 January 1824, para 20.
58 *Ibid.*, para 21.
59 *Ibid.*, 23 February 1824, para 30.
60 *Ibid.*, F.P.P., 17 January 1824, No. 6.
61 Secret Letters to the Court of Directors, 23 February 1824, para 34.
62 *Ibid.*, also 9 January 1824, paras 10-2.
63 F.P.P., 31 October 1823, Nos. 15-6.
64 *Ibid.*, 28 November 1823, No. 5.
65 *Ibid.*
66 *Ibid.*, 17 January 1824, No. 6.
67 Letter from the Burmese Governor to Scott, quoted in Lahiri, n. 8, 49.
68 Banerjee, n. 28, 215.
69 *Ibid.*
70 Secret Letters to the Court of Directors, 9 January 1824.
71 F.P.P., 17 January 1824, No. 6,
72 Secret Letters to the Court of Directors, 9 January 1824, para 10.
73 *Ibid.*, Para 11.
74 *Ibid.*, Para 12.
75 *Ibid.*
76 *Ibid.*, 23 February 1824, para 34.
77 *Ibid* , para 37.
78 *Ibid.*
79 *Ibid.*
80 *Ibid.*, para 38.
81 H.H. Wilson, *Documents illustrative af the Burmese War*, Calcutta. 1827, No. 28.
82 *Ibid.*
83 *Ibid.*, Nos. 21-5.
84 Banerjee, n. 28, 215-25.

85 Aitchinson, n. 7, No. XII.

86 *Ibid.*

87 H.K. Barpujari, *Assam : In the Days of the Company*, Gauhati, 1963, 10,

88 *Ibid.*, 10-1.

89 Banerjee, n. 28, 250-9.

90 F.P.P., 20 April 1824, No. 6.

91 Banerjee, n. 28, 253.

92 Wilson, n. 81, No. 96. It is not clear why the Burmese so hurriedly evacuated Cachar. Dudpatil was strongly fortified, and probably ten thousand Burmese troops were living there on the eve of their departure. *Ibid.*, No. 97.

93 *Ibid.*, No. 104.

94 Banerjee, n. 28, 290-320,

95 Article 2, Treaty of Yandaboo : "His Majesty the King of Ava renounces all claims upon, and will abstain from all future interference with the principality of Assam and its dependencies, and also with the contiguous petty states of Cachar and Jynta. With regard to Manipore, it is stipulated that, he shall be recognised by the king of Ava as Rajah thereof."

96 F.P.P., 23 June 1826, No. 18.

Chapter Three : Paramountcy

1 F.P.P., 23 June 1826, No. 18.

2 R.B. Pemberton, *Report on the Eastern Frontier of British India*, Calcutta, 1835, 196.

3 F.P.P., 3 November 1827, No. 42.

4 *Ibid.*, 3 July 1829, No. 6.

5 *Ibid.*

6 *Ibid.*

7 *Ibid.* To quote Scott : "From all now I can learn if the whole of South Cachar were fully cultivated, it would not produce at ordinary rates of rent a small gross revenue of one lakh of rupees and also that such a state of things could not be brought about under the best management in a much larger period than ten or twelve years."

8 *Ibid.*, 23 November 1827, Nos. 43-4.

9 *Ibid.*, No. 44.

10 *Ibid.*

11 *Ibid.*, 14 May 1832, Nos. 100-7; also Pemberton, n. 2.

12 *Ibid.*, 9 April 1824, No. 8; also H.K. Barpujari, *Assam : In the Days of the Company*, Gauhati, 1963, 74.

13 *Ibid.*

14 *Ibid.*

15 *Ibid.*, also 14 May 1832, No. 79.

16 *Ibid.*, 30 May 1829, No. 1.

17 *Ibid.*, 14 May 1832, No. 87.

18 *Ibid.*

19 *Ibid.*, 31 July 1829, No. 22.
20 *Ibid.*, 26 February 1830, Nos. 2-3.
21 *Ibid.*, 23 July 1832, Nos. 64-9.
22 *Ibid.*, 14 May 1832, No. 95.
23 *Ibid.*, 23 July 1832, No. 68.
24 *Ibid.*, 9 April 1832, No. 37.
25 *Ibid.*, 30 May 1829, No. 4.
26 *Ibid.*, 14 May 1832, No. 86.
27 C.R., No. 35 of 1837; 78 of 1844.
28 F.P.P., 14 May 1832, No. 82.
29 *Ibid.*, No. 100.
30 *Ibid.*, 9 April 1829, No. 44.
31 *Ibid.*, 30 May 1829, Nos. 2-5.
32 *Ibid.*, 14 May 1832, No. 83A.
33 *Ibid.*
34 *Ibid.*
35 *Ibid.*, Tucker's letters to Govindachandra.
36 *Ibid.*, No. 104; R.M. Lahiri, *Annexation of Assam*, Calcutta, 1954, 126.
37 *Ibid.*, Nos. 85-6.
38 *Ibid.*
39 *Ibid*, 28 May 1830, No. 84.
40 *Ibid.*, 14 August 1829, Nos. 5-7.
41 *Ibid.*, 11 February 1831, No. 86.
42 *Ibid.*, 30 May 1829, No. 6.
43 *Ibid.*, No. 2.
44 *Ibid.*, 4 May 1832, No. 107.
45 *Ibid.*, 30 May 1829, No. 6.
46 *Ibid.*, 14 August 1829, No. 5.
47 *Ibid.*
48 *Ibid.*, 14 May 1830, No. 38; also India Political Despatch to the Court of Directors, No. 25 of 1830.
49 *Ibid.*, 21 May 1830, No. 9.
50 *Ibid.*, 14 May 1830, No. 45.
51 *Ibid.*, 4 June 1830, No. 30.
52 *Ibid.*, 28 May 1830, No. 84.
53 B.R.C., 7 September 1830, No. 1; 28 June 1831, No. 1-3.
54 F.P.P., 18 June 1830, No. 48.
55 *Ibid.*, 23 May 1830, No. 84.
56 *Ibid.*, 14 May 1830, No. 38.
57 *Ibid.*
58 *Ibid.*, 9 April 1832, No. 44.
59 *Ibid.*
60 *Ibid.*
61 *Ibid.*, No. 56.
62 *Ibid.*
63 Lahiri, n. 36, 137.
64 F.P.P., 14 May 1832, No. 100.

65 *Ibid.*, 25 November 1832, No. 63.
66 *Ibid.*, 14 May 1832, No. 100.
67 *Ibid.*
68 *Ibid.*, No. 99.
69 *Ibid.*, 29 October 1832, No. 142.
70 *Ibid.*, 14 May 1832, No. 100.
71 *Ibid.*
72 *Ibid.*
73 *Ibid.*, No. 98.
74 *Ibid.*, 25 November 1831, No. 60.
75 *Ibid.*, 14 May 1832, No. 98.
76 *Ibid.*, No. 109.
77 *Ibid.*, To quote Pemberton : "...a task involving so much trouble with so little profit, that the attempt to take it upon ourselves, when it may so easily and advantageously be transferred to another, would be nothing more than a species of political quixotism."
78 *Ibid.*, No. 110.
79 *Ibid.*
80 *Ibid.*, No. 117.
81 *Ibid.*, No. 118.
82 *Ibid.*, 9 July 1832, No. 15.
83 *Ibid.*, No. 17.
84 *Ibid.*, 29 October 1832, No. 142.
85 *Ibid.*, 23 July 1832, No. 65.
86 *Ibid.*, 9 July 1832, No. 7.
87 *Ibid.*, 23 July 1832, No 65
88 *Ibid.*, No. 64.
89 *Ibid.*, No. 66.
90 *Ibid.*
91 *Ibid.*, 27 December 132, No. 12.
92 Secret Letters from the Court of Directors, No. 14 of 1834.
93 *Ibid.*
94 Barpujari, n. 12, 100.
95 F.P.P., 14 May 1832, Nos. 85-6.
96 *Ibid.*, 20 August 1832, No. 94.
97 *Ibid.*
98 *Ibid.*
99 *Ibid.*, 18 June 1832, No. 4.
100 *Ibid.*, 17 September 1832, No. 95.
101 *Ibid.*, 28 May 1832, No. 104.
102 *Ibid.*, 12 November 1832, No. 46.
103 *Ibid.*, 16 January 1832, No. 2.
104 *Ibid.*, 20 August 1832, No. 95.
105 *Ibid.*, 17 September 1832, No. 136.
106 *Ibid.*, No. 137.
107 *Ibid.*
108 *Ibid.*, 29 October 1832, No. 132.

109 *Ibid.*, No. 133.
110 *Ibid.*, 12 November 1832, No. 46.
111 *Ibid.*, 30 May 1833, No. 100.
112 *Ibid.*, 7 November 1832, No. 127-8.
113 Letters from the Court of Directors, No. 14 of 1834.
114 *Ibid.*
115 A.S.R., Vol. X, No. 368; F.P.P., 29 October 1832, No. 133; also Governor-General's Minute on Cachar of 19 March 1833.
116 C.U. Aitchinson, *A Collection of Treaties, Engagements and Sanads*, vol. II, Calcutta, 1872, No. XLII.
117 F.P.P., 6 February 1839, No. 60.
118 *Ibid.*, 27 February 1839, No. 164.
119 *Ibid.*, 6 February 1839 London, 1855, No. 60; also J. Butler, *Travels and Adventures in the Province of Assam*, 104-6.
120 *Ibid.*, 1 January 1840, No. 112; B.J.P., 19 March 1851, No. 223.
121 Butler, n. 119.
122 F.P.P., 14 October 1853, No. 42.
123 B.J.P., 6 November 1850, No. 51.
124 *Ibid.*, No. 127; India Political Despatch to Court of Directors, No. 7 of 1852.
125 F.P.P., 14 October 1853, No. 42; B.J.P., 19 March 1851, No. 225.
126 B.J.P., 6 November 1850, No. 127.
127 *Ibid.*, 128.
128 Minute of Lord Dalhousie, the Governor-General, of 6 March 1853.
129 *Ibid.*
130 F.P.P., 14 October 1853, No. 42.
131 Political Letters from Court of Directors, No. 5 of 1854.
132 F.P.P., 14 October Nos. 45-6.
133 A.S.R., Letters received from Government, Vol XXXIV, No. 726.
134 F.P.P., 14 October, 1853, No. 45.
135 *Ibid.*, No. 46.
136 *Ibid.*
137 B.R.C., 10 August 1854, No. 56.
138 F.P.P., 14 October 1853, No. 48.
139 *Ibid.*, Extract from Mills Report.
140 *Ibid.*, No. 49; Lord Dalhousie's Minute of 27 August 1853.
141 B.R.C., 20 July 1854, No. 8; Letter from Court of Directors, No. 56 of 1855.

Chapter Four : New Regime

1 B.R.C., 7 September 1830, No. 1.
2 F.P.P., 18 June 1830, No 62; B.R.C., 28 June 1831, Nos. 1-3.
3 B.R C., 7 September 1830, No. 1; also F P.P., 30 May 1833, No 30.
4 D Datta, (ed), *Cachar District Records*, Silchar, 1969, 22.
5 J.B. Bhattacharjee, *The Garos and the English, 1765-1874*, Unpublished Ph.D. dissertation of Gauhati University, 1971, 25-36.

6 C.E. Buckland, *Dictionary of Indian Biography*, Oxford, 1937, 146.

7 A.S.R., Letters received from Government, Vol. 10 (b) No. 1835.

8 F.P.P., 14 May 1832, Nos. 81-107.

9 J.B. Bhattacharjee, *Some Aspects of Heramba Government on the eve of British Rule*, Shodhak, Vol. 2 pt. B. Jaipur, 1973, 189-95.

10 A.S.R., File No. 636 of 1872.

11 *Ibid.*

12 W.W. Hunter, *Statistical Account of Assam*, Vol. II, London, 1879, 395-7.

13 B.C. Allen, *Assam District Gazetteers*, Vol. 1, Cachar, Allahabad, 1905, 30.

14 A.S.R., File No. 606 of 1872; C,R,, No. 36 of 1850.

15 Hunter, n. 12.

16 *Ibid.*

17 A.S.R., File No. 636 of 1872.

18 F.P.P., 3 September 1830, No. 38.

19 *Ibid.*, 12 November 1832, Nos. 46-7.

20 *Ibid.*

21 *Ibid.*

22 B.R.C., 20 December 1836, Nos. 61-3.

23 *Ibid.*

24 Datta, n. 4, 21.

25 A.S.R., File No. 636 of 1872.

26 B.R.C., 15 February 1842, No. 120; 9 January 1843, No. 87; 27 August 1844, Nos. 7-8; 9 January 1844, No. 42; 20 November 1843, Nos. 5-6.

27 *Ibid.*, 13 November 1844, Nos. 26-9.

28 A.S.R., File No. 636 of 1872.

29 *Ibid.*

30 C.R., No. 62 of 1836.

31 A.S.R., File No. 636 of 1872.

32 C.R., No. 174 of 1838.

33 *Ibid.*

34 *Ibid,*, No. 221 of 1839.

35 *Ibid.*, No. 17 of 1840.

36 *Ibid.*

37 *Ibid.*, No. 23 of 1840.

38 *Ibid.*, No. 80 of 1857.

39 B.R.C, 6 June 1844, Nos. 7-8. The monthly pay of the *Tehsildar* was Rs 10 and his *Peadah* Rs 7. See C.R., No. 15 of 1844.

40 A.S.R., File No. 636 of 1872.

41 *Ibid.*

42 F.P.P., 12 November 1832, Nos. 46-7; 14 May 1832, No. 106.

43 *Govinda Chandrer Ain* appended in A.C. Choudhury, *Shrihatter Itibritta*, Sylhet, 1317 B.C., 120-38.

44 F.P.P., 12 November 1832, Nos. 46-7.

45 *Ibid.*

46 *Ibid.*

47 *Ibid.*
48 *Ibid.*
49 Datta, n. 4, 20.
50 C.R., No. 64 of 1837.
51 *Ibid.*,No. 84 of 1837.
52 *Ibid.*, No. 146 of 1838.
53 *Ibid.*
54 *Ibid.*, No. 4 of 1839.
55 *Ibid.*, No. 108 of 1840.
56 *Ibid.*, No. 336 of 1842.
57 *Ibid.*
58 *Ibid.*, No. 349 of 1842.
59 *Ibid.*, No. 472 of 1842.
60 *Ibid.*, No. 512 of 1842.
61 *Ibid.*, No. 13 of 1843.
62 *Ibid* , No. 3 of 1845.
63 *Ibid.*
64 *Ibid.*, No. 10 of 1851.
65 *Ibid.*,No. 8 of 1852.
66 *Ibid.*, No. 184 of 1858.
67 *Ibid.*, No. 1 of 1840.
68 *Ibid.*, No. 27 of 1851.
69 *Ibid.*, No. 118 of 1848.
70 *Ibid.*, No. 62 of 1837.
71 *Ibid.* The tax to be levied was at the following rates : Silchar *thana,* Rs 4-12-0; Hailakandi, Rs 6-11-0; Katigorah, Rs 4-10-0.
72 *Ibid.*, No. 335 of 1842. The offices of the *Darogas* from the very beginning were manned by the local people.
73 *Ibid* , No. 52 of 1850.
74 L. Cachar, Allen, n. 13, 143.
75 L.W. Shakespeare, *History of Assam Rifles,* London, 1929, 8.
76 *Ibid.*, 9; P.P.P., Pol. A, June 1866, Nos. 37-9.
77 *Ibid.*, 10.
78 F.P.P., Pol. A, June 1866, Nos. 37-9.
79 *Ibid.*
80 *Ibid.*, C.R., No. 78 of 1844.
81 *Ibid.*
82 *Ibid.* , No. 22 of 1847.
83 *Ibid.*
84 *Ibid.* , No. 74 of 1849.
85 Shakespeare, n. 75, 19-22.
86 C.R., No. 78 of 1849.
87 Shakespeare, n. 75, 21-4.
88 C.R., No. 52 of 1850.
89 F.P.P., 28 May 1832, No. 105.
90 *Ibid.*
91 *Ibid.*, No. 106.
92 *Ibid.*, No. 105.

93 *Ibid,*, Pol. A, June 1866, Nos. 37-9.
94 *Ibid.*
95 *Ibid.*
96 *Ibid.*

Chapter Five : Transition

1 F.P.P., 19 December 1823, No. 21.
2 B.R.P., 20 May 1833, No. 6.
3 *Ibid.*, Robertson to Megnathen, 28 April 1833.
4 *Ibid.*, Extract from the Proceedings of Right Hon'ble Governor-General in Council, 16 May 1833.
5 C.R., No. 214 of 1839.
6 *Ibid.*, No. 215 of 1839.
7 *Ibid.*, No. 158 of 1858.
8 F.P.P., 12 November 1832, No. 46.
9 *Ibid.*, 8 March 1832, No. 70.
10 *Ibid.* To quote Robinson : "*Jamuna Mukh, or Dharumpur,* includes that portion of the Nowgong district bordering on the Kapili, Jamuna, and Dayung rivers, having the Mikir Hills on the north, and the hills of Kachar on the south.
The present division, includes the Hozai, covers an area of $580\frac{3}{4}$ square miles. The Hozai was a grant of Dhurmuter, or Nankar land, given during the reign of the last Raja of Kachar to a member of Tularam family, for the performance of certain religious services. It is at present farmed by Tularam's nephew, Durgochurn, on a settlement liable to periodical revision.
Dharumpur, together with the adjoining territories of Tularam Senapati, was at one time included in the possessions of the Raja of Kachar. It was then divided into twelve districts, placed under the management of as many chiefs.
The whole of this tract of country is remarkably fertile, producing rich crops of rice, mustard seed, and sugar cane; while the hilly parts yield an abundance of cotton, which forms a staple article of export. The products of northern Kachar, are said to form a very large portion of the trade of Assam." See W. Robinson, *A Descriptive Account of Assam,* Calcutta, 1841, 312.
11 C.R., No. 285 of 1839.
12 *Ibid.*, No. 187 of 1839.
13 *Ibid.*, 27 December 1832, No. 12.
14 C.R., No. 35 of 1837.
15 H K. Barpujari, *Annexation of Jayantia,* Proceedings, Indian Historical Records Commission, 1954.
16 K.N. Dutta, (ed.), *A Hand Book to the Old Records of the Assam Secretariat,* Shillong, 1959, 12-3. The Raja of Jayantia was, however, allowed to retain the hills (Jaintia) portion of the kingdom, but as he declined

to preside over the 'fallen empire' the same was placed under the Political Officer of Khasi Hills whose jurisdiction now came to be known as the United Khasi and Jaintia Hills, and the Raja pensioned off.

17 A.S.R., Bengal Government Papers, File No. 336 of 1835; also File No. 379 of 1866.

18 A.C. Choudhury, *Srihalter Itibritta*, Sylhet, 1317 B.C., 44.

19 C.U. Aitchinson, *A Collection of Treaties, Engagements and Sanunds*, Calcutta, 1872, 148-9.

20 A.S.R., Bengal Government Papers File No. 351 of 1856.

21 F.P.P., Pol. A, June 1866, Nos. 37-9.

22 *Ibid.*

23 A.S.R., Letters issued to the Government of Bengal, Vol. 121, No. 137 of 1856.

24 A.S.R., Bengal Government Papers, File No. 351 of 1856.

25 F.P.P., Pol. A, June 1866, Nos. 37-9; also A.S.R., Bengal Government Papers, File No. 351 of 1856.

26 W.J. Allen, *Report on the Administration of North Cachar*, Harkaru, 1859; also F.P.P., Pol. A, June 1866, Nos. 37-9.

27 F.P.P., June 1866, No. 38.

28 *Ibid.*, No. 37.

29 A.S.R., Dacca Commissioner's Papers, File No. 969 of 1872-73.

30 A.S.R., Letter No. 834 of the Officiating Under Secretary to the Government of Bengal to the Commissioner of Assam, 23 September 1867.

31 C.R., No. 47 of 1868.

32 *Ibid.* The establishment would include 1 *Tahsildar* @ Rs 50, 1 *Mohurir* @ Rs 20, 1 *Jemadar* @ Rs 10 and 4 *peadahs* @ Rs 8 per *mensem.*

33 *Ibid.*; also Report on the Revenue Administration of Cachar, 1872.

34 *Ibid.*

35 *Ibid.*, Letter No. 5928 of 5 November 1868; Secretary to the Government of Bengal to the Deputy Commissioner, Cachar.

36 *Ibid.*

37 *Ibid.*, No. 395 of 1868.

38 A.S.R., Assam Commissioner's Papers, File No. 636 of 1872.

39 *Ibid.*

40 Cachar Administrative Report, 1882.

41 B.C. Allen, *Assam District Gazetteers*, Vol. I, (Cachar) Allahabad, 1905, 35-6.

42 C.R., No. 78 of 1844.

43 *Ibid.*, No. 34 of 1845.

44 *Ibid.*, No. 22 of 1847.

45 *Ibid.*, No. 74 of 1849.

46 *Ibid.*, No. 78 of 1849.

47 *Ibid.*, No. 83 of 1849.

48 *Ibid.*, No. 78 of 1849.

49 *Ibid.*, No. 83 of 1849.

50 *Ibid.*

51 *Ibid.*, No. 5 of 1850.

52 *Ibid.*, No. 26 of 1852.
53 *Ibid.*, No. 5 of 1850.
54 J. P., 12 April 1855, Nos. 95-101.
55 B.C. Chakravarty, *British Relations with the Hill Tribes of Assam since 1858*, 52-3.
56 J.P., March 1870, Nos. 80-4.
57 *Ibid.*, July 1870, Nos. 117-8.
58 *Ibid.*
59 A. Mackenzie, *History of the Relations of the Government with the Hill Tribes on the North-East Frontier of Bengal*, 300-14.
60 A.S.R., Bengal Government Papers, File No. 267/538 of 1871.
61 *Ibid.*, Bengal Government Papers, File No. 25/29 of 1871-74. "The policy unanimously recommended by the local officers was that raids should be met by condign punishment, in the shape of a military occupation of the raiders' villages during as long a period as possible, the seizure of their crops and stored grain, and the forced submission of their chiefs; after that by the steady endeavour of the frontier officers to influence them and promote trade; and finally, by a system of frontier posts combined with a line of road running north and south from Cachar frontier to that of Chittagong." C.E. Buckland, *Bengal under the Lieutenant Governors*, 461-2.
62 Mackenzie, n. 59, 314.
63 *Ibid.*
64 F.P.P., Pol. A, 30 July 1873, Nos. 10-51, 216.
65 A.S.R., Bengal Government Papers, File No. 192/328 of 1872.
66 Mackenzie, n. 59, 312-6.
67 *Ibid.*
68 *Ibid.*
69 *Ibid.*
70 F.P.P., Pol. A, August 1882, Nos. 88-91. J.K. Wight, Deputy Commissioner of Cachar, explained the cause of the famine in the following words : "After certain intervals of time the bamboo plants swell considerably, and a sort of seed is formed within them resembling ordinary paddy seed. The existence of such rich supply attracts rate in swarms, and as these animals were naturally very prolific, abundance of food causes a still greater number to appear, which of course increases in a geometrical proportion. The rats then spread and consume everyting that is eatable, sparing neither paddy crops, *Kachu* (arum), nor even cotton seeds...."
71 *Ibid.*, August 1890, Nos. 1-46; Allen, n. 41, 39-41.
72 *Ibid.*, June 1891, No. 139.
73 *Ibid.*, Extl. A, January 1891, No. 123.
74 *Ibid.*, Pol. A, December 1893, Nos. 37-62.
75 *Ibid.*, September 1899, Nos. 1-4; also Extl. A, November 1900, No. 1.
76 *The Indian Daily News*, 12 June 1901.
77 J.P., June 1866, Nos. 113-4.
78 F.P.P., January 1873, No. 528.
79 Chakravarty, n. 55, 189-91.

80 F.P.P., August 1877, Nos. 123-32.
81 Mackenzie, n. 59, 131-6.
82 *Ibid.*
83 R. Reid, *History of the Frontier Areas Bordering on Assam*, Shillong, 1942, 173.
84 Chakravarty, n. 55, 191.
85 C.R., No. 470 of 1842.
86 *Ibid.*, No. 43 of 1839.
87 *Ibid.*, No. 102 of 1840.
88 *Ibid.*, No. 115 of 1841.
89 *Ibid.*, No. 205 of 1841.
90 *Ibid.*, No. 232 of 1841.
91 *Ibid.*, No. 82 of 1843.
92 *Ibid.*, No. 13 of 1844.
93 *Ibid.*, No. 15 of 1844.
94 *Ibid.*, No. 116 of 1844.
95 *Ibid.*, No. 15 of 1850.
96 *Ibid.*, No. 34 of 1850.
97 *Ibid.*, No. 94 of 1850.
98 *Ibid.*, No. 115 of 1850.
99 *Ibid.*, No. 118 of 1850.
100 *Ibid.*, No. 121 of 1850.
101 *Ibid.*, No. 163 of 1850.
102 *Ibid.*, No. 165 of 1850.
103 *Ibid.*, No. 180 of 1850.
104 *Ibid.*, No. 187 of 1850.
105 *Ibid.*, No. 192 of 1850.
106 *Ibid.*, No. 179 of 1852.
107 *Ibid.*, No. 61 of 1851.
108 *Ibid.*, No. 73 of 1851.
109 *Ibid.*, No. 57 of 1852.
110 *Ibid.*, No. 64 of 1852.
111 *Ibid.*, No. 69 of 1852.
112 *Ibid.*, No. 31 of 1851.
113 *Ibid.*, No. 152 of 1852.
114 *Ibid.*, No. 69 of 1852.
115 Letter No. 81 dated 24 November 1851, from Political Agent, Manipur.
116 *Ibid.*, No. 115 of 1852.
117 *Ibid.*, No. 157 of 1852.
118 *Ibid.*, No. 194 of 1850.
119 *Ibid.*, No. 157 of 1852.
120 *Ibid.*, No. 162 of 1852.
121 *Ibid.*
122 *Ibid.*, No. 11 of 1853.
123 *Ibid.*, No. 12 of 1853.
124 *Ibid.*, No. 18 of 1853.
125 *Ibid.*

126 Mackenzie, n. 59, 157-9.
127 E. Gait, *A History of Assam*, Calcutta, 1925, 401.
128 *Ibid.*, 402.
129 W.W. Hunter, *A Statistical Account of Assam*, *Vol. II*, London, 1879, 363.
130 L.W. Shakespeare, *History of Assam Rifles*, London, 1929, 250-1.
131 Allen, n. 41, 143.
132 Shakespeare, n. 130.
133 Chakravarty, n. 55, 176.

Chapter Six : Consolidation

1 Regulation X of 1822. For details see J.B. Bhattacharjee, "Pattern of British Administration in the Garo Land", *Journal of Indian History*, Vol II, 511-5.
2 Minute by John Lawrence, 19 February 1868, para 12; H. Pub. P. 28 March 1868, No. 150.
3 H. Pub. P., 1873, Nos. 517-33.
4 Minute by G.N. Taylor, 27 February 1868.
5 H. Pub., 1873, No. 533.
6 A.C. Choudhury, *Shrihatter Itibritta*, Sylhet, 1317 B.S., 92. Assam was divided into 3 Divisions, viz. Surma Valley Division consisting of Cachar and Sylhet; Brahmaputra Valley Division consisting of Goalpara, Kamrup, Nowgong, Darrang, Sibsagar and Lakhimpur; and Hills Division consisting of Garo Hills, Khasi-Jaintia Hills, Naga Hills and Lushai Hills.
The province of Eastern Bengal and Assam had 5 Divisions, viz. Dacca Division consisting of Dacca, Faridpur, Bakerganj and Mymensing; Chittagong Division, consisting of Tripura, Chittagong, Hill Chittagong and Noakhali; Rajshahi Division consisting of Dinajpur, Rajshahi, Rangpur, Bogura, Pabna, Maldah and Jalpaiguri; Surma Valley Division consisting of Cachar, Sylhet, Khasi-Jaintia Hills, Naga Hills and Lushai Hills; and Assam Valley Division consisting of Goalpara. Kamrup, Darrang Sibsagar, Nowgong, Lakhimpur and Garo Hills.
7 F.P.P., 5 April 1825, No. 24.
8 *Ibid.*
9 H.K. Barpujari, *Assam : In the Days of the Company*, Gauhati, 1963, 188-9.
10 D. Datta, (ed.), *Cachar District Records*, Silchar, 1969. Mainwarring to Louis.
11 Sir John Strachy, *India : Its Administration and Progress*, London, 1903, 83-4.
12 B.R.P., 20 November 1843, Nos. 5-6.
13 *Ibid.*, 24 December 1857, No. 3.
14 *Ibid.*, No. 4; also 18 February 1858, No. 42.
15 C.R., No. 242 of 1858.

16 *Ibid.*, No. 17 of 1860.
17 *Ibid.*, No. 19 of 1860.
18 *Ibid.*
19 *Ibid.*, No. 170 of 1862.
20 Letter No. 3825 dated 17 July 1866.
21 A.S R., File No. 115/212 of 1872-73.
22 Notification No. 683 dated 13 May 1875.
23 B.C. Allen, *Assam District Gazetteers*, Vol. II (Cachar), Allahabad, 1905, 142.
24 *Ibid.*
25 E. Gait, *A History of Assam*, Calcutta, 1925, 387.
26 *Ibid.*
27 C.R., No. 624GJ dated 21 January 1930.
28 *Rules for the Administration of Justice/Police in the Autonomous Districts of Assam*, 49-56.
29 C.R., 178 of 1858.
30 *Ibid.*
31 Allen, n. 23.
32 *Ibid.*
33 S.K. Bhuyan, (ed.), *Kachari Buranji*, Gauhati, 1938, 48-65, 88-98 and 106-15.
34 *Ibid.*, *Tripura Buranji*, Gauhati, 1936, viii.
35 R. Pemberton, *Report on the Eastern Frontier of British India*, Calcutta, 1835, 51-3.
36 *Ibid.*, 77.
37 *Ibid.*
38 *Ibid.*
39 C.R., No. 13 of 1862.
40 A.S.R., Bengal Government Papers, File No. 157/293 of 1872.
41 *Ibid.*, File No. 7/485 of 1872; Letter No. 1415 dt. 23 November 1872.
42 *Ibid.*, No. 276½ dated 16 December 1872.
43 *Ibid.*, File No. 157/293 of 1872; No. 3352 dated 1 August 1872.
44 *Ibid.*
45 *Ibid.*, Bengal Government Papers, File No. 127/237 of 1872.
   The following were the receipts the Committee, by leasing out the ferries, during 1868-73.

Year	Rs. As P.
1868-69	11,656 8 0
1869-70	11,986 0 0
1870-71	11,986 0 0
1871-72	12,682 0 0
1872-73	9,830 0 0

46 C.R., No. 109 of 1866.
47 A.S.R., Bengal Government Papers, File No. 192/328 of 1872; Letter No. 483T dated 24 November 1872.
48 *Ibid.*, No. 6865 dated 16 December 1872; also B.J.P., December 1872, No. 845.

49 C.R. Revenue B, June 1935, No. 1542-57..

50 *Ibid.*, December 1935, Nos. 321-31.

51 *Ibid.*, June 1935, Nos. 881-92.

52 A.S.R., Bengal Government Papers, File No. 127/237 of 1872; Pemberton. R.B., n. 35, 53.

53 Allen, n. 23, 107-8.

54 Datta, n. 10, 24.

55 C.R., No. 72 of 1852.

56 Allen, n. 23.

57 C.R., Bundle No. 558; D.C.'s Order No. 4749 dated 19 September 1929.

58 Revenue Report of Cachar, 1903-04.

59 General Administration Report of Cachar, 1862.

60 Report on the Re-settlement of Cachar for 1894-99.

61 Pemberton, n. 35.

62 B.C. Allen, *Assam District Gazetteers*, Vol. I, Allahabad, 1905, 128.

63 *Ibid.*, 89.

64 Report on the Reassessment of Cachar, 1913-18.

65 *The Assam Land Revenue Manual*, Vol. I, cxxxii-ix.

66 *Ibid.*, clxii-i; C.R., December 1935, Nos. 1551-8.

67 *Report on Revenue Administration of Cachar*, 1872-3.

Year	No. of mahals	Amount for which leased
		Rs. As.
1852-53	42	619 8
1857-58	43	834 8
1862-63	98	3,733 0
1867-68	79	8,731 0
1871-72	93	7,396 0

68 *The Assam Land Revenue Manual*, Vol. 1, cxxxix.; C.R., Rev. B, December 1935, Nos. 761-4.

69 A.S.R., File No. 626 of 1872.

70 Allen, n. 23.

71 A.S.R., Bengal Government Papers, File No. 201/352 of 1872-74.

72 *Ibid.*, Letter No. 140R.

73 *Ibid.*, No. 4936.

74 C.R., No. 184 of 1836.

75 A.S.R., Revenue Papers, File No. 636 of 1872.

Year	No. of mahals	Revenue (in rupees)
1852-53	9	1030
1857-58	2	840
1862-63	2	340
1867-68	2	143
1871-72	1	95

76 A.S.R., Revenue Papers, File No. 636 of 1872.

Year	Revenue (in rupees)	Year	Revenue (in rupees)
1831-32	3,200	1856-57	9,050
1836-37	5,085	1861-62	16,000

1841-42	4,010	1866-67	5,520
1846-47	5,955	1870-71	14,800
1851-52	7,917	1871-72	10,244

77 *Report on the Revenue Administration of Cacher, 1872*
78 C.R., No. 10 of 1861.
79 *Ibid.*, No. 170 of 1862.
80 *Ibid.*, No. 15 of 1874.
81 C.R., Seperate Revenue B, March 1936, No. 228-30.
82 *Ibid.*, No. 170 of 1862.
83 *Ibid.*, No. 47 of 1853.
84 *Ibid.*, No. 107 of 1853.
85 Allen, n. 23, 75-7.
86 W. Hamilton, *Description of Hindostan*, Vol. II, London, 1820, 764.
87 A.S.R., Bengal Govt. Papers, File No. 157/303 of 1872, No. 865.
88 *Ibid*, Notification No. 2865T.
89 *Ibid.*, Government of Bengal's Order No. 995, dated 20 February 1868.
90 *Ibid.*, No. 866.
91 *Ibid.*, No. 196.
92 *Ibid.*, No. 2110.
93 *Ibid.*, No. 865.
94 *Report on the Revenue Administration of Cachar, 1872.*
95 Cachar Administrative Report, 1902.
96 A.S.R., Bengal Govt. Papers, File No. 167/303 of 1872; No. 865.
97 C.R., D.C.'s letter No. 3188, 21 December 1891.
98 *Ibid.*, Chief Commissioner's Order No. 160, 13 April 1892.
99 Assam Administrative Report, 1830-31.
100 Assam Gazettee, 4 August 1877.
101 *Ibid.*, 5 July 1879.
102 *Ibid.*, 22 September 1877.
103 H.P.P., 18 May 1882, No. 1912.
104 *Ibid.*
105 A.S.R., Bengal Govt. Papers, File No. 157/293 of 1872, No. 3352.
106 *Ibid.*, No. 1415.
107 Assam Gazette, 11 May 1878.
108 *Ibid.*, 22 September 1877.
109 *Ibid.*, 19 May 1885.
110 *Ibid.*, 4 June 1883.
111 General Administration Report, Cachar, 1920-21.
112 C.R., Chief Commissioner's No. 1330M, 18 March 1915.
113 *Ibid.*, Commissioner's Letter No. 4329, 7 June 1915.
114 Annual Report of Local Boards (Assam), 1927-28, v. Venkate Rao, *A Hundred Years of Local Self-Government in Assam*, Gauhati, 1965, 70-103 and 187-215.
115 *The Assam Code*, Vol. II, 12-39.
116 *The Assam Land Revenue Manual*, Vol. I, 175.
117 C.R., Notification No. 5204E, dated 24 September 1923.
118 *Ibid.*

119 *Assam Legislative Council Proceedings*, Vol. VI, 485-7.
120 C.R., No. 1851-52, dated 23 May 1929.
121 *Ibid.*, No. VA-7/41-VA, dated 31 August 1929; Rao, n. 114, 30-8.

Chapter Seven : Material Progress

  1 F.P.P., 23 June 1826, No. 18.
  2 *Ibid.*, 14 May 1832, No. 84.
  3 *Ibid.*, No. 106.
  4 R.B. Pemberton, *Report on the Eastern Frontier of British India,* Calcutta, 1835, 212-3.
  5 C.R., No. 99 of 1837.
  6 A.S.R., File No. 636 of 1872.
  7 C.R., No. 80 of 1846.
  8 *Ibid.*, No. 35 of 1846.
  9 *Ibid.*, No. 2 of 1848.
10 Report on the Re-assessment of Cachar, 1913-18.
11 *The Assam Land Revenue Manual*, Vol. I.
12 B.C. Allen, Assam District Gazetteers, Vol. I (Cachar), Allahabad, 1905, 65.
13 C.R., No. 50 of 1857.
14 *Ibid.*, No. 18 of 1862.
15 *Ibid.*, No. 99 of 1837.
16 *Ibid.*, No. 46 of 1839.
17 F.P.P., 11 February 1831, No. 27.
18 H.K. Barpujari, *Assam : In the Days of the Company*, Gauhati, 1963, 210-7.
19 F.P.P., 11 February 1835, No. 82.
20 Tea Committee Consultations, 21 August 1839, No. 84.
21 C.R., No. 40 of 1835.
22 D. Datta, *Beginning of the Tea Industry in Cachar*, Purbasee, Silchar, 1965, 2-3. In Goongoor in Chatla, Haokara and Nowalla near Gagra, Burrahangun in Hailakandi and Infang in Rajnagar the plants in plenty.
23 A.S.R., Bengal Government Papers, File No. 345 of 1864-67.
24 C.R., Nos. 111-2 of 1856.
25 *Ibid.*, No. 197 of 1856.
26 B.R.C., 6 December 1856, No. 13; A.S.R., Dacca Commissioner's Papers, File No. 26 of 1856.
27 C.R., No. 35 of 1861. The most important of their grant was Adeleide Tea Estate.
28 *Ibid.*, No. 118 of 1856.
29 Datta, n. 22.
30 C.R., No. 50 of 1857.
31 A.S.R., Bengal Government Papers, File No. 373 of 1861.
32 C.R., No. 101 of 1858.

33 *Ibid.*, No. 230 of 1858.

34 *Ibid.*, No. 158 of 1858.

35 *Ibid.*, No. 101 of 1858; 178 of 1858.

36 *Ibid.*, No. 35 of 1861.

37 A.S R., Bengal Government Papers, File 373 of 1861.

38 C.R., No. 35 of 1861.

39 A.S.R., Bengal Government Papers, File No. 373 of 1861.

40 *Ibid.*, Dacca Commissioner's Papers (Cachar Papers), File No. 38 of 1862.

41 *Ibid.*

42 *Ibid.*, Bengal Government Papers, File No. 318 of 1873.

43 *Ibid.*

44 Report on the Annual Revenue Administration of Cachar, 1872.

45 *Ibid.*

46 A.S.R., Bengal Government Papers, File No. 103/199 of 1871-73.

47 *Ibid.*, File No. 102/198 of 1872-74.

48 *Ibid.*, File No. 100/106 of 1871-72.

49 *The Assam Land Revenue Maunual.*

50 Allen, n. 12, 78-80.

51 *Ibid.*, Papers relating to tea industry in Bengal, 1873.

52 Tea Report, Cachar, 1873.

53 A.S.R., Dacca Commissioner's Papers, File No. 38 of 1861.

54 Tea Report, Cachar, 1873.

55 C.R., No. 145 of 1838.

56 *Ibid.*, No. 90 of 1848.

57 *Ibid.*

58 Quoted in Datta, n. 22, 3.

59 H.A. Antrobus, *A History of the Assam Company*, 388.

60 C.R., No. 50 of 1857.

61 *Ibid.*, Superintendent's Letter of 13 May 1858.

62 Quoted in Datta, n. 22, 4.

63 *Ibid.*

64 Allen, n. 12, 80.

65 *Hindu Patriot*, 18 August 1873.

66 Allen, n. 12, 80-2.

67 P.M. Rajgopal, "Role of the Indian Tea Association," *The Statesman* (Tea Supplement), 31 July 1973.

68 *Ibid.*

69 S.P. Sen, (ed), *Dictionary of National Biography*, Vol. III, Calcutta, 1923, 285-7.

70 Allen, n. 12, 82.

71 Provincial Tea Report (Assam), 1878.

72 Allen, n. 12, 80.

73 Tea Report, 1885.

74 *Ibid.*, 1895.

75 *Ibid.*, also *Assam Land Revenue Manual.*

76 Allen, n. 12, 80.

77 *Ibid.*, 85.
78 *Kacharer Cha Shilpa*, Hairamba (Puja Special), 1373 *Bangabda* 33.
79 Allen, n. 12, 86.; J.B. Bhattacharjee, "The Genesis and Beginning of the Tea Industry in Cachar," *Shodhak*, Vol. 5 Pt. B., 671-85.
80 *Assam Land Revenue Manual*, xxvi.
81 Allen, n. 12, 90.
82 *Ibid.*, 96.
83 *Ibid.*
84 F.P.P., 18 June 1830, No. 60.
85 *Ibid.*, 14 May 1832, No. 109.
86 Pemberton, n. 4, 213.
87 R.M. Nath, *The Background of Assamese Culture*, Shillong, 1949, 75.
88 Pemberton, n. 4. To quote Hamilton, in 1820 : "A communication exists by water through Assam to the centre of both Cachar and Gentiah, although usually deemed inaccessible even by land. Formerly the commerce between Bengal and Cachar was carried on by land from Silhet; the Assamese being so jealous of the Bengal neighbours, that no access whatever was allowed through the Brahmaputra."
89 F.P.P., 11 February 1835, No. 82.
90 C.R., No. 34 of 1845.
91 F.P.P., 14 May 1832, No. 81.
92 *Ibid.*, 8 March 1832, No. 70.
93 F.P.P., 4 November 1831, No. 54.
94 *Ibid.*
95 *Ibid.*
96 *Ibid.*
97 C.R., Bundle No. 59, File No. 45 of 1829-30.
98 *Ibid.*
99 *Ibid.*, File No. 87 of 1929-30.
100 *Ibid.*
101 *Ibid.*, No. 149 of 1929-30.
102 *Ibid.*, No. 187 of 1929-30.
103 *Ibid.*, No. 158 of 1858.
104 D. Datta, (ed.), *The Cachar District Records*, Silchar, 1969, 25; Abstract of salaries of the Civil Establishment of Cachar for the month of May 1836.
105 C.R., No. 212 of 1839.
106 Datta, n. 104, 29; Burns to Louis.
107 C.R., No. 151 of 1838.

Chapter Eight : Impact of British Rule

1 R.B. Pemberton, *Report on the Eastern Frontier of British India*, Calcutta, 1835, 195-6.
2 *Ibid.*, 200.
3 F.P.P., 18 June 1830, No. 59.

4 *Ibid.*, 14 May 1832, No. 109.

5 *Ibid.*

6 *Ibid,*, No. 89.

7 C.R., No. 91 of 1837; 100 of 1837.

8 F.P P., 14 May 1832, No. 98; Fisher's letter dated 11 January 1831.

9 *Ibid.*, No. 104; Fisher's letter of 3 March 1831.

10 *Ibid.*, Scott's letter of 22 March 1831.

11 A.S.R., File No. 636 of 1872-73.

12 C.R., No. 91 of 1837.

13 *Ibid.*, No. 341 of 1842.

14 *Ibid.*, No. 111 of 1845.

15 *Ibid.*, No. 69 of 1851.

16 *Ibid.*, No. 50 of 1857.

17 Pemberton, n. 1, 204.

18 C.R., No. 91 of 1837.

19 *Ibid.*, No. 69 of 1851.

20 Census of India, 1891, Vol. I (Assam), 67.

21 *Ibid.*, 74.

22 *Ibid.*, 197.

23 *Ibid.*, 62.

24 *Ibid.*, 1901, Vol. I (Assam) 65.

25 B.C. Allen, *Assam District Gazetteers*, Vol. I (Cachar) Allahabad, 1905, 44.

26 Census of India, 1891, Vol. I (Assam), 74.

27 Census of India, 1931, Vol. III, Part II, Table II, 4.

28 *Ibid.*

29 *Ibid.*, Table IV, 8.

30 *Ibid.*, 1921, Vol. III, Part I, 121.

31 Pemberton, n. 1, 195-7.

32 S.N. Sen, (ed.), *Prachin Bangala Patra Sankalan*, Calcutta, 1942, Letter Nos. 65, 77, 80, 100, 107-9, 112-8, 120-2, 124, 133, 141, 148, 153, 157-8 and 160-8.

33 A.C. Choudhury, *Shrihatter Itibritta*, Sylhet, 1317 B.S., see Appendix.

34 Allen, n. 25, 45.

35 *Ibid.*, 181.

36 C.R., No. 91 of 1837. Robinson wrote in 1841 : "The present inhabitants of Cachar are, with few exceptions, Bengalis." See W. Robinson, *A Descriptive Account of Assam*, Calcutta, 1841, 405.

37 D. Datta, *History of the Silchar Government Higher Secondary School*, Silchar, 1963.

38 Allen, n. 25.

39 Census of India, 1931, Vol. III, Part II, Table II, 4.

40 *Ibid.*, 1921, Vol. III, Part II, 121.

41 *Ibid.*, 1931, Vol. III, Part I, 184.

42 *Ibid.*

43 Census of India, 1891, Vol. I (Assam) 87-92.

44 Allen, n. 25, 56.

45 *Ibid.*, 58.

46 R.M. Nath, *The Background of the Assamese Culture*, Shillong, 1949, 72.

47 Allen, n. 25.

48 *Ibid.*

49 J.B. Bhattacharjee, "Some Important Sources of the History of Medieval and Modern Cachar," *Shodhak*, Vol. 4, pt A, (Jaipur) (1975) 466.

50 Allen, n. 25.

51 *Ibid.*

52 *Ibid.*

53 C.R., No. 42 of 1861.

54 Allen, n. 25, 59.

55 Census of India, 1891, Vol. I (Assam), 88.

56 *Ibid.*

57 *Ibid.*

58 Allen, n. 25.

59 Census of India, 1931, Vol. III, Part II, 214.

60 Allen, n. 25, 48.

61 *Ibid.*, 48-51.

62 C.R., No. 23 of 1843.

63 Allen, n. 25, 101.

64 C R., No. 233 of 1858.

65 *Ibid.*, No. 16 of 1862.

66 *Ibid.*, No. 106 of 1844; Allen, n. 25, 104.

67 Cachar Re-Settlement Report, 1898.

68 C.R., No. 106 of 1844.

69 *Ibid.*, No. 90 of 1848.

70 Allen, n. 25, 100,

71 Revenue Report of Cachar, 1853.

72 C.R., No. 15 of 1852.

73 Allen, n. 25, 101,

74 *Ibid.*

75 *Ibid.*, 102.

76 D. Datta, *Cachar District Records*, Silchar, 1969, 25 ; see Abstract of salaries of the Civil Establishment of Cachar for the month of May 1836.

77 Allen, n. 25, 107.

78 *Ibid.*, 102.

79 U.C. Guha, *Cachar Itibritta*, Gauhati, 1971, 119.

80 *Ibid.*, 120.

81 F.P.P., 14 May 1832, No. 81.

82 Datta, n. 76, 19.

83 Guha, n. 79.

84 *Ibid.*

85 Allen, n. 25, 103.

86 *Ibid.*

87 Extract quoted in *Ibid.*

88 Datta, n. 37, 51-2.

89 A.K. Naug, *Prachin Cachare Bangla Bhasa 0 Sahitya*, *Sambhar*, 1367 B.S., 25-7.

90 J. Dev. *Heramber Itikatha*, *Azad*, *Nava Varsa* Special, 1370 B.S.. 8.

91 *Ibid.*

92 Datta, n. 76. 17.

93 Quoted in *Ibid.*, 17-8.

94 C.R., No. 100 of 1837.

95 *Ibid.*, No. 140 of 1838.

96 Report on the General Administration of Cachar, 1853.

97 *Ibid.*

98 *Ibid.*

99 C.R., No. 234 of 1862.

100 *Ibid.*

101 *Ibid.*

102 Superintendent's letter dated 16 September 1862, quoted in Datta, n. 76.

103 Datta, n. 76.

104 *Ibid.*

105 *Ibid.*, 10.

106 C.R., No. 512 of 1863.

107 *Ibid.*, Superintendent's letter of 3 February 1864.

108 Datta, n. 76, 11 ; see Secretariat Circular No. 31, General Department dated 2 May 1879.

109 *Ibid.*, 12.

110 A.S.R., Cachar Papers, File No. 89 of 1864-65.

111 *Ibid.*

112 *Ibid.*, Superintendent's letter dated 2 May 1864

113 W.W. Hunter, *A Statistical Account of Assam*, London, 1879, 455-7.

114 Census of India, 1891, Pt. I (Assam), 146.

115 Datta, n. 76, 52-3.

116 *Ibid.*, 24.

117 *Ibid.*, 12.

118 Allen, n. 25, 146.

119 Datta, n. 76, 27-8.

120 Census of India, 1931, vol. III, Part II, 214.

121 Datta, n. 76, 54.

122 *Ibid.*

123 *The Assam Tribune*, 6 March 1976.

124 Datta, n. 76, 57. To quote Datta : "It was late Hara Kishore Gupta who took the initiative in starting a press and with this aim in view subscription was raised from the public. Even the Maharaja of Manipur made a handsome contribution to the fund. Incidentally it may be mentioned here that at that time the Ruler of Manipur had a closer tie with Silchar, and during his visits to this town he used to stay at the 'Rajbari' situated on the land opposite to the 'Sivabari' at Malugram. With the fund raised in 1883, a printing machine was purchased from

Dacca, and the arrival of the machine, strangely enough, coincided with the arrival of two Manipuris being released from the Alipore Central Jail. As convicts the Manipuris had been trained in the art of printing in the Jail, their presence in Silchar at the right moment was regarded by the owners of the press as God-sent. The press now could be run without bringing any expert from outside."

125 *Ibid.*, 166.
126 *Silchar*, issue dated 29 July 1903.
127 Datta, n. 76, 67.
128 Quoted in *Ibid.*
129 Head Master's letter No. 23, dated 17 April 1900, quoted in *Ibid.*
130 *Ibid.*
131 *Surma*, issues dated 1 July 1912 and 13 April 1914.
132 S.P. Sen, (ed.), *Dictionary of National Biographies*, Calcutta, 1924, vol. IV, 422.
133 C.R., 1929-30, Bundle No. 559.

Declaration made in the Zilla Court

  Name: Brahman Parishat Patrika.
  Language: Bengali.
  Editor: Bhuban Mohon Vidyarnava.
  Subject: Social Reform of Brahmin Society
  Place of Publication: Silchar.
  Pages: 56 pages.
  Size: 1/8 demy.
  First Published: 25-4-1929.
  Copies: 1000.
  Price: 4 annas.

134 *Ibid.*
135 *Ibid.*
136 *Ibid.*
137 *Ibid.*, Notification No. 8180/6-R/8 of 1929.
138 *Ibid.*, No. 10492/6-R/2 of 1829.
139 Datta, n. 76, 32.
140 *Ibid.*, 64.

Chapter Nine : Epilogue

1 C.R., No. 252 of 1855. The fall of Sebastapol during the Crimean War was celebrated in Cachar by illuminating the houses.
2 K.N. Dutta, *Landmarks of the Freedom Struggle in Assam*, Gauhati, 1958, 23.
3 C.R., No. 46 of 1861.
4 C.R., Deputy Commissioner's Report for 182-3,
5 B.C. Allen, *Assam District Gazetteers, vol. I* (Cachar) Allahabad, 1905, 39 ; also *Ananda Bazar Patrika*, 2 February 1936.

6 *Ibid.*, Allen, n. 5, 41.

7 S.P. Sen, (ed.), *Dictionary of National Biography*, vol. I, Calcutta, 1922, 259-60.

8 *Ibid.*, 260-1.

9 H.C. Datta, Souvenir, Bipin Chandra Pal Centennary Celebration Committee, Silchar, 1958, 6.

10 R.C. Majumdar, *History of the Freedom Movement in India*, Vol. II, 5-6.

11 *Ibid.*, 6.

12 *Ibid.*, 25-6.

13 *Ibid.*, 62.

14 *Ibid.*, 64.

15 *Azad*, Bengali weekly, Silchar, 5 March 1963.

16 *The Bengalee*, 20 July 1906. A big pandal, spacious enough to accomodate 500 delegates, was constructed in the private compound of Babu Suroj Kumar Das, a *Zamindar*.

17 *Azad*, 15 August 1974.

18 Souvenir, n. 9, 19.

19 *Ibid.*, 16.

20 *Ibid.*, 61-2.

21 D. Datta, *History of Silchar Government Higher Secondary School*, Silchar, 1963, 62. Babu Apurba Kumar was the eldest son of Kamini Kumar Chanda. He had a distinguished career in Bengal Education Service and retired as the Directior of Public Instruction, Government of West Bengal.

22 *Azad*, 5 March 1963. From Cachar, Kamini Kumar Chanda, Mahesh Chandra Datta and Kali Mohan Dev attended the session.

23 *The Indian People*, 12 October 1907.

24 *Ibid.*

25 *The Bengalee*, 11 March 1908.

26 *The Eastern Chronicle*, 20 March 1908.

27 *The Bengalee*, 19 April 1908. Babu Paresh Nath Das, *Zamindar* of Panchakhanda, and Babu Ramani Mohon Das, a *Zamindar* of Karimganj, were the President and Secretary respectively, of the Reception Committee and a big pandal was constructed in the Secretary's compound.

28 Sen, n. 7, 416.

29 R.C. Majumdar, *An Advanced History of India*, 981.

30 Souvenir, n. 31.

31 Mazumdar, n. 10, 251-64.

32 *Azad*, 15 August 1974.

33 Report on the Administration of Assam, 1925-26.

34 Dutt, n. 2, 41.

35 Sen, n. 7, 416-7.

36 Majumdar, n. 10, 348.

37 See Letter of Mohamed Ali of Mahmudabad to K.K. Chanda, dated 30 November 1916, appended in *History Seminar Magazine*, Gurucharan

College, Silchar, 1966.

38 Majumdar, n. 29, 915.

39 Dutt, n. 2, 91.

40 Majumdar, n. 10, 416-7.

41 *Azad*, 15 August 1974.

42 Sen, n. 7, 398.

43 *Azad*, 15 August 1974.

44 *The Indian Daily News*, 30 May 1921.

45 Majumdar, n. 10, vol. III, 203-5.

46 *The Musalman*, 2 September 1921.

47 *Azad*, 15 August 1974.

48 *The Bengalee*, 10 September 1928.

49 *Ibid.*, 30 November 1926.

50 *Ibid.*, 21 November 1926.

51 *Ibid.*, 3 December 1926.

52 *The Bengalee*, 18, 19, 20, 22, and 23 June 1929.

53 *Ibid.*, 2 July 1929.

54 *Ibid.*

55 *Ibid.*, 13 June 1929.

56 *Ibid.*, 14 July 1929.

57 *Ibid.*, 2 July 1929.

58 *Ibid.*, 2 February 1930.

59 Dutt, n. 2, 74.

60 *Azad*, 15 August 1974.

61 Dutt, n. 2, 70.

62 *The Bengalee*, 8 January 1931.

63 Dutt, n. 2, 71.

64 *Ibid.*, 72.

65 Majumdar, n. 10, vol. III, 289.

66 *The Bengalee*, 10 September 1930

67 *Azad*, 1 *Baisak*, 1370 B.S.

68 *Majumdar*, n. 10, 472.

69 Sen, n. 7, 413.

70 *Azad*, 15 August 1974

71 Sen, n. 7, 416.

72 *Ibid.*, 294.

73 *Azad*, 15 August 1974.

74 Some of these letters were published by Professor D. Datta in the *History Seminar Magazine*, Gurucharan College, Silchar, 1966.

75 Dutt, n. 2, 83.

76 *Azad*, 15 August 1974.

77 *Ibid.*

78 Dutt, n. 2, 106.

79 M.A.K. Azad, *India Wins Freedom*, New Delhi, 1959, 156.

80 *Azad*, 1 *Baisak*, 1370 B.S.

81 Azad, n. 79, see Appendix.

82 *Azad*, 15 August 1974.

83 *Ibid.*

84 To quote Dr. Triguna Sen : "...the transfer of Sylhet to Pakistan and already been secretly decided upon and accepted by the Congress High Command and also by many in the Assam Congress to reduce Bengalee element in Assam's Population. See Sen, n. 7, 355.

Glossary

Adalat, court.
Agrahayan, the tenth month of the Bengali calendar.
Amin, a revenue officer.
Amlah, a court officer.
Arzee, a petition or an application.
Aswin, the sixth month of the Bengali calender.
Baksha, waste land.
Bangabda, the Bengali Year.
Barbhandari, Prime Minister.
Bari, homestead.
Barkendaz, an armed retainer or mercenary soldier.
Bazar, a daily market.
Beel, a small lake.
Bepari, trader.
Bhandari, minister.
Bhit, homestead.
Bigha, a measured area of land, one-third of an acre.
Bildar, a peon attached to the receipt and delivery of bills.
Bising, a deity of the Dimachas.
Bitra Daloi, a revenue officer.
Brahmattara, rent-free tenure given for the support of the Brah
　　mins.
Bundabast, settlement.
Chaitra, the last month in the Bengali Calender.
Chandy, a form of *Durga*, the mother-goddess of the Hindus.
Chaprasi, a peon or an orderly.

Chaukidar, a watch-man.

Chokeiy, a frontier outpost.

Choudhury, a revenue officer in charge of a *Pargana*.

Dak, mail.

Dakua, mail-runner.

Daptari, a peon entrusted with preparing and maintaining records.

Darbar, court, assembly.

Daroga, a police officer.

Dastavez, a document.

Debottara, rent-free tenure for the support of the temples and deities.

Desh, country, state.

Dewan, chief executive, revenue collector, Governor.

Dewani, revenue administration.

Dhoti, a loin cloth.

Dola, palanquin.

Durga, the ten-handed mother goddess of the Hindus.

Ejahar, petition.

Ejara, mortgage.

Fakir, a Muslim mendicant.

Fouj, army

Fouzdar, criminal administrator, also revenue collector.

Fouzdari, criminal administration.

Gadi, throne.

Ganja, a drug.

Ghat, a hill pass or a landing place on the bank of a river.

Goanburha, a village headman.

Goondaboo Bia (*Gandharva Bibaha*), a marriage by mutual consent.

Govinda, a Hindu deity, equivalent to *Vishnu*.

Guru, a spiritual guide.

Hal, a measured area of land being twelve times of a *Keyar*.

Haor, a large lake.

Hat, a periodical market.

Havildar, a non-commissioned army officer.

Ilaka, a jurisdiction.

Iman, a Muslim prophet.

Jagir, an assignment.

Jalkar, a tax in fisheries.

Jamadar, a junior commissioned army officer.

Jammadar, one who is in charge.

Jheel, a marshy land.

Jhum, the system of agriculture prevalent among the hill people.

Jumma, assessed revenue.

Juvaraj, heir-apparent.

Kacha-kanti, a shrine at Udharband dedicated to goddess *Kali*.

Kali, the four-handed mother goddess, a form of *Durga*.

Kamakhya, a mother goddess, originally a deity of the Khasis but equated with *Durga* or *Kali* by the Sanskritists.

Kartik, the seventh month in the Bengali calender.

Kashaokhati, the tutelar deity of the Bodos (including Dimachas).

Katchari, office, court of justice.

Khas, principal, main.

Khat, an estate.

Kheddah, elephant catching.

Khel, a self-governing revenue division.

Khitmatgar, servant.

Kshatriya, a Vedic Hindu caste.

Kulbah, a measurement of land equivalent to 4.82 acres.

Kulanji, family chronicle.

Kutcha, metal.

Lakhiraj, a rent-free grant.

Laskar, a civil and revenue officer.

Latbandi, a document of purchase.

Mahajan, a merchant.

Mahal, a division of land.

Maharani, chief queen.

Majumdar, a fiscal officer.

Manjhi, a boat-man.

Mantri, minister.

Mauza, a fiscal unit.

Mauzadar, a fiscal officer in charge of a *mauza*.

Mel, an assembly.

Mirasdar, a land-holder.

Mohurir, a supervisor, clerk.

Mukhtar, a revenue officer in charge of a *khel* or *Raj*.

Mukhtear, a agent, a spokesman or pleader.

Muni, a saint.

Munshi, a judicial officer.

Nallah, a minor stream, natural drain.

Narayana, a name of *Vishnu*.

Nazir, a cash officer in the court.

Nizzamat, revenue.

Omlah, an agent.

Paik, a tenant whose duty was to render services to the King and State at a fixed period of the year.

Paltan, platoon of infantry.

Panchali, chronicle.

Panchayat, a village tribunal.

Pargana, a revenue division.

Parvati, a name of *Durga*.

Pandit, a scholar.

Patgiri, a minor revenue officer.

Pathshala, a primary school.

Patit, fallow land.

Patwari, a village accountant.

Patra, a minister.

Patta, a lease deed.

Paus, the ninth month in Bengali calender.

Peadah, peon, orderly, messenger.

Pie, an Indian monetary unit; 192 *pies* make a rupee.

Pucca, concrete.

Puja, worship, Hindu festival.

Punji, a tribal village.

Qazi, a Muslim magistrate.

Quran, the Holy scripture of the Muslims.

Raj, a country.

Raja, king.

Rajkumar, prince.

Ranachandi, the tutelar deity of Cachar, equivalent to *Kali*.

Rani, queen.

Ryot, tenant.

Sadar Dewani Adalat, chief civil court.

Sadar Nizamat Adalat, chief criminal court.

Samanta, feudatory.

Sankhya, a school of Indian philosophy.

Sarak, road.

Sardar, a chief or headman.

Sarkar, a district in the Mughal Empire.

Sayer, miscellaneous cesses.
Senapati, general, commander.
Seristadar, keeper of records.
Sezwal, revenue collector.
Shastra, scripture
Siva, a Hindu deity, husband of *Durga* or *Kali*.
Sravana, the fourth month in Bengali calendar.
Subadar, a non-commissioned army officer.
Subah, a province in the Mughal Empire.
Subahdar, governor.
Tahsil, revenue office.
Tahsildar, a revenue officer.
Tamsuk, a deed of money-lending.
Thana, a police station.
Thanadar, officer in charge of a police station.
Teelah, hillock.
Tol, an institution of Sanskrit learning.
Umananda, a deity of the Bodos, equivalent to *Siva*.
Uzir, minister.
Vakeel, a pleader.
Varsa, a country.
Visaya, a province or administrative division.
Vishnu, a Hindu deity, also known as *Krishna*.
Zilla, a district.
Zamindar, landlord.

Select Bibliography

Primary Sources

UNPUBLISHED DOCUMENTS

(a) *National Archives of India, New Delhi.*
Agricultural, Revenue and Commerce Department Proceedings.
Bengal Political Consultations.
Despatches to and from the Court of Directors.
Despatches to and from the Secretary of State.
Foreign Department Proceedings.
Home Department Proceedings.
Revenue Department Proceedings.

(b) *State Archives, Government of West Bengal, Calcutta,*
Bengal Judicial Consultations.
Bengal Revenue Consultations.

(c) *Records Office, Assam Secretariat Shillong.*
(i) Pre-1874 Files received from (a) Bengal Board of Revenue, (b) Bengal Government, and (c) Dacca Commissioner's Office.
(ii) Selected Letters (a) issued to the Government of Bengal, (b) received from the Government of Bengal, (c) issued to District Officers, and (d) received from miscellaneous quarters.

(d) *District Records office, Silchar.*
Cachar Records, 1835 to 1935.

These include volumes and files of letters issued and received
by the Superintendents and Deputy Commissioners of
Cachar, besides various survey reports.

PUBLISHED

(a) *Assamese.*

Bhuyan, S.K., ed., *Kachari Buranji*, Gauhati, 1936.

————, *Tripura Buranji*, Gauhati, 1938.

Datta, S.K., ed., *Jayantia Buranji*, Gauhati, 1937.

(b) *Bengali.*

Bhattacharjee, P.N., *Heramba Rajyer Dandavidhi*, Gauhati,.
1920.

Dekhial Phukan, H., *Assam Buranji*, Calcutta, 1829; edited
by J.M. Bhattacharjee, Gauhati, 1962.

Sen, S.N., ed., *Prachin Bangla Patra Sankalan*, Calcutta,.
1942.

Singha, K.C., ed., *Rajamala*, Calcutta, 1898.

(c) *English.*

Aitchinson, C.U., *Treaties, Engagements and Sanands*,
Vol. II, Calcutta, 1872.

Allen, B.C., *Assam District Gazetteers*, Vol. I (Cachar),.
Allahabad, 1905.

Azad, M.A.K., *India Wins Freedom*, New Delhi, 1959.

Banerjee, S.C., ed., *Collection of Statutes relating to India*,
2 vols., Calcutta, 1913.

Baruah, B.C., *The Assam Code*, Vol. II, Shillong, 1961.

Bhuyan, S.K., tr., *Tungkhungia Buranji*, Gauhati, 1933.

Borah, M.I., tr., *Baharistan-i-Ghaibi*, Gauhati, 1936.

Bruce, C.A., "Report on the Manufacture of Tea and on the
Extent and Produce of Tea Plantation in Assam", *Journal
of the Asiatic Society of Bengal*, 1839.

Buchanan, F.H., *An Account of Assam*, London, 1820.

Butler, J., *Travels and Adventures in the Province of Assam*,
London, 1855.

Clarke, R., *The Regulations of the Government of Fort William
in Bengal*, London, 1854.

Das, J.N., ed., *The Assam Land Revenue Manual*, Shillong,

1965.

Datta, D. ed., *The Cachar District Records*, Silchar, 1969.

Dutt, K.N., ed., *A Hand Book to the Old Records of Assam Secretariat*, Shillong, 1959.

Firminger, W.K., ed., *Sylhet District Records*, 4 vols., Shillong 1913-1919.

Fisher, T., "Memoir of Sylhet, Kachar and the Adjacent Districts," *Journal of the Asiatic Society of Bengal*, Vol. IX, 1840.

Grange, G.L., "Extracts from the Journal of an Expedition into the Naga Hills on the Assam Frontier," *Journal of the Asiatic Society of Bengal*, 1840.

Hamilton, W., *Historical Geographical and Descriptive Account of Hindostan*, London, 1820.

Hunter, W., *A Statistical Account of Assam*, 2 vols., London, 1879.

Mackenzie, A., *A History of the Relations of the Government with the Hill Tribes on the North East Frontier of Bengal*, Calcutta, 1884.

Medhi, J.C., ed., *The Assam Code*, Vol. I, Shillong, 1956.

Michel, J.F., *Report on the North East Frontier of India*, Calcutta, 1883.

Mills, A.J.M., *Report on the Province of Assam*, Calcutta, 1854.

Neufvile, J.B., "On the Geography and the Population of Assam," *Asiatick Researches*, Vol. XVI, 1828.

Pemberton, R.B., *Report on the Eastern Frontier of British India*, Calcutta, 1835.

Reid, R., *History of the Frontier Areas Bordering on Assam, from 1883-1941*, Shillong, 1942.

Robinson, W., *A Descriptive Account of Assam*, Calcutta, 1841.

Wade, J.P., *An Account of Assam*, edited by B. Sarmah, Sibsagar, 1927.

White, A., *Memoir of late David Scott*, London, 1832.

Wilcox, H., "Memoir of a Survey of Assam and the neighbouring countries 1825-1828," *Asiatick Researches*, Vol. XVII, 1832.

Wilson, H.H., *Documents Illustrative of the Burmese War*, Calcutta, 1827.

GAZETTEES, JOURNALS AND NEWSPAPERS

Azad (Bengali).
Eastern Chronicle.
Hindu Patriot.
Indian People.
Journal of the Asiatic Society of Bengal.
Journal of the Assam Research Society.
New India.
Purbasree (Bengali).
Silchar (Bengali).
Surma (Bengali).
The Assam Gazettee.
The Assam Review.
The Bengalee.
The Calcutta Review.
The Indian Daily News.
The Musalman.

Secondary Sources

Acharya, N.N., *The History of Medieval Assam*, Gauhati, 1968.

Antrobus, H.A., *A History of the Assam Company*, Edinburgh, 1957.

Baden-Powell, B.H.I., *The Land Systems of British India*, 3 vols., Oxford, 1892.

Banerjee, A.C., *The Eastern Frontier of British India*, Calcutta, 1946.

Barooah, N.K., *David Scott in North East India*, New Delhi, 1970.

Barpujari, H.K., *Assam : In the Days of the Company*, Gauhati, 1963.

Bhattacharjee, J.B., *The Garos and the English, 1765-1874*, Unpublished Doctoral Thesis, University of Gauhati, 1971.

———, "Jayantia-Heramba Relations," *Proceedings*, Indian History Congress, Muzaffarpur, 1972.

———, "Some Aspects of Heramba Government on the eve of British Rule," *Shodhak*, Vol. 2, pt. B, Jaipur, 1973.

———, "Early History of Tea Industry in Cachar," *Proceed-*

ings, Indian History Congress, Chandigarh, 1973.

————, "The Vakeels and Social Exploitation in the Non-Regulated Province of Cachar (1832 to 1874)," *Proceedings*, Indian History Congress, Calcutta, 1974.

————, "Some Important Sources of the History of Medieval and Modern Cachar," *Shodhak*, Vol. 4, pt. A, Jaipur, 1975.

Bhattacharjee, S.N., *A History of Mughal North-East Frontier Policy*, Calcutta, 1929.

Bhuyan, S.K., *Early British Relations with Assam*, Shillong, 1928.

————, *Anglo-Assamese Relations*, Gauhati, 1949.

Buckland, C.E.,

————, *Bengal under the Lieutenant Governor*, 2 vols., Calcutta, 1901.

Dictionary of Indian Biography, Oxford, 1937.

Chakravarty, B.C., *British Relations with the Hill Tribes of Assam since 1826*, Calcutta, 1964.

Chakravarty, B.P., *Annexation of Cachar (1832)*, Proceedings, Indian Historical Records Commission, 1942.

Chatterjee, S.K., *Place of Assam in the History and Civilisation of India*, Gauhati, 1955.

Chaube, S.K., *Hill Politics in North Eastern India*, Calcutta, 1974.

Choudhury, A.C., *Shrihatter Itibritta* (Bengali), Sylhet, 1317, B.S.

Dalton, E.T., *Descriptive Ethnology of Bengal*, Calcutta, 1872.

Datta, D., *Beginning of Tea Industry in Cachar*, Purbasree 1965.

————, *History of Silchar Government Higher Secondary School*, Centenary Volume, Silchar, 1963.

Debi, L., *Ahom—Tribal Relations*, Gauhati, 1968.

Dutt, K.N., *Landmarks in the Freedom Struggle in Assam*, Gauhati, 1958.

Elwin, V., *India's North East Frontier in the Nineteenth Century*, Bombay, 1959.

Endle, S., *The Kacharis*, London, 1911.

Furber, H., *John Company at Work*, Harvard, 1951.

Gait, E.A., *A History of Assam*, Calcutta, 1925.

Gohain, U.N., *Assam under the Ahoms*, Jorhat, 1942.

Guha, U.C., *Cacharer Itibritta* (Reprint), Gauhati, 1971.

Hamilton, W., *The Eastern India Gazetteers*, Vol. I, Calcutta, 1828.

Johri, S.R., *Where India, China and Burma Meet*, Calcutta, 1962.

Kaye, J.W., *History of the Administration of the East India Company*, London, 1853.

Lahiri, R.M., The Annexation of Assam, Calcutta, 1954.

Majumdar, N., *Justice and Police in Bengal*, Calcutta, 1960.

Majumdar, R.C., *Glimpses of Bengal in the Nineteenth Century*, Calcutta, 1961.

————, *History of Ancient Bengal*, Calcutta, 1971.

————, *History of Medieval Bengal*, Calcutta, 1973.

Martin, M., *History, Antiquities, Topography and Statistics of the Eastern India*, 3 vols., London, 1838.

Misra, B.B., *The Central Administration of the East India Company*, Manchester, 1959.

Muir, R., *The Making of British India*, Manchester, 1915.

Nath, R.M., *The Background of the Assamese Culture*, Shillong, 1949.

O'Malley, L.S.S., *Modern India and the West*, London, 1942.

Philips, C.H., *The East India Company*, Manchester, 1940.

Rao, V. Venkata, *A Hundred Years of Local Self-Government in Assam*, Gauhati, 1965.

Roy, J., *The History of Manipur*, Calcutta, 1958.

Sen, S.P., ed., *Dictionary of National Biography*, 4 vols., Calcutta, 1972-1974.

Shakespeare, L.W., *A History of the Assam Rifles*, London, 1929.

Singh, L.I.G., *An Introduction to Manipur*, Imphal, 1960.

Strachey, J., *India, its Administration and Progress*, London, 1903.

Sword, V.H., *Baptists in Assam*, Chicago, 1935.

Ward, W.E., *Note on the Assam Land Revenue System*, Shillong, 1897.

Woodruff, P., *The Men who Ruled India*, London, 1953

Index